Unwin Education Books: 18

MORAL EDUCATION

A Sociological Study of the Influence of Society, Home and School

Unwin Education Books

Series Editor: Ivor Morrish, BD, BA, Dip.Ed. (London), BA (Bristol)

Unwin Education Books: 18
Series Editor: Ivor Morrish

Moral Education

A Sociological Study of the Influence of Society Home and School

WILLIAM KAY
Nottingham College of Education

London
GEORGE ALLEN & UNWIN LTD
RUSKIN HOUSE   MUSEUM STREET

First published in 1975

ISBN 0 04 370052 7 hardback
     0 04 370053 5 paperback

Printed in Great Britain
in 10 point Times Roman type
by Cox & Wyman Ltd,
London, Fakenham and Reading

To Pamela

Author's Preface

In writing a book based on both the published and unpublished research of himself and others, it is inevitable that an author should feel indebted to a host of researchers. As a beneficiary of such work I would like to record my gratitude to all who contributed in this way. As there are too many to mention in a preface, suffice it to say that whenever their names appear in the text they do so with my admiration, respect and gratitude—even though at times I may profoundly disagree with them.

I would, however, like to mention four individuals by name. First, my colleague Brendan Magill who, during the writing of this book, offered the benefits of his erudition and clarity of thought. Second, Frances Scott of Nottingham University, who read the manuscript as it was written and made many valuable suggestions and comments. Third, Dr John Daines of Nottingham University, who applied his keen mind to reading the final script and assured me that the problems discussed here were of fundamental importance. And last, my wife Pamela of Loughborough University, whose extensive reading in the social sciences was always placed at my disposal.

Since this book will be of interest to both American and British readers I have drawn on published and unpublished research evidence available on both sides of the Atlantic. The problem of nomenclature was partly overcome by omitting terms which would be ambiguous for such a mixed readership; but one could not be avoided.

British *Public Schools* are known as *Private Schools* in America. Here I have retained the British term with a note directing American readers to this fact.

One final point must be made for the benefit of readers who may think that insufficient attention has been paid to moral education in primary schools. The explanation is simple. This aspect is dealt with in the author's forthcoming *Nursery and Infant Education* (Routledge and Kegan Paul).

Nottingham   WILLIAM KAY

Contents

12 / *Moral Education*

Chapter 1

Introduction and Overview

It is now axiomatic that moral education should be an established element in the curricula of schools in every country that has advanced beyond the 'folk-society' stage. Until very recently advocates of this view had to advance complex and compelling arguments to support their policy. This is no longer the case. Cultural and moral crises throughout the world have made it clear that schools can no longer evade their responsibilities in this area of education. Unfortunately such a situation can easily be exploited. The need for moral education is so clamant that an increasing volume of inadequate curricular material is currently being published and disseminated through our schools.

The present volume has been written to help those who wish to assess the relative validity of such material, and also to enable parents and teachers to identify those elements in a child's social environment which either help or hinder his moral growth. Together with the companion volume, *Moral Development* (1), it provides a composite psychological and sociological view of both the insights and the problems facing those who are concerned with the moral growth of children. Furthermore both volumes provide the research data on which these views are based.

The Preconditions of Morality
Apart from the opening chapter of Part One, the material in the present volume follows a chronological course. It begins with infancy and shows that the preconditions of morality must be established before moral growth is possible. These preconditions are: identity, self-acceptance, identification, a fully formed conscience, success and achievement.

A sense of identity is necessary before an individual can become autonomous. Self-acceptance enables him to make valid moral judgements. Identification facilitates those paradigmatic experiences without which a child has little to guide his early conduct. A mature and informed conscience provides the inward validation of such judgements. Success and achievement cause all the elements to cohere which are then confirmed by the attendant positive reinforcement.

All this takes place in the miniscule society of the family, which is why child-rearing techniques are so crucial to later development and also why the quality of home life in infancy is such a powerful determinant of later moral conduct.

Primary Moral Traits

When social-class differences in moral conduct are examined carefully it is clear that five moral traits emerge as characteristic of moral maturity. These are: (1) moral judgement, (2) deferred gratification and future orientation, (3) moral personalism, (4) moral flexibility, and (5) moral dynamism and moral creativity. When the preconditions of morality have been established, these traits emerge not only as empirically observed facts but also as logically necessary sequences.

First, a mature form of moral judgement is needed before any moral decision can be made. This then requires the moral agent to be future orientated because the implementation of the decision may require some personal gratification to be deferred in order to accomplish this. Other people are always an inevitably and inextricably involved element in any moral decision, and so they too must be considered. Therefore the quality of moral personalism is required which always takes account of the welfare of the person involved in a moral situation; but both moral personalism and moral judgement, as the altruistic and rational elements in reaching a moral decision, must be based on moral principles. Thus moral flexibility is essential for this is characterized by the facility to abstract moral principles from the welter of legal fiats and authoritarian dicta which are intended to control our behaviour. However, the ability to abstract moral principles is inadequate unless they are then creatively applied in everyday life. Therefore such an individual requires not only the competence to make a moral decision, but also the ability to apply moral principles to specific situations.

With the relevant evidence it can be demonstrated that the social classes of any advanced society are clearly divided in terms of these moral traits. It can also be shown that the process of embourgeoisement does not affect morality. Although there does appear to be an economic merging of some higher and lower-status social groups, this conflation does not seem to characterize morality. Higher social status is still correlated with greater moral maturity; and, equally, lower-status with greater moral immaturity. However, if any deduction is to be drawn from this evidence, it is not that the middle classes are a superior breed—it is simply that the economic, educational and cultural privileges which they enjoy, should become the property of all.

Primary Moral Attitudes

One of the arguments contained in *Moral Development* presented a case for establishing that the morally mature person must be autonomous, rational, altruistic and responsible. It was further argued that one has here four primary moral attitudes whose co-existence in a fully developed form mark the morally mature individual.

It is possible to demonstrate why this should be so. Autonomy is essential, for anything done under compulsion can never be classified as moral, but once an autonomous decision is to be made it must be subject to the requirements of reason. Only in this way can a valid moral judgement be assured. Then, since other people are always involved in such decisions, concern for their welfare is another essential ingredient. Therefore altruism is needed to modify or augment the rational decision. Finally, because an autonomous, rational and altruistic moral decision is effete until it has been acted upon, it is essential for the individual concerned to implement the decision by acting upon it.

This argument is taken a step further in the present book. It is stressed that since both rationality and altruism are essential to morality, it is possible that an entirely new psychological trait may be emerging—'rational-altruism'–which depicts that orientation of personality which responds to people with love and to problems with reasons. These, however, are not different psychological traits; they are, as it were, different facets of a single central construct.

The Influence of School

Having then presented evidence to indicate how both the family and society influence an individual child's moral development, attention is turned to the school. Here it is primarily the influence of the school as a social system, which is examined. The evidence suggests that a democratic milieu is essential for the emergence of the moral traits and attitudes listed above. The ideal school is then described as a familial organization which has eliminated all forms of elitism, and involves both teachers and pupils in policy and decision making. Such a system, it is concluded, can only operate in an ideal comprehensive school.

Structure of the Book

By means of a strategy such as this, the chronological, developmental sequence of moral maturation is traced in terms of the effects exerted by sociological factors. Consequently, the social influences affecting the moral preconditions, traits and attitudes are all traced through the home, society and school. However, since this volume is primarily concerned with social-class differences in morality, it begins with a non-analytical study of social class. It then reverts to a study of the influence of family, social class and school in order to explain the structured nature of sub-cultural variations in moral conduct.

Moral Education and Social Stability

In conclusion it must be stressed that moral education is not intended to be a panacea merely for the ills of society. At the beginning of 1973, for example, the Lord Chief Justice in London, stated that if the present trend in crime continued it could reach such a rate of growth that civilization itself would be in jeopardy. The courts would be unable to cope with the amount of work involved, and there could well be a total breakdown of law and order. It is this, which many fear; and the recent 'law and order' debates of the past few years underline the seriousness of the situation. Indeed, so serious has it become that in March 1973, President Nixon revealed his plans for a massive onslaught on crime, which contained the following controversial passage: 'I am convinced that the death penalty can be an effective deterrent.' In the same week the British Lord Chancellor, Lord Hailsham, also outlined what he called 'a strategy to get tougher' with criminals, and stressed that he was speaking against a background of 'bombs in Whitehall and the Old Bailey'. Furthermore, as we shall see, violence is now entering the schools, where vicious teenagers can vitiate any attempt by teachers to control and educate them. This alone proves that some form of compulsory moral education is urgently required.

That is the negative side, and without intending to belittle those whose advocacy of moral education springs from such considerations, there is also a positive side. Professor Liam Hudson in Britain has recently highlighted the aridity of education which is purely practical and scientific. When further related evidence is added it is clear that the acquisition of facts and skills alone is not enough. Children should not be educated for work alone; their leisure activities and personal growth in society must be cultivated just as assiduously as we now tend their garnering and digesting of factual data. Here is the positive side of moral education. It must not only eliminate crime and social disorder, but also cultivate personalities who can enjoy the fruits of our culture to the full.

REFERENCES

1 Allen & Unwin (1968). Schocken Books Inc. (1969).

Bibliography
HUDSON, LIAM, *Contrary Imaginations* (Methuen, 1966).
HUDSON, LIAM, *Frames of Mind* (Methuen, 1968).

Part One
Social-class Determinants of Morality

Chapter 2

Morality and Social Class

The Nature of Social Class

Almost every society known to man has been stabilized by the presence of a hierarchical social structure. In some it is imperceptible; in others it seems to be the most dominant characteristic. According to Wootton, Britain and America, despite their democratic protestations, belong to the latter group. Since Marx and Weber made an analysis of social stratification, researchers here have faced inordinately complex problems. Not only are many criteria of social class evanescent and unstable, but social mobility, the process of embourgeoisement (see Chapter 10), and the disdain of any such fissiparous structure, by the young, make many current and wittily relevant papers on social stratification obsolete the moment they are printed. Yet it is still possible to analyse social stratification, if in that analysis, one establishes that class, status and power are three crucial dimensions.

The most obvious criterion in Britain is that of the Registrar General who classifies citizens on the basis of occupation. This may be a crude yard-stick, but it does indicate the general life-style, educational level, intelligence and background of the persons involved. Of course, there are inconsistencies, for inherited privilege or the parvenu can blur the system. Yet this sole criterion is invariably the rationale of every other criterion. A brief perusal of these will make this clear.

It has variously been argued that income ought to replace occupation as the official criterion of social class. Again, local authorities have stressed that housing, and even the residential area, should locate one on the social-class scale. More sophisticated, psychologically-orientated commentators have argued that one's attitudes, values and beliefs are the most potent and relevant criteria. They plead that it is personal qualities and not status symbols which signify where a man should be placed in the hierarchy of social excellence. Finally, there is the immediately apparent difference in speech, for both linguistic structure and verbal accent are an immediately identifiable index of social class.

It is self-evident, however, that an occupation which bestows relative affluence, status and power inevitably not only establishes one's social position but at the same time confers all the characteristics which are inherent in it. For example, the offspring of a well-educated, successful professional man is likely to enjoy the benefits of affluence; occupy a fine house in a select neighbourhood; express general assent to parental attitudes, values and beliefs; and couch such assent in the appropriate grammatical forms and accents affected by that particular sub-culture.

This, of course, is only one stratum in the complex of social stratification, but immediately it can be seen how social class affects morality. Passing through the socialization processes embedded in their complex of roles, values, attitudes, beliefs, traits and life-style, the members of each social class are likely to emerge with similar patterns of conduct. This is further endorsed by the fact that members of the same social class depend upon this membership to both establish their identity and confirm their social acceptance. Both of which, of course, not only ward off the depredations of alienation, but also in the process, further guarantee the behavioural cohesion of its members. It is thus inevitable that each social class should have its peculiar mores and ethos to which all but the aberrant members subscribe. But why, it is often asked, should there be so much animosity between the social classes?

The Origins of Class Consciousness and Conflict

It is somewhat surprising to learn that this apparently ineradicable element of contemporary social life is a modern phenomenon! Most researchers, omitting any reference to the French Revolution, locate its origin as recently as the nineteenth century. Foster, for example, alleges that it could only arise with the establishment of a dominant industry in one locality, imparting a sense of solidarity and unity to those who worked for the owners. Asa Briggs thinks it likely that the conflict arose when urbanization reached the point where it facilitated social interaction and contact between disparate economic groups. Scott affirmed that she had identified it as a feature of urbanization, wherein the clerk's or artisan's attachment to a city or town contrasted with the peripatetic life of an unskilled labourer.

From some such circumstances as these may have developed the typically distinct havens of security. In such a situation the principal determinants of the working-class mores would be poverty and insecurity. As a natural consequence kinship ties and neighbourly co-operation would be woven into a secure web to offset the erosion of social and economic fear. The much vaunted working-class *bonhomie* is thus a psychological bastion against adversity, which, as Coates and Silburn found in Nottingham, is soon abandoned when its defensive function fails. The middle classes, however, tended to amass property as a source of economic security. Consequently, in an inflationary economy their source of security became even more financially supportive. Thus a subtle social-class difference emerged at the point where men are most vulnerable—their need for security. Now a current finding relating to the 'lucrative orientation' of delinquents adds more supportive evidence. Shoham found that the one significant difference between the middle- and working-class boys concerned, was the former's insatiable desire to possess property.

However, upon this skeletal analysis one must place the flesh of human feeling. Such a juxtaposing of the deprived and privileged would generate intense feelings of hostility; the least offensive of which would be sheer unadulterated envy. Indeed, it is to this that Schoeck appeals to explain the motivation of most human behaviour, arguing that it is responsible for social stratification since by it the lower orders detach themselves from the higher and make it the target of their malevolence. Then in turn the higher protect themselves against any erosion of their privilege. Consequently both groups are defined by their mutual antagonism. Inevitably harnessed with envy comes greed and in an atmosphere of competitive greed the social classes close ranks and glare at each other with mutual animosity.

A more subtle explanation is offered by Shils. It is now known from the work of Karen Horney that men employ various strategies to cope with dangerous people. The two most popular are dominance and deference. Thus although modern militant unions, flexing their political muscles, are a frightening spectacle, this is their way of coping with those they fear and envy. An equally adequate way of coping with the situation employs deference. Each are emasculating the social and economic threat. The first says, 'I'm so strong that you can't hurt me.' The second pleads, 'I'm so defenceless that you won't hurt me.' Thus one must not overlook the fact that deference is a vital link in the chain of social stratification. Indeed it may be true to argue that deference is also responsible for the class and strata formation of modern society and emerges in the phenomenon of the working-class Tory. Since dominance and deference are two sides of the same coin, the plebeian folk-hero who demeans himself before his 'betters' and then reviles them behind their backs, is wholly explicable.

Finally, one can now see that sub-cultural mores would exacerbate the situation. Two socially distinct and hostile groupings in society would become not only socially, economically and politically hostile but morally antipathetic too. The differing life-styles of each would inculcate different norms, attitudes and values. Consequently the groups already predisposed to be mutually non-interactive, would become positively antagonistic towards each other, particularly if social upward mobility was denied to the bulk of the lower-status group.

Social-class Stereotypes

As a natural consequence of this, one finds a polarizing of social-class groupings in school. Oppenheim and Lacey present the evidence for this with particular care, and the reasons for this appear to be both educational and personal.

It is now axiomatic that socially deprived children will also be educationally retarded. Consequently the gap between the deprived and the privileged will grow. Given this situation, tribal tendencies come into operation and, as is now known, members of groups will only effectively co-operate if they are from similar or almost identical sub-cultures. Various researchers disclose the obvious fact that this is because varying sub-cultures use different signals for pleasure, distress and gratitude (1). One final curious contributory factor lies in the nature of social mobility. It has been repeatedly shown that any increased upward social mobility results in an increased disparity between the ability levels of the classes and therefore intensifies social stratification.

One could also show that the members of each social class establish their identity and life-style in contrast to non-members. In order to explain the complex social structure which emerges from such a situation, recourse is made to recondite theorizing by erudite sociologists, much of which simply tells us what we already know. Indeed it sometimes confuses that which had previously been clear. Take for example the now notorious comments that Prince Charles is the 'scion of an upper middle-class family'; and the difficulty of keeping up with the Joneses since Princess Margaret married one! For such reasons many people resort to stereotypes and mould their social-class concepts accordingly.

In a research project the writer found that the women on both a council and a private estate had these stereotypes of each other. The working-class women were convinced that the privileged middle-class mothers neglected their children and delegated the housework to a 'daily', while they attended interminable coffee mornings and committees of 'do-gooders'. They were invariably visualized as slender, well-groomed, manicured, coiffured and smelling faintly of expensive perfume. When they smoked, they did so elegantly. When they spoke it was with well-modulated voices. In every crisis they kept tantalizingly cool.

The middle-class women had an equally distorted view of their lower-status compatriots. They all seemed to have an image of a golden-hearted slut given to bouts of vicious temper. Hence she was thought of as alternating between indulging and thrashing her children, while gossiping over the garden fence. Her appearance was always deemed to be the same. She wore a grubby apron, shuffled on loose slippers trimmed with pink fur and completed her attire with a head full of rollers, corrugating her chiffon headscarf. When smoking it was with eyes crinkled against the smoke rising from the cigarette in the corner of her mouth. When dressed to go out she wore patent leather shoes and sported a brittle hair-do.

This, it appears, is the coinage of class consciousness, which has become the common currency of humour. Gibb, for example, has provided a series of humorous contrasts between upper-status and lower-status man. In these he portrays the characteristic attitudes, values, occupations, social and family life, holidays, homes and dress of the two classes. Such, too, is the more modulated theme of Burton who lavishes scorn on the pine kitchens and exotic pets of both the aspirants to, and the members of, the middle classes. The reservoir from which such writers can draw deeply, is the incipient snobbery ineluctably conjoined with social class which distils itself into what Hoggart called the 'us' and 'them' mentality. For if identity depends on establishing what one is not, as well as what one is, then snobbery is the delineating fence around each in-group.

One cannot refer to social-class stereotypes without quoting Melly, who had encapsulated them perfectly.

'In a street market,' he says, 'I watched a working-class mum and her daughter. The mother waddled as if her feet were playing her up. Outside a Knightsbridge Hotel I watched an upper-class mum and her daughter come out from a wedding reception and walk towards Hyde Park Corner, the mother on very thin legs slightly bowed as though she had wet herself. She controlled her body as if it might snap if moved too impulsively. Both daughters walked identically.'

Thus most people know the difference between higher- and lower-status persons, just as they know the difference between men and women, and knowing the difference they cater for it. Experts of every kind may then show how complex are the distinctions between men and women: but this would only try our patience—we know the difference, and we accommodate our behaviour to this difference. The multiplicity of both male and female types does not blind us to this basic fact. It is the same with social class. When all the theorists have polished their neologisms on the subject, the actual participants of social intercourse are rarely any wiser. This does not mean that they are unaware of the subtle gradations within each class, but this awareness is garnered from experience rather than research reports.

The Two-class Tool

If different members of society actually employ some such stereotypes as those outlined above we would expect this to emerge in research reports: and, indeed, this is so. Some time ago Centers investigated what members of different social classes actually thought about themselves, and produced the following predictable data (2). Almost all the respondents classified themselves as either middle class or working class. Clearly, such subjective assessments are as important as objective criteria, for this psychological approach establishes the reference group of the individual in question.

A number of other researchers have observed that the two-class tool is blunted by the fact that many researchers have displayed insufficient courage to investigate the lower lower-class and upper middle-class groups, and still more have pointed out that once we have excluded the vagaries of aristocrats, the greatest social contrast exists between the lowest lower class and all the rest. Further social-class refinements can be added. Zweig, for example, classified workers on the basis of their attitudes to property. The top group tries to acquire it. Lower down on the same scale the acquisition is thought to be an unrealizable pipe-dream. Still further down, working men are antipathetic to the idea, considering that such ownership is a liability: and even at that level, sub-divisions can be found. Stott, for example, in studying unsettled families, distinguished between two kinds of slum-dweller. The first he called the 'medieval' family, which appeared to thrive under those conditions. The second he termed the 'break-down' family, which only seemed to survive when nursed by social workers. Then to complicate the picture still further, Leggett, in true Marxian fashion, believes that class consciousness is indexed by economic insecurity and organized working-class militancy. On this basis he proceeds to permutate these and demonstrates the complex structure of class consciousness. However, rather than make this study more complex by examining the different strata within each social class of society, this simple dichotomy between higher-and lower-status groups will serve as a research tool.

Such a tool has already been used by Newcomb to analyse social-class groups and roles. Jackson and Marsden employed it to discover the effects of social class on educational opportunities. Klein utilized this simple dichotomy in order to clarify her evidence relating to the different child-rearing practices, family life and occupational characteristics found in Britain. Sugarman applied it specifically to moral, as distinct from cultural, social-class characteristics. In all of these one finds a simple dichotomy between the higher-status and lower-status levels. The former is predominantly middle class and the latter working class. That such a breakdown is legitimate is shown by the ease and clarity with which the above researchers were able to deploy their material.

The advantages of such a tool are obvious. When classified by occupation, according to the Registrar General's categorization, the population forms a curve of normal distribution. The bulk of those people in the centre are very similar. It is only as one moves outwards to the higher and lower extremes that sharp differences appear. Thus a study of these can throw light on the nature of the bulk of the population. A simple example should suffice to make this clear. When Betty Spinley studied both public school boys and slum school children, her results not only told us more about the contrasts to be found between the educationally deprived and the educationally privileged, but also much more about education and social class in general and how they affected the bulk of the school population.

An equally telling example comes from Bechhofer, who dealt with income as a social-class determinant. Taking the range of income as a baseline he says, 'At the bottom, and to some extent at the very top, of the income distribution, one can deduce quite a lot. But in the middle, where most people are to be found, it is a great deal harder. The extremes of the distribution yield more predictable behaviour, because there are cut-off points above and below.' This is equally true of status when it is determined by occupation. Indeed it may well be that the crude and clumsy two-class tool of investigation may yield more verifiable and valuable results than a more sophisticated research technique.

SOCIAL-CLASS DIFFERENCES IN BEHAVIOUR

At first it seems superfluous to discuss social-class variations in conduct. The stereotypes presented above seem to be adequate. However, such a rapid dismissal of a polarized form of the social classes is inadequate because the differences are more structured than would at first appear. The ramifications of socio-economic class extend well beyond the range of economic considerations and include human relationships, home-life, attitudes to work, moral convictions and value-systems in an all embracing coherent web. As we shall see, upper-status occupational levels provide the income and leisure to enjoy both recreation and home life, and so bestow the further benefits which accrue from this. Equally the poorly paid labourer derives lowly status from a task which provides little pleasure and successfully excludes him from many cultural and recreational delights. Consequently, the former's success is more likely to induce positive and dynamic attitudes towards people and situations, while the latter will more frequently approach them with grudging resentment.

Experience in School

It is now accepted that the lower-status child has less chance of succeeding in school than his more privileged peer. Arid reports and documentary records repeatedly reiterate the sad fact that not only do higher-status children enter schools with many genetic advantages which successful parents bestow, but then proceed to widen the gap between them and the manual worker's offspring by improving their performance relative to the rest of the children. It is thus no surprise to find that a disproportionate minority of lower-status children enter grammar schools, and that the proportion of children reaching tertiary education is six times as great among the middle class as among the working class.

Probably the most potent contributory factor to this is the nature of the speech structures in both social groups. Through the work of Bernstein it is now axiomatic that middle-class children have an elaborated, flexible code of language, which lends itself to the formulation and articulation of complex ideas and conceptual structures. On the other hand, working-class children have only the stilted, inadequate, restricted, linguistic code which fails to equip them for the demands of educational advance. However, middle-class children also have the facility to use this code, and hence they may communicate with their peers in one system, and with their teachers and parents in the other. Consequently some critics have suggested that although the restricted code is limited it may be an equally efficient means of communication. However, the research on this point is inconclusive. One point, however, is crystal clear. The different social systems generate different linguistic structures.

At first this seems to be a minor consideration, but it has two profound consequences. The first is educational and the second personal. The educational corollary of this is self-evident. Since language is the most frequently employed medium of expression, any inadequacy here disqualifies the linguistically maladroit from making any substantial educational progress. Furthermore the linguistically, and thus educationally, privileged children are further stimulated by the interest and encouragement of their parents. Though on this point the writer has some misgivings. It is repeatedly noted that children succeed because of their parents' approval and encouragement, thus suggesting that parental attitudes are crucial, but nowhere is it ever suggested that this *causal nexus* may be reversed. Might it not be that parents encourage successful children, thus making the responsibility devolve on them? Might not some treat successful children as status symbols and so then encourage them in much the same way as they polish their cars? Could it even be that these bourgeois, compulsive encouragers-of-the-young, are seeking to enhance their own limited success? However, whether it is approving parents or striving, competent children who create the parent/child motivating force, it is invariably the middle-class family which purveys the inducements to emerge successfully from the educational obstacle race.

The personal consequence is even more tragic. It has been found that because lower-status children are unable to express their feelings (even to themselves) they become frustrated. The more articulate swear to compensate. This can range from explosive, vehement cursing, to a sustained, intoned, monotonous liturgy of sexual and sanguineous expletives. Many cannot even reach this level, and, since they cannot express themselves with the suave aplomb of their privileged peers, resort to the other means of expression which inarticulacy has caused them to cultivate. They give vent to violent emotions. Or, if they are sufficiently inhibited, the obverse occurs. They can only recognize and respond to the emotions of hatred, anger and fear, the more sophisticated feelings of sensitivity and sympathy becoming alien and atrophied. As a natural corollary they eventually tend to use emotion rather than reason in the ordering of their lives—a fact which distinguishes them sharply from their middle-class peers who avoid displaying emotion, particularly in its potent sexual and aggressive forms. Thus the educational system, commited to eliminating disparity, further polarizes the social classes. On one side stands the successful higher-status child, dedicated to the pursuit of education as both a means to the good life, and an end in itself; while his less fortunate peer is not only branded as a failure but is forced into aberrant means of achieving success as the educational ladder crumbles beneath him.

It might be thought possible to compensate for such linguistic ineptitude by intensive language courses, but little advantage would result, for this problem revolves around two foci. One may be language, but the other is comprised of value-systems. For the simple fact is that, despite the lower-status origins of many teachers, most schools and their staffs subscribe to middle-class values and norms. Children from working-class homes, it should be remembered, are thus compelled by law to enter culturally *alien* institutions.

We shall see that young children inherit their value-system, with its internal regulator, from their parents. We thus have the unseemly spectacle of lower-status children baffled by the language, values and norms of the authority figures, in the high-prestige institution, all being antithetical to those which are not only familiar to them, but constitute the fabric of their personality. At best they are forced into bemused and befuddled confusion. At worst such a conflict situation leads to anxiety, uncertainty and a sense of rejection; all of which, we shall see, are inimical to moral growth. The sense of estrangement is inevitable for it also occurs when a child identifies with an admired teacher, and this time the attendant whole or partial incorporation of a value-system estranges him from his family mores, leaving him a moral outcaste.

This added function of schools, whereby they inadvertently impose and reinforce the conventional morality of the middle class, has further moral consequences. Success at school tacitly becomes a mark of the degree to which pupils conform to higher-status standards of conduct. It follows from this that middle-class children are further favoured by the system. If a working-class pupil wished to attain a measure of success he would necessarily have to do violence to his own moral code.

It has not unnaturally been noticed that many such pupils are unwilling to be sacrificed on the altar of bourgeois respectability. Yet they still cannot emerge morally unscathed. This further disability is called a 'value-stretch'. It is characteristic of lower-class children, who can only subscribe to the values of society by developing an alternative parallel value system. In effect the victim of this cognitive dissonance develops flexible values which can become so stretched that lesser levels of success are acceptable. These alternative values then enable such a child to adjust to his deprived circumstances: but it is an emasculated adjustment, for such a child sinks into academic and moral torpor. Unwilling to strive, their lives become patterns of monotonous mediocrity.

Experiences in the Home

Obviously the physical conditions of the home have a direct effect on moral conduct. It is extremely difficult to be reasonable and loving when home life is chaotic; and exceptionally hard not to steal from a supermarket when one's home is bereft of toys and comfort. Leaving aside all the ramifications of economic disparity, however, there are some fundamental differences between the classes which influence moral conduct.

Higher-status children, it seems, have more loving parents. It is true that the practice of sending them to boarding schools seems to belie this, but the bulk of the evidence suggests otherwise. First, adoption is essentially a middle-class practice. Both adoptive and natural parents smile much more often when speaking to their children and consequently the offspring are early assured of their acceptance, and nestle cosily in the security of this love. This does not mean that working-class mothers are neglectful. It is merely that their affection is displayed in other ways. The Newsons are a fruitful source of information here. Studying infants in Nottingham they found that although enlightened child-rearing practices were filtering down the social scale, class differences were nevertheless apparent. Higher-status parents were angelically patient with temper tantrums, but steadfastly refused to dispense a regular supply of sweets. Furthermore they had high tolerance levels for bedtime crying and would only comfort a child when it was clear that he really was in distress. On the other hand, the lower-status parent provided an endless supply of sweets, and rushed swiftly with a dummy to a crying infant but tended to round furiously on a child in a temper-tantrum and dispensed immediate, incommensurate corporal punishment. Even with less offensive misdemeanours such parents tended to resort to immediate smacking, while middle-class mothers cuddled their infants out of the emotional morass into which their disobedience had led them.

With older children the differences are still marked. Lower-status children are threatened with the withdrawal of love or the imposition of authority (usually the policeman) to induce obedience, while their privileged peers are provided with explanations for the inevitable disapproval. As a consequence the former's concept of authority is chaotic, being usually thought of as the incomprehensible imposition of an alien power. The latter's penchant for explanations further enhances the differences. Depending, as it does, on the more sophisticated language of the middle-class child, it both expresses and reinforces his ability to conceptualize from specific experiences. Take a simple example. Bernstein presents a simple social-class contrast. He imagines a mother–child situation on a 'bus. The first are working class; the second, obviously middle class

1. Mother: 'Hold on tight.' Child: 'Why?' Mother: 'Hold on tight.' Child: 'Why?' Mother: 'I told you to hold on tight didn't I?'
2. Mother: 'Hold on tightly darling.' Child: 'Why?' Mother: 'If you don't you'll be thrown forwards and then you'll fall.'

Clearly the first child feels subject to the authoritative whim of his parent, while the latter may begin to suspect that we must have *reasons* for behaving as we do. In one sense the latter could be considered dishonest, for not even a brilliant child can win such an argument with its parent, and a fair charge might be that this is the middle-class equivalent of a slap, since both are essentially intended to induce a specific form of conduct. Yet even with its emotional blackmail such procedures are preferable to those experienced by a child living in a deficient house in a deprived area whose parents assert their feelings rather than explain their reasons. Every prohibition is accompanied by, 'Because I say so', 'You've got to, that's why', 'Wait till your father gets in'. Therefore, it is obvious and predictable that as the former child is dozing into sleep he will realize, vaguely, remotely, imperfectly but inexorably, that identifiable areas of concern for people matter. He will catch a glimmer of the truth that their feelings should be considered in any of his activities, and in this way begin to discern principles behind the moral precepts. Whereas the latter will stumble into bed bemused by a further series of unconnected fiats and so assume that conduct is only subject to authoritative dicta. As an adult he may well become one who lives blindly by the Bible, the union book and the law of the land. One is not thereby justified in assuming that the moral development of the former is assured, while that of the latter is not. However, the parallel with language is apparent. Without conceptualizing language, intellectual growth is stultified. Equally, without the ability to abstract and comprehend moral principles, moral growth is impossible. These parallel incompatible processes are perpetuated by both sets of parents, since one unequivocable fact is that our own experience of socialization is the norm for the child-rearing practices of our subculture.

There is a further aspect of these experiences which will be considered in detail when examining the notion of deferred gratification. The parental tendency to induce good conduct by the promise of future benefits, is not limited to either class, but its practice differs markedly between them. The structured, ordered life of a middle-class home lends itself to this system, since promised rewards are invariably given. If they were not, this cultivation of deferred gratification would obviously break down. Hence promises are honoured and members of such families keep their word to each other. This is not the case in lower-status homes, where the chaos, confusion, neglect, negligence and sometimes sheer stupidity cannot sustain such a sophisticated system.

Thus the homes also exacerbate the differences between the social classes. On the one hand is a higher-status child living in economic security and comfort. His educational and cultural development are assured within a stable, loving family and a school which is little more than the institutionalized form of his home. His structured life leads to the regulation of his conduct. Achievement motivation and deferred gratification rest lightly on his shoulders like accolades of future success. Mature value judgements and long-term goals induce in him a wisdom beyond his years, and yet the joys of childhood are not denied him. If he stands beside a peer whose life is the negation of these privileges one would soon see that the differences penetrated to the heart of their consciousness. Their attitudes, prejudices and concept of the 'good life' would emerge as diametrically opposed. It is not only economics, but also morality which divides society into at least two nations. For the former, life is a coherent sensible whole, trustworthy and reasonable. For the latter it is senseless, unpredictable and treacherous. The conduct of each may well reflect this tragic dichotomy. The ramifications of these differences, when both go to work, are complex, fascinating and depressing. Two facts, however, throw more light on this problem: boredom and noise both at work and home appear to interact one upon the other and affect personal relations.

It is now known that lower-status workers cannot accurately assess the passing of time. Because of this they are less patient and more easily bored. Many who have taken part in lightning strikes are now known to have done so because their 'action orientation' affects their 'subjective clock', leading them to believe that a job takes longer than it really does. Higher-status workers, on the other hand, are more sensitive to noise. This came to light when complaints concerning airport noise were analysed. One can see why this should be so. A factory worker surrounded by machinery would be less aware of noise than a bank clerk or office worker. Consequently the latter is less able to resist the stress of high noise levels.

Social Class and Human Relationships

This is an extremely delicate subject not only because relationships depend upon the personalities of the participants, but also because it would seem natural to suppose that although the classes were socially distinct they would still enjoy rich and warm relationships amongst themselves: but this is not so. The relationships of the two groups are markedly different.

One can see why this should be so. In explaining the origins of class conflict above, it was noted that the working classes were thrown back on to their families for security. This social pattern has survived to the present wherein most lower-status children find themselves born into the kinship web of an extended family and thus have no need to learn the social graces needed to attract and retain friends.

It has been tacitly assumed that the middle classes were bereft of such benefits, but now Bell has shown, with meticulous research support, that the middle class is also built upon extended families. Bott has shown how familial dynamics of a complex nature result in these focusing on the father in contrast to the working-class family web, which centres on the mother. It is a further fundamental difference which has such a profound influence on interpersonal conduct. The middle class are geographically mobile while the working class are not. Hence the extended family of the latter usually straddles a clutch of back streets while the former can extend from national boundaries. However, the point is this. They need to make friends in their locale. The lower-status family does not.

A number of recognized sociological experts have commented on this phenomenon. Some say that the middle-class extended family is bound together by regular telephone calls, occasional visits by car, and financial support and help from the dominant father figure. Local friends, outside the kinship-web, are essential. Others have noted that whereas a working-class wife can alleviate her marital problems in conversation with a sibling, cousin or maternal figure, the middle-class husband and wife have to keep their relationships in good repair. The antiseptic term 'mental hygiene' describes this, but the process does ensure that at the parental level there is a sustained sensitivity to persons and interpersonal relationships.

It is almost superfluous to add that the massive and uncoordinated findings concerning middle-class social dynamism fit into the pattern here. Such children and adolescents have been found to realize very rapidly the value of extra-familial group cohesion. They are thus more acceptable to their peers and possess what is generally termed 'high social desirability'. Hence they judge friendliness as the prime social virtue and prefer this to be laced with scholastic competence or at least a veneer of cultural sophistication.

By contrast the working classes tend to dismiss the benefits of group membership while the family is firmly established. They are consequently less friendly to those peers who do not share the privilege of kinship with them. This almost amounts to anti-social conduct for not only do they rank lower in 'social desirability' but do not seem to comprehend the nature of this personal quality. With this sensitivity blunted it follows naturally that they prefer any 'friends' to be sociable rather than friendly. Then because the tribalism, endemic to an extended family mentality, still remains, such 'friends' are usually cherished for their aggressiveness.

Expressed thus the tragic truth can be too easily overlooked. This kinship-based system induces a despairing negativism in many lower-status children. It has been repeatedly noted that at school they are characterized by passivity. They make no more creative ventures in social relationships than they do in intellectual or aesthetic activity. Kerr speaks of them as in 'retreat from sociability', and Spinley says rather more bluntly, 'Their relations with other people are coloured by negativism'. Naturally there are many exceptions, but the overall pattern of personalism seems to be clear. Once again the middle classes emerge triumphant.

Aggression, Authority and Sex

These are the three generally accepted foci around which revolve extremes of both feeling and conduct. It was noted immediately above that working-class relational preferences list aggression highly. Apart from being the natural response of one tribe to another, and thus a desirable quality in defensive warrior reactions, there are more subtle explanations of this. The one most relevant to this chapter will be expanded later. Apparently the inconsistent and irregular moral training of the lower-status child not only provides no secure framework for him, but also has the added distinction of containing little real recognition or concern for him as an individual. Consequently self assertion, denied the middle-class channel of articulacy, issues in the aggression so natural to 'action orientated' people. Further support for this is provided by the 'frustration–aggression' hypothesis. Confirmation of this has shown that both are significantly correlated. Aggressive men are invariably frustrated, and since the experiences of economically-deprived low-status men are of necessity frustrating, one would expect to find them more aggressive. Then to this must be added the recently confirmed fact that aggression is also correlated with anxiety, and the working-class life-style is known to be conducive to both anxiety and stress. Thus one ought always to treat an aggressive man as if he were anxious; and view with some sympathy the violent picket action of striking workers, and the destructive hooliganism of teenagers cast on the social scrapheap.

However, whatever the cause, working-class children are much more aggressive than their middle-class peers. As one would expect in a sub-culture where this was admired, they are much more ready to admit to being aggressive. When higher-status people possess that level of aggression required for success in business, they try to conceal it, self-control is a prime middle-class virtue. On this basis Merton argued that middle-class parents suppress aggression in their young, not because it is destructive, but simply because it leads to a loss in self-control. Such children then grow up, as Spinley reported, obsessively concerned to inhibit or conceal any aggressive traits.

Consequently, the bourgeoisie have devised subtle but highly successful means of canalizing it (except, it seems, when driving a car). Instead of becoming involved in abusive arguments or physical brawls, they casually challenge a friend to a game of squash and proceed to thrash the ball instead of him. It has also been noticed that the sacred hour, for many, has now been moved from Sunday to Saturday, when tribal combat takes place on a football field, or local champions lock in conflict on the wrestling ring floor. Observers thus vicariously enjoy a bar-room brawl and dissipate their hostility and aggression in the urban gladiatorial conflict of wrestlers: a fact which has no doubt not escaped the notice of the shrewd showmen who manipulate and enhance this element.

The differing attitudes to authority are rather more complex. Conditioned, as we have seen, into accepting authority as the fixed point to which one is either subservient or against which one rebels, the working-class child is 'authority-orientated'. Conversely the middle-class child's experience of authority figures, who were invariably willing to discuss their dicta and fiats, leads him to view authority as a device for easing social life, rather like the routine processes of tying shoes and ties, which render dressing a less arduous activity. Here, of course, developmental factors enter, and these are inordinately complex. Subscription to authority, as the prime moral sanction, is the mark of moral immaturity; conceptualizing is a necessary precursor in those who outgrow it, and this depends on intellectual maturation. The neurotic security seeker makes for the haven of clear authority to guide him, and this is a measure of personal disequilibrium.

A number of studies have found that any working-class community, with a genuine grievance, either sit back passively or, using authority as that against which they must rebel, resort to acts of aggression and crimes of violence. All this is sanctioned by opposition to the authoritarian 'them' who are deemed to be responsible. Middle-class communities, on the other hand, form a committee, elect a chairman, write to their Member of Parliament, ventilate their grievance through the local Press and then approach the offending body after having taken due care to consider the complexity of the situation in the light of all the relevant information. Of course one can expect this where the lawyer, architect, doctor, teacher, business-executive and social worker combine. It is, however, extremely difficult to imagine such action coming from labourers and factory workers. This should not, however, conceal the underlying and fundamental difference in social-class attitudes to authority.

One final point fits rather neatly into this scheme. When authority impinges on family life less dramatically, it is invariably the middle-class *husband* or the working-class *wife* who face 'them'. This is precisely what one would expect because the former family is orientated around the father, while the latter revolves around the mother.

In a period of sexual permissiveness social-class differences here may be diminishing. Yet these are still sufficiently identifiable to be important. One sharp difference is easily defined. Numerous researchers into contemporary working-class life have recorded one single fact with impressive unanimity. Whereas non-marital heterosexual relationships amongst the middle classes are accepted as not necessarily based on carnality, it is invariably the case that no such relationships are tolerated by the working class outside the familial circle. All of these are deemed to be based on active sexual practices. The middle classes, it seems, pride themselves on their sexual restraint and refrain from telling smutty stories in mixed company.

Yet even this simplistic picture can be misleading. Cynics may speak of middle-class hypocrisy and allude to week-end parties nocturnally throbbing with portly figures groping towards each other's wives. It is certainly true that such people with abundant leisure-time, ample facilities, sufficient money and social graces, have tended to view extra-marital, heterosexual relations as one of the more pleasant aspects of social intercourse; except, of course, where a stultifying, puritanism acted as an irrational inhibitor. However, since the Kinsey reports on sexual conduct more data have been added with social class variables to analyse them, and we now know that although much of this is overtly sensuous, many sustained, romantic sexual relationships do not depend upon carnal congress. Whether it ranges from the purity of platonic love to a mutually abandoned pagan worship of human flesh, cultivated men and women have always delighted in the sexuality of exploring each other's minds and bodies. Much of this may now result from a current fundamental change. Sexual intercourse is no longer the primarily procreative or need-reduction activity of earlier generations. Instead it appears to be emerging as a recreational activity for both sexes, in very much the way that Aldous Huxley predicted.

This social-class anomaly, however, reaches down into childhood. The working classes, who seem to acknowledge sexuality as a public feature of life, display an almost taboo-mentality on nudity. Not only do adults retain some garment, even during the most intimate activities, but they prohibit nudity and semi-nudity in the home. Consequently, many such children rarely see the naked bodies of both sexes and their first experience of making love is unlikely to remedy this. Equally vehement is the lower status embargo on even the innocent display or manipulation of infant genitalia. By contrast middle-class parents are permissive with genital play and treat adult and child nudity with nonchalance. (Indeed some reports claim that one has here sexual manipulation in the guise of innocent fondling.)

At first the inconsistencies seem to be irreconcilable, but a brief consideration of the different life-styles throws light on them. On the one hand the higher-status home treats children as persons in their own right. Thus just as their emotional, aesthetic and intellectual needs are catered for, their sexual growth is also fostered. Consequently sexuality grows with the other personal attributes and furthermore contributes towards a clear definition of male and female roles. As a natural consequence sexuality is seen in the context of mature personal relationships. In this milieu all the features of bourgeois sexuality are perfectly explicable.

In sharp contrast to this, one has a lower-status home where children are treated as things rather than persons. This becomes marked in a deprived economic setting where financially distressed parents tend to treat children as expensive objects, who wear out valuable commodities, eat expensive food and add to the familial lack of amenities by functioning as vomiting, defecating, urinating, noisy and attention-demanding sources of irritation. This infantile offensiveness then coalesces with the economic depredations of pregnancy and leads parents to suppress sexuality in the young.

It has been reported quite explicitly that lower-status overcrowded lack of amenities means that incest is a real danger; and many cases of girls citing their fathers and brothers as initiators of the process have been reported. The simple psychological fact is that when levels of inhibition fall, aggression and sexual activity rise. Rape and war have, after all, been correlated throughout man's history, but for the working-class 'action-orientated' male, both sex and aggression are the stereotype methods of asserting his masculine identity, and establishing his community role. Consequently, one has the curious fact that such children are trapped in the ambivalence of overt adult sexuality, with a taboo on its infantile manifestations. Hence one is led logically to the last point which enables all these curiously conflicting points to cohere. Sexuality is essentially an assertion of aggressively tinctured personal and social traits. It is not, for them, a tender and intimate expression of human relationships experienced at depth, as it is for the bourgeoisie.

Life-styles and Morality
The above evidence points to a fundamental sociological truth. Many of the maladies of modern man are correlated with different life-styles and modes of cognition. On a telluric scale one can see that they are often extensions of societal attitudes which remain unexamined. Amongst these one may place the stereotyping of man and nature so that violence is done to racial and cultural norms. Hence both the rape of our species and planet, and our failure to recognize the pathology of both urbanization and industrialization, follow as a natural consequence. At the level of social class, our reluctance to

accept the economic consequence of social reformation and organization leads to the moral impasse implied above. It is simply tragically true that moral, cultural and economic advantages are all correlated; and despite the process of embourgeoisement (see Chapter 10) this structure appears to be an epiphenomenon of advanced societies today.

There is an abundance of evidence to confirm that culture determines morality. We have seen above that a child sensitized to people's feelings, made aware of first-order moral principles, and linguistically and intellectually equipped to conduct himself according to these insights, has the potential to become a morally mature man; while the child deprived of some, or of all, has not. But this concept probes deeper. It implies that moral values are the internalized components of a common culture. Hence cultural and moral deprivation or privilege are positively correlated.

Observers of western society are unanimous in their approval of this conclusion in its various forms. Long ago Durkheim demonstrated beyond all doubt that the morality of each human being is correlated with the social structure of which he is a part. MacIntyre has recently argued cogently that the pluralistic nature of contemporary morality has served to highlight an important fact. There is, he says, one morality for the middle class and another for the working class. It is, therefore, not surprising to find sociologists mostly arraigned against those who explain crime and immorality in terms of individual differences. Instead they insist that such phenomena can only be properly understood as the product of social factors. These may impinge upon individuals with different degrees of potency, but even this variable is socially determined, for an individual's role and status within his class are determinants here. Such a sanguine view does tend to minimize human culpability and present man in an ennobled light, but, equally, it enables one to recoil with less horror from the mass atrocities which characterize our history.

Such determinants are also, it seems, operative in sub-systems and reference groups. Army euphemisms for theft indicate clearly how soldiers view stealing. The crunch comes when one realizes that middle-class morality is not only different from, but also superior to that of the working classes. It is unnecessary to explicate all that is implicit in the above discussion. Suffice it to say that numerous researchers have reached this conclusion.

There is conclusive evidence to show that working-class boys are more delinquent than their privileged peers. Of course, the evidence can be manipulated. One may argue, for example, that working-class boys are also less intelligent and are, therefore, more likely to be caught by the police. Or again it may be stressed that deprivation is an incentive to steal; but this is an argument which is emasculated by the disappointment of those who thought that crime would atrophy in an affluent society. Hence it is repeatedly said that the middle classes are characterized by high morality; though it is intriguing to note that none who say this care to define their terms.

One social-class characteristic here is the pattern of theft. Numerous researchers have pointed to the fact that working men steal from their factories with insouciance. There is on record one report of a visit to a semi-slum home painted cream within and without. The puzzled interviewer, suspecting some form of virulent colour blindness, was soon enlightened. The husband worked at a paint factory. Cream was the colour of the paint batch when the painting was done. He could only bring home one colour in a jam-jar; the rate of work presumably then being one jam-jar of paint per night. Higher-status protestations of scrupulous honesty then stand in stark contrast. However, this may well be a principle honoured in the breach. Hotel managers, librarians and office storekeepers can testify to the fact that towels, books and stationery are deemed to be middle-class perquisites.

Only one final point needs to be stressed here. This does not mean that the middle classes are moral and the working classes are not. Both have rigid standards whereby crime and immorality are judged. These are relative phenomena and must be assessed with reference to the morality of the specific group. Even delinquency is relative to the culture, but still assessed as such. An obvious example of this is student behaviour. When the middle classes dominated university life, student rags were violent, sometimes immoral and even vicious, but they were tolerated as the exuberance of the next generation of leaders. Today, if working-class students behave in a similar fashion they are castigated as louts, and doubts are cast on the state of their underwear, and the occupation of their fathers. Even if bourgeois disapproval is justified, it often emerges that the plebeian undergraduate is involved in a pathological attempt to conceal the fact that he is already diverging morally upward from his social class.

CONCLUSION

If these moral distinctions seem to be either artificial or exaggerated, it is salutary to note that the same pattern exists in non-moral activities. The cultural differences are constantly seen to diverge and form coherent entities, each of which characterize the sub-culture. It is now known that disease patterns, religious views, mourning customs and responses to tragedy, are all correlated with class. Eating patterns and alcoholic consumption are too. On the whole the middle-class man rarely drinks to excess. His fundamental sense of economy proscribes an expensive habit, and anyway he flinches from the aggressive traits which may lie dormant until drink relaxes his inhibitor. Even if he does become drunk, social class also determines precisely the way in which he will conduct himself for he tends to behave as his particular society expects him to behave. This is also true of the facial expressions used as sensitive responses to a range of verbal stimuli, and any middle-class man hoping to escape from his class by controlling his facial muscles, ought to remember that the times of his rising and retiring, and the use he makes of his evenings and week-ends are equally conditioned by this factor.

Sport too, comes under the same influence. Jackson and Marsden found that the two social classes in a grammar school came into conflict here. In contrast to the enthusiastic, lithe-limbed compulsive athlete who reverenced sportsmanship and team-spirit, the working-class pupils listed all the games and then observed somewhat earthily, 'Load of crap the whole lot!' Even when such a lad indulges in sport the forms it takes are stylized, with soccer dominant in Britain and baseball in America. And finally it is known that even the forms and modes of children's play are subject to clear social-class variables.

Thus one could continue. Hygienic practices vary too and the characteristic smell of a workman in the home reminds one of the different patterns of washing and bathing. Two further related facts support this. First, it has been discovered that cervical cancer is significantly more common amongst working-class women. Second, male smegma (obviously removed by regular bathing) is listed as a carcinogenic agent (3). Of course the evidence is inconclusive, but it does support the general contention. All of this confirms that such moral variations occur. Perhaps one does not meet these stereotypes in isolation since we are only most truly ourselves when embedded in the matrix of our own sub-culture.

However, all the features, listed above, have glossed over the most fundamentally important moral qualities. They alluded to them but did not explicate them. Take one strand of this complex. A middle-class child, reared in a stable home looks forward to promised rewards. At school he anticipates later academic successes. Facing problems, he considers long-term consequences. When this is added to the temporal dimension of his use of money and leisure, or the weight he gives to future advantages, which may require a temporary sacrifice, it is clear that he is 'future-orientated', or, as many sociologists prefer, he is characterized by a 'deferred-gratification' pattern of conduct.

Now when all the research has been sifted and analysed with care, the five primary social-class differences in morality listed on p. 58 emerge. So important are these traits for the development of moral maturity, that they will be considered in detail later. Consequently we shall then pass from a purely *descriptive* account of social-class differences, to one which makes a detailed *evaluative* analysis on the basis of sociological evidence (see Chapters 4–9). In effect this will constitute a sociological analysis of the educative processes which lead an individual towards moral maturity. As education is a cumulative process an investigator is necessarily compelled to examine the evidence in a chronological sequence. Consequently we must first consider those infant, familial experiences which constitute the preconditions of morality, and then, since as a child grows his social experience widens, we shall consider the influence of social-class factors upon the development of the primary moral traits. Lastly, since compulsory education forces all children into schools, we must examine the way in which, as systems, they affect the moral maturation of their pupils.

Before passing on to consider these aspects of moral education a final, qualifying point must be stressed. Our task as moral educators and socializers has recently been made more arduous and complex. It is now abundantly clear that both Britain and America are overtly pluralist societies. Purists may baulk at the term but cannot surely refute the view that we are becoming increasingly both multi-cultural and multi-racial in form with violently conflicting mores existing within the same society. Hence the moral education of children must of necessity take place in a society which is infinitely more complex than that of our fathers who had only to consider the idiosyncrasies of varying social classes within the one culture. The elaboration of this point requires a volume of evidence and argument and thus does not properly belong to the present book, so, therefore, the admittedly simplistic approach of a two-class tool is used in this section, with the added proviso that such polarizations are found in each pluralistic social element.

One predictable sociological fact is an extension of this point. Most sub-cultures are orientated towards either religious or secular ideologies. It is only when one is actually faced with a classroom of children from Christian, Muslim, Hindu and Buddhist sub-cultures that one realizes how deeply morality is affected by religious *mores* and beliefs. The question of religion and morality will be considered later (Chapter 18), but once again it must be stressed that a consideration of such complexities belongs properly to a further book. It will be seen there, however, that the terms 'religion' and 'morality' are used with such wide connotations that the arguments may be acceptable to all except the most exclusive sectarians, be they atheistic humanists or Muslims bent on a holy war.

REFERENCES

1 An example of this emerged from a standard intelligence test. An item showed two men, one digging and the other reading. A child was asked to indicate which man was working. She pointed to the one who was reading and was marked wrong until it was discovered that her father was a college tutor who dug the garden for relaxation.
2 Cf 94% who came into this category, 43% classified themselves as lower status and 51% deemed themselves to be higher status.
3 It can, of course, be argued that this evidence points to lower-status reluctance to submit to regular screening by cervical smears. Even if this is so it only highlights a further facet of hygienic differences amongst the social classes.

Bibliography
BECHHOFER, F., 'A Sociological Portrait: Income', in *New Society*, No. 472, October 1971.
BELL, C. R., *Middle Class Families* (Routledge & Kegan Paul, 1971).
BERNSTEIN, B., 'Language and Social Class', *British Journal of Sociology*, Vol. XI, 1960.
BERNSTEIN, B., 'Social Structure, Language and Learning', in M. Craft (Ed.), *Linking Home and School* (Longmans, 1967).
BERNSTEIN, B., *Class, Codes and Control* (Routledge & Kegan Paul, 1971).
BOTT, E., *Family and Social Networks* (Tavistock, 1964).
BRIGGS, A., *Victorian Cities* (Odhams, 1963).
BURTON, A., *The Jones Report* (Secker & Warburg, 1970).
CENTERS, R., *The Psychology of Social Classes* (Princteon Univ. Press, 1949).
COATES, K. and SILBURN, R., *Poverty, Deprivation and Morale* (Nottingham Univ. Dept. Adult Education, 1967).
DURKHEIM, E., *Moral Education* (Free Press, Glencoe, 1925).
FLOUD, J. E., HALSEY, A. H. and MARTIN, F. M., *Social Class and Educational Opportunity* (Heinemann, 1956).
FOSTER, J., 'Nineteenth Century Towns', in H. S. Dyos (Ed.) *A Study of Urban History* (Int. Round Table Conf. Proceedings, Leicester, 1968).
GIBB, L., *The Jones: How to Keep up with Them* (Frederick Muller, 1959).
GIBB, L., *The Higher Joneses* (Frederick Muller, 1961).
HOGGART, R., *The Uses of Literacy* (Pelican, 1957).
HORNEY, K., *The Neurotic Personality of Our Time* (Routledge & Kegan Paul, 1962).
JACKSON, B. and MARSDEN, D., *Education and the Working Classes* (Routledge & Kegan Paul, 1962).
KERR, M., *The People of Ship Street* (Routledge & Kegan Paul, 1958).
KINSEY, A., *et al., Sexual Behaviour in the Human Female* (Saunders, 1953).
KINSEY, A., *et al., Sexual Behaviour in the Human Male* (Saunders, 1953).
KLEIN, J., *Samples from English Culture*, 2 Vols (Routledge & Kegan Paul, 1965).
LACEY, C., 'Some Sociological Concomitants of Academic Streaming in a Grammar School', in *British Journal of Sociology*, Vol. 17, 1966.
LEGGETT, J. C., *Class, Race and Labour* (Oxford Univ. Press, 1968).

MACINTYRE, A., *Secularisation and Moral Change* (Oxford Univ. Press, 1967).

MELLY, G., 'Gesture goes Classless', *New Society*, 17 June 1965.

MERTON, R., *Social Theory and Social Structure* (Free Press, Glencoe, 1957).

NEWCOMB, T. M., *Social Psychology* (Tavistock, 1959).

NEWSON, J. and NEWSON, E., *Patterns of Infant Care in an Urban Community* (Allen & Unwin, 1963).

OPPENHEIM, A. N., 'A Study of Social Attitudes of Adolescents', Unpublished Ph.D. thesis, London, 1956.

SCHOECK, H., *Envy: A Theory of Social Behaviour* (Secker & Warburg, 1969).

SCOTT, J., 'The Glass Workers of Carmaux', in S. Therstrom and R. Sennett (Ed.), *Nineteenth Century Cities* (Yale Univ. Press, 1969).

SHILS, F. C., 'Deference', in J. A. Jackson (Ed.), *Social Stratification* (Cambridge Univ. Press, 1968).

SHOHAM, SHLOMO, *et al.*, 'The Etiology of Middle Class Delinquency in Israel', *Human Relations*, Vol. 24, No. 4, 1971.

SPINLEY, B. M., *The Deprived and the Privileged* (Routledge & Kegan Paul, 1953).

STOTT, D. H., *Unsettled Children and their Families* (Univ. London Press, 1956).

SUGARMAN, B., 'What the Sociologist has to Say', in J. Wilson, N. Williams and B. Sugarman (Eds), *Introduction to Moral Education* (Pelican, 1967).

WOOTTON, B., *Contemporary Britain* (Allen & Unwin, 1971).

ZWEIG, F., *The Worker in an Affluent Society* (Heinemann, 1961).

Chapter 3

The Preconditions of Morality

In this chapter we shall be concerned primarily with those familial experiences in infancy which will enable children to make progress along a path of increasing moral maturity. Immediately, the question arises, 'What should we expect of such a child?' Leaving aside the philosophical problem of *defining moral maturity*, it is possible to isolate certain qualities which appear to be essential. He should have a developed sense of individual identity and a realistic appraisal of his own personality. He needs to be amenable to that moral guidance which will enable him to develop sufficient character and insight to make and defend his own moral judgements. Finally, a mature conscience should help him to control his conduct by supplying *subjective* confirmation or rejection of his *objective* alignment to moral values, standards and norms. These and other qualities should be cultivated to ensure that they perpetually mature as he grows. And it is these which will form the basis of that moral education which must be the essence of socialization.

THE PRIMARY PRECONDITIONS

Such a description of the preconditions of moral maturity could continue into the minutiae of analysis within many academic disciplines. But from such a discussion the same basic pattern will invariably emerge, even though the terminology changes. James Hemming, for example, speaks of the processes of identification, self-differentiation and socialization. Professor Morris refers to the three basic needs to identify oneself, experience acceptance and make an adequate identification. Charlotte Fleming emphasizes this 'need-reduction' in her theory of social maturation, which Maslow then erects as a hierarchy of needs. Susan Isaacs, among others, stresses the need to comprehend the increasing complexity of components which contribute towards the process of socialization. Finally, Havighurst refers to 'development tasks' which have to be accomplished before growth can proceed—although, as we shall see, this last view must be qualified.

Such an analysis could be endlessly computed. For convenience, and in the interests of clarity, it is useful to present these concepts distilled in the form of questions. The reason for this is obvious. We are dealing with young children and their prime characteristic seems often to be the ability to ask an unabating stream of almost unanswerable questions: 'Where do we come from? What are we? Where are we going?' These and similar questions haunt every human being until he faces his own death and wonders then whether they will finally be answered. We may ignore them, summarily dismiss them, or be satisfied with glib and facile answers. Yet they return and insist upon being answered: and the degree to which we answer them 'rightly' often establishes the level of our morality.

Obviously infants are not exempt from this experience. For them process may be less conscious, but the questions remain the same. 'Who are you? Who am I?' These are questions which must be answered before any human growth is possible; and by implication they must be answered before any moral growth is apparent. The first basic moral question is a simple one, 'What must I do?' we ask. Such a simple question is naturally made more sophisticated by philosophers. Thus Braithwaite prefers it in the form 'what moral principles shall I adopt?' (1) but like Nowell-Smith, he too affirms that this primary question constitutes the avenue of morality. Yet this presupposes that a series of prior questions have been asked and answered; the first of which is 'Who am I?' Therefore, it will be convenient for the material of this chapter, dealing as it does with the preconditions of morality, to be couched in the form of questions.

We noted above that all analyses in this sphere can be reduced to a common pattern, and such a conclusion is clearly apparent at this point. There are at least five questions asked by all potentially moral beings, and they must be satisfactorily answered before children can become mature moral agents. Fortunately, by a simple series of correlations it is possible to discover that these questions highlight at least five preconditions of morality. For simplicity they may be listed as follows:

1 The establishment of one's identity. ('Who am I?')
2 The ability to accept oneself. ('What am I really like?')
3 The accessibility of moral models. ('How must I behave?')
4 The formation of a mature conscience. ('What is the right thing for me to do?')
5 The experience of achievement and success. ('How am I doing?')

The pre-eminence of love
Before passing on to consider these themes, two important points must be made. This analysis is based not on rationality but upon

relationships. Their essence is compounded not of logic but of love. This point will be pursued below, but the primacy of love at this point must be stressed. It is also relevant to point out that because of this all children are at risk in an alienated (2) society, but that the establishment of these preconditions can do much to end the contingent alienation of modern man. Hence it is argued here that moral education must make a sustained effort to establish and perpetuate these preconditions.

It must be remembered, however, that the above is not an exhaustive list. It is an analytical model. Yet its accuracy is partly confirmed by Robert Ardrey who studied the animal origins of our society, with its complex structure built on property and tribes, and his conclusions were clear. Even animals need to establish and maintain their identity, security and source of stimulatory approval.

Personal Identity

The primary human question, 'Who am I?' can only be answered in a social context for our identity is established in relationships. As Aristotle said, 'Man is a social animal' and the oft quoted phrase of Teilhard (3) that 'union differentiates' sums this up graphically: the two words contain the fundamental truth that a man's uniqueness emerges from his corporate life. In the terms of this book we may say that it is in a family that children ought to find the conditions under which their 'selves' can be established.

Obviously this can induce an imbalance between self and society. In neurotic forms such disparities can lead to the immorality of either gross egocentricity or extreme submissiveness. Identity is established in relationships and is thereby intimately and indissolubly bound up with morality. As T. S. Eliot said, 'There is no life that is not lived in community'. The problem of autonomy is therefore relevant here. Community life must be lived by autonomous individuals who act responsibly. Thus irresponsible and unbridled individuality must not be confused with mature identity. A cell which goes its own way is cancerous. It ought to operate symbiotically within an homeostatic organic system, but it does not. Thus it is with children. The differentiation of their 'selfhood' must proceed in union with their social environment.

Self-acceptance

While answering this question a child also needs to accept the self which is emerging: he asks, 'What am I like?' Unfortunately the clues provided by his environment and consciousness present ambivalent evidence. His most terrifying experience is that of recognizing that he can hate the object of his love. It does seem to be literally true that we, 'Always hurt the one we love'! Psycho-analysts provide evidence of the fact that this sentiment is true. A child drawn from the warm security of breast-feeding can develop into a knotted paroxysm of fury and murderous rage when a nipple is finally pulled from his suckling lips. He thus learns the truth that children (and adults) are all an amalgam of good and evil. This is a terrifying truth to face. Consequently few children are able to accept themselves *as they really are*. Obviously loving acceptance by his family can help a child to do this, and it is this 'unconditional acceptance' (4), which, as Ingleby later discovered, enables children to learn to love. For the simple truth is that we can only love because we are loved. Thus paradoxically a 'good' home is one in which a child can be bad for the disciplined, unqualified love, he finds there, is a constant corrective. This should be true of a classroom too. However, unless self-acceptance is genuine, moral growth is jeopardized. Until a child can accept himself realistically as a person he cannot treat others as persons in their own right.

Identification

In this process of establishing his identity and accepting himself, the child asks the next crucial question. 'How must I behave?' It is at this point that he needs moral models on which to base his conduct. The psychological term for this unconscious process is 'identification'; but sociologists speak of models or paradigms. Naturally parents provide children with their first paradigmatic experiences, but this is not an exclusively parental function. Later, other figures emerge from the widening social environment of a growing infant and fulfil this role. Clearly the accessibility of such moral models is an essential precondition of moral growth; and it is becoming increasingly recognized that 'ideal figures' are important in this respect. They flow imperceptibly into the child's own ego-ideal and ideal-self, and so reinforce his self-image as they subtly affect his morality.

Conscience

The next question follows naturally from this, for a child's paradigms could range from a Jesus Christ to a pathological Ché Guevara. Thus he must ask 'What is the right thing for me to do?' Here many say simply that his conscience will be a reliable guide in this respect. Indeed some contemporary eminent educators are saying that moral education should have as its primary aim, 'The formation of a mature personal conscience' (5).

Unfortunately recent investigation into this human phenomenon reveals how exceedingly complex a concept it is. On the surface the term 'conscience' appears to refer to a simple human experience. We all know the difference between right and wrong, even though social relativity, of the kind discussed in Chapter 5, eliminates absolute objectivity from the knowledge provided. But, says the layman, we know that there is a difference because we each possess a conscience. The complexities of this deceptively simple opinion will be disclosed later. For the moment we have only to consider how recorded history presents us with a saga in which men have pillaged, tortured, murdered and damned each other at the behest of conscience. The cynic may perhaps be forgiven for wryly suggesting that we might well be better off without one; it has been said that we spend our infant years acquiring a conscience, and the rest of our lives trying to get rid of it! Yet the stark fact remains that, without some internalized control of this kind, morality is impossible.

ACHIEVEMENT AND SUCCESS

Finally, having acquired an identity, accepted himself as he is, modelled himself on ideal figures and developed an internalized control, the child asks plaintively, 'How am I doing?' Hitherto, loving acceptance in the family met his needs, now in order to develop a positive self-concept he must experience both success and achievement and that loving approval which accompanies it. For infants the answers to this question are therefore most effective; parents in supplying a range of positive and loving responses perpetually meet this need. In this way a sense of personal dignity and worth is born in each child by the experience of parental acceptance and love.

The common experience of finding infants being excessively mischievous and annoying appears to be linked with this. In such situations children may simply be testing the degree of their acceptance as persons, despite their faults. The ridicule, sarcasm and personal belittling of children, common in many homes and schools, clearly hinders the establishment of this precondition. Every child, however inadequate, should enjoy the dignity of some personal success, no matter how meagre it may appear to be. Ego-wounds, of any kind, inflicted so often without any realization of the profound damage they do must inevitably affect individual morality. Hemming has presented the dark side of this picture. 'A child's self-respect and confidence,' he writes, 'can be undermined by too much criticism, which makes him feel worthless.' (6) In any class of any school on any day the observant teacher can find children who behave immorally because they are treated as such; or, conversely, who behave as responsible and intelligent human beings because they feel themselves to be respected and accepted *as they are*.

A Life-long Process

It must be added here that the above outline, and its elaboration below, may appear to subscribe to the Freudian view that character is indelibly established in infancy. This depressing view is expressed forcibly in the conclusion, that by the seventh year, 'children will have absorbed the basic attitudes and values of their sub-culture' (7). There is some truth in this conclusion, particularly, as we shall see, for lower-status children. Thus the importance of the early years cannot be devalued. If this were the whole truth moral educators would be impotent and moral education a non-viable activity in school. Fortunately, this maxim is only partly true. The full truth is that we spend *all our lives*, as both children and adults satisfying these needs, and establishing more firmly the preconditions of infant, child and adult morality. The explorer Nansen highlighted this fact, by saying simply that 'We ought to regard our most important task in life as the discovery of our ego' (8).

Recent psychological investigation, particularly by Erik Erikson and others, endorses this; they show that the establishment of our identity, for example, is a life-long process. Indeed we can now speak without reserve of the 'identity-crises' which perpetually face us. This is also true of the other preconditions of morality. Hence the qualification mentioned earlier when speaking of Havighurst's 'development tasks' can be added.

A Second Chance

We now know that there are two periods of personality 'plasticity'. One, as we have seen is at the beginning of childhood. The other is on the threshold of adulthood. Hence teachers can be encouraged by the knowledge that adolescence is a second phase of personal malleability in human growth. It is at that stage that some of the deficiencies of childhood can be augmented by education and the personal influence of a teacher.

There is, however, a negative side to this second chance. In Part Two of the book we shall see how adolescent, delinquent sub-cultures tend to remedy these deficiencies and produce the violent gangs characterized by socially aberrant conduct. The positive side is that while primary school teachers have the tremendously important educational task of allying themselves with parental influence in establishing these preconditions with the very young, the secondary school teacher may literally have to act *in loco parentis moralis* to perform this task. He can then help to provide that which had been withheld in infancy. Indeed it is becoming increasingly apparent that teachers will also need to fulfil a secular equivalent of the function hitherto reserved for priests and doctors, and perhaps the movement towards the appointment of personal tutors and counsellors in schools is highlighting this trend. The fact remains, however, that deficiencies in infancy may be remedied in adolescence.

These preconditions can lead to either moral or immoral conduct. Inadequacies here lead inevitably only to amoral behaviour. Deprivation can produce personalities characterized by schizoid or psychopathic structures. In discussing the former Laing is quite specific; expressing views repeatedly presented in his published work, he said quite simply, 'Schizophrenia is not in a person but is between people. It represents a broken-down relationship'(9). Stephenson is equally precise, 'The psychopath,' he writes, 'tends to be insensitive to interpersonal and moral considerations' (10).

This, of course, is a simplification of a complex matter. Psychopathy and schizophrenia are both generic terms used to describe complex pathological states. For the moment, however, we can say with certainty that failure to establish the preconditions of morality, either in infancy or early adolescence, militates against a child's attainment of moral maturity. In its mildest form deprivation leads children to be alienated both in school and society at large. In its severest manifestations they may pass through the apathy of amorality on to the total moral inadequacy inherent in schizoid and psychopathic personalities.

SOCIAL-CLASS DIFFERENCES

Despite the numerous and meticulously documented reports on child rearing in recent years, it is difficult to make any other than tentative affirmations. Those involved in this work will know how readily discussions here degenerate into an exchange of uninformed prejudice, but some general conclusions can be reached on the basis of the following chapters.

There is clearly some correlation between the preconditions and the moral traits enumerated below. Hence it would seem that social class is a determinant here too. One interesting current project is that of my colleague Frances Scott, whose doctoral dissertation is devoted to this theme, but for the moment all that one can say is that the moral preconditions appear to resolve themselves down to a consideration of personal identity. Equally, the moral traits apparently revolve around the concept of personalism (see Chapter 7). Then we find that higher-status children are more likely to be accorded the dignity of personal worth, and are equally accepted as persons in their own right, Any relationship with them must include rational discourse and individual concern.

Thus it would seem that the preconditions of morality are most surely established in those homes which will also encourage the development of the primary moral traits (see Chapter 4), and if this is so it necessarily follows that their inculcation is most assured in a middle-class home.

REFERENCES

1 Braithwaite (1971), p. 145.
2 An alienated society is one in which individual members are sociologically disposed to structure their own self-awareness in terms of impotence, depersonalization, purposelessness, meaninglessness, anomie, isolation and self-estrangement.
3 Teilhard (1966), p. 262.
4 Ingleby (1967), p. 109.
5 Berridge (1969), p. 13. This actually sums up *one* theme of this delightful and valuable book.
6 Hemming (1969), p. 98.
7 Lewis (1966), p. 21.
8 Quoted by de Terra (1964), p. 138.
9 See especially Laing (1967).
10 Stephenson (1966), p. 45.

Bibliography

ARDREY, ROBERT, *The Territorial Imperative* (Collins, 1967).
BERRIDGE, DOROTHY M., *Growing to Maturity* (Burns & Oates, 1969).
BRAITHWAITE, R. B., 'An Empiricist's View of the Nature of Belief', in J. Bowden and J. Richmond (Eds), *A Reader in Contemporary Theology*, Student Christian Movement, 1971).
FLEMING, CHARLOTTE, *Adolescence: Its Social Psychology* (Routledge & Kegan Paul, 1967).
HAVIGHURST, R. J., *Human Development and Education* (Longmans, 1953).
HEMMING, JAMES, 'The Development of Children's Moral Values', *British Journal of Educational Psychology*, June 1957.
HEMMING, JAMES, *Individual Morality* (Nelson, 1969).
INGLEBY, A. H. B., *Towards Maturity* (Hale, 1966).
INGLEBY, A. H. B., *Learning to Love* (Hale, 1967).
ISAACS, SUSAN, *Social Development in Young Children* (Routledge & Kegan Paul, 1961).
LAING, R. D., *The Divided Self* (Penguin, 1965).
LAING, R. D., 'Helping the Split Mind to Cure Itself', in *Observer*, 12 February 1967.
LAING, R. D., *Self and Others* (Tavistock, 1969).
LEWIS, OSCAR, 'The Culture of Poverty', in *Scientific American*, October 1966.
MASLOW, ABRAHAM H., *Motivation and Personality* (Harper & Row, 1970).
MORRIS, B., *Preconditions of Moral Education* (Farmington Trust Research Unit, Oxford, 1966).
NOWELL-SMITH, P. H., *Ethics* (Penguin, 1959).
STEPHENSON, G. M., *The Development of Conscience* (Routledge & Kegan Paul, 1966).
TEILHARD, PIERRE DE CHARDIN, *The Phenomenon of Man* (Collins, 1960).
TERRA, HELMUT DE, *Memories of Teilhard de Chardin* (Collins, 1964).

Chapter 4

Social-class Variations in Primary Moral Traits

In passing from a consideration of crucial childhood experiences to social-class differences in morality, one negotiates an area of national life of which many are rightly ashamed. Over a decade ago Douglas reported on the progress and life-styles of children born in 1946. Now Davie, *et al.*, have augmented this work with a longitudinal study of all children born in 1958. It is a depressing document for its most pungent observation is that the disadvantaged children in our land are further penalized for being already deprived. It is axiomatic that lower-status children suffer from physical, intellectual and emotional deprivation, and now we learn that the gap between higher- and lower-status infants continues to widen during their years at school.

Lower-status children are found not only to be more likely to come from inferior homes, with a minimum of amenities, but to suffer more from physical and emotional neglect. They are shorter, more prone to respiratory disorders, squints and speech defects and inadequate linguistic skills, little general knowledge, find it difficult to adjust to school and display many symptoms of neurotic stress, including enuresis.

It is immediately apparent that such stark social-class differences will affect the quality of those experiences which qualify as moral preconditions. Obviously love and affection can exist independently of physical conditions, but there is here an inevitable and undesirable correlation. Although no statistical evidence is available it is still possible to conclude that those preconditions, based as they are on love, patience and ordered discipline, constitute some of the privileges which are present in higher-status homes and absent in the lower. Indeed, like all the other advantages they naturally cohere with the rest. Now since this is also true of moral advantage and deprivation, it is possible to continue the argument advanced in Chapter 2 and consider the social-class differences in those primary moral traits already outlined.

In turning to consider these one takes the first tentative step into a controversial area. Many of us are peculiarly sensitive in this respect. Whenever a lecturer or writer makes an evaluative reference to social-class differences in behaviour of any kind, he can be assured of a violent response. At its best it can take the form of accusing him of snobbery; at its worst personal vilification may be heaped upon him. However, the evaluative nature of the material under discussion cannot be avoided. Nor should personal and academic caution induce us to gloss over these apparently unpleasant truths.

As we have seen, it is now axiomatic that the academic ability and attainment of children are positively correlated with their position in the social stratification which characterizes our society. It has also been shown that even such a peculiarly human, individual, yet universal phenomenon as linguistic development is also determined by differing sub-cultural experiences. One would not therefore expect morality to be exempt from this influence. In morality, as in all areas of human behaviour and development, there are distinct social-class differences. It is an unfortunate fact that, on the whole, human moral qualities appear to deteriorate with a fall in social status.

In one sense it is curious to find opposition to this view. We have already accepted that simple cultural variations are apparent in morality and behaviour. We are not, however, quite so willing to admit that sub-cultural differences, of a fundamental kind, exist within the same culture, and must be the object of evaluative analysis. Perhaps it is the ambivalence of the perennially snobbish, white, anglo-saxon attitude which leads to such an *impasse*. We readily divide and sub-divide our nation into classes and sub-classes. Yet the harsh and stark corollaries of this are then ignored because each individual blithely evades the consequences of this analysis by assuming that the lower-status category begins on the level just below him. However, when viewing the five primary moral traits it becomes obvious that the maturation of each reflects clear socio-economic factors.

When the psychological, developmental pattern of moral growth was outlined in an earlier volume it was discovered that one of its dimensions was that of moral judgement (1). This element must now be examined more closely, for, since the early 1930s, it has become increasingly recognized that the moral judgement, exercised by an individual, is closely related to his sub-cultural experiences. Now more evidence has been accumulated to substantiate this view by sociologists who have studied human morality in a social context.

Before proceeding any further, however, the methodological approach outlined above must again be emphasized. The majority of citizens in any society fall into the large category of the middle groupings of social class. This may range from the blue-collared worker at the lower end of the scale to the relatively wealthy lower-professional man at the upper end. Between these two extremes there is a considerable amount of socially upward and downward mobility in our dynamic society. In this process those becoming socially degraded may still take their higher-status attitudes with them, and those who are upwardly mobile may also take their lower-status attitudes with them. Thus such an investigation as the one currently being undertaken is facilitated by the use of the 'two-class' tool, which was described in Chapter 2. This enables us to sharpen distinctions and dissect the coherent elements embedded almost inextricably, in the evidence provided by investigations into the morality of the great majority of people lying in this central heteronomous grouping. A further advantage accrues from this. By extending the extremes of the groupings under consideration one may speak generally of 'higher-status' children on the one hand, and 'lower-status' children on the other, and so avoid a perpetual concatenation of qualifications and footnotes to avoid misunderstanding. It must not be forgotten, however, that this is merely a tool and like all tools its value lies not in any inherent worth it may possess, but simply in the function it performs. Hence if this tool helps us to understand the morality of children within the context of social stratification, it can be used even though it may be a clumsy and blunt instrument. When this is done, in the area of morality, an interesting fact emerges. There are clear social-class differences in terms of the five fundamental facets of moral behaviour outlined in Chapter 1 (see p. 58).

The fact that moral judgement is fundamental to any consideration of morality is self-evident, but this may not be so with the other terms used. Those familiar with philosophy or sociology will recognize the general areas delineated by the other terms, but because they are being used here in a new and specific way they must all be defined and described before a detailed examination is made of each one.

Moral Judgements

In the matter of moral judgement one has to keep two concepts sharply distinguished. The first is that different sub-cultures have varying ideas about what is right or wrong. It is imperative that the sociologist discovers just why it is that in some lower-status, urban sub-cultures, it is considered normal and right for a boy to lie to the authorities, steal from public corporations and be sexually promiscuous.

Then there is the second psychological consideration. Moral judgement, as a cognitive process, passes through sequential, developmental stages. First it is based on prudence, then authority, then equality and finally on considerations of equity (2). The rather disturbing sociological fact then emerges that, statistically speaking, this developmental hierarchy is reflected in that of social class. Given a group of children with only their social class as a variable (i.e. with all matched for intelligence, age, sex, school-background, etc.) any test of moral judgement will reveal a trend towards this positive correlation. Therefore, since moral judgement is basic to any moral decision it looks as though the higher-status child may be significantly more morally mature than the lower-status child.

Personal Gratification

Studies in the area of what is termed either 'gratification' or 'orientation' reveal that higher-status and lower-status children are sharply divided in terms of an attitude which is also equally fundamental to morality. Children have been tested to discover the degree to which they are able to defer the gratification of their desires. This was first done in the USA, hence Americans speak of the deferred gratification pattern. In Britain, however, it is more usual to refer to a child as either present orientated or future orientated. If he is the former then he cannot defer his gratifications—if he is the latter, he can. Because the moral implications are made more explicit by the term 'gratification', the latter will be used here.

The ramifications of this quality are enormous. It can be related to both the educational system and the practice of child rearing. As a process of preparing men and women for the elitist world of higher-status occupations, education requires children to be future orientated. This is basically because the system stresses present deprivation for future gratification. Such people glide smoothly into the higher-status groups through the process of future-orientated examination procedures. Then they, in their turn as parents, establish the ordered home-life, with its anticipation of regulated pocket-money and anticipated outings, which replicate this attitude in their offspring. Consequently higher-status children are likely to be future orientated because they have learnt to defer these gratifications, and the lower-status child tends to be present orientated because he has not.

How far the immediate gratification of a hire-purchase economy will affect this situation is problematic. This apparently simple analysis is made even more complex by some recent findings, which may relate to the concept of a counter-culture. There are already suggestions, based on impeccable evidence (3) that the traditional deferred-gratification pattern of the pupil role is being displaced by a present-gratification contra-pupil role. One thing, however, is perfectly clear. The 'I-want-it-now' mentality has fundamental moral implications, ranging from theft to extra-marital sexual relationships.

Here again the social-class pattern is clear. The higher-status person is invariably one who has had to learn to defer personal gratification. The lower-status person has not. Consequently the former can be deemed to be the more morally mature.

Moral Personalism

This term, although a technical one in modern philosophy, is used here to describe the degree to which an individual is capable of treating others as persons. This is self-evidently one aspect of the essence of morality. When one either demeans a person by treating him as an object, or elevates a thing to the personal level, there can be little morality. This quality naturally depends upon the degree to which the preconditions of morality have been established in each child, for it is only after a child has been loved and accepted that he can love and accept others. Indeed the degree to which we can treat others as persons is directly related to the extent to which we, as children, were treated as persons ourselves.

This quality, too, follows a pattern of social-class differences. On the whole, the lower a child's social status, the more probable it is that less recognition and concern will have been shown for him as a person in infancy. Consequently his conduct is less likely to be characterized by this quality of personalism. Hence there appears to be a positive correlation between this moral quality and social status: both are high or low, as the case may be.

Moral Flexibility

Children may also be classified according to the degree of competence they display in abstracting moral principles from specific moral regulations. The term used here is intended not only to convey the degree of this ability, but also to distinguish it from the rigidity which marks the authoritarian personality. As one would expect, rigidity in children is correlated with the degree to which parents insist on the total submission and immediate unqualified obedience of their offspring. Clearly this is linked with the quality of moral personalism for such an authoritarian parental attitude can take little account of children as persons.

One would therefore expect flexibility to be highest in a home where parental regulations are based on the application of moral principles and are themselves amenable to reasoned, personal analysis. Even punishment, when it is applied under such circumstances, becomes a structured device helping children to establish socially acceptable, and mature moral attitudes. Equally important is the fact that the experience of success is assured by the parental accommodation of moral demands to the maturity of the children concerned. With such a process of positive reinforcement to encourage them, children rapidly develop this facility to discern the moral principles which extend beyond the specific situation. By contrast, lower-status children are controlled with dogmatic, specific commands and punishment for misdemeanours then becomes a retributive device. Under such conditions it is inevitable that conduct here is regulated at the level of authoritarian specificity (4).

Obviously varying home conditions and parental experiences of this kind will produce variations in morality. On the one hand are the higher-status children who, even in the primary school, begin to realize that moral principles can be abstracted from the welter of moral regulations. On the other hand, there are the lower-status children who are likely to grow up convinced that authority is all that matters. The latter may either subscribe to it or reject it, according to their inclinations. If, however, they become normal, 'decent' citizens their behaviour is more likely to be regulated by reference to authority, whether it be enshrined in a legal system, the Bible or a union rule book. This, however, is more rightly discussed in the context of moral dynamism. Therefore, because mature morality is concerned with subscription to moral principles rather than to authority of any kind, the higher-status child, given every opportunity to discover these underlying principles, has a greater opportunity to become morally mature.

At this point a brief mention should be made of an apparent anomaly concerning lower-status home life. There children experience the ambivalence of both permissive freedom and authoritarian restrictions. This point will be raised in the following chapters and so discussed in specific contexts. For the moment all that one needs to add is that the two apparently contradictory qualities are related. The permissiveness results from a number of factors. Lack of parental oversight results from fatigued, working parents giving their children considerable freedom to live in an unsupervised way. The present orientation of the parents also endorses this, since they tend to follow the 'anything for a quiet life' philosophy. Inevitably, things can easily get out of hand in such a situation, and when they do, these parents usually resort to authoritarian demands, to restore order. Hence the fundamental disorder of a *laissez-faire* policy requires authoritarian correctives. These two qualities are also conceptually related: both are the antitheses of the fundamentally democratic ambiance of the typical middle-class family and, therefore, are related in that both are non-democratic procedures.

Moral Dynamism

When one turns to the quality of 'dynamism', in morality, the social-class differences are clearly discerned. It is the terminology which is elusive. Using the model of physics one may speak of a 'dynamic' or a 'static' state. Alternatively, the mathematical terms 'positive' and 'negative' might be used. All the evidence suggests that a higher-status child adopts positive attitudes to his environment, while those of the lower-status child are negative. However, the term 'dynamism' is used here since recent publications in sociological circles have tended to speak of the dynamic middle classes.

In terms of this criterion people may be classified according to the degree to which they creatively assert themselves against a passive environment. On the one hand static personality types tend to endure whatever fate may bring. Caught in the web of a complex, incomprehensible, and apparently hostile society, against which they feel any struggle will be ineffective, they decline towards a fatalistic and resentful passivism. In contrast to this the dynamic personality is perpetually rolling up his sleeves, as it were, and saying, 'Now what can we do about this?' So they draw up plans to dam rivers, bridge ravines, build railways and alleviate the lot of man in every sphere.

In moral matters this distinction becomes more pronounced. The passive person tends to fall back upon the security of past practice as a guide. And since such practices are invariably codified, or form structured 'folk-ways', this moral quality is closely related to that of 'flexibility'. The passive person is happiest when he can refer to tradition or law to guide him and does not have to apply any moral principles. All who have chaired club or church meetings will recognize this quality immediately. Whenever a new idea or procedure is proposed and the dynamists are sprinting along discussing its advantages and how best to implement them, voices may be heard protesting, 'But, Mr Chairman, we've never done that before.' Such people naturally fall back on tradition or precedent to guide them.

Naturally, the dynamists rise in the social scale, for this dynamic attitude brings its own rewards in industry or commerce; the professions also need such people to serve society. Hence it is found that like the other primary moral qualities, outlined above, the degree of moral dynamism is inevitably correlated with social class. Thus higher-status children, reared in such a milieu, tend to be more dynamic in their moral attitudes than children from lower-status families.

Moral Creativity

There is another reason why this quality is an extremely important one. By its nature it must be linked with the related notion of creative thinking. Just how far moral dynamism is related to creativity of thought is not known. However, the difficulty here is that although considerable work is being done on the concept of creativity in itself, there is some doubt concerning the degree of correlation between the incidence of this type of thinking and socio-economic class.

THE INTERRELATION OF MORAL TRAITS

Finally, it must be added that although each of these traits is clearly distinct they are all basically interrelated. One can see why this should be so. Valid *moral judgements* will always consider the possibility that any deferred benefits may outweight immediate *gratifications*. In its turn, personal gratification may often be deferred because *personalism* requires that some account ought to be taken of the feelings and circumstances of the other persons involved in any situation. This concern for people then becomes one important basis of the moral *flexibility* whereby principles are abstracted from specific and concrete situations. Finally, moral *dynamism* is marked by the degree to which individuals are willing to apply moral principles creatively, instead of merely abiding by the law, precedent or accepted practice.

These traits, it will be seen, must be cultivated and grafted on to the personal preconditions of morality, if moral maturity is to be a possibility for the child. However, since the interaction of all the socially determined elements produce an inescapable consequence, and since the process of socialization, sub-cultural life-style, and the inherent system of norms and values cohere within each social class, it is self-evident that the offspring of each will be characterized by a normative moral ethos. The inevitability of this moral legacy is one factor which will make effective moral education so extraordinarily difficult. Under such circumstances it may be employed merely as an instrument of social control, whereby pupils will be induced to subscribe and conform to a specific code of conduct. *This must never be allowed to supplant true moral education, wherein children are enabled to apply perpetually valid and self-authenticating moral principles, with due regard to the specific circumstances, subject to the requirements of reason and love.* It is precisely at this point that the five primary moral traits become relevant, for each is required, in a developed form, before an individual can practise such a sophisticated morality.

REFERENCES

1 Kay (1968), Chapters 6 and 7.
2 The distinction between 'equality' and 'equity' is crucial in any understanding of morality. Equality is essentially a rational consideration. It expresses the 'golden rule' of Jesus and argues that justice is served if we do to others as we would have them do to us. Equity emerges from the application of altruism. It transcends equality by insisting that we ought to treat others as we would like to be treated *if we were in their situation and subject to the identical circumstances*. Here reason is transcended by altruism. At its lowest it is marked by empathy; at its highest by self-disregarding love. See Kay (1968), Chapter 6.
3 See Sugarman (1965).
4 In morality the term 'specificity' refers to conduct which is specific to a situation. Hence it is determined more by circumstances than any moral trait. See Kay (1968), Chapters 2 and 9.

Bibliography

DAVIE, R., BUTLER, N. and GOLDSTEIN, H., *From Birth to Seven* (Longmans, 1972).
DOUGLAS, J. W. B., *The Home and the School* (McGibbon & Kee, 1964).
KAY, WILLIAM, *Moral Development* (Allen & Unwin, 1968).
SUGARMAN, BARRY, 'Teenage Boys at School', Unpublished Ph.D. thesis, Princeton, 1965.

Chapter 5

Moral Judgement:
Social-class Differences

As already observed it is essential at this point to distinguish between two aspects of moral judgement. First, there is the simple fact that the concepts of 'right' and 'wrong' vary with sub-cultures; and, second, the rather more complex notion that different levels of moral judgement form a developmental hierarchy (1).

UNCOORDINATED VARIATIONS

On the first point the evidence of the Newsons is quite clear. They discovered that there were clearly 'class differences in the moral attitudes expressed by mothers in the handling of their children' (2). This began in the early years when the moral evaluation of infantile conduct disclosed social-class differentiations. For example, some regarded 'demanding' babies as tyrants and 'passive' ones as models of perfection and goodness; while others preferred to be needed by their children, for any kind of social interaction, and so approved of 'demanding' infants. The standards of behaviour tolerated in these years varied, but the same variations were either allowed or checked in different social milieux.

As already reported, 'various social classes have different ideas of what is right and wrong' and therefore 'have somewhat different sets of values' (3). Such differences must also include general cultural variations. A folk society, for example, with its less fragmented sub-cultural structure, would be less likely to display these differences in a vivid and stark form. Thus, as will be seen below, investigations into such a society can produce disparate conclusions. Consequently one set of investigators can say of another, 'we do not find as sharp differences between social classes as he found' (4), but even so they still conclude that social-class differentiations in morality can be discerned in their sample. Indeed they go on to speak of a minority sub-culture with norms antithetically opposed to those of the rest of society.

It is when one turns to the urban areas that such differences become even more pronounced. Lower-status life in large cities appears to be so disorganized that it virtually becomes a tangled web of disintegrated social and moral values. Taking Liverpool as an example, Madeline Kerr found extreme deviations in the moral judgement of her lower-status sample. John Mays, in his study of children growing up in that city, found these deviations to be sufficiently structured and constant to enable one to speak of a delinquent sub-culture in which the normal standards of moral judgement did not apply. Indeed he found this to be so integrally structured that a decade later he was able to report on the positive correlation of crime with the social structure of such cities in this country. However, this is not an evil epiphenomenon of urbanization, for Peck and Havighurst echoed the same conclusion in their study of a folk society (5).

Such judgements as these are inevitably made by higher-status sociologists and school teachers, but these sub-cultural variations of moral judgement are an established fact. This was confirmed by Barry Sugarman in his research with over 500 London schoolboys. He discovered that their moral judgements were positively correlated with socio-economic status. Furthermore, the higher the social class of the family the higher the teacher rated the conduct of the child. One could, of course, dismiss this as evidence underlining the fact that higher-status children fit snugly into schools where middle-class values and judgements are the norm: but it cannot be dismissed for it points once again to the social-class differences to be found in moral judgements.

STRUCTURED VARIATIONS IN MORAL JUDGEMENT

As was observed earlier, moral judgements can also be understood in a more structured and technical way. Here there appears to be a clear developmental hierarchy. Judgements are first based on prudence. Here the 'right' thing to do is that which is rewarded. Then they are based on subscription to authority, so that the 'right' thing here is simply that which is demanded by a credible representative of the law. Third, judgements are based on considerations of equality, i.e. conduct is deemed to be 'right' if the golden rule of reciprocity can be applied. Finally, there is the mature stage at which the notion of equity operates, i.e. where moral judgements are based on universally valid principles. Thus there appears to be a progression from the crass heteronomy of prudential and authoritarian considerations, through the stage of what Norman Bull calls socionomy, until finally judgements are based on moral principles.

Now it is precisely this structured hierarchy which appears to be reflected in that of social status. It is, of course, legitimate to argue that there is a social-class pattern in the distribution of intelligence, and therefore that moral judgement, as a cognitive activity, will inevitably reflect this. However, all the available evidence underlines this fact in a much more positive and structured way.

General Research from Piaget (1932) to Lydiat (1971)

Piaget's pioneering research in this area managed to evade this issue by using a sample of lower-status children who were all from 'the poorer parts of Geneva'. As a natural consequence, Harrower then selected children from the different social classes and tested their moral judgement with Piaget-type tests. As one would expect she was able to highlight the deficiency of Piaget's results and show that his conclusions could not be applied indiscriminately to different socio-economic groups of children. Her positive results, however, were much more valuable. Taking two sample groups (one from London's east-end and the other from middle-class suburban areas) she was able to show that children from the higher-status families tended to display relatively mature moral judgements, and that this disparity was apparent in infancy and remained so throughout childhood. Thus she showed conclusively, within two years of Piaget's work, that social-class differences must be accepted as a salient factor in the maturity of a child's moral judgement.

Within a few years of this Lerner disclosed a further deficiency in Piaget's work. He was convinced that not enough attention had been directed to the quality of parental control exercised. Basing his work on Harrower's conclusions, he studied the importance of social-class differences in terms of the different kinds of parental control which constituted the essence of what Piaget had called moral (i.e. adult) restraint. His general results are fascinating for a number of reasons. The most relevant here, however, is that he again showed that social status and moral judgement are correlated. He found, quite simply, that children living in higher-status families tended to display more mature forms of moral judgement than their lower-status contemporaries. Having carefully matched his two samples he was quite adamant about his conclusions. This difference, he insisted, depended upon social-class factors and not primarily on any hidden factors such as, for example, individual intelligence.

These general conclusions were also confirmed later by Barkley who discovered that moral judgement was directly associated with socio-economic status. An important forward step was taken at this point. Barkley had studied college students and so evidence now became available from a wider age range of samples. Consequently the work of Hollingshead is also relevant. His study of the teenagers in Elmtown (6) confirmed that there were distinct social-class differences evident in the moral judgements of the adolescents who constituted his sample. The only qualification that needs to be added here is that Peck and Havighurst, who researched contemporaneously with a sample from the same town, recorded that they observed 'much less social-class differentiation than is usually found'.

However, this difference of opinion must be considered in the light of two facts. First, this was a 'folk society' in which such differentiation is less pronounced than that found in urban areas. Second, they admit that their sample contained 'practically no upper middle-class youth'. However, further confirmation was soon forthcoming.

McRae, who later specifically tested Piaget's theories of moral judgement, now added his evidence. Recognizing, as we have seen, that no facet of a child's development can be considered in isolation from the parental influence exercised, he studied moral judgement in the context of parent–child relationships and clearly revealed the influence of socio-economic factors.

Such were also the conclusions of Morris. For him, value judgements were essentially moral judgements and his testing involved him in studying the latter in samples from both lower-status secondary modern pupils and higher-status grammar school children. His conclusions were almost predictable. He found that the secondary modern school pupils were much more conformist in their moral judgements than their grammar school counterparts. The former tended to base their judgements upon authoritarian and social sanctions, while the latter displayed a facility for perceiving the principles upon which such judgements needed to be founded.

Thus research conclusions can be heaped one upon the other to produce a formidable mass of evidence for this general thesis. However, before turning to the work of perhaps the two most eminent researchers in this field, mention should be made of four more who worked in this area of morality.

Kohn, although more concerned to show social-class variations in the kind of parental control exercised over children, still provided evidence to support this general thesis. Because of differences in this respect, lower-status children tend to evaluate actions in terms of their consequences, while higher-status children are more likely to consider motive and intent to be crucial to any moral judgement.

Johnson, in his turn, was primarily concerned to discover the degree of consistency in moral judgements made in different areas of experience. In passing, he too showed that such activities must always be assessed in the context of the family situation, but his relevant conclusion for us was decisive. He discovered that on an ascending scale 'parental occupations were positively and significantly correlated with mature moral judgements in all areas' (7).

Boehm, too, was able to isolate some social-class factors in her analysis. One of her results here is particularly interesting in the light of Kohn's findings. She discovered that Catholic children matured much earlier in their moral judgement. This, she concluded, is explained by the necessity of every Catholic child to be prepared for confession when he is seven years old, and who is thus introduced early to the need to consider motives as well as actions, in making any moral judgement. Clearly, although Bull showed that intelligence exerts as important an influence as social class, it is still possible to educate children into making more mature judgements.

Finally, a recent study by Lydiat confirms these conclusions. Setting himself the task of extending Piaget's work in this field, he constructed six Piagetian-type tests and applied them to 368 Sheffield children, mostly of primary school age. Throughout his reporting of a very sophisticated research project Lydiat makes his conclusions perfectly clear. Moral judgement is positively correlated with social class. This conclusion forms a chain running through the whole dissertation. 'It can be seen clearly', he writes, 'that children from middle-class homes show fewer immature responses than those from working-class homes' (8). He confirms this by insisting that in tests of moral judgement 'middle-class children had an advantage over working-class children' (9). Like Bull, he found a not entirely un-expected correlation between moral judgement and intelligence, but his final conclusion, in relation to the theme of this chapter, is pellucidly clear, 'There was', he writes, 'a correlation between greater moral maturity in the child and a middle-class family background' (10).

The Work of Lawrence Kohlberg

Kohlberg's general developmental theory is relevant here since he equates his six stages of development with 'six types of moral judgement' (11). Thus although his theory is generally commended because it endows each child with a dynamic, active role in the structuring of his social environment, its greatest value for us lies in this equation of moral maturation and the development of moral judgement. 'In an initial study', he writes, 'six types of moral judgement were defined after extensive case study. They fell into three major levels of development as follows:

Level I. Premoral:

Type 1. Punishment and obedience orientation.

Type 2. Naïve instrumental hedonism.

Level II. Conventional role conformity:

Type 3. Good boy morality of maintaining good relations, and the approval of others.

Type 4. The placation of authority to avoid guilt and censure.

Level III. Morality of moral principles:

Type 5. The morality of contract, individual rights and democratically accepted law.

Type 6. Individual moral principles approved by one's conscience' (12).

Kohlberg subsequently affirmed that middle-class children were found to negotiate these stages with greater ease than matched working-class children. Hence he related these differing levels of moral judgement to the vantage points of people located at different levels in the hierarchical social scale. He cites as evidence varying responses to the question, 'Should someone obey a law if he doesn't think it is a good law?' The responses are as follows:

Lower-class boy: 'Yes, a law is a law and you can't do nothing about it. You have to obey it, you should. That's what it's there for.' This he classifies as type 1 moral judgement, observing that such a child feels impotent before the law.

Lower middle-class boy: 'Laws are made for people to obey and if everyone would start breaking them . . . Well, if you owned a store and there were no laws, everybody would just come in and not have to pay.' This he classifies as type 4 moral judgement, noting that it is the perspective of a storekeeper who has a stake in the existing order.

Upper middle-class boy: 'The law's the law but I think people themselves can tell what's right from wrong. If you don't believe in a law, you should try to get it changed, you shouldn't disobey it.' This is classified as type 5 moral judgement, with the observation that this is the perspective of the democratic policy-maker (13).

The Work of Norman Bull

Finally, reference must be made to the now classical study of moral judgement undertaken by Norman Bull. Taking a sample of 360, to cover the whole range of school population, he set out with three primary aims. He wanted first to test the levels of moral judgement displayed by the children throughout this chronological spectrum. Then, as a natural consequence, he attempted to establish a developmental hierarchy of maturity in moral judgement. Here he referred to a four-grade scale of anomy, heteronomy, socionomy and autonomy. Finally, however, he attempted to correlate these conclusions with five controlled variables: age, sex, intelligence, religious beliefs and social class.

His conclusions can be criticized from a number of vantage points. As in all psychological investigations, philosophers can point out the conceptual inadequacies. Nowhere, they could claim, does he define what he means by 'morality' and 'moral maturity'. This criticism leads to a more trenchant one; it can be argued that the whole notion of developmental stages results not from experimental observation but from the nature of human thought. This, of course, is no new discovery. Eddington's view that even the laws of physics are conditioned by the nature and structure of our minds has been confirmed by subsequent research (14). It is thus no surprise to find Dearden, for example, arguing that developmental stages are logical necessities rather than empirical discoveries. Here one becomes trapped in a further tangle of those antinomies which lead protagonists of opposing views to argue that the other is conditioned by his nature to do so.

However, one must not forget that the former criticism has some validity. It is crucial to define what it means to be moral, if one is to speak in terms of maturational developmental levels. Speaking of definitions on moral autonomy and prerequisites, Bailey, although he too is generally critical of the notion of development implicit in most research into morality, concludes that 'Empirical studies might yield helpful information about factors causally connected *with* these prerequisite processes'. Thus in this qualified sense it is possible to agree with him when he continues that 'the stages of moral development are not things to be ascertained by empirical methods alone' (15).

However, despite criticisms of this kind, Bull's findings are fruitful for the investigation in hand. He discovered too, that socio-economic factors were relevant in any consideration of moral judgement, and that social-class factors were a significant variable even with the youngest of his sample. His conclusions, however, reveal a more complex picture.

The sexes differ significantly in this respect. The moral judgement of boys is influenced far more by social-class factors than is that of girls. They, it seems, reveal a much more significant correlation between intelligence and moral judgement. This is not entirely unexpected. Moral judgement is a cognitive activity, which must by its nature reflect the level of the arbiter's intelligence. Hence Bull finally concludes that his results are 'of a piece with the broad statistical finding that socio-economic class is in far closer association with the judgements of boys than of girls. Given the greater reliance of boys upon environmental influences, it follows that socio-economic class must inevitably be of greater significance for them' (16).

However, with this qualification, the general thesis still stands. With any given sample having social class as the only variable, the statistical probability is that maturity of moral judgement will be positively correlated with a concomitant rise in social status.

Parental Influences

It was mentioned above that one basis upon which Lerner conducted his research, was his conviction that Piaget had not directed enough attention to the nature of parental control, as a correlate of the moral judgement of their offspring. This in turn led Kohn to concentrate on disclosing the social variations of this influence. Now this line of inquiry can be taken a little further.

Hoffman found that higher-status children develop their own (non-prudential) standards of right and wrong early in life. Then familial experiences tend to confirm and endorse both the standards and the moral techniques required to apply them to specific moral problems. Bandura and McDonald showed how this operated. Such children adopt the types of moral judgement expressed by the parent. In doing this, the child immediately gains the approval of similar adults. Obviously learning theories have much to say here, but in a sociological context the process is clear. The approving intervention of adults induces such children to learn to make the appropriate moral judgements more quickly.

Such adult interventions can also be seen to help in other ways. Higher-status parents and adults have disclosed a distinct tendency to offer guidance *in advance* and so ensure that their children attain the level of success, which is the heart of positive reinforcement. These are called *proactive* parents, whose influence leads not only to more success, but also a positive response to such encouragement. Equally, when a higher-status child inquires why a particular decision or course of action is deemed to be the right one, his question is taken seriously, and the explanation gives him some insight into the fact that first reasons, and then principles, undergird all mature moral judgements.

In contrast to this Hoffman found that lower-status children evaluated the morality of their conduct by direct reference to prudential considerations. Whether or not he would be caught and punished, was the primary criterion here. Consequently, Hoffman found that such children were unable to develop their own standards of right and wrong. Furthermore, he found that such children regarded their parents as harsh and dominantly authoritarian. This too is a line of thought which can now be developed.

It has been found that working-class parents usually only tell their children *afterwards*, whether they are right or wrong. Thus they confirm the child's image of harsh parental authoritarianism. Such experiences lead to frustration, and this soon induces antipathy to learning the right responses. Thus *reactive* parents successfully debar their offspring from developing mature forms of moral judgement. These attitudes are then negatively reinforced by related experiences.

If such a child queries a demand made by the parent, he is usually simply told, 'Because I said so'. This then is further reinforced by parental recourse to authority figures who are used as threats against disobedience. Consequently such a child soon considers that questions are useless. At school he lacks curiosity, asks few questions, listens to fewer answers and generally considers any learning to be a painful process. Consequently, he rarely learns to make mature moral judgements either at home or at school (17).

Intelligence as a Factor
Since moral judgement is essentially the end product of a cognitive process one would expect to find a correlation between intelligence and moral judgement. Yet hitherto the research conclusions have varied on this point. Durkin, for example, found hardly any evidence at all that a child's intelligence was correlated with the level of his moral judgement, and Lerner dismissed individual intelligence as a relevant factor. Yet standard intelligence tests contain questions which are clearly tests of moral judgement.

Consequently, in an earlier work (18) it was observed that a partial solution to this apparent inconsistency is that this failure to find any significant correlation underlines a deeper truth. This truth may be that when one describes moral judgement as a cognitive activity, one is referring to the *mode* of activity, not to its intellectual *level*. Thus a stupid boy who is willing to reason about moral problems is involved in cognitive activity of a kind which cannot be found in an infinitely more intelligent child who only makes intuitive or authoritarian judgements. However, since then two parallel research findings have clarified the issue.

Bull investigated the possibility of finding a correlation between intelligence and moral judgement, and reached a simple conclusion. 'Statistical evidence', he says, 'showed intelligence to be the most noteworthy of the various factors in its positive association with moral judgements' (19). Such too were the findings of a research project designed to measure rationality in the context of moral judgements. Here it was found that intelligence was significantly correlated with this measure of moral judgement (20). Finally, Lydiat discovered a significant correlation between intelligence and maturity of moral judgement.

One other relevant finding was the fact that the girls in Bull's sample were more intelligent than the boys. It is thus suggested that they are apparently less dependent on social-class factors than boys; but this need not follow. To say that high intelligence is more potent than socio-economic factors only serves to underline the dichotomy between the higher- and lower-status samples. For when one adds to this the statistical fact that intelligence is correlated with social class, this datum emerges as a further confirmation of the thesis that more mature moral judgements are found amongst middle-class children.

Implications for Morality

The moral implications of the above information is self-evident. If children are fixated at the authoritarian level of moral judgement, they live by prudence or authority. Those who make their judgements on the basis of equity, are applying moral principles. Now since mature morality consists in applying moral principles to concrete situations the facility to discern, explicate and then apply these principles is an essential prerequisite of moral maturity. Consequently the lower-status child can never become morally mature, so long as he lives by authoritarian dicta. Whereas the higher-status child can. He may not, of course, always do so but the potential is present in his ability to see beyond the law, to the principle underlying it.

REFERENCES

1 The former is implicit in the findings of Jones (1943). The latter results from the work of Piaget (1932).
2 The Newsons (1963), pp. 177 ff.
3 Peck and Havighurst (1964), pp. 24 ff.
4 Ibid., p. 26. The town is variously designated as Elmtown by Hollingshead (1949), i.e. the 'he' to which Peck and Havighurst refer when they call this Prairie City. Both, in fact, refer to Morris, Illinois.
5 op. cit., p. 27.
6 See note (4) above.
7 Johnson (1962), p. 353.
8 Lydiat (1971), pp. 254 ff.
9 Ibid., pp. 316 ff.
10 op. cit., pp. 397 ff.
11 Kohlberg (1966), p. 9.
12 Kohlberg (1964), p. 400.
13 Kohlberg (1966), p. 29.
14 Kay (1970), p. 30 ff, presents a fully documented account of this argument. Pinker (1972) claims that this is also true of absolutes in social psychology. Its policies, he claims, are derived from ideological rather than empirical data.
15 Bailey (1969 a), p. 76.
16 Bull (1969 a), p. 283. For any who wish to read a résumé of this research a more palatable form appears in Bull (1969 b). The first half of this work incorporates a summarized account of the research reported in the larger volume, to which reference has been made here.
17 There is an abundance of evidence to show that such confused and inconsistent forms of family control lead to delinquency. See Wright (1971).
18 Kay (1968), p. 185.
19 Bull (1969 a), p. 71.
20 Kay (1969), pp. 179 ff, contains the statistical evidence for this.

Bibliography

BAILEY, C., 'The Notion of Development and Moral Education', in *Proceedings of the Philosophy of Education Society of Great Britain*, January 1969.

BANDURA, A. and MACDONALD, F. J., 'The Influence of Social Reinforcement and the Behaviour of Models in Shaping Children's Moral Judgment', in *Journal of Abnormal and Sociological Psychology*, No. 67, 1963.

BARKLEY, K. L., 'The Development of Moral Judgements of College Students', in *Character and Personality*, No. 10, 1942.

BOEHM, L., 'The Development of Conscience: A Comparison of Students in Catholic Parochial Schools and in Public Schools', in *Child Development*, No. 33, 1962.

BULL, N. J., *Moral Judgement from Childhood to Adolescence* (Routledge & Kegan Paul, 1969).

BULL, N. J., *Moral Education* (Routledge & Kegan Paul, 1969).

DEARDEN, R. F., *The Philosophy of Primary Education* (Routledge & Kegan Paul, 1968).

DURKIN, D., 'Children's Concepts of Justice', in *Journal of Educational Research*, 1959.

HARROWER, M. R., 'Social Status and Moral Development', in *British Journal of Educational Psychology*, No. 4, 1934.

HOFFMAN, M. L., 'Child Rearing Practices and Moral Development: Generalizations from Empirical Research', in *Child Development*, No. 34, 1963.

HOLLINGSHEAD, A. G., *Elmtown's Youth* (John Wiley, 1949).

JOHNSON, RONALD C., 'A Study of Children's Moral Judgements', in *Child Development*, Vol. 33, No. 2, June 1962.

JONES, A. H., 'Sex, Educational and Religious Influences on Moral Judgements Relative to the Family', in *American Sociological Review*, Vol. 8, 1943.

KAY, WILLIAM, *Moral Development* (Allen & Unwin, 1968).

KAY, WILLIAM, 'An Investigation into the Moral Attitudes of Primary and Secondary School Children', Unpublished thesis, Nottingham 1969.

KAY, WILLIAM, 'A Teilhardian Resolution of the Naturalistic Fallacy', in *Teilhard Review*, Vol. 5, No. 1, 1970.

KERR, M., *The People of Ship Street* (Routledge & Kegan Paul, 1958).

KOHLBERG, L., 'Moral Development and Identification', in H. Stevenson (Ed.), *Child Psychology* (Univ. Chicago Press, 1963).

KOHLBERG, L., 'Development of Moral Character and Moral Ideology', in M. and L. Hoffman (Eds), *Review of Child Development Research* (Russell Sage Foundation: New York, 1964), Vol. 1.

KOHLBERG, L., 'Moral Education in the Schools', in *The School Review*, Vol. 74, No. 1, 1966.

KOHLBERG, L., 'The Developmental Approach to Moralization', in M. Hoffman (Ed.), *Moral Processes* (Chicago Aldine Press, 1966).

KOHLBERG, L., 'The Development of Children's Orientations Toward Moral Order', in *Vita Humana*, Vol. IX, 1966.

KOHN, M. L., 'Social Class and Parental Values', in *American Sociological Review*, Vol. XXIV, 1959.

KOHN, M. L., 'Social Class and the Exercise of Parental Authority', in *American Sociological Review*, Vol. XXIV, 1959.

LERNER, E., *Constraint Areas and Moral Judgement in Children* (Manasha: Wisconsin, Banta, 1937).

LYDIAT, M., 'The Development of Moral Judgements in Children', Unpublished Ph.D. thesis, Sheffield, 1971.

MAYS, J. B., *Growing Up in a City* (Univ. Liverpool Press, 1956).

MAYS, J. B., *Crime and the Social Structure* (Faber, 1963).

MCRAE, D. Jnr., 'A Test of Piaget's Theories of Moral Development', in *Journal of Abnormal and Sociological Psychology*, Vol. 49, 1954.

MCRAE, D. Jnr., 'The Development of Moral Judgement in Children', Unpublished Ph.D. thesis, Harvard, 1950.

MORRIS, J. F., 'A Study of Value Judgements in Adolescents', Unpublished Ph.D. thesis, London, 1955.

NEWSON, J. and NEWSON, E., *Infant Care in an Urban Community* (Allen & Unwin, 1963).

PECK, R. F. and HAVIGHURST, R. J., *The Psychology of Character Development* (John Wiley, 1964).

PIAGET, JEAN, *The Moral Judgement of the Child* (Routledge & Kegan Paul, 1932).

PINKER, R. A., *Social Theory and Social Policy* (Heinemann, 1972).

SUGARMAN, B., 'Teenage Boys at School', Unpublished Ph.D. thesis, Princeton, 1965.

WRIGHT, DEREK, *The Psychology of Moral Behaviour* (Penguin, 1971).

Chapter 6

Gratification and Orientation

We may now turn to another fundamental personal attitude which also appears to be characteristic of the higher-status, rather than the lower-status child. This is simply the ability to defer one's desire for gratification. Obviously this is also extremely important for the future moral maturation of children. Leaving aside the clear social-class differences for a moment, it may be observed that all children vary in the degree to which they are able to postpone the gratification of their desires. Some are able to consider the future consequences of conduct and in the light of this can often defer the immediate fulfilment of an impulse or desire, in order to obtain a more adequate and enduring satisfaction in the future. In sharp contrast to these are those children who seek the immediate gratification of their whims, with little thought for the future consequences. The former as we have noted, are thus accurately described as future oriented in their conduct. The latter may be described as present orientated in their actions.

Such a feature of conduct could, of course, be ascribed merely to individual differences, and Raymond Cattell discusses this point in his complex scientific analysis of human personality. At a simple level one may observe this in the eating habits of children. On the one hand are those who eat the tastiest morsels as soon as the plate of food is placed before them. While in contrast, there are others who leave the choicest titbits until they have eaten the rest of the meal. At a more mature level one finds athletes, ascetics and religious devotees displaying this conduct. Athletes deny themselves food, alchohol and other indulgences in order to win a race in the future. Ascetics allow their natural appetites little gratification in order to achieve a later but higher level of personal or spiritual integrity. In an extreme form one may find adherents of many religions depriving themselves of present worldly gratification in order to obtain more lasting pleasure in the world to come (1). Yet we must anticipate the evidence and observe that if this future orientation is simply a personality trait, it is interesting to note that it appears to emerge most strongly in members of the middle classes, who have perpetually supplied society with its athletes, warriors, saints and religious devotees.

At this point one could embark on a sterile debate concerning the nature of the causal nexus between this personality trait and social-class status. On the one hand, it could be argued that the deferred rewards intrinsic to a protracted educational process which leads to higher-status occupations, produces this complex of attitudes in the successful citizen. On the other hand, it could be averred that those already possessing this attribute naturally accommodate themselves to a system, which then leads to success in what Michael Young has called the 'meritocracy'. One thing appears to be certain. The deferred gratification personality trait sharply distinguishes the higher-status from the lower-status social groups in the quality of their emotional, intellectual and moral lives.

Schneider and Lysgaard were amongst the first sociologists to have discussed this behavioural pattern in terms of social class. Their work was conducted in America and consisted of testing children to see whether they were able to renounce their impulses or were prone to following them. The lower-status subjects tended to find it impossible to renounce their impulses, and this reflected a general sub-cultural pattern in which higher education was not pursued and money was not saved. Hence they showed clearly that the lower-status person tended to be present-orientated while the higher-status person was not. This work, however, was not entirely original. Exactly a decade before this Whyte had described how his lower-status street corner gangs were characterized by a pattern of embarking on unpremeditated and impulsive action with apparently no regard paid to the later consequences (2).

In England these conclusions were simultaneously confirmed by Betty Spinley. After investigating the educational experiences of both higher- and lower-status pupils she disclosed the intra-class pattern. She noted that:

'These differences may be most clearly seen in the following two sets of descriptive phrases, the first of which contains statements which are true of the slum group only. The individual shows a marked unwillingness and inability to deal with disturbing or unpleasant satisfactions. For the public school group these descriptions must be discarded and the following statements substituted. The individual faces disturbing situations and attempts to deal adequately with them. Present satisfactions are postponed for the sake of greater ones in the future' (3).

However, the ramifications of this simple dichotomy are enormous and have led investigators to penetrate the complexities of social-class differences in home life. For the moment, however, we must be content to study these differences in isolation from the life-styles, familial structures and sub-cultural norms of the different social classes. As Richard Farley so rightly concluded in his study of adolescent consumption habits and personal aspirations, 'The deferred-gratification pattern is of cardinal importance' (4).

SOCIAL-CLASS DIFFERENCES

The higher-status pattern of future orientation can easily be described. The future consequences of any action are invariably deemed to be of paramount importance. This in turn distils itself down to the simple conviction that self-discipline and hard work in the present lead inevitably to success in the future.

This, of course, tinctures the whole of life. 'The children of upper middle-class parents gradually learn the habits of impulse renunciation, deferred gratification, saving, ambition, hard work for future rewards, patience' (5). Hence such citizens are unlikely to be impulsive. For them it is the long and tedious haul to success which gives life meaning. This is only to be expected, for they mostly belong to the professional or executive classes where status can only be achieved through long and arduous training. Their fine homes, and other valued possessions are invariably obtained only by the sustained sacrifice of minor, inessential luxuries. These activities provide life with meaning and purpose and so lead inexorably on to the puritan view that hard work is intrinsically virtuous.

Indeed this is the conclusion which Schneider and Lysgaard reached. In their discussion of the higher-status modes of behaviour they found two further important elements. First, that the postponement of gratification involved one in positive as well as negative corollaries: it implied not only negative deprivation but also positive present sacrifices. Second, that these 'sacrifices' in terms of hard work and applied industry, were in some way deemed to be more than merely prudent. They were morally meritorious. Indeed one may find many references to this view in the studies of higher-status communities. Hughes, for example, says quite bluntly that amongst them 'work is a moral activity'.

In contrast to this orientation of the middle classes, which stresses the long-range goals, and life-span ambitions, the working classes emerge as more inclined to take the short-term view and yield to present desires. Again, this life style imbues the whole of life. Time orientation is foreshortened. Jobs providing immediate rewards, but little security, are preferred. Conduct bringing brief but present pleasure is indulged in place of that which brings lasting, later happiness. This attitude ranges from eating habits, on which point it has been observed that 'there is said to be more obesity among the lower class presumably reflecting a failure to inhibit gustatory impulses' (6), right through to their leisure activities which Hughes points out are in general pursuits which provide temporary but immediate escapes and emotional releases from the tedium of life.

Evidence of this can be indefinitely multiplied; Richard Hoggart, for example, found that 'working-class life puts a premium on the taking of pleasures now, discourages planning for some future goal, or in the light of some ideal; they assume 'tomorrow will take care of itself'; on this side the working classes have been cheerful existentialists for ages' (7). Even Zweig's affluent workers were mostly characterized by 'present-day mindedness'. It should therefore be no surprise to find that in times of industrial unemployment and redundancy manual workers, who have been earning wages in the £2000–3000 per annum bracket, should be found bereft of savings, with homes denuded by firms calling in the goods acquired on hire-purchase.

However, before proceeding any further, it would be an advantage to anchor all these assertions in empirically confirmed researches. Schneider, Lysgaard and Spinley virtually ploughed virgin soil, but others soon harrowed and reaped a harvest. Amongst these one may place Oppenheim. Comparing working-class with middle-class grammar school boys in England his results overwhelmingly confirmed the earlier findings that higher status appears to confer the ability to resist implementing one's impulses.

Thus the concatenation of evidence can grow. Paneth found her Branch Street slum dwellers desiring sophistication, but unable to sustain any effort to attain it. Dennis and his colleagues reported that their colliers had a constricted horizon and lived in a perennial present. Madeline Kerr discovered her slum denizens of Liverpool incapable of realistically planning ahead. Pearl Jephcott records how even bright young working-class adolescents become increasingly unable to break away from the present orientation of their cultural milieu; a point which Mogey affirmed with his young families in Barton. Willmott and Young touched a raw nerve here; even when future orientation emerges it is always circumscribed. Lower-status people save for a *small* car, or a *short* holiday, or a *minor* addition to the home. They cannot sustain the effort required in the long haul. Zweig found that the 'ideal of a worker is that he must be of a happy-go-lucky nature. He should not worry about the future' (8). Thus the present orientation of the lower-status personality is delineated. At this point evidence adduced to support the view that higher-status individuals are future orientated is redundant. It not only follows necessarily from this evidence, but since most readers of the present book will belong to that category it would also be superfluous. Thus we may proceed to a more general discussion.

Contrasting Social-class Conduct

It was mentioned earlier that the middle classes not only learn to inhibit their impulses, resist their temptations, apply themselves to attaining excellence and defer their gratifications, but turn all of this into a virtue compounded of industry and morality. It is this point which McCandless emphasizes in reporting his conclusions. Speaking of the middle classes, who abstain from gratifying their immediate pleasurable desires and canalize their energy into hard work, he says that such people 'will in the long run be happier, have more money in the bank and be more esteemed by the community' (9).

A more succinct account of the protestant, puritan ethic outlined by Max Weber would be difficult to find. The minutiae of this view could be traced through such work as that of Vaz, where this typically higher-status attitude is outlined in detail. Here one reads, for example, that such parents use regulated pocket money as a 'device for teaching the child that money is to be used carefully and wisely'. Thus they deliberately 'inculcate in their children the belief that money is not to be spent recklessly and, if not immediately necessary, should be put away for future use' (10). Such a system makes little appeal to the lower-status child. Not only does he rarely experience success as a result of hard work, but he must seize money and opportunities as they arise, for both are transitory elements in his social life.

This view could be expressed even more bluntly. It seems that our society is not organized in such a way that it can demonstrate to lower-status children the value of sustained hard work and self-discipline. Indeed the reverse is more true. It may even suggest to them that they should seize those things which society reveres, but which they, by natural inadequacy, are not capable of achieving through legitimate means. Furthermore, the lower-status sub-culture provides the environment within which this attitude is fostered.

Here the apparently inevitable lower-status child's experience of perpetual failure within our educational system is a potent factor. It is now axiomatic that lower-class children frequently meet with little but failure when they are at school, and the results of this, argue Schwebel and Bernstein, are far-reaching. Constant failure of this kind leads such children to adopt the view that they will continue to fail. As a natural consequence they adopt aberrant attitudes to school work, the most dominant of which is a defensive pose. The primary characteristic of this appears to be the emergence of 'impulsivity'. Here, with nothing to lose, the child responds, impulsively to any problem. Believing that sustained application to the task in hand will only lead to failure, he tends to eliminate the chore of learning and answer a question on impulse. Such a situation is well known to any teacher in an educationally deprived area.

As one would expect, a natural development of this impulsivity leads to cheating. Here immediate gratification can be obtained without recourse to the tedious process of learning. It is not surprising, therefore, to find that Mischel and Gilligan report this tendency in an experiment where children were forced into cheating in order to gain attractive prizes. Although the lure of the prizes proved too great for a substantial number there was yet a significant correlation. These children who were able to delay their gratification in order to obtain a later better prize, cheated much less than those who preferred small immediately conferred rewards. There is, it seems, a direct correlation between deferred gratification and resistance to temptation.

Berkowitz extended this beyond the school situation when he argued in a similar way. He suggested that a history of protracted failure and frustration would inevitably cause such an individual to lose all hope of ever succeeding. Consequently such a person anticipating further failure and frustration, is more likely to develop the view that he should seize his opportunities while they are possibilities. Such experiences of failure are thus, it seems, conducive to the formation of a present-orientated personality in which the need for immediate gratification becomes of paramount importance.

CONDITIONS IN THE HOME

The development of this impulsivity, and its attendant practice of acquiring immediate gratification, is also inculcated by the home conditions of lower-status children. With economic necessity requiring both parents to be at work, such a child is left largely unsupervised during the day. Consequently the powerful physical appetites of children are unchecked by adults in the vicinity. Or, if any attempts are made to check them, they emanate either from authority figures (park-keepers, policemen, etc.) or representatives of middle-class families, and are thus resented and opposed.

After an exhaustive study of this aspect of lower-status life LeShan concluded that such a child 'is to a large degree at the mercy of his own impulses with reward or punishment following immediately on his actions' (11). Such a situation inevitably reinforces the tendency towards immediate gratification which such deprived children develop in a capitalist economic system. Hence the total milieu, within which such a child lives, will endorse the view that immediate physical gratification constitutes the essence of a fulfilled life.

This in turn is further endorsed by his experiences within the intimacy of home life. Weekly celebrations invariably lead to over-indulgence in drinking, and these in turn precipitate a situation in which overt aggression and sexuality are manifest. Two points, however, need to be noted with care. Such a characteristic lower-status situation must be analysed in the light of two distinct, yet related concepts. The first is that such conduct is the result of a desire for immediate gratification. The second, that such gratification is invariably indulged through physical media. Both are manifestations of the view that everyday problems ought to be evaded rather than faced.

The first point is amply illustrated by the view that in such communities 'drinking is the model recreational pattern. The drinking in turn leads to fighting, another way of attempting to obliterate rather than solve problems. Recreation, then, when enjoyed at all tends to be at either end of two extremes; the drinking which soon results in oblivion, or the fighting and related types of violent action' (12).

The second point is clothed in the flesh and blood of autobiographical experience in Claude Brown's book. Here he makes it abundantly clear that the lower-status child will inevitably find his pleasure and gratification in those activities (like drinking, violence, aggression and sex) which are immediately available in an economically deprived stratum of society. Clearly children growing up in such an environment are unlikely either to acquire the habits of self-denial and restraint, or to develop a life-style in which intellectual satisfaction plays a prominent part. Consequently, the deferred gratification pattern of conduct is hardly likely to be established.

In its starkest form, this inadequacy has recently been exposed by Oldman, Bytheway and Horobin. In their attempt to disclose more fully the relationship existing between family structure and educational achievement, they discounted the view that family size *in itself* was of any significance. The size of the family, they argued, resulted from parental personality characteristics. It was *these* which were inherited from parents rather than induced by the family structure. Their results suggested that large lower-status families represented parental lack of concern for the future. Where present orientation and the failure to use contraceptives had such palpably self-evident results, it was clear that children in these families also acquired the parental characteristic of present orientation and so become destined to form part of the flotsam and jetsam of our educational system.

Further interesting relevant evidence of the view that lower-status home life leads invariably to the formation of present orientation in individual personality traits, comes from Madeline Kerr. In her study of slum children she concluded that the restricted number of roles, accessible to the children, resulted in their possession of an unstructured and weak ego. Her full documentation of the evidence need not be duplicated here. Suffice it to say that the lack of role differentiation, which resulted in the weak ego control of her slum children, led her to subscribe to the view that 'their impulses demand immediate gratification; postponement is impossible, and their regard for right and wrong is wholly subordinated to instinctual satisfaction' (13).

A final comment can clinch this phase of the argument. The Newsons, in their study of urban children, observed that many lower-status parents now probably over-indulge their children with material goods as a natural reaction to their own childhood deprivation as a result of war or poverty. If this is so, one may find abundant evidence of it by visiting a lower-status shopping centre. There, children have only to wail for a lollipop to have one thrust into their hands. The pay-desks of the larger stores are bedecked with 'impulse' purchases for children, and the ice-cream van has only to sound its chimes to presage a horde of children and mothers streaming towards it. For any with the time to spend in uninvolved observation, the private housing estate of the higher-status segment of society provides a sharp contrast. There, with regulated pocket money, the children rarely scream for sweets or salivate at the sound of an ice-cream vendor's van. It would be difficult to find a more vivid exemplification of the difference in conduct between the present- and the future-orientated child.

Parental Influence
The paramount importance of parental influence cannot be ignored here, since it has been implicit in all the above evidence. Yet the point must be made explicit. Parental self-indulgence or denial is replicated in the personalities of the offspring. The latter, as Eaton and Weil have shown, can persist for generations and sustain a frugal Puritan attitude to life through the vagaries of political and economic change. Further evidence was also later provided by Mischel who showed that both parents and children of three distinct sub-cultural groups displayed the same levels of gratification. (1) Highly indulgent parents had children who developed a marked preference for immediate rewards. (2) Impulsive parents had children who disclosed little concern for the future. (3) The disciplined home life, characterized by consistency of parental training, produced children who later

preferred larger rewards to immediate, lesser ones. All of this, however, is only a confirmation of Miller and Swanson's affirmation that Schneider and Lysgaard's discovery also indicated patterns of parental control.

Of course, mental health enters as a factor as soon as parental consistency is mentioned, and Wagner has pointed to the relevance of parental pathology in this respect. He concluded that a pathological parent hindered the development of impulse control in children, so that present orientation and immediate gratification characterized their conduct. However, this is entirely predictable. The consistency of parental demands, including the subsequent keeping of their promises, is extremely relevant to the development of a deferred gratification pattern of conduct.

Future orientation neccessarily depends upon the certainty of a promise being kept and a 'deferred gratification' being 'realized' later (14). If it is not then the present-orientated attitude, which is contingent upon perpetual frustration, will itself emerge as a personality trait. Peck and Havighurst describe such a disorganized and chaotic home which is characteristic of the amoral child. In such a situation, they conclude, 'the only avenue of gratification left open to him, is immediate impulse gratification, which he tries to find wherever he can' (15).

Mischel's evidence also adds weight to this point. He found that children of absentee fathers chose immediate rather than deferred rewards. Assuming that such paternal neglect (characteristic of urban slum areas), implies lack of order in the home, one may conclude with the view that the deferred-gratification pattern of conduct requires a stable and organized home life within which to develop. Here the evidence is conclusive. Higher-status homes are characterized by parental consistency and regularity of conduct, while lower-status homes are not. Thus the former induce a future orientation of life, while the latter tend to emphasize present gratification as a mode of living.

THE MORAL IMPLICATIONS

The relevance of this consideration for morality is immediately apparent. Unless gratification can be ultimately assured by legal methods a child may turn to crime in order to attain it. Long ago Robert Merton argued that delinquency may be explained in this way. The delinquent is merely an instrumental deviant. He desires the socially approved rewards but lacks the ability to attain them. Hence, rather than save, or study and so acquire them by legitimate means, he turns to crime to facilitate this immediate gratification.

In his researches into the correlation between the level of social responsibility expressed and the degree of delayed rewards tolerated, Mischel confirmed this fact. He found that, in comparison with his control group of non-delinquents, delinquent adolescents were more likely to display both socially irresponsible attitudes and also a tendency towards desiring immediate gratification. More recently, West has described the young offender as being characterized by impulsiveness and an inability to defer gratification.

Charis Frankenburg also adds her evidence to confirm the view that the immediate-gratification syndrome leads to juvenile delinquency. In fact she sub-titles her book 'Spoilt Baby into Angry Young Man' in order to stress this point. We have already noted that the Newsons discovered a high degree of indulgence, displayed by lower-status parents, for their children. McCandless bluntly opposes Bronfenbrenner's view and argues that 'the lower-status child is more likely to have been breast-fed on demand, weaned relatively late, toilet-trained later and less urgently, and given more freedom' (16).

Frankenburg builds her thesis upon this foundation and from it surveys the mounting tide of crime and delinquency. Abstracting the essential from her book one may discern a simple pattern. She argues that immediate gratification progresses from an over-indulged infancy to a criminal adulthood. When an infant cries for gratification a dummy is popped into its mouth. When a child does so, a lolly is provided as a substitute. When, as an adolescent, an individual craves for oral gratification, a cigarette replaces the dummy or lolly. In some such way as this, she argues, an 'I-want-it-now' mentality is nurtured, and this, she argues, is invariably the root cause of many of the delinquent cases she has tried as a magistrate in Oxford.

After having heard her lecture on this theme the present author began to collect newspaper cuttings to illustrate this point. These now form a file of considerable proportions, but the contents can all be distilled down to the sentiment expressed by one young man who was arraigned before the court for maliciously wounding an elderly tobacco kiosk attendant. When asked why he had done such an awful thing, he replied nonchalantly, 'I wanted a fag, then, and didn't have any money on me'.

That these are not merely the fulminations of an elderly middle-class magistrate of the law has been recently confirmed by Mark Messer in his analysis of the increased misuse of drugs. Studying the personality of drug-addicts in colleges and universities he found that they displayed all the qualities which we have already outlined as characteristic of the present-orientated personality. His marijuana smokers believed that the lot of the average man was deteriorating, hence present pleasures should be sought; they placed no importance at all on prudent planning, since the future was uncontrollable and unpredictable; and finally they attached no value to the practice of deferred gratification.

On the other hand, children characterized by their future orientation not only avoid such overt forms of delinquency, but display positive moral virtues. Miller and Swanson found that middle-class children, with personalities moulded around the ideal of goal deferment, tended to inhibit their aggressive tendencies. They did not give way, as easily as the lower-status child, to the gratification provided by temper tantrums or physical violence. Such, too, were the findings of Livsen and Mussen, some years earlier. In their study of ego-control and aggression, they found that children able to defer gratification, in the form of rewards, were also those who displayed less aggressive conduct.

It would not be honest to omit any mention of the fact that one cannot form a simple equation in which future orientation and deferred gratification are equated with moral maturity. There are many reasons for this, some result from stupidity, others from hedonism. It is possible, for example, to find a child who acts to gratify his needs simply because he does not comprehend the consequences of deferring them. Equally, another child may defer them because he can find no way to gratify his needs. Thus irrational and unreasonable considerations can complicate the picture, and because of this one needs to qualify the views presented above and say that future-orientated conduct must be conscious and considered, if it is to qualify as moral behaviour.

Hedonism too can play a part. Prompted by similar motives children may be either present or future orientated. Thus while one child derives pleasure from gratifying his desires, another may defer them to achieve the same end. In adult life many examples of this spring readily to mind. The complex, elegant protracted rituals leading up to and characterizing a sophisticated dinner party; the restraint exercised during the course of the meal; the slow savouring of the fare provided only serve to enhance the gratification obtained from excellent wine, good food and stimulating conversation. Lovers will prolong their caresses and delay a sexual climax in order to derive the most intense and rich satisfaction from the experience. So again, it must be added that conduct tinctured in this way cannot really be classified as moral in the sense outlined above. Maslow has pointed out, 'The higher the need and the less imperative it is for sheer survival, the longer gratification can be postponed' (17).

Before concluding, a further complexity must be mentioned.

Future orientation depends upon a degree of intellectual sophistication not attainable by all children. Indeed all the evidence suggests that this necessary conceptual and linguistic proficiency is the prerogative of the higher-status child. Consequently, it is natural to expect the correlations outlined above.

Since any discussion of children's language today cannot help but be indebted to the work of Basil Bernstein, we can begin with him, even though his work is the latest in this particular field. He discovered that the complexity of higher-status language enabled children to place themselves in a spatial and temporal 'structure of relationships'. Conversely the lower-status child had no conceptual-linguistic structures to help him thus, 'a more volatile patterning of affectual and expressive behaviour will be found in the working classes' (18).

It is this consideration of impulsivity, with which we began, which now becomes relevant again. Baldwin built a sophisticated theory upon this by extending the notion. Many years previously the work of Hartshorne and May had employed techniques of investigation into child morality, which the present writer considers to have been little more than measures of a child's resistance to temptation (19), but which are relevant to the present discussion. When faced with a choice between following or renouncing an impulse a child is faced with a real temptation.

The sophistication of Baldwin's view now becomes apparent. He argued that 'Temptation occurs only when there is a conflict between two alternatives, one of which is more immediate or more concrete or more impressive and the other more remote, or abstract' (20). The crucial equations here are: (*a*) immediate = concrete and (*b*) remote = abstract. From what we have already learned above the linguistic-conceptual structures of children clearly accommodate themselves to these equations

Lower status = concrete = immediate = present orientation.
Higher status = abstract = remote = future orientation.

But this argument is not dependent upon moving cyphers around the paper in this way. All the evidence accumulated from studies in which social class and linguistic development have been correlated confirm it. Luria's work may serve as one example of this, since it is pertinent on this point. He discovered that the growth of what Bernstein called an 'elaborated-code' (21) became a behavioural regulator as well as an efficient medium for communicating and manipulating conceptual structures. As an internal regulator it transformed a child's conscious and voluntary activity since language which would otherwise have been interpreted as simple specific commands, was transformed into media for transmitting abstract notions. These included not only ideals and principles, but abstractions concerning the non-existent, intangible future. Thus, in this semantic framework, the *future* became a prime determinant of conduct. Dollard and Miller expressed this in a much more homely way when they reported that language, for such children, introduced them to both abstract moral concepts and future considerations.

With Jane Mathison, I have elsewhere argued this point in an academic paper. Rather than cite the tedious references required in such a publication, it might be valuable to present an eclectic quotation. Interested readers could then follow the complexities of the argument in the original work. The context needs some explanation. We were there concerned to rebut Desmond Morris's argument that man is merely a naked ape and argued that man's language, conceptual structures and moral sense could not be accommodated in this reductionist model. We argued that

'Vigotsky was among the first to suggest that there was an inter-dependence of thinking and speech in the historical development of human consciousness. Thus, however extrapolative the evidence, however hypothetical some of the bases on which the argument rests, it still remains philosophically and empirically tenable that the use of words transformed the naked ape into a moral, conscious ape. This must have been a factor involved in the breakthrough into the noosphere in which cultural evolution plays a dominant part. Man is, therefore, the possessor of a new adaptive mechanism, culture, and this sets him totally apart from other animals. Desmond Morris has almost the last word, "So there he stands, our vertical, hunting, weapon-toting, territorial, neotenous, brainy naked ape, a primate by ancestry and a carnivore by adoption, ready to conquer the world". However, his conquest of the world has involved him in a struggle to achieve moral autonomy from the imperatives of taboo, and intellectual autonomy from his native egocentricity. So there he stands, our symbolizing, logical, moral ape, not only ready to conquer the world but also to enrich the milieu in which values and principles hold sway' (22).

However, as we shall see below (see Chapter 10) the matter is not so simple as this would suggest. Srauss found over a decade ago that working-class aspirants for middle-class status learnt to defer their gratifications. Achievement-aspiration appears to be inextricably related to future orientation. Indeed, as we have seen, in a situation where sustained study and training is a necessary prerequisite for social ascent by members of the working class in a mobile society, need deferment is obviously functional.

All this evidence only serves to underline a single point. The 'I-want-it-now' attitude of mind has moral corollaries ranging from simple theft to complex sexual promiscuity. It is therefore perfectly natural for Halloran to conclude that 'it is important to note that the ability to postpone gratification is frequently associated with moral maturity' (23). This is indeed a salutary observation for even middle-class, adult males suspect that if they did not restrict their personal gratifications they would soon become 18-stone, alcoholic lechers. The point is that such men do defer such gratifications! We know too that cigarette smoking—the epitome of immediate gratification—also differs according to social class. At the height of the smoking/lung-cancer scare, the percentage of higher-status smokers, who stopped smoking, was over 65 % of the estimated total; while smokers amongst the lower-status groups showed only a minimal percentage who were prepared to forego immediate gratification in order to ensure future health. Of course, individual differences are salient here but the statistically significant variable is social class. Thus even a practice as common as smoking indicates the correlation between socio-economic status and the manifestation of this crucial moral trait.

REFERENCES

1 'For I reckon that the sufferings of this present time are not worthy to be compared with the glory which shall be revealed to us' (Romans 8:18).
2 Whyte (1943), p. 106.
3 Spinley (1953), pp. 129–30.
4 Farley (1969), p. 85.
5 Berelson and Steiner (1964), p. 486.
6 Ogburn and Nimkoff (1964), p. 357.
7 Hoggart (1957), p. 110.
8 Zweig (1948), p. 135.
9 McCandless (1969), pp. 382–3.
10 Westley and Elkin (1967), pp. 18–19.
11 LeShan (1952), p. 591. For a macabre and horrifying account of a child's environment where there is no protective adult influence, see Ray Bradbury's *The Playground*.
12 Hughes (1960), p. 307.
13 Kerr (1958), p. 179. See Chapter 25 for the full range of evidence.
14 A curious semantic problem arises here. If gratification is *deferred* it must necessarily be assumed that satisfaction follows later. Therefore, if it is not satisfied later it is not deferred; it is simply never satisfied. However, the complication of the chronological implications of linguistic usage belong properly to philosophy rather than sociology.
15 Peck and Havighurst (1964), p. 110.
16 McCandless (1969), p. 596. Bronfenbrenner (1958) is relevant here. He was

perplexed by the fact that researchers in the 1940s had found that permissiveness was characteristic of lower-status child rearing; while a decade later this was described as a feature of the process in higher-status homes. In his report on social-class variations in socialization he reached a simple conclusion. The researchers in both decades had been accurate in their observations and conclusions. The later results merely revealed the extent to which higher-status parents had been affected by the advocates of permissiveness (e.g. Benjamin Spock). As a natural consequence it seemed that lower-status parents were less permissive than they had hitherto been deemed to be. In conclusion Bronfenbrenner (1961) later expressed the view that less permissive modes of child rearing would ensure greater degrees of personal maturity (cf. Chapter 11).

17 Maslow (1970), p. 98.
18 Bernstein (1958), p. 168.
19 Kay (1968), Chapter 2.
20 Baldwin (1956), p. 49.
21 This 'elaborated' code is contrasted with the 'restricted' code. The former is that familiar mode of language in which educated individuals, both adults and children, can couch their complex ideas. The latter is inadequate for this and employs clichés, repetitions and stereotyped forms of emphasis to communicate emotional states. It is argued that all children can use the latter, but only higher-status children can also use the former.
22 Mathison and Kay (1968), pp. 67–73.
23 Halloran (1967), p. 130.

Bibliography

BALDWIN, A. L., *Behaviour and Development in Childhood* (Holt, Dryden, 1956).

BERNSTEIN, B., 'Some Sociological Determinants of Perception', in *British Journal of Sociology*, Vol. IX, 1958.

BERNSTEIN, B., 'Language and Social Class', in *British Journal of Sociology*, Vol. XI, 1960.

BERELSON, B. and STEINER, G. A., *Human Behaviour* (Harcourt, Brace & World, 1964).

BERKOWITZ, L., *The Development of Motives and Values in the Child* (Basic Books: New York, 1964).

BROWN, CLAUDE, *Manchild in the Promised Land* (Macmillan: New York, 1965).

BRONFENBRENNER, URIE, 'Socialisation and Social Class Through Time and Space', in E. Maccoby, T. M. Newcomb and E. L. Hartley (Eds), *Readings in Social Psychology* (Holt, Rinehart & Winston, 1958).

BRONFENBRENNER, URIE, 'The Changing American Child', in *Journal of Social Issues*, No. 17, 1961.

BROWN, CLAUDE, *Manchild in the Promised Land* (Macmillan: New York, 1965).

CATTELL, R. B., *The Scientific Analysis of Personality* (Pelican, 1965).

DENNIS, N., HENRIQUES, S. F. and SLAUGHTER, R. C., *Coal is Our Life* (Eyre & Spottiswoode, 1956).

DOLLARD, J. and MILLER, N. E., *Personality and Psychotherapy* (McGraw-Hill, 1950).

EATON, J. W. and WEIL, R. J., *Culture and Mental Disorders* (Free Press, New York, 1955).

FARLEY, R. M., 'Television and the Consumption Habits and Aspirations of a Selected Sample of Adolescents', Unpublished M.Ed. thesis, Leicester, 1969.

FRANKENBURG, C. U., *I'm All Right* (P. R. MacMilland, 1961).

HALLORAN, J. D., *Attitude Formation and Change* (Leicester Univ. Press, 1967).

HARTSHORNE, H. and MAY, M. A., *Studies in the Nature of Character*: Vol. 1, *Studies in Deceit*; Vol. 2 *Studies in Service and Self Control*, with Maller; Vol. 3, Unavailable in Great Britain. With Shuttleworth (Macmillan Company: New York, 1928, 1929 and 1930, respectively).

HOGGART, R., *The Uses of Literacy* (Chatto & Windus, 1957).

HUGHES, C. C., *et al.*, *People of Cove and Woodland: Communities from the Viewpoint of Social Psychiatry* (Basic Books: New York, 1960).

JEPHCOTT, P., *Some Young People* (Allen & Unwin, 1954).

KERR, M., *The People of Ship Street* (Routledge and Kegan Paul, 1958).

KOHN, M. L., 'Social Class and the Experience of Parental Authority', in *American Sociological Review*, Vol. XXIV, 1959.

LESHAN, L. L., 'Time orientation and Social Class', in *Journal of Abnormal and Social Psychology*, No. 47, 1952.

LIVSON, N. and MUSSEN, P. H., 'The Relation of Ego Control to Overt Aggression', in *Journal of Abnormal and Social Psychology*, No. 55, 1957.

LURIA, A. R. and YUDOVITCH, F., *Speech and the Development of Mental Processes* (Staples, 1959).

MCMANDLESS, BOYD R., *Children: Behaviour and Development* (Holt, Rinehart & Winston, 1969).

MALLER, J. B., *see* Hartshorne and May.

MASLOW, A. H., *Motivation and Personality* (Harper & Row, 1970).

MATHISON, JANE and KAY, WILLIAM, 'The Evolution of Consciousness', in *Teilhard Review*, Vol. 3, No. 2, 1968.

MERTON, R. K., *Social Theory and Social Structure* (Free Press, New York, 1956).

MESSER, MARK, 'The Predictive Value of Marijuana Use', in *Sociology of Education*, Vol. 42, No. 1, 1969.

MILLER, D. R. and SWANSON, G. E., *The Changing American Parent* (John Wiley, 1958).

MILLER, D. R. and SWANSON, G. E., *Inner Conflict and Defence* (Holt, Rinehart & Winston, 1960).

MISCHEL, W., 'Preference for Delayed Reinforcement and Social Responsibility', in *Journal of Abnormal and Social Psychology*, No. 62, 1957, p. 61.

MISCHEL, W., 'Preference for Delayed Reinforcement; An Experimental Study of a Cultural Observation', in *Journal of Abnormal and Social Psychology*, No. 56, 1958.

MISCHEL, W. and GILLIGAN, C. F., *Delay of Gratification and Resistance to Temptation* (Stanford Univ. Press, 1962).

MOGEY, J., *Family and Neighbourhood* (Oxford Univ. Press, 1956).

MORRIS, DESMOND, *The Naked Ape* (Jonathan Cape, 1967).

OGBURN, W. F. and NIMKOFF, M. F., *A Handbook of Sociology* (Routledge & Kegan Paul, 1964).

OLDMAN, D., BYTHEWAY, B. and HOROBIN, G., 'Family Structure and Educational Achievement', in *Journal of Biosocial Science,* Suppl. No. 3, 1971.

OPPENHEIM, A. M., 'Social Status and Clique Formation Among Grammar School Boys', in *British Journal of Sociology*, Vol. 6, 1955.

PANETH, M., *Branch Street* (Allen & Unwin, 1944).

PECK, R. F. and HAVIGHURST, R. J., *The Psychology of Character Development* (John Wiley, 1964).

SCHNEIDER, L. and LYSGAARD, S., 'The Deferred Gratification Pattern', in *American Sociological Review*, No. XVIII, 1953.

SCHWEBEL, A. I. and BERNSTEIN, A. J., 'Effects of Impulsivity on performance of lower class children on the W.I.S.C. Test', in *American Journal of Orthopsychiatry*, No. 40, 1970.

SHUTTLEWORTH, F., *see* Hartshorne and May.

SPINLEY, B. M., *The Deprived and the Privileged* (Routledge & Kegan Paul, 1953).

SPOCK, BENJAMIN, *Baby and Child Care* (Bodley Head, 1958).

SRAUSS, M. A., 'Deferred Gratification, Social Class and the Achievement Syndrome', in *American Sociological Review*, Vol. 27, 1962.

VAZ, EDMUND W. (Ed.), *Middle-class Juvenile Delinquency* (Harper & Row, 1967).

WAGNER, N. N., 'Developmental Aspects of Impulse Control', in *Journal of Consultant Psychiatry*, No. 24, 1960.

WEBER, MAX, *The Protestant Ethic and the Spirit of Capitalism* (Allen & Unwin, 1930).

WEST, D. J., *The Young Offender* (Duckworth, 1967).

WESTLEY, W. A. and ELKIN, F., 'The Protective Environment and Adolescent Socialization', in E. W. Vaz (Ed.), *Middle-class Juvenile Delinquency* (Harper & Row, 1967).

WHYTE, W. F., *Street Corner Society* (Univ. Chicago Press, 1943).

WILLMOTT, P. and YOUNG, M., *Family and Class in a London Suburb* (Routledge & Kegan Paul, 1960).

YOUNG, MICHAEL, *The Rise of the Meritocracy* (Thames & Hudson, 1958).

ZWEIG, F., *Labour, Life and Poverty* (Gollancz, 1948).

ZWEIG, F., *The Worker in an Affluent Society* (Heinemann, 1961).

Chapter 7

Moral Personalism

In turning to consider this third primary moral characteristic a technical term has been purloined from the sphere of philosophy. As we shall see later, this is a legitimate course of action to take because complex philosophical theories have been erected upon the view that respect for the integrity of persons is the *sine qua non* of a morally sound society. However, in this context, the term simply refers to the degree to which parents regard their children as persons. It seems that even this moral experience can be correlated with social class.

SOCIAL-CLASS DIFFERENCES

During his research into the effects of parental conduct on the maturity of a child's moral judgement, Lerner found a sharp difference of attitude amongst the parents investigated. He discovered that higher-status parents tended to be flexible in their moral demands. They were not exactly permissive in Frankenburg's sense of being over-indulgent, but they did provide considerable latitude in their moral requests. This took cognisance of the child as a person and made allowance for his intellectual, physical and psychical levels of maturation.

In contrast to this, he found that lower-status children were treated as though they were objects rather than persons. Their general parental attitude seemed to imply that children were an expensive, irritating inconvenience. As a natural consequence lower-status parents displayed a high degree of dogmatic specificity in the control of their children and tended to ignore the situational circumstances or personal condition of the child involved. Such parents naturally made specific, dogmatic, inflexible demands and expected to be unquestioningly obeyed. In this relationship, there was no room for personal encounter. Authoritarian parents expected their partially depersonalized offspring to slip like cogs into the right gear as smoothly as any piece of complex machinery.

As will be seen below, such authoritarianism is consistently characteristic of lower-status familial life (1). However, for the moment this theme may be taken up where Adorno and his colleagues left it. Here a connection between socio-economic status and authoritarianism was established. Accepting that authoritarian techniques are orientated more towards preserving legal requirements than satisfying personal needs (2), one can see how such a correlation would emerge.

Lower-status parents practise stricter and less love-orientated child-rearing techniques. As a natural consequence, their children become vulnerable to authoritarian and legalistic techniques of social control. But, for the purposes of our arguments, this diminution of love, in the relationship, also indicates a diluting of the personalism to be found there.

A few years later Eleanor Maccoby and her colleagues found similar evidence in their investigation of child-rearing practices in higher-and lower-status families. They too noticed this lowering in the level of personalism amongst lower-status mothers, whose child-rearing practices were, on the whole, more rigid than their higher-status counterparts. They used more physical punishment, made more inflexible demands, and refused to allow the children opportunities to express their own will.

Evidence supplied later by Winterbottom, and then by Kohn, emphasized the next obvious point. In higher-status families the treatment of children implied that they were maturing moral agents. Hence they were treated as though they were *people in the process of becoming good citizens*. Winterbottom's findings are important since they indicate that children need the perpetual experience of success if they are to mature. In this case, she argued, such achievement enabled children to become more independent of their parents. The important point here, made by Duvall a decade earlier, is that higher-status parents appear to be more sensitive to their children as developing persons, and thus more realistic in the moral demands which they make of them. As a natural consequence these parental demands are matched to the level of each child's capabilities. In this way both the constant motivation to achieve, and also a sustained experience of success, were assured. Such flexible, realistic demands, however, were characteristic of higher-status families only.

Kohn also developed this point, but concentrated his attention on social-class variations in the exercise of parental authority. Like Winterbottom, he too found higher-status parents viewing their children as moral agents with developing personal powers, and contrasted this sharply with the lower-status view. Concentrating on the varying nature of punishment in each sub-culture, he discovered a sharp and fundamental difference of emphasis. Lower-status parents tended to punish retributively so that punishment became an impersonal device employed to minimize the inconvenience caused in the home by inconsiderate children. On the other hand, higher-status parents appeared to use punishment as a means of ensuring that socially acceptable behavioural patterns were established in their children. Clearly it is only in the latter case that personal concern could be displayed and experienced by both parents and children.

Two years later Elder returned to the theme of authoritarian, impersonal control. It was mentioned above that Adorno and his colleagues traced a correlation between socio-economic class and authoritarianism. Elder developed this theme in terms of what he called the exercise of either coercive or legitimate parental authority. Put simply, he argued that when parents reject a child's request without considering its validity they are exercising *coercive* authority. But when they display a willingness to consider any such request, discuss its merits and grant it on the basis of reciprocity (i.e. the child must do something for the parents in return for the favour), they are exercising *legitimate* power. Thus in any given familial situation one has parental power exercised through a continuum ranging from autocratic, coercive techniques to democratic legitimate processes.

Elder's findings are extremely relevant here since he found that the legitimate use of democratically exercised, parental authority induced a greater degree of personal autonomy, in the children, than did the autocratic, coercive techniques. Clearly, in the former higher-status situation, the children were treated as persons who had a valid point of view and a right to be heard. In the latter, they were not. Thus personalism, in this context, developed as an essential moral trait in the children who experienced it.

Further evidence for moral personalism also emerges from the Newsom Report, where, once again, it appears to be correlated with social class. One headmaster, concerned with the diminished personal contact between lower-status parents and children, lamented that 'as one examines the background of these pupils, descending from the able to the less able, the more one finds them being left to their own devices'. This is precisely what LeShan had found with his lower-status children. They invariably played in the streets away from adult supervision because parents were either at work or unaware of their children's activities. Consequently, as the Newsom Report goes on to record, 'Boys and girls left continually on their own tend to get into more or less serious mischief'.

A cursory reading of such comments, made by headmasters in active educational work, can leave one with the impression that social-class differences are blurred here. One, for example, describing a typical educationally-deprived, slum area, says 'I feel that the large majority of parents are doing their best and that there is a wholesome atmosphere in the homes'. This is echoed by a further comment from another headmaster to the effect that 'The parents are fond of their children and go to great lengths to provide them with the things they want—football boots, uniforms, bicycles, pocket-money'.

At this point the two elements have to be disentangled. First, parents who neglect their children by going out to work, are thereby enabled to obtain the means to provide such material compensation for their absence from the home. Second, one must distinguish sharply between the warm personal relationships, which are the seeds of moral personalism, and the bestowing of material benefits which are a *substitute* for this. Indeed, the headmaster who painted the picture of parental care in such glowing colours went on to say, 'but it is not generally their custom to be with their children very much. Nobody worries very much unless the child gets into trouble of some sort'. It is this personal deprivation which is so crucial.

As we have already seen, it is the loving acceptance of themselves as persons, which is crucial to the moral growth of children. The bestowal of material benefits, no matter how lavish, can never compensate for the absence of this expression of personal love and care.

It is precisely this inadequate substitute, which absentee, working lower-status parents offer to their children. As one further head-master concluded, 'The parents are often over-generous in material things, and under-generous in giving their time to their children' (3).

Thus a gloomy picture of personal neglect, amongst lower-status children, is painted by the contents of this official report, which only serves to add weight to the conclusion of Peck and Havighurst. Outlining the conditions in such a home, characterized by the inconsistent moral training, with material goods as substitutes for affection and immediate gratification necessarily being encouraged by the process, they make the same point in a pungent, forceful way. 'This general parental support,' they conclude, 'since it is combined with irregularity and leniency, does not contain much real recognition or concern for the child as an individual' (4).

Now to this one may add the evidence provided by John and Elizabeth Newson from their investigation of four-year-old urban children. They found sharp social-class differences in the way mothers reacted to inconvenient quarrels between their offspring. The characteristic, higher-status maternal reaction was entirely predict-able. Mothers intervened and tried to reach a settlement by verbaliz-ing the difficulties, and then, if necessary, separating the children into topographically distinct areas. In doing this they made it clear all the time, that everybody concerned had personal rights, privileges and responsibilities.

The lower-status mothers on the other hand, did almost the exact opposite. Instead of intervening, they left the children to fend for themselves. Instead of attempting to establish some personal *rapprochement* between their children the mothers actively encouraged them to indulge in aggressive physical violence. Instead of verbalizing the difficulties in order to reach a solution, they only verbalized in order to continue the child-squabble on the plane of adult bickering.

Implications for morality

Clearly, any significant advance in moral development can only be assured by the higher-status-type experiences which have been outlined above. The personal nature of the child–parent relationship enables the children concerned to develop an awareness of their obligations to all others, as persons in their own right. It was argued earlier that nobody can love unless they have first been loved; nor accept others until they have first been accepted.

This argument is equally valid here. It is only when children have first been accepted as persons, that they can enter into genuinely personal relationships with others. One fundamental law of all social intercourse seems to be not merely that we ought to treat others as we would wish them to treat us, but that in fact *we treat others as we ourselves have been treated*. The inevitable corollary of being accepted and treated with the dignity accorded to a person, is that children will naturally extend this courtesy to others. Furthermore, since the parents, who establish such a personal relationship, ensure that constant motivation and sustained success characterize their child's moral experience, this positive reinforcement will ensure that this development is sustained. Such experiences also develop the quality of moral flexibility, which is equally essential for moral maturity. A relationship, which is characterized by concern for persons, leads the participant inevitably and naturally to consider the moral principles which are inherent in a concrete situation and which, of necessity, extend beyond the specific circumstances of the moment.

One final point, which is relevant to the argument here, results from the fact that personalism depends not only upon the degree to which a child is treated as a person, but also *the extent* to which he is thus treated. There are thus two variables. The first indicates the quality; the second the quantity, of personalism in the relationship. When conflated these then produce a continuum characterized at one end by the loving higher-status parent who sustains a personal relationship with his child; and, at the other end, by the irascible lower-status parent whose infrequent encounters with his offspring make it clear that he deems them to be little more than an extension of the things which irritate him in his already difficult life (5).

This, of course, is not exclusively unilateral. It has often been observed that children also fall into two categories. There are those who can enter into personal relationships with adults by attracting attention without at the same time annoying them, but there are also those who cannot. The whining, demanding, selfish child is the paradigm of the latter group. It has been recently discovered that on the whole it is the higher-status child who is more accomplished in this respect. Thus the two elements cohere. The experiences of the higher-status child enable him to establish more firm and frequent personal relationships with his parents; the lower-status child's experiences do not.

However, this consideration of the correlation of personalism in terms of social-class distribution cannot be left there without further comment. The degree to which we treat other people as persons is central to the value system of any given culture. Arnold Toynbee subscribed to the view that civilizations declined and finally disappeared when this moral quality became so diluted that it ceased to be a cohesive force in society.

This, after all, is what common sense would conclude. In societies, where men manipulated each other and their relationships were characterized by exploitation and mutual scorn, there is not only no cohesive element present but there is in fact a negative disruptive force at work. Conversely, where men and women revere each other's individual worth, and display this by mutual respect and co-operation, there one finds a healthy, morally mature community.

A healthy ego must transcend itself in relationships if it is to remain so. On this theme Angyal is eloquent. He discovered that 'ego-transcendence' was as necessary for the health of individuals as love and autonomy. Furthermore, in this situation, which he called one of homonomy, individuals displayed less neurosis. Now Maslow has taken the argument a stage further. He argues that we need to go beyond the limits of our ego in search of persons. Their love can then enable us to transcend our ego, and this, he says, 'may be a need in the same sense that we have need for vitamins' (6).

The thread binding these ideas together is that of personalism. Individual and social health depends upon this expression of human love. Lives are wrecked when it dies and cultures collapse when it is eroded. It is the essential prerequisite of any morality, for morality is compounded of relationships and relationships can only exist between people who treat each other as persons.

THE PHILOSOPHY OF PERSONALISM

Such an important cultural concept has naturally been systematically studied since it is essential for any system of morality. If, as the previous paragraphs implied, it is a self-authenticating value, one would expect a school of thought to be erected upon its basic presuppositions as, indeed, is the case.

A number of writers have argued that the fundamental nature of an individual is derived not from personal qualities, but interpersonal activities, in which all express their nature as persons. Of these Emmanuel Mounier stands out as the most cogent advocate. Better known in this country for his studies of such French existential writers as Malraux, Camus, Sartre and Bernanos, in which he discusses the hope lying behind the innately desperate human condition, he has coined the term used as the title of this chapter.

In his book *Personalism*, he discusses the virtues of 'personal' living. For him the essence of life is constituted by our perpetual need to be treated as persons, and the concomitant need to treat others as persons in their own right. He, of course, is not the only advocate of this ideal. Maslow's 'self-actualizing' morally mature individual lives by this code, and it is in this personal interaction that all the virtues, which make mortality bearable, have their origin.

Long ago Henry Thoreau expressed the pessimistic view that 'The mass of men lead lives of quiet desperation' (7), and much more recently Jean Paul-Sartre caustically observed that hell consists of other people (8). Yet out of this desperate hell of life, argues Mounier, we can salvage virtue, happiness and hope. Thus for one who elevates personal worth, the obstructions formed by egotism, self-interest and impersonalism are thrust aside. This personalism, he argues, 'disarms refusal by offering to another what is of eminent value in his own estimation, at the very moment when he might expect to be over-ridden as an obstacle, and he is himself caught in its contagion' (9). For it is in situations of this kind, continues Mounier, that one finds the liberating value of the highest personalist values of love, forgiveness and concern.

The core of Mounier's argument, that 'The person only exists thus towards others, it only knows itself in knowing others, only finds itself in being known by them' (10) was later expounded by Jourard. As a psychological researcher who turned to psychotherapy, he found that his patients invariably felt more human and integrated when they had disclosed something about themselves which had hitherto been kept a secret. They had, it seems, pulled down a barrier which divided them from other people and had hitherto diminished their personal status. As a result he too became more open to them in this cultivation of what he terms 'the transparent self', and, contrary to all the canons of psychiatric practice, this worked.

He found that when he and his patients stopped approaching each other in the stereotyped roles of doctor and patient, they met each other as people (11). From this work he reached two conclusions: (1) that much mental ill-health results from the fact that our society inhibits the self-disclosure which genuine personal confrontation requires; and (2) that while such honesty in personal relationships has its dangers, it is essential for both individual and social morality, leading, as it does, to an increase in psychic and spiritual energy.

Such a philosophy has been endowed with cosmic proportions by the speculations of Teilhard de Chardin. It is impossible to convey the grandeur and subtlety of his thought in the compass of one paragraph. Adherents of his world-view must thus forgive what may appear to be a cavalier treatment of his work. However, he argues that the whole process of evolution leads to a personalized goal. All existence, he says, is being drawn forward by an 'attractive centre which has personality'. It is this evocation of the personal element in all existing forms, which will ultimately overcome the eroding force of an apparently inevitable cosmic disintegration, prophesied by subscribers to the second law of thermo-dynamics.

These two notions cohere in his conclusion where he argues that we must conceive of 'a noogenesis rising upstream against the flow of entropy, to provide evolution with a direction, a line of advance and critical points; and finally to make all things double back upon *someone*' (12). Consequently in other works he is led to speak of autonomy and socialization as forces which impel man more firmly along the pathway of cultural evolution so long as they do 'not take the form of anarchical individualization but of personalization' (13).

Contra-personalism
Such an attitude of mind is increasingly difficult for western, urban-ized man to adopt. Living, as he does, in the industrial age of space-technology and cyberculture, he is subject to two forces which militate against personalism. In the academic world of science this idea is increasingly bedevilled by the erosion of reductionism; and man in society is increasingly characterized by a sense of alienation.

Reductionism, in the study of man today, has been described by Sir Peter Medawar as the philosophy of 'nothing-buttery' which he stigmatizes as symptomatic of the bogus in scientific work. According to its tenets every organization is reduced to nothing but a complex association of more primitive elements which in their turn can be reduced to simpler, more basic components. Undoubtedly there is some value in this exercise. As Lord Brain has said, what man has in common with other animals may prove to be just as important for our understanding of his behaviour as are his distinctly human characteristics (14). However, man is deemed to be little more than a naked ape and the complexity of his nature can be fully explained, so it is thought, by reference to animal behaviour.

Ardrey, Lorenz, Leonard Williams, Tiger, Goodall and the Russells are all protagonists of this view, but the high-god in this pantheon is undoubtedly Desmond Morris, whose trilogy of books argues explicitly that man can be fully understood if his primate, animal nature is taken as the base line from which he operates.

Such a reductionist view has been vigorously opposed by many eminent scholars. Apart from Medawar, Koestler, Sinnott, Towers and Lewis have all argued that such an approach to man ignores the essentially human elements in his make-up. With Jane Mathison (15) I have elsewhere argued that part of this uniqueness consists of man's self-consciousness, and that this can only be understood, not in reductionist terms, but in the light of his linguistic competence and moral sense. Yet the publications of Desmond Morris have attained such a high degree of popularity that the reductionist 'nothing-buttery' view appears to be gaining ground.

This view of man is furthermore endorsed by the behavioural school of psychologists, headed by Skinner. Here findings from experiments with rats and pigeons are indiscriminately applied to man. It is true that as a result of this work, tremendous advances have been made in our understanding of the techniques to employ in programmed learning; but the basic presupposition dehumanizes man. And now, in his latest publication, provocatively called *Beyond Freedom and Dignity*, Skinner crowns his life's work. For him man is clearly nothing but a product of environmental circumstances which induce specific modes of conduct and then reinforce them: moral praise and blame being irrelevant concepts except in so far as they act as positive or negative forms of reinforcement. Thus despite the ambiguity of his contiguous statements that 'Science does not dehumanize man' and 'What is being abolished is autonomous man' (16) it is clear that he rejects what we normally mean by 'man'.

Consequently there is a tendency, in academic circles, to eliminate the human element in both psychological and sociological investigations. This reduces individual men and women to the level of elements in complex social interactions and as products of operant-conditioning. As a result the findings of many academics are passed over if such men become personally involved with the subjects of their researches. The essence of such research, it is argued, is the establishment of empirically confirmed, objectively assessed data, and complicated batteries of machinery and tests are devised in order to do this and so eliminate the human element (17).

One spirited reaction to this is that of Professor B. Morris, whose work in educational psychology has been a constant source of inspiration for the practising teacher. In his analysis of the contribution of psychology to the process of education, he argues that the central stream of educational psychology has now 'reached the level of the personal'. This implies that 'the concept of individual and society disappear, being transformed into the notion of persons and community (i.e. persons in relation)'. In this way the self is recognized not merely as a passive receiver of impressions, but as an active agent. Furthermore, he argues, psychology as a conceptual system can only be rightly interpreted when 'the all inclusive concept is that of the person'. He concludes that even 'psycho-analytic thought is undergoing transformation from an original largely organic form to one that is unmistakably personal' (18). Obviously there are certain human actions, like the reflexes enabling us to avoid physical harm, which can be legitimately analysed on the basis of some such mechanistic model as the behaviourists employ. But many of them cannot, and it is the distinction between the two which is crucial here.

In his discussion of the divided self, Laing has argued that, 'Man seen as an organism or as a person disclose different aspects of human reality. However, one must be alert to the possible occasion for confusion' (19). Yet in psychological investigation today, the methodological techniques appear to cluster around the former concept. It is this against which Robert Phillips has reacted. He pleads for experimental psychologists to take a 'great leap backwards' because he fears that the complex gadgets of the psychologist are preventing him from comprehending the people he seeks to understand. Hence he concludes that 'The need for protest is urgent, as the number of machines that bleep, warble, twitter, whistle, hum, click, whirl, and flash, in the laboratory, increases daily'.

Alienated Man

But contemporary man is not only reduced to the level of 'nothing but' a complex structure of stereotyped reactions, circumscribed by his primate, animal nature. He is also becoming alienated both from himself and society, and in this process too he is becoming depersonalized.

This pathway through recent cultural evolution can be clearly and easily traced. Firstly, Galileo pointed out that the earth was not the centre of the universe, it was merely one orb in a minor planetary system. While still reeling from the humiliation of being dethroned from the centre of the universe, and perhaps comforting himself with the thought that at least he was unique on this planet, Darwin struck the second blow. Man, it seemed, was merely one of the proliferating species with which earth abounded. Denied cosmic uniqueness, he was now also stripped of terrestrial uniqueness.

This loss of dignity was then increased by Freud and his contemporary psycho-analysts. Having perhaps taken comfort in the fact that at least he was the most rational of all creatures, man was now assured that he was not guided by reason. Much of his conduct, it seemed, had its roots in sources inaccessible to the intellect, and not amenable to logical analysis. This was not the end in the downgrading of man. Caught in a technological revolution, he first found that machines were able to replicate his physical actions with greater competence, and computers could usurp his mental function by storing data with greater accuracy and reaching calculated conclusions with greater speed.

The latter development, of course, need not be entirely detrimental. When machines freed man from the tedium of physical labour they liberated his mind, and cultures emerged which did not depend upon the degradation of a slave class. Today, computers, still in their infancy, may ultimately free men from the drudgery of mental calculation, data-storing and decision making. Then just as his brain was earlier liberated, so now man's personal qualities may be freed. In this situation art, music, religion, morality, even hitherto unexplored powers of the human personality may flourish and help man to become truly 'personalized'.

At the moment, however, man's alienation is a fact. In contemporary society he feels impotent and isolated. His interior life seems to be characterized by self-estrangement. Life appears to be bereft of purpose and meaning, and he is thereby becoming depersonalized. He is no longer deemed to be a real person (20).

Wright Mills gives a cutting edge to this fact with his view that the 'salesman ethic' determines man's behaviour in a commercial setting. Here, the individuals concerned dispassionately and impersonally manipulate each other in order to sell their commodities. Those concerned in the transaction, are no longer treated as people. They are merely means to be used for economic ends. It is here that the acid of alienation bites most deeply and erodes that personalism without which moral conduct becomes a utopian chimera.

Thus, in the different spheres of his life, each man suspects that he is no longer a person and that genuine personal relationships are fast becoming *passé*. Not only may we be deemed to be little more than cyphers in a bureaucratic system, but science views us as nothing more than material for objective inquiry. Industry treats us as extensions of automated machines or computers; and commerce assumes that we are depersonalized units to be manipulated in an impersonal system.

Two Cultural Aberrations

There are, of course, a number of escape routes leading out of that depersonalization, which constitutes a moral *impasse*. Two of these are particularly interesting to both sociologists and anthropologists for they constitute a polarization of personalism in terms of cultural diversity. Either we may assert our individuality or we may become totally absorbed in society. Although the latter seems commendable, both, in fact, are travesties of man's nature as a social being.

The former is more familiar to us in the western world. Our major religion, Christianity, emphasizes the need for personal salvation, and recently has produced the individualistic, autonomous independent non-conforming protestant. Indeed many Christians would say that such a description is not inaptly applied to the Founder Himself. Thus in the West we can trace a line of aberrant social development in which individuals asserted their own will and identity to the ultimate detriment of society.

To avoid unnecessary complexity a consideration of this phenomenon will be limited to the nineteenth and twentieth centuries. It began with Schopenhauer's philosophical conclusion that ultimate reality was a cosmic evil will and all phenomena were objectifications of it. Thus for him life consisted of individual man's egotistic assertions against this by his 'will to live'.

Nietzsche outgrew his predecessor's pessimism and altered this concept into the affirmation that it was a man's 'will to power' which constituted the ultimately real essence of life. For him the ideal man was the incarnation of this 'will to power'. As such he could use force and pain to achieve his ends; and for him society was merely the means whereby an individual could attain this personal excellence. The path could follow the sado-masochistic track mapped by the Marquis de Sade, or straight to Belsen, Buchenwald and Dachau. Nietzsche was a great admirer and friend of Wagner and it takes little imagination to see that Wagner's hero, Siegfried, was modelled on Nietzsche's superman. Hitler too was inflamed with this vision of a superman and a super-race.

Contemporaries describe how, before he came to power, Hitler would stride up and down his room with eyes blazing, in manic euphoria, gesticulating wildly to the blaring tones of Wagner's records. This aberrant solution led directly to the concentration camps, the SS torture chambers and the brutalizing of a whole nation.

This is the egotism which Max Stirner had earlier advocated. Paterson has recently made it perfectly clear that Stirner really did believe that each man had the right to treat others solely as material for his own gratification. Indeed his parody of religion consisted of the view that we should demolish all ideologies except those which facilitated an individual's self-aggrandisement. Some have expressed surprise that such a notion should have sprung from the heart of the Romantic Movement. Yet Romanticism could lead not only towards the ideal of union with the natural world, but also express a reaction against reason. Schopenhauer and Nietzsche expressed the notion philosophically; de Sade and Stirner, pathologically; and Byron and Wordsworth, poetically: but the essence of this movement was its emphasis of the human will at the expense of the intellect. Impatient with sequences of logic and chains of reasoning, it asserted the centrality of the ego. Today, the trendy expression of this same idea emerges as the view that everybody ought to be doing 'their own thing': and from this, many argue, stems drug addiction, promiscuity and a general rejection of social norms.

The other extreme alternative is that more familiar to the eastern world. There, it is said, the teeming masses of mankind think naturally of the group, rather than the individual, as the basic social reality. This idea is central to the major religions of the east. They advocate that an individual should seek not personal salvation and eternal life, but absorption in the ultimately real cosmic whole, and thus escape from an isolated, individual existence. Indeed the basic view that permanence is an illusion and hence no static 'personality' exists, pervades both the teachings of Hinduism and Buddhism. The Buddha preached that nothing has an 'ego' since all is caught in the panorama of illusion and change. Therefore, he concluded, we must cease to desire any individual existence.

Such a view is clearly reflected in the sayings of Mao Tse-tung (21). We are told that 'masses are the real heroes', that they alone 'have boundless energy', man must 'act in accordance with the needs and wishes of the masses', true leadership must 'Take the ideas of the masses and concentrate them, then go to the masses'. Thus to live the good life one must be totally absorbed in society and have no personality, will, ideas or motivation of one's own.

This philosophy naturally commends itself to the underfed, underprivileged, politically and economically impotent individuals who make up the masses of Asia, for they can find both political and economic solvents in its teaching, even though they abdicate their status as individuals, when they subscribe to it; but this is no worse than the immorality of western egotism and individualism.

Both trends are aberrant extremes. Man as an individual must not seek to establish his uniqueness either by eulogizing or by denigrating society. In the former he would experience what Whyte calls 'the imprisonment or brotherhood'. This is the essentially oriental ideal which appears to be taking root in the establishment of 'organization man' in the western world. In the former he would become either a maverick, and so deplete the herd; or a cancer which would ultimately destroy the parent body. Just as the mass organization mentality has invaded the western world in every facet of its life, so also this occidental individualism has become a feature of the eastern world. Kruschev derisively referred to this as the 'cult of personality'. This discussion, however, only highlights the problem of personal autonomy. We must learn to be autonomous without being egotistic, we must remain as social creatures without at the same time losing our identity. In a sentence, we must establish personalism as a quality of life while avoiding these two aberrant extremes into which it could lead us.

The Problem of Autonomy

It must be said immediately, that Rousseau faced this problem squarely when he said, 'The problem is to find a form of association in which each, while uniting himself with all, will remain free as before, and obey only himself' (22). This threat to autonomy must be recognized, for as an essential element of mature morality, autonomy must be assured. It would be useless to eliminate personal alienation as the enemy of morality only to destroy with it that autonomy which is its most powerful ally.

Many writers have pointed to this danger. Both Whyte and Kornhauser have done so by arguing that many modern organizations erode individual autonomy by demanding total allegiance to the organization. Riesman has rubbed salt into this sore by implying that associations which seize man's autonomy may give him nothing in its place. We can, he argues, be more lonely amongst other people than anywhere else, and to imagine that we can end our loneliness amongst an association of our peers, is like attempting to quench our thirst by drinking from the sea. It exacerbates rather than alleviates the condition. For it is a simple fact that mere belonging is not enough. We must be organically united with our fellows. So paradoxically it is only when we seek to lose our lives in community that we find them, as individuals.

Teilhard de Chardin comes to the rescue here with two words: '*Union differentiates*'. Standing alone they mean little. Italicized, as they are in the argument of his book, they shine like a beacon to men in danger of shipwreck.

It is only in union with our fellows that we attain a differentiated personality.

MORALITY REQUIRES RELATIONSHIPS

The implications of this are enormous. It suggests that the primary moral reality is a relationship and affirms that Martin Buber's use of the term 'I–thou' is indeed the 'primary word' he deemed it to be. Thus when John MacMurray spoke of the form of the personal he had to speak of *persons in relation*. Indeed the essence of personalism, and hence of morality, may be a primary relationship of this kind.

This need not be too outrageous an idea. There is a paradigm existing already in the theology of Christian marriage, when it is affirmed that two individuals become one person and live a richer, fuller life as a consequence of this. It is, after all, only a natural development of the Confucian view that 'There was no man until there were two men'; and of the Hebrew view that a man is not a person in isolation from society (23). But all of this distils down to a simple proposition. Morality can only exist between persons in relationships. Unless this level of personalism is established, moral maturity is an unattainable ideal. There are, of course, two trends which militate against this, both are aberrant, and are the converse and obverse sides of the same coin. When people are treated as things there can be no morality. Equally, when things are treated as people, morality becomes impossible.

If one demeans a fellow human being and uses him as a tool for gratification or self-advancement there is no relationship and therefore no morality. The moral point being made here probes deeper still. It *depersonalizes* and *degrades* both at the social and cosmic level. Mounier argued that when we treat people as objects we despair of them, and when we despair of them we evacuate their lives of meaning, purpose, hope and potential. 'To despair of anyone is to make him desperate' (24). Maslow found that the mature 'self-actualizing' person always acknowledged the worth of others by according them the personalist respect they deserved, for this, he found, 'acknowledges another person as an independent entity and as a separate and autonomous individual' (25). With his cosmic perspective Teilhard makes the same point by arguing that when people abuse human relationships 'they fritter away, by neglect or lust, the universe's reserves of personalization' (26).

The implications of this insight obviously range from the simple prostitution of an individual to the industrialization of a whole society, and it needs little acquaintance with the concept of alienation to make one realize that this is the moral malady of our age. Alienated man is depersonalized man, and this diminution of personalism constitutes the essence of this ethical erosion. Perhaps it is our familiarity with the experience which makes us unaware of its corrosive influence. Hence it takes a novelist with William Golding's imagination and deft literary touch, to bring this home to us with the full impact of a revelation.

In his novel, dealing with the emergence of the true hominoids from the complex of Neanderthals, he examines this theme and reminds us how fortunate we are to be *The Inheritors*. For most of the story we follow the fortunes of a neanderthal family group. We come to know them by name; we learn of their relationships and mode of life. They are referred to as Lok, Fa, Oa, Mal, and Liku. Then the dominant hominoids arrive and in the closing pages of the novel William Golding drops his psychological bombshell.

These members of the familial neanderthal group suddenly cease to be people and become *things*. Thus in the closing pages the sole survivor is referred to as *it:* '*It* moved faster, broke into a queer loping run. *It* stopped at the end of the path. *It* put up a hand and scratched under *its* chinless mouth' (27). One would have difficulty in finding a more appropriate and vivid allegory of modern man's depersonalized condition, or a more emphatic affirmation of Kant's dictum that we should all treat each other as ends, rather than as means to an end (28).

Relationships are not necessarily Moral

It is equally true that if we personalize impersonal objects we still do not achieve a relationship, and thus cannot attain morality, but here a caveat must be added. Buber has been accused of personalizing nature, for he says that the I–thou relationships can exist between man and natural objects. 'Thou', he writes, 'can be an animal, a plant, a stone' (29), but the point he is making is that the immanental reality G.O.D. is met when our understanding of the natural world is heightened by a sensitive awareness that life for man must include in it a 'dialogue' with nature.

Such an argument would naturally commend itself to those who spend excessive amounts of money on pet-food and fertilizer, while one third of mankind starves. They would not understand a word of Buber's mystical notions, but they could take comfort in thus justifying a basic human desire to nurture plants and animals. Hence one must ask why it is that we appear to have this innate tendency; and why it is that primitives assume that all existence is personal.

Young and Monod have recently provided an interesting and

plausible explanation of this. Young concludes that all human language, and therefore the conceptual structures which determine the nature of thought expressed by it, emerge in children at a stage when the most important elements in their lives are people. Hence our primary mode of human expression is that form of language which is permeated with our experience of people. Consequently, he argues, all our language is 'people language'. Whatever we think or say is irradiated by the sense of a personal essence.

To a child a table can be naughty, when he bumps against it: a rose can be angry, when its thorns prick.

Monod also believes that men tend to personify everything, but primarily because they want to find a comprehensive explanation to cover all events in the phenomenal world. Monod's work is important if only because controversy is currently raging around the book in which he expressed this idea. It claims that recent discoveries concerning organic matter demonstrate that all forms of life are the product of pure chance, and therefore exclude the possibility of assuming that life does or should follow a master plan. He argues that primitive animism, infantile anthropomorphism, pathological fetishism and the proposition that the universe is under the beneficent control of a personal God, are all manifestations of this one innate desire for a comprehensive, personal explanation of the phenomenal world (30).

Personalism and Morality

It can thus be seen that personalism is crucial to morality. It is correlated with both cultural and sub-cultural factors, and is of such central importance that academic schools of thought have been erected around its basic premise. Its thesis is simply that people matter and that sound personal relationships are the *sine qua non* of any society! If any society is to develop aright, the line of its growth must be in the direction of establishing genuine relationships with individuals who are accepted as persons.

This is only the sociological facet of Mounier's philosophy; but it was this same view which was expressed by Bonhoeffer from the loneliness of his prison cell—'To feel that one counts for something with other people is one of the joys of life. What matters here is not how many friends we have, but how deeply we are attached to them. After all, personal relationships count for more than anything else' (31). The tragedy disclosed by our sub-cultural analysis of this primary moral quality is that it is only the higher-status sector of society which appears to produce children who possess it to a marked degree.

One final observation is relevant at this point. Many contemporary institutions are almost wholly instrumental in that the personal element is subordinated, by depersonalized administrators, to the impersonal requirements of impersonal systems. In the context of the above evidence and argument it is immediately apparent that such organizations are inimical to morality. We must therefore first ensure that schools are organizations or systems which place such an overwhelming emphasis on personal values, welfare and relationships, that moral personalism flourishes amongst the members.

If this limited objective can be achieved, through the medium of moral education, then it should follow that academic institutions at the tertiary level may also be characterized by a sincere concern for the individual members. Then, if this quality can become characteristic of all human organizations, even a technocratic culture may ultimately be composed of members who display this moral personalism to a marked degree.

Each member of such a society must also have a developed and secure sense of identity. The connection is clear. It is only when children have been treated as persons that such an identity is established, and it is only after being treated thus that they can treat others as persons in their own right. Therefore it follows that the more securely their personal identity is established, the more socially potent will be that moral personalism which can transform those arid, impersonal organizations which characterize modern society.

REFERENCES

1 This authoritarian/permissive dichotomy as a feature of non-democratic lower-status social structures is a recurring theme.
2 Jesus also found this, cf. 'The Sabbath was made for man and not man for the Sabbath', i.e. institutions should always be subservient to human need.
3 All the quotations are from the Newsom Report (1966), paras. 180–2.
4 Peck and Havighurst (1964), p. 111.
5 The difficulties of lower-status home life have already been outlined, e.g. Chapter 1.
6 Maslow (1970), p. 194.
7 Thoreau (1886), p. 6.
8 We can, I think, ignore the existential paradox, as exemplified in Morris and Sartre, that hell is found both in isolation and in other people.
9 Mournier (1952), p. 22.
10 *op. cit.*, p. 20.
11 Stafford-Clark (1972) recently described doctors now emerging from the Medical Schools as 'plumbers and technicians'. They lacked personalism because 'The students' first contact with people is a corpse in the dissecting room. They should deal right from the beginning with people who are alive', p. 680.
12 Teilhard (1960), p. 290.

13 Teilhard (1970), p. 175.
14 Lord Brain (1966), p. 11.
15 Kay and Mathison (1968), pp. 62 ff.
16 Skinner (1971), p. 164.
17 This theme is echoed in Cox's and Jeffreys' criticism of the work of the Farmington Trust Research Unit, Oxford.
18 Morris (1966). All the quotations come from pp. 148–52.
19 Laing (1960), p. 73.
20 This is the most rigorous criticism which can be levelled at contemporary sexual permissiveness. In essence this reduces both men and women to the level of sex objects. Hence the apparent stress on sexuality de-sexualizes our culture, for only *persons* can be sexual. The demeaning of 'people' to the level of objects, whereby sexual gratification may be achieved is the most potent and profound form of depersonalization.
21 Mao Tse-tung (1967), pp. 67 ff. This point is developed by Ballard (1972), pp. 324 ff.
22 See his *Social Contract and Discourses*, Book 1, Chapter 6.
23 This is the more accurate translation of 'It is not good for man to be alone'. See Genesis 2:18.
24 Mounier (1952), p. 23.
25 Maslow (1970), p. 196.
26 Teilhard (1969), p. 75.
27 Golding (1964), p. 241.
28 cf. Maslow (1970). 'Horney in a lecture has defined un-neurotic love in terms of regarding others as *per se*, as ends in themselves rather than as means to an end', p. 198.
29 Buber (1954), p. 10.
30 See Kay (1970), where it is argued that the 'personalistic' view of all phenomena is integral to our understanding of human personality.
31 Bonhoeffer (1960), pp. 128–9.

Bibliography
ADORNO, T. W., *et al.*, *The Authoritarian Personality* (Harper & Row, 1950).
ANGYAL, A., *Neurosis and Treatment: a Holistic Theory* (John Wiley, 1965).
ARDREY, ROBERT, *The Territorial Imperative* (Collins, 1967).
ARDREY, ROBERT, *The Social Contract* (Collins, 1970).
BALLARD, ROGER, 'Hierarchy', in *New Society*, 9 November, 1972.
BONHOEFFER, D., *Letters and Papers from Prison* (Fontana, 1960).
BOWLBY, JOHN, *Child Care and the Growth of Love* (Penguin, 1965).
BRAIN, LORD, *Science and Man* (Faber, 1966).
BUBER, MARTIN, *I and Thou* (Clark, Edinburgh, 1937).
BUBER, MARTIN, *Between Man and Man* (Routledge & Kegan Paul, 1954).
DUVALL, E. M., 'Conceptions of Parenthood', in *American Journal of Sociology* Vol. LII, 1971.
ELDER, G. H., 'Parental Power Legitimization and its Effect on the Adolescent', in *Sociometry*, No. 26, 1963.
FRANKENBURG, C. V., *I'm All Right* (Macmillan, 1961).
GOLDING, WILLIAM, *The Inheritors* (Faber, 1964).
GOODALL, JANE, *In the Shadow of Man* (Collins, 1971).
JEFFREYS, M. V. C., *Personal Values in the Modern World* (Pelican, 1963).
JOURARD, S. M., *The Transparent Self* (Van Nostrand, 1971).
KAY, WILLIAM, 'A Teilhardian Resolution of the Naturalistic Fallacy', in *Teilhard Review*, Vol. 5, No. 1, 1970.

KOESTLER, ARTHUR and SMYTHIES, J. R., *Beyond Reductionism* (Hutchinson, 1969).

KOHN, M. L., 'Social Class and Parental Values', in *American Journal of Sociology*, Vol. LXIV, 1958.

KORNHAUSER, WILLIAM, *The Politics of Mass Society* (Routledge & Kegan Paul, 1960).

LAING, R. D., *The Divided Self* (Tavistock, 1960).

LESHAN, L. L., 'Time Orientation and Social Class', in *Journal of Abnormal and Social Psychology*, No. 56, 1958.

LEWIS, J. and TOWERS, B., *Naked Ape or Homo Sapiens* (Garnstone Press, 1969).

LORENZ, KONRAD, *Studies in Animal and Human Behaviour* (Methuen, 1970).

MACCOBY, E. E., *et al.*, 'Methods of Child Rearing in Two Social Classes', in W. E. Martin and C. B. Stendler (Eds), *Reading in Child Development* (Harcourt, Brace & World, 1954).

MACMURRAY, JOHN, *Persons in Relation* (Faber, 1957).

MAO TSE-TUNG, *Quotations from Chairman Mao Tse-tung* (Bantam, 1967).

MASLOW, A. H., *Motivation and Personality* (Harper & Row, 1970).

MATHISON, JANE and KAY, WILLIAM, 'The Evolution of Consciousness', in *Teilhard Review*, Vol. 3, No. 2, 1968.

MEDAWAR, PETER B., *The Art of the Soluble* (Methuen, 1967).

MILLS, C. WRIGHT, *The Power Elite* (Oxford Univ. Press, New York, 1959).

MILLS, C. WRIGHT, *White Collar: The American Middle Class* (Oxford Univ. Press, New York, 1964).

MONOD, JACQUES, *Chance and Necessity* (Alfred Knopf, New York, 1971).

MORRIS, B., 'The Contribution of Psychology to The Study of Education', in J. W. Tibble (Ed.), *The Study of Education* (Routledge & Kegan Paul, 1966).

MORRIS, DESMOND, *The Naked Ape* (Corgi, 1969).

MORRIS, DESMOND, *The Human Zoo* (Corgi, 1971).

MORRIS, DESMOND, *Intimate Behaviour* (Cape, 1971).

MOUNIER, EMMANUEL, *Personalism* (Routledge & Kegan Paul, 1952).

MOUNIER, EMMANUEL, *Malraux, Camus, Sartre, Bernanos: L'espoir des Désespérés* (Seuil, 1953).

NEWSOM REPORT, *Half Our Future* (HMSO, 1963).

NEWSON, J. and NEWSON, E., *Four Years Old in an Urban Community* (Allen & Unwin, 1968).

NIETZSCHE, F. W., *Thus Spake Zarathustra* (Penguin, 1961).

PATERSON, R. W. K., *The Nihilistic Egoist: Max Stirner* (Oxford Univ. Press, 1971).

PECK, R. F. and HAVIGHURST, R. J., *The Psychology of Character Development* (John Wiley, 1964).

PHILLIPS, ROBERT E., 'Comparison of Direct and Vicarious Reinforcement and an Investigation of Methodological Variables', in *Journal of Experimental Psychology*, Vol. 78, No. 4, Part I, 1968.

RIESMAN, DAVID, *et al.*, *The Lonely Crowd* (Univ. Press, New Haven, 1964).

ROUSSEAU, J. J., *The Social Contract and Discourses* (Dent, 1935).

RUSSELL, C. and RUSSELL, W., *Violence, Monkey and Man* (Macmillan, 1968).

SCHOPENHAUER, A., *The World as Will and Idea*, 3 Vols. (Humanities Press, New York, 1968).

SINNOTT, E. W., *Cell and Psyche: The Biology of Purpose* (Harper & Brothers, 1961).

SKINNER, B. F., *Science and Human Behaviour* (Free Press, 1953).

SKINNER, B. F. and HOLLAND, J. G., *The Analysis of Behaviour* (McGraw-Hill, 1961).

SKINNER, B. F., *Beyond Freedom and Dignity* (Alfred Knopf, 1971).

STAFFORD-CLARK, J., *What Freud Really Said* (Schocken, New York, 1966).

STIRNER, MAX, *The Ego and His Own* (Jonathan Cape, 1971).

TEILHARD, PIERRE DE CHARDIN, *The Phenomenon of Man* (Collins, 1960).

TEILHARD, PIERRE DE CHARDIN, *Human Energy* (Collins, 1969).

TEILHARD, PIERRE DE CHARDIN, *Activation of Energy* (Collins, 1970).

THOREAU, HENRY D., *Walden* (Walker Scott, London, 1886).

TIGER, LIONEL, *Men in Groups* (Nelson, 1969).

TOYNBEE, ARNOLD J., *A Study of History* (Oxford Univ. Press, 1954).

TOYNBEE, ARNOLD J., *Civilization on Trial* (Oxford Univ. Press, 1957).

WHYTE, WILLIAM H., *The Organization Man* (Jonathan Cape, 1957).

WILLIAMS, L., *Man and Monkey* (Panther Science, 1969).

WINTERBOTTOM, M., 'The Relation of Need Achievement to Learning Experience in Independence and Mastery', in J. W. Atkinson (Ed.), *Motives in Fantasy Action and Society* (Princeton: Van Nostrand, 1959).

YOUNG, J. Z., *An Introduction to the Study of Man* (Clarendon Press, 1971).

Chapter 8

Moral Flexibility

RIGIDITY AND FLEXIBILITY

The term 'flexibility' is used here primarily as an index of the competence children display in abstracting moral principles from specific regulations. Since its use is also intended to distinguish between flexible and authoritarian children, a word of explanation must be added.

After reading Penelope Leach's definitive survey of the complex, concept *rigidity*, one is left with a number of clear impressions. For our purposes, the most valuable of these is her conclusion that rigidity must be understood in a moral, as well as a socio-psychological sense. Children with a high degree of rigidity in their personality are basically authoritarian. They are happiest when it is possible for them to continue with a familiar mode of conduct or behaviour, and they feel most secure when this is clearly described and stipulated. Hence they are conformists, who wish to remain subscribing to a specific authority.

Outside this uniform framework they feel insecure. They cannot tolerate the ambivalence which the introduction of a new idea brings and readily revert to traditional modes of behaviour in order to escape from a situation which they find extremely unpleasant. In Penelope Leach's own words, they see 'black and white as recognizable and manageable, and grey the colour of threat' (1). That such people can accommodate themselves to the conditions of modern industry is clearly apparent, and many of its tediously monotonous but essential tasks are performed by them. But rigidity is inimical to morality for it prevents children from abstracting moral principles from concrete regulations.

This second attribute of rigidity builds upon the first. Not only are such children authority orientated, but they wish to remain that way, and so resist the introduction of any dissonance (2) which a consideration of moral principles would bring. This is because such principles are intangible and indecisive, and have to be applied by individuals in a new way to changing circumstances. It is this which a 'rigid' child cannot accept. He prefers to keep to the safety of accepted stereotypes and social norms, and does not want to be involved in new situations demanding novel modes of conduct. Thus he dislikes change, is intolerant of innovation, and prefers authority to autonomy. Rigidity is common today in multi-racial communities where intolerance or prejudice are common. Rigid children are intolerant of change in any form.

When these attributes are combined a clear picture emerges. A rigid child is intolerant of any change in his social environment, and this leads him to subscribe to authoritarian regulations. Yet moral maturity implies that intolerance must be eliminated and moral problems solved by recourse to principles rather than formal, legal prescriptions. Hence Leach concludes 'In the field of social rigidity, most work is concerned with combating ethnic prejudice and teaching people to consider social issues in themselves rather than accepting current stereotypes' (3).

Thus the term 'rigidity' indicates both a tendency to subscribe uncritically to an authoritatively imposed codified directive, and also a reluctance to press beyond it to discover the moral principle upon which it is based. Clearly, as we have said, this is not only inimical to morality, but it is diametrically opposed to it. For this reason the term *flexibility* has been used here.

A flexible child, unlike a rigid one, will look for the principle behind the regulation. In this process he will feel neither inadequate nor insecure, even though this experience provides him with no clear guidance. On the contrary, he will be willing to abandon the security of an authoritarian structure, if the application of a moral principle requires him to do so.

Working-class Authoritarianism

Leaving aside the fact that rigidity, in its technical sense, is a variable which must be considered in any evaluation of a child's morality, we may now note a clear pattern of social-class differences here. In the terminology outlined above, higher-status parents tend to be *flexible*, while lower-status parents display a high degree of *rigidity*. Consequently these attributes emerge in their children.

An examination of the available research reports makes it clear that lower-status parents tend to be authoritarian, rigid and inflexible in their demands, and enforce obedience with techniques which prevent a child from discerning the moral principles upon which such fiats are based. Kent and Davis found this present to a marked degree. They present children with rigid regulations and are intolerant of any departure from them. Kohn described the lower-status homes as being characterized by specific regulations. In them children were made acutely conscious of the fact that only specific types of conduct were permissible.

This feature of moral specificity will be discussed below. For the moment one only needs to add that such children will accept, for example, that ink must not be flicked on the kitchen floor, but will need a further specific instruction to dissuade them from inking the bedroom floor! Consequently they can only learn by rote, and, as Frenkil-Brunswik found, tend to retain parental favour and approval by a piecemeal learning of the specific forms of behaviour required.

This inflexible rigid form of control naturally produces the 'authoritarian personality' which Frenkil-Brunswik and her colleagues outlined in the book ascribed to Adorno. But it does more. It produces authority-orientated children. Almost a decade after this Rosenthal *et al.* concluded that the rigid and over-controlling techniques, typical of lower-status mothers, produced children who were submissive to authority, and thus extremely conventional in their conduct. Years before this, Lerner too had discovered that lower-status children were less sensitive to the circumstantial and motivational aspects of moral judgement, and one can see why this should be so. Specific commands produce a specificity-orientated form of conduct, wherein each individual act is seen in isolation from the rest.

Such child-rearing and socializing techniques have a further deficiency. The inflexible and specific commands of the lower-status parent are not always intelligible or attainable. It has already been noted that Winterbottom found lower-status parental demands less realistic than those of higher-status parents. Frenkil-Brunswik now adds her evidence at this point. She found that the authority-orientated family was characterized by parental demands which, being neither easy to understand, nor easy to obey, only confused children. If then a lower-status child asked for further elucidation he would be met by a reply couched in the 'restricted code' wherein, as Bernstein showed, both explanation and conclusion cohere into a specific categoric statement.

Questioned in this way a parent would reply, 'Because I say so', or 'Do as I tell you'. Thus confronted by a further display of authority, which only endorsed the specificity of his moral orientation, the perplexed child became a certain candidate for parental punishment. This is made worse by the fact which Josephine Klein observed, 'The child's request for explanation may be treated as insolent, disobedient or otherwise challenging the parent's authority' (4). Hence, as we have repeatedly observed, the social classes are divided. The middle class, democratic, basically non-authoritative ethos welcomes such questions. The working class, fundamentally non-democratic, authoritarian milieu does not.

Leaving aside the paradox that such a lower-status non-democratic environment also produces the *laissez-faire* environment, in which permissiveness follows such an 'anything for a quiet life' attitude, we must note a further point. Those who eulogize middle-class parental recourse to smooth reason forget that this is as powerful and often unfair a control as violence. In the one superior intellect is employed; in the other greater physical strength is used.

Obviously where authoritarian parents resent any questioning of their commands, the elucidation of moral principles becomes a more remote possibility, but when punishment is introduced it does even more. It actually dissuades the child from attempting to find any explanation for the regulation.

We have already looked at the different techniques of punishment, as practised by higher- and lower-status parents. It only needs to be added here that the threatening or retributive punishment, character-istic of the lower-status parent, is not only usually attached to incomprehensible or unattainable demands, but is also unpredictable or illogical, as shown by LeShan.

Clearly, children in such a predicament, no matter how intelligent they may be, would soon despair of trying to make sense of the situation. Being unable to predict either parental requests or reactions, they would inevitably become disinclined to find any rationale in the system. Since lower-status children are already averse to using their reasoning powers, such inconsistent punishment would endorse this rejection of reason and make the elucidation of moral principles an even more unlikely practice.

Lerner also underlined this fact and argued that such lower-status parental demands, supported by inconsistent, retributive or threaten-ing punishment, led to *moral specificity*. As a result of such experi-ences it is inevitable that lower-status children would behave as they do, almost entirely in order to avoid angering a parent; or even simply to appease one who was already irate. There would conse-quently be little opportunity for them to discern that behaviour in the home should be directed by a principle of familial concern. Therefore, they would also be blinded to the fact that principles can be abstracted from the welter of authoritarian dicta which assailed them while at home.

Moral specificity, in working-class homes

At this point the question of *moral specificity* must be faced. I have elsewhere described this feature of morality (5) and shown that almost all the research into child morality has concluded that at some stage child conduct is specific to the situation in which it occurs. That is, conduct is determined by the circumstances in which it takes place, rather than by the application of any moral principles. There are two elements which have to be disentangled here: the first is developmental; the second is sociological.

It is now known that although all morality is tinctured by this specificity, it becomes less evident as children grow. Norman and Sheila Williams call this a 'generalization effect' (6). The most primitive, inchoate form of morality is essentially specific, and in a more developed form it can be seen that behavioural responses become attached to more general concrete circumstances than those in which they were first formed. In its most fully developed form there is an abstract generalization in which principles are formulated. Such a view clearly follows the familiar pattern of growth through pre-operational, concrete operational and formal operational thought, which has been made familiar through the work of Piaget.

It is the second element which is of importance here. Sociological investigations have suggested that not only is moral specificity a characteristic of infant morality, it is also the most dominant feature of lower-status conduct. As one behavioural corollary of specific, authoritarian parental demands, this is to be expected.

The evidence for this is so voluminous that its abundance is more of an embarrassment than a help. However, one illustration comes readily to mind. Madeline Kerr describes in great detail how her slum dwellers were meticulously honest amongst themselves, but accepted unequivocally the fact that stealing from their place of work was legitimate (7).

Bronfenbrenner concluded that Piaget's two-stage morality, of restraint and co-operation, reflected the fact that dominant authoritarian parents led children to adopt a morality of adult restraint in infancy. In lower-status homes this was perpetuated into adulthood; but in higher-status homes the rational, egalitarian treatment offered to older children finally displaced it.

Clearly under lower-status circumstances of this kind moral beliefs are formulated from concrete reactions to specific situations, and this necessarily prevents children from consciously formulating a generalized code of conduct based on moral principles. Thus moral learning takes place with reference to isolated, concrete acts. No effort is made to help children to generalize from these situations and so develop a coherent philosophy of life.

Such experiences, however, are not limited to lower-status homes. They can exist elsewhere, in schools, for example, with a 'lower-status' ethos. This is the conclusion that Havighurst and Taba reached concerning the children they studied in their folk society. They realized that 'The development of a personal and rational code, when it does take place, grows out of the accidents of personal make-up and patterns of adjustment' (8).

Higher-status Experience

With middle-class children one finds the conditions almost entirely reversed. Here, instead of perpetuating authoritarian, specific modes of moral conduct and thought, parents seem unwittingly to encourage their children to elicit the moral principles which underlie human conduct. One can see the structured reason for this quite clearly. The higher level of intelligence, articulacy and toleration naturally produces an environment in which inquiring minds converse with each other. When to these qualities one adds the fact that higher-status parents are usually less authoritarian, one has a situation in which as Sugarman says, 'parents permit their children more say in decision making' (9).

The introduction of reasoned discussion also leads inevitably to a consideration of motives. Thus whereas Kohn found that working-class parents stressed the importance of behavioural factors (presumably to ensure the social respectability of their children), Boehm found that middle-class parents and children disclosed more genuine concern for the motivational element in conduct. This is also evident in Catholic homes where, from the age of seven, children are treated as rational creatures and encouraged to evaluate a deed in terms of its motivation.

As a consequence parental commands and punishment facilitate this process. The dogmatic, reiterated demands of the lower-status parent ('Because I say so'), pass through an intermediate stage where emotional pressure is exerted ('Because I've got a headache darling') until they emerge as reasoned explanations for requesting a particular form of conduct. This, at least, is what Henderson and Bernstein found.

Beginning with Bernstein's thesis that linguistic usage is a relevant determinant of social conduct, they showed that the social classes employ language, as a means of socialization, in quite distinct ways. The traditional middle-class stress on autonomy and the application of moral principles is, it seems, a direct corollary of this. Higher-status mothers were found to welcome verbal interaction with their children and were also more willing (and able) to explain why particular forms of behaviour were required.

This is equally true even when punishment is administered. Higher-status parents tend to explain why it is given. It could be equally true, of course, that intelligent, articulate, confident middle-class children naturally insist on an explanation to account for the indignity of being thus punished. However, one may conflate both points and argue that parent and child probably both endorse this same attitude in each other. Whatever the cause, the line of research from Lerner to Sugarman makes this point clear. In contrast to the vagaries of punitive punishment in a working-class home, middle-class children experience consistent, explicable forms of punishment with accompanying explanations, and therefore grow up with a much more flexible view of moral sanctions. Thus they are led inexorably to the point where they can discern the fact that moral regulations are expressions of moral principles and that these are applicable beyond the immediate situation.

One final research project can add to the sum of evidence here. It is extremely valuable since its findings virtually sum up the argument which has been presented thus far. Kohn and Schooler decided to extend the research which had confirmed that while working-class parents tend to emphasize submission to authority, middle-class parents stress the autonomous elucidation of moral principles. Out of this ambitious and complex research project a number of findings emerged, all of which are relevant to the thesis of this chapter.

It was found that the higher a man's social class, the more likely would he be to stress self-direction, and the less he would accept subscription or conformity to authority as a moral norm. As a natural corollary to this such high-status parents valued a sustained interest in the reasons which lay behind events. Thus they stressed intellectual curiosity, moral responsibility and self-reliance, and made it quite clear that they wanted their children to display these same qualities. For them the ideal child was one who showed personal consideration; was interested in the principles which lay behind all events (whether they were physical or moral); consistently displayed a high degree of self-control; and behaved responsibly to his fellows.

It needs little imagination to set such a child in his home environment and contrast a day in his life with that of a lower-status child. The latter would have been assailed by a stream of dogmatic, inflexible, authoritarian demands, which were only repeated with stereotyped emotive force, if explanations were asked for. Thus his day would be punctuated with specific, unqualified requests. 'Don't play with your ball.' 'Come inside.' 'Go to bed.' 'Shut up.' These and many similar fiats would be issued by parents to assail the working-class child.

In contrast, one can imagine a middle-class child going through similar situations on the same day, but instead of reiterated directives, explanations would accompany parental requests. 'I'd prefer you not to play with your ball darling. You might damage daddy's flowers.' 'I think you ought to come in sweetie. It's getting damp and cold, and you might catch a chill.' 'We think you ought to go to bed now. You were tired this morning.' 'Please don't interrupt us, when we're talking. We try not to interrupt you.' These and similar, well-modulated, reasonable requests, with an accompanying explanation, replace the barrage of orders.

Of course, as we have already noted, it could be objected that whereas lower-status parents resort to authority to ensure obedience, those of the middle class do the same but simply use a different weapon. For them it is the force of reason, and since they are invariably more intellectually mature than their offspring, they usually get their way. This may even be true in those cases where the explanation is little more than emotional blackmail, e.g. 'Do be quiet dear, I've got a headache'. But it is difficult not to see the sharp contrast between these two stereotyped situations. However, as we noted above, the important thing is this. At the end of the day the lower-status child would conclude that all that mattered was subscription to authority, but the higher-status child would conclude that people and their welfare were of pre-eminent importance—and thus morality would be born and nurtured.

This is the consensus of opinion amongst all who have worked in this field. Frenkel-Brunswik expressed the plight of the former child in one vivid sentence. Long before she started her work with Adorno on authoritarianism, she said 'The requested submission and obedience to parental authority is only one of the many external, rigid and superficial rules which such a child learns' (10). At the other extreme one finds experiences which are diametrically opposed to this. 'The middle-class mothers', say Henderson and Bernstein, 'are more likely to explain to the child why they want a change in his behaviour' (11). Such a child ends the day less authority orientated, and more autonomy orientated, than his less fortunate peers. Consequently, the level of his moral flexibility is considerably higher.

An Inner Control
This leads naturally to a consideration of the inner control, which such potentially autonomous children must have. This is a tricky concept for whereas a psychologist could immediately shuffle through his voluminous notes on 'conscience' (12) the sociologist has to shrug his shoulders and beg to be excused such an exercise, for 'conscience' is a concept which has little validity for him (*see* Chapter 3).

Obviously there must be a non-cognitive element in a child's personality, which leads him to reach intuitive conclusions concerning the rightness or wrongness of an action. Here, we must limit the discussion to considering the fact that if a child is freed from the tyranny of legalism and no longer amenable to the compulsion of external authoritative commands, he must have some internalized component which corresponds to this. Penelope Leach contrasts these in a vivid way. She speaks of 'obedience to external demands rather than to internalized standards' (13), as typical of the lower-status child's conduct.

This too, was the conclusion which Kohn and Schooler reached. They found that the higher-status family lived in a milieu wherein self-direction rather than blind subscription to authority, characterized behaviour. They further developed this theme and argued that the occupational conditions and circumstances of the higher-status, autonomous, professional man reinforced this attitude. Conversely, the employment of lower-status men, who were being perpetually told what to do, tended to promote an increase in their evaluation of conformity to authority. Consequently, the inner control of middle-class men and women became an established feature of their home lives.

Kohn had already confirmed this fact and concluded that working-class parents trained their children so that they would fear to violate the prescribed norms of family life. On the other hand middle-class parents emerged as being concerned to ensure that their children internalized the standards of behaviour, of which they approved. Consequently, Kohn continues, the lower-status child becomes obsessed with the immediate consequences of his action, while the higher-status child tends to review it in the light of motivational elements and factors: i.e. the former is present orientated; the latter is future orientated.

This distinction ran even deeper, Kohn found that the higher the mother's status, the more probable it was that she would emphasize the moral virtues of curiosity, self-control and consideration for others; while the lower-status mother would stress cleanliness, neatness, and obedience. The former would be concerned with subjective qualities; the latter with objective, tangible factors. These features fit snugly into the pattern wherein middle-class children stressed intent, and working-class children emphasized physical consequences. Consequently, we find again that middle-class children not only discern the principles which undergird moral requirements, but also possess the inner resources to implement the imperative which such principles place upon them.

At this point a most pertinent research conclusion emerges. Higher-status children, as we have seen, possess an autonomous regard for moral principles, and so need an inner control to take the place of prudent subscription to, or evasion of, authority, but these two facts are positively correlated. The same child-rearing practices which produce the one, also induce the other. Sears *et al.* found that the experiences most likely to develop an internal control system in children, were those which we have already listed as most likely to develop moral flexibility in a child. They virtually summarize their monumental work in this final conclusion. Thus we may say that *such an internal control is created by the same conditions which make it necessary!* They found that there was a statistically significant correlation between a highly developed conscience and the child-rearing techniques which resorted to reasoned explanations and made little recourse to physical punishment.

In his work in the same area Kohlberg confirmed these findings. He preferred to say that the non-physical forms of control, employed by the middle classes, not only elicited sensitivity to moral principles, but also produced the powerful guilt control which compelled such children to subscribe to them. However, it comes to the same thing in the end. *The conditions which enhance moral flexibility in a child, also propel him towards that autonomy which it requires.*

In conclusion here, it only needs to be observed that both sub-cultural and cultural factors are operative. The negligent, indulgent practices of the lower-status families do not cultivate such an inner control in their offspring. Indeed, as Sprott observes, such practices are liable to induce their children 'to associate wrongdoing with an exciting atmosphere of risk, rather than with a sense of sin' (14).

On the other hand the loving, discipline of middle-class parents creates a powerful internal control. Over thirty years ago Bateson said simply, that the 'persistent inculcation of cultural norms, predominantly reinforced by punishments, inflicted by a limited number of adults who are also loved by the child' produced the west European puritan conscience. Of course this dichotomy between permissiveness and discipline does not exhaust the content of the complex spectrum of parental attitudes. Wall claims that the former abdication of parental obligations not only erodes the assurance that a framework of sensible rules would give, but also removes the structure within which a child can strengthen his character. Yet on the other hand such supervision must not be too strict otherwise children may interpret, as morally culpable, those actions which merely irritate adults, which, he claims, produces a most deleterious effect. Whereas the permissiveness of the lower-status child associates free expression with excitement, it is often associated in the higher-status child, with neurotic guilt and anxiety.

Hence one can feel the force of Riesman's remark that 'Parents who try, in inner-directed fashion, to compel the internalization of disciplined pursuit of clear goals, run the risk of having their children styled clean out of the personality market' (15). Inner direction of this neurotic kind can stultify the growth towards true autonomy. However, this must be read against the background of Riesman's general thesis that neither the inner nor the outer-directed man can be truly moral.

AUTHORITARIAN MORALITY

Clearly modern society must have some authoritative system for enforcing law and order, or it would not survive. This was brought home most forcibly on two of the occasions when the police went on strike. Reynolds and Judge have recently recorded what happened when the British Police struck years ago. In order to secure better pay, more welfare benefits and the recognition of their union the London police downed truncheons and went on strike in August 1918. Their own conduct was not entirely exemplary. In London they first went on strike and then used force and physical violence to compel reluctant strikers to stand firm. This was during the closing phases of the war, and Lloyd George promised to consider their grievances when it ended. However, when, ten weeks after the Armistice, nothing had yet been done for them, the police went on strike again.

The need for authority then became patently clear. In the previous year criminals had naturally taken advantage of the strike in London, but now the mobs did so. Whereas London had been quiet, Liverpool and Birkenhead became centres of indiscriminate mob violence, looting and arson. Lest we should dismiss this as natural in a society which had hardly emerged from the nineteenth century and was still seething with the brutalizing influence of a world war, we need to be reminded that this can still happen.

Only a few years ago the police went on strike in Canada. Reports reaching England told exactly the same story. An otherwise law-abiding community suddenly became involved in widespread arson, looting, violence and murder. The grievance was all too familiar. The Montreal police wanted to receive the same rate of pay as the Toronto police, so they went on strike in support of this claim. The morning contingent failed to arrive and left the city without police protection. It was the first emergency of this kind for almost half a century so nobody really took the move seriously. It is true that armed bandits held up some banks, but that was normal. The city traffic was in chaos, with an exceptionally high number of accidents, but that too was not entirely unique.

Then the sinister tones were heard. World news agencies reported that Montreal was 'dazed by what happened last night'. Without police protection it lay virtually defenceless in the face of an upsurge of public disorder and anarchy. The sporadic law-breaking became a wave of violence, looting, arson, murder, rape, riots, destruction of property and senseless mob hysteria. The situation became so serious that the premier of Quebec, Mr Bertrand, had to intervene by threatening to call in troops to maintain public order. An emergency cabinet meeting deemed this to be the only expedient possible, but fortunately the law could be invoked and the police were ordered back on duty. (The guardians of the law were clearly amenable to its sanctions.) No mention was made of their wage claim yet the point had been made. The police, it seems, are an essential restraint preventing the simmering pot of society from boiling over (16).

Although expediency makes such authoritarianism essential, one must not be blind to its disadvantages. The restrictions and limitations of a legal code are clearly apparent in the life of any society; and we all try to evade its stifling demands. The first-century Jews disclosed this clearly. Since the law forbade them to carry any burdens on the Sabbath, devout Jewesses sewed their brooches on. This expedient then made these brooches part of the garment and thus technically not a burden (17).

Gentiles are also culpable. The recent legislation concerning the breathalyser test made it clear that authoritarian dictates can be thus evaded. Within a year of its promulgation the 'breath-test' law became a tattered legal shred as motorists found more and more ways of evading its requirements. Hence it had to go back to the House of Lords to have the bigger loop-holes closed (18). The most popular was the 'hip-flask' device. A motorist, stopped by police, would hand them his ignition key, step out of the car, which he claimed he was pushing, and then drink some alcohol from a container in his pocket. Of this device Mr Justice Bridge blandly observed 'The action of a motorist in drinking whisky with the object of frustrating the carrying out of the provision of the Road Safety Act is clearly a wilful obstruction of the police in the execution of their duty' (19). By this means the original breathalyser test was invalidated. One cannot avoid thinking of the executioner who complained that his victim kept moving his head. Man's sense of self-preservation has sustained him for 500,000 years, and it is therefore difficult to discard it lightly.

Even when genuine moral principles are enshrined in a legal code, the code can distort them, as Tawney showed in his survey of our acquisitive society. He pointed out that the law relating to private property was originally intended to ensure that a man could serve his community. In a peasant society, the craftsman needed to own the tools of his trade otherwise they would never be available when his services were needed. Now, observes Tawney, the application of this law in a technological society reverses its original intention.

The law, which was intended to enable men to serve society now enables them to exploit it. This results simply from the fact which Cooley noted, that laws cannot be taken from one culture to another without being distorted. Only principles can operate in such a situational manner. The Mosaic law forbidding us to covet our neighbour's ass, means little to contemporary man, living in his semi-detached house with a second-hand car parked outside, but it is still true that the principle of non-covetousness should guide our conduct. Thus whereas there are many occasions when an authoritarian fiat is appropriate, since one cannot always stop and explain (20), it is invariably dangerous.

Zaehner sums up the position neatly. Although he is speaking specifically about religious authoritarianism, his words are still applicable. 'Dogmas', he writes, 'cannot be eternal but only the transitory, distorting, and distorted images of a truth that transcends not only them but all verbal definition' (21). Thus it is with secular authoritarian fiats; they only imperfectly and inadequately express the perpetually valid principles upon which our culture is based. The authoritarian child's frame of mind may make him amenable to discipline, but once matured, such a population would be ripe for the dictator. Passively subservient and subject to any authoritarian fiat it would fall into the hands of any demagogue who could support his demands with the necessary authority.

Here social-class distinction becomes acute again. The Newsons have shown that lower-status parents tend to employ threats of recourse to an authority figure, in order to obtain the obedience of their children, with the policeman being the most frequently mentioned, in this context. The authors then point out that this not only tends to perpetuate the 'us' and 'them' sub-cultural dichotomy of society, but also ensures that higher-status children tend to identify with authority, while lower-status children do not. Indeed for the latter, authority is invariably the dominant consideration even though it may be an enemy to outwit as well as a sanction to fear. Moral principles just do not merit any consideration.

The Anomaly of Freedom and Authority
From the above survey of research it seems clear that the degree of flexibility displayed by children is directly related to the quality of parental control and family life. At its highest this emerges in children who are able to discern that behind and beyond specific regulations lie the principles upon which they are based. At its lowest it is apparent in the authoritarian children who tend, as Adorno showed, to be conventional, uncritical of the accepted mores, willing to submit to authority, hasty in condemnation of those

who do not subscribe to their ethos, prone to think in clichés or stereotypes, and who are bigoted and prejudiced (22).

Before continuing, two points need to be added by way of clarification. First, Eysenck criticized Adorno's analysis on the ground that it confused psychological and sociological factors. Thus it must be reiterated that the psychological factor of *rigidity* must be inserted here as a relevant variable. This then modifies the effect of social class, family structures and parental attitudes on the development of flexibility.

Second, Lipset's confirmation of Adorno's views were rebuffed by Miller and Riesman on the grounds that Adorno's 'F' Scale (23) meant different things to different social classes. Hence they argued that authoritarian scales were invalid when applied to working-class respondents. However, Lipset later wrote a spirited and effective reply to his critics and reaffirmed the original view with which he had begun his chapter on working-class authoritarianism. There he had said that 'intolerant movements in modern society are more likely to be based on the lower classes' (24). However, this point will be considered again in the next chapter when we examine the nature of moral dynamism.

With this proviso the situation might appear to be clear. But this is not so. When one examines the available relevant research reports two anomalies emerge. First, Sugarman says that *middle-class* families enable children to develop the independence which will enable them to assert their individuality. Yet this is precisely the conclusion reached by Boehm when studying her *working-class* children. Second, the ideal family, says Sugarman, is one in which the parents share power between themselves and allow their children to participate in decision making. Such a structure, he argues, is essential for moral flexibility to develop. Yet Schuham has recently discovered that the egalitarian family is basically inimical to moral growth.

Now why should such anomalies emerge? If we can answer this it will enable us to understand a little more clearly how parental and familial factors effect the emergence of moral flexibility. Indeed, it is in the resolution of these paradoxes that the family structure, most conducive to this, can be discerned.

Let us first consider the lower-status situation. From what has already been suggested, it would be natural to conclude that working-class children would be authority orientated. Yet the work by Boehm, on the development of moral judgement, suggests that this is not so. She found that such children had a very sophisticated attitude to authority. This resulted, she explained, from the fact that such children were given more latitude than their middle-class contemporaries (25). There were few checks on their friends and activities, and home life was generally chaotic.

Hence these factors, with the inevitable growth in peer-dependence, made them *appear* to be more independent and mature, but this is a false impression. If we return to the work of the Newsons for a moment, and consider the working-class penchant for using authority figures as a disciplinary threat to their children, one can see how the impression is created for no matter how much his intervention may be threatened, *the policeman rarely actually appears*. Perhaps it is here that one should seek for the genesis of lower-status ambivalence towards authority in general. It is, as Duncan Dallas shows, both a sanction to be feared and an enemy to be outwitted. And even if it appears to be a rejection of authority this authority is still a dominant consideration (26).

Wann and his colleagues have also shown that this is so. They found that even young children are aware of the delicate balance of power within any social institution and will play parent against parent, or teacher against teacher with considerable expertise. Thus even their apparent freedom is authoritarian. It is *licence* to evade the law, rather than *liberty* to act independently, which characterizes their conduct. They are, therefore, fundamentally tied to the authoritarian mores of their sub-culture.

At other extremes one should find higher-status children becoming increasingly independent of their family. Indeed this is what Sugarman found. His research, amongst teenagers, suggests that higher- and lower-status children are distinguished in terms of individualism as opposed to dependence on parents or peers. The pathway leading to this is clearly marked. Pear found that middle-class parents were not so much the instruments of authority as the admired models on whom children moulded themselves. This may simply be because, as he discovered, parents and children in the middle-class home have a friendly relationship based on a mutual desire to please each other. Spinley developed this theme further. She found that the privileged middle-class child was less subject, than her deprived slum child, to experience spasmodic, parental authoritarianism. Indeed both writers found evidence of the fact that the higher-status parent tended to accept that children must be allowed to grow in independence, and then modified their conduct accordingly.

Leaving aside the developmental fact that younger children, as the Newsons found, are treated more indulgently, an important point emerges. The lower-status family is characterized by extremes of conduct. The father is as Kohn showed, both permissively absent and punitively present. He not only allows a *laissez-faire* situation to develop but when he enters as a social control it is as an authority figure who merely supports the mother (27). Indeed it is usual in these homes to find misdemeanours admonished with the threat, 'wait until your father gets home'.

On the other hand in the higher-status family the father complements the mother's role and together they establish the conditions in which their children can display genuine liberty and not merely the licence to flout authority. Clearly only in the former can moral flexibility develop, since the latter is still authority orientated, even when permissiveness prevails.

On this point of role-segregation, Elizabeth Bott is particularly informative. Her research consisted of asking husbands and wives to describe their roles. Despite the uncertainty of spouses living in a mobile society, with role definition in an imprecise, fluid state, like Kohn she found distinct and sharp class differences. The middle-class father saw his role as complementary to his wife, for both acted in harmony. The working-class husband, on the other hand was merely supportive and the filial roles of him and his spouse did not actually overlap. In sociological terms, they were merely *contiguous* and *contingent*.

On this same point it is interesting to note that Chapman found a clear correlation. As social status rose, so also did the likelihood that both husband and wife co-operated in the purchase of possessions for the home and the maintenance of its condition. Clearly these two models of complementarity and supportive marital relations would affect the processes of child rearing and the ethos of the home.

In turning to consider the anomaly of familial structures further, one finds a similar paradox. Sugarman developed his argument by adding that in addition to being less authoritarian, higher-status families 'permit their children more say in decision making. The father and the mother also share power between themselves, instead of there being one dominant partner, as is usual among the lower-status families' (28).

This view cites the support of Strodtbeck who discovered that families with authoritarian fathers produced children with a diminished sense of their personal potency and worth. (This point is taken up in the next chapter.) There the matter would appear to be concluded. *But this is not so.* Careful reading of Strodtbeck makes it clear that he found high personal aspirations in the children of families where the mother was dominant. Her authority and influence, it seems, provided not a brake but an incentive to achievement: and this despite the fact that Marsden has shown, that mothers had peculiar difficulty in adopting the dual role of supportive, succurant providers of affection, and also the sources of authority for their children. He was, of course, speaking of fatherless families, but the point is still relevant.

To this one can now add the finding of Schuham. He discovered that an egalitarian family structure was related to psychopathic behaviour in the children. One can see how this would result. A family of such a kind could not resolve its internal conflicts and the psychopathic child would inherit this absence of family guidance in the form of a deficient conscience. Here is the other side of the coin. Just as inadequate lower-status families produce children who appear to be independent but are in fact merely rebelling against authority; so the inadequate higher-status family can produce children who appear to be independent but are actually bereft of any genuine autonomy. In neither case can moral flexibility develop fully.

The only possible conclusion that one can draw here is that extremes of authoritarianism or permissiveness are both unable to produce children who will develop the facility to think for themselves and so adopt that morally mature stance which looks ultimately to principles, rather than laws, to guide their conduct.

Parental Control

This, in fact, is the implicit conclusion of Schuham's research. Beginning, as he did, with the research question 'How do the families of psychopathic offspring differ from those with normally adjusted children?' he found that the latter had a clear-cut power structure. There was first the father, then the mother and finally the children, all forming a stable hierarchy. Thus he supported the view that the normal family was 'mildly authoritarian'.

Therein lies the clue. It is *mildly* authoritarian, and allows democratic procedures, but only within the structure of a stable hierarchy of authority. Indeed this too is the conclusion of Josephine Klein, who concluded that 'Mothers who let their children run wild do not produce socially successful children; neither do indulgent overprotective mothers; neither do the restrictive and overconcerned' (29). Despite his arguments to the contrary even Barry Sugarman appears to support this view. In his sensitive and penetrating analysis of Daytop Village, a therapeutic community for drug addicts, he records the need for a familial authority structure: 'There must be some clear authority structure so that residents know whose orders they are required to follow' (30).

It seems clear then that it is the structured-democratic, rather than the crassly authoritarian or *laissez-faire* family which succeeds in this way, for it provides a firm and secure framework within which the children can exercise their emerging autonomy. Roy Farrant uses the analogy of a ship in the shipyard. Like any structure, it needs scaffolding while it is being built, but when the work is completed the scaffolding becomes redundant. Only then can it be removed to allow the ship to slide into the sea and begin its life. Removed before this, it would have hindered the building process. Had it remained in place, the ship would never have fulfilled its destiny (31). Thus, the semi-authoritarian structure of a family should also make itself redundant, and merely be used to prepare children for the day when they can be launched on life and be guided by their own inner-controls and make their own autonomous voyages of social discovery.

This too is the conclusion Erikson reached. Discussing the need for a child to exercise autonomy within a stable structure he concluded that if this autonomy is denied pathological forms of conduct occur. 'This is the infantile source of later attempts in adult life to govern by the letter, rather than by the spirit' (32).

To clinch this argument recourse can be made to one final research report. Williams *et al.* based their research on one assumption of the symbolic interaction theory which suggests that both high and low parental permissiveness is likely to lead to misconduct in children. This argues that in a restrictive situation a child would perpetually fail and so develop a faulty self-concept. In a permissive situation the child would have no guide-lines for conduct and would also assume either that parents had rejected him (as in high-status homes) or were indifferent to him (as in lower-status homes). Again, he would consequently form a faulty self-image. Both high and low levels of parental permissiveness resulted in a faulty self-concept which prohibited the growth of moral maturation, or, in the terms of this chapter, of moral flexibility.

Thus, leaving aside such variables as intelligence, it is clear that there is a correlation between the form of parental control and the degree of moral flexibility which children display. It appears to be a simple correlation, but the balance is a delicate one. Both an excess or a deficiency of either permissiveness or authoritarianism jeopardize the child's chance of moral maturation. It is neither the permissiveness which apparently leads to independence, nor the authoritarianism, which appears to facilitate autonomy, which is most effective.

The permissiveness must operate within a stable framework, or, put another way, the authoritarianism must take cognisance of a child's personal views and desires, if moral maturity is to be assured. Alone the former leads to negative assertiveness and the latter to passivism. Together and properly balanced they provide the environment in which moral flexibility may flourish. Clearly the family, like society, needs authority to provide a stable structure within which the individual can exercise his freedom. This stable structure provides the stability and security within which children can exercise their moral autonomy and so gradually learn to live by the application of moral principles rather than by subservience to rigid demands from authority. If there is a perpetual and rigid, authoritarian imposition of group norms upon them, then, as Klein has shown in her study of groups, the moral life of the community is jeopardized.

IMPLICATIONS OF MORAL FLEXIBILITY

The implications for morality are clear. The working-class tendency to punitive aggression, which is primarily an expression of adult, indiscriminate power, leads to specificity. Here the child only learns that a particular offence results in punishment and so, rather than comprehend the nature of moral prohibitions, merely seeks to evade punishment in the future. On the other hand, the typical middle-class parental use of reason, attempting simultaneously to inculcate some form of internal control, leads to that perception of moral principles upon which moral flexibility is founded.

As will be argued in the next chapter, it is the use of these moral principles which characterizes moral maturity. Thus the family which enables children to attain that freedom of inquiry and discussion (which leads them to probe behind the regulations governing conduct to the principles upon which they are erected and sustained) is the one which produces morally mature citizens. Alas, it appears to be again the case that higher-status families are those in which this is most likely to occur.

The only final qualification which needs to be added is the one which will be elaborated in Chapter 10. There it will be shown that the privatization (33) which enhances personal contact between parents and children, affects only a segment of society, which for convenience, may be described as the blue-collar/white-collar area of overlap. Since the social-class differences, described in these chapters, only result from the application of a two-class tool, such a realignment in the area between these extremes indicates the greater complexity of the problem, and necessarily invalidates the argument.

REFERENCES

1 Leach (1967), p. 18.
2 This is a complex notion. Klein (1967 Vol. I, pp. 237 and 247) presents it as a conflict between approved and actual behaviour.
3 Leach (1967), pp. 19 ff.
4 Klein (1967), Vol. II, p. 525.
5 See Kay (1968), pp. 35–9, 60–9, 191–2, 231–8, etc.

6 Williams and Williams (1970), p. 99.
7 See also references to such conduct in Fraser (1968) and Kerr (1958), p. 125.
8 Havighurst and Taba (1963), p. 95.
9 Sugarman (1967), p. 357.
10 Frenkil-Brunswik (1949). See the critique of Jahoda and Christie (1954).
11 Henderson and Bernstein (1969).
12 See Williams and Williams (1970), and Kay (1968).
13 Leach (1967), p. 18. A valuable parallel research project confirms this. Eslinger, Clarke and Dynes (1972) found that bureaucratic (lower-status) students were inclined to be 'other-directed', while entrepreneurial (higher-status) students were self-directed and adopted a flexible attitude to their social environment.
14 Sprott (1958), p. 175.
15 Riesman (1950), p. 47.
16 *Times*, 8 and 9 October 1969.
17 Equally only three-legged stools could be used in the open. These did not rock and so scrape or 'plough' the earth. Nor could women look into a mirror. They might see a grey hair, pluck it out and so 'reap'. Such casuistry is present today. The following is taken from *Ask the Rabbi* in the Jewish Chronicle of 22 January 1971.

Question: Is a Jew permitted to go to the Synagogue by motor-car on Saturdays and Holy Days if he is an invalid and unable to walk?
Answer: This is forbidden; it is better for an invalid to pray at home than to ride to the Synagogue, although many Orthodox Rabbis in this country turn a blind eye to the infringement of these rules. The solution to this is for the invalid to be driven to Synagogue by a non-Jewish driver who has no obligation to keep the Jewish Sabbath.

18 *Guardian*, 4 December 1969.
19 *Guardian*, 17 November 1971.
20 Every parent and teacher knows from experience that there are occasions when one just has to say 'No! Because I say so'. There just is not enough time for protracted explanations and reasoned analyses.
21 Zaehner (1966), p. 3.
22 This aspect of Adorno's work was developed by Jahoda (1954, 1960).
23 This is the scale used by Adorno *et al.* to assess authoritarianism.
24 Lipset (1959), p. 97.
25 See Chapter 9. Especially the references to Ford and Miller.
26 Dallas (1971). 'It is as if they recognized no authority at all, rather than deliberately tried to deceive or else to avoid it', p. 892.
27 Again one meets this paradoxical antinomy of working-class authoritarianism and permissiveness. As was noted earlier both are fundamentally antidemocratic. Lipset (1960) makes this point. 'The lower classes are much less committed to democracy than are the urban middle and upper classes', p. 102.
28 Sugarman (1967), p. 357.
29 Klein (1967), p. 604.
30 Sugarman (1970), p. 80.
31 Farrant (1968) uses this analogy of the Church; 'I see the Church as a ship, but still on the stocks. Over the centuries of her building, people have grown so accustomed to the framework around her that when, bit by bit, men have knocked away this support many have felt the ship itself to be in danger. Now the last of the chocks are being hammered away and the ship

wobbles and slips. Many of the most loyal church workers cry 'woe' but others see that her time has come, that a new stage has been reached, for she is entering her true element, the sea of life', pp. 745–6.
32 Erikson (1965), p. 244.
33 Privatization is the term used to describe that home-centredness which has little time for extra-familial activity. Thus privatized persons belong to no clubs or associations, have little social contacts beyond their kin and make home and family devotion a way of life. A popular description of such anomic segments of the population is expressed in the songs 'Little Boxes' and 'Eleanor Rigby'.

Bibliography
ADORNO, T. W., et al., *The Authoritarian Personality* (Harper & Row, 1950).
BATESON, G., 'Cultural Determinants of Personality', in J. M. Hurt (Ed.), *Personality and Behaviour Disorders* (Ronald Press, 1940).
BERNSTEIN, BASIL, 'Language and Social Class', in *British Journal of Sociology*, Vol. XI, 1960.
BOEHM, L., 'The Development of Independence', in *Child Development*, No. 28, 1957.
BOTT, ELIZABETH, 'Urban Families: The Norm of Conjugal Roles', in *Human Relations*, Vol. IX, 1956.
BRONFENBRENNER, URIE, 'Freudian Theories of Identification and Their Derivatives', in *Child Development*, No. 31, 1960.
CHAPMAN, D., *The Home and Social Status* (Routledge & Kegan Paul, 1955).
COOLEY, C. H., *Social Organizations* (Schocken, 1962).
DALLAS, DUNCAN, *The Travelling People* (Macmillan, 1971).
DALLAS, DUNCAN, 'The Gaff Lads', in *New Society*, 4 November 1971.
ERIKSON, E. H., *Childhood and Society* (Penguin, 1965).
ESLINGER, K. N., CLARKE, A. C. and DYNES, R. R., 'Principle of Least Interest, Dating Behaviour and Family Integration Settings; in *Journal of Marriage and the Family*, Vol. 34, No. 2, 1972.
EYSENCK, H. J., *The Psychology of Politics* (Routledge & Kegan Paul, 1954).
FARRANT, ROY, 'Friends' Role in a Dying Church', in *The Friend*, Vol. 126, No. 25, 1968.
FORD, JULIENNE, *Social Class and the Comprehensive School* (Routledge & Kegan Paul, 1969).
FORD, J., YOUNG, D. and BOX, S., 'Functional Autonomy, Role Distance and Social Class', in *British Journal of Sociology*, Vol. 18, 1967.
FRASER, R., *Work*, Vols I and II (Penguin, 1968).
FRENKIL-BRUNSWIK, E., 'Intolerance of Ambiguity as an Emotional and Perceptual Personality Variable', in J. S. Bruner and D. Krech (Eds), *Perception and Personality* (Duke Univ. Press: North Carolina, 1949).
HAVIGHURST, R. J. and TABA, H., *Adolescent Character and Personality* (John Wiley, 1963).
HENDERSON, D. and BERNSTEIN, B., 'Social Class Differences in the Relevance of Language to Socialization', in *Sociology*, Vol. 3, No. 1, 1969.
JAHODA, MARIE, *Race Relations and Mental Health* (HMSO, 1960).
JAHODA, MARIE and CHRISTIE, R., *Studies in the Scope and Methods of the Authoritarian Personality* (Free Press, 1954).
KAY, WILLIAM, *Moral Development* (Allen & Unwin, 1968).
KENT, N. and DAVIS, D. R., 'Discipline in the Home and Intellectual Development', in *British Journal of Medical Psychology*, No. 30, 1957.
KERR, MADELINE, *The People of Ship Street* (Routledge & Kegan Paul, 1958).

KLEIN, JOSEPHINE, *The Study of Groups* (Routledge & Kegan Paul, 1956).

KLEIN, JOSEPHINE, *Samples of English Culture*, 2 Vols (Routledge & Kegan Paul, 1967).

KOHLBERG, L., 'Development of Moral Character and Moral Ideology', in M. Hoffman and L. Hoffman (Eds), *Review of Child Development Research*, Vol. 1 (Russell Sage Foundation, New York, 1964).

KOHN, M. L., 'Social Class and Parental Values', in *American Journal of Sociology*, Vol. LXIV, 1958.

KOHN, M. L. and SCHOOLER, C., 'Class, Occupation and Orientation', in *American Sociological Review*, Vol. 34, 1969.

LEACH, P. J., 'A Critical Study of the Literature Concerning Rigidity', in *British Journal of Social and Clinical Psychology*, No. 6, 1967.

LERNER, E., *Constraint Areas and Moral Judgement in Children* (Manasha, Wisconsin, Banta, 1937).

LIPSET, S. M., *Political Man: The Social Bases of Politics* (Anchor Doubleday, 1959).

LIPSET, S. M., *Political Man* (Heinemann, 1960).

LIPSET, S. M., 'Working Class Authoritarianism: A Reply to Miller and Riesman', in *British Journal of Sociology*, Vol. 12, 1961.

MARSDEN, DENNIS, *Mothers Alone* (Allen Lane, 1969).

MILLER, W. B., 'Lower-class Culture as a Generating Milieu for Gang Delinquency', in *Journal of Social Issues*, Vol. 14, 1958.

MILLER, S. M. and RIESMAN, F., 'Working Class Authoritarianism: A Critique of Lipset', in *British Journal of Sociology*, Vol. 12, 1961.

NEWSON, J. and NEWSON, E., *Four Years Old in an Urban Community* (Allen & Unwin, 1968).

PEAR, T. H., *English Social Differences* (Allen & Unwin, 1955).

PIAGET, J., *Logic and Psychology* (Manchester Univ. Press, 1965).

REYNOLDS, G. W. and JUDGE, A., *The Night the Police Went on Strike* (Weidenfeld & Nicolson, 1968).

RIESMAN, DAVID et al., *The Lonely Crowd* (Yale Univ. Press, 1964).

ROSENTHAL, M. J., FINKELSTEIN, M. and ROBERTSON, R. E., 'A Study of Mother-Child Relationships in the Emotional Disorders of Children', in *Genetic Psychological Monographs*, Vol. 60, No. 1, 1959.

SCHUHAM, A. I., 'Power Relations in Emotionally Disturbed and Normal Family Triads', in *Journal of Abnormal Psychology*, Vol. 75, No. 1, 1970.

SEARS, R., MACCOBY, E. and LEVIN, H., *Patterns of Child Rearing* (Harper & Row, 1957).

SPINLEY, B. M., *The Deprived and the Privileged* (Routledge & Kegan Paul, 1953).

SPROTT, W. J. H., *Human Groups* (Pelican, 1958).

STRODTBECK, F. L., 'Family, Integration, Values and Achievement', in A. H. Halsey, J. Floud and C. A. Anderson (Eds), *Education, Economy and Society* (Collier-Macmillan, London, 1969).

SUGARMAN, B., 'Social Class and Home Background', in Wilson, Williams and Sugarman (Eds), *Introduction to Moral Education* (Penguin, 1967).

SUGARMAN, B., 'The Therapeutic Community and the School', in *Interchange*, Vol. 1, No. 2, 1970.

TAWNEY, R. H., *The Acquisitive Society* (Bell, 1952).

WALL, W. D., *Child of Our Times* (National Children's Home Convocation, 1959).

WANN, K. D., *Fostering Intellectual Development in Young Children* (New York Teachers' College, Columbia Univ., 1962).

WILLIAMS, J., ALLEN, BEAN, FRANK and RUSSELL, CURTIS, 'Impact of

Parental Constraints on the Development of Behaviour Disorders', in *Social Forces*, Vol. 49, No. 2, 1970.

WILLIAMS, N. and WILLIAMS, S., *The Moral Development of Children* (Macmillan, 1970).

WINTERBOTTOM, M., 'The Relation of Need Achievement to Learning Experience in Independence and Mastery', in J. W. Atkinson (Ed.), *Motives in Fantasy Action and Society* (Van Nostrand: Princeton, 1959).

ZAEHNER, R. C., *Hinduism* (Oxford Univ. Press, 1966).

Chapter 9

Moral Dynamism and Creativity

The final distinction to be drawn in terms of morality, between the two social classes, is easily recognizable in practice, since it is a direct development of the moral flexibility described in the last chapter. There it was shown that the familial experience and parental relationships of higher-status children enabled them more readily to discern that moral principles lie behind specific moral regulations. Here we will now be concerned with their capacity to apply these principles; and then show that such a moral quality requires creative, positive attitudes to life which are unhampered by the rigid restrictions of authoritarian legalism.

Although this is easily recognizable in practice, appropriate terminology is difficult to find. Perhaps the terms *positive* and *negative* are suitable. The higher-status child learns to be positive towards life and people: the lower-status child does not. The former becomes an activist asserting his human potential against his environment, convinced that it will succumb to his creative activity. The latter tends, on the other hand, towards a fatalistic and resentful negativism because he feels trapped in a complex, only partially comprehended society which will not yield to his efforts to master it.

However, the term 'positive' is too limited. It does not suggest the sustained, dynamic, confident striving which characterizes the middle classes. John Raynor for example speaks of the 'dynamic' middle classes, because he considers them to be a significant force for change in our political and social life. Consequently, we shall use the term 'moral dynamism'. The higher-status child is essentially dynamic: the lower-status child is not. This assertion has implications which range far beyond the concerns of morality. The dynamism of a higher-status family with its wide cultural and social interests, forms a base from which they launch forays of personal achievement at every level and in every sphere, and contrasts vividly with the unsophisticated lower-status home with its limited range of interests and ambitions.

The former will badger their MP, write to *The Times* or form a local action-group to redress a wrong. The latter will usually limit their response to futile complaints, and only make recourse to the power of their trade unions when a specific, clearly understood wage issue is raised. Barber contrasts these two stereotypes with his stark and pithy observation that 'Lower-class people often give "don't know" answers. They know less about matters that concern their economic and social interests'. To this Lipset adds his ruthless observations that 'The hard core of "chronic know-nothings" comes disproportionately from the lower socio-economic groups. These people are not only uninformed but harder to reach, no matter what the level or nature of the information' (1).

These different life styles obviously each form a spectrum of correlated attitudes ranging from personal ambition to personal morality. The static, present orientation of the working man, content to leave his economic well-being in trade union hands, contrasts sharply with middle-class ambitions, fostered and sustained by the conviction that industry and the application of rationally determined principles results in both economic and cultural advancement (2).

The previous chapter made it clear that the familial experience of higher-status children enabled them to see beyond the authoritarian structure, which delineated the lives of lower-status children, and discern the principles of which this was a tangible expression. Here we shall show that the negativism of working-class children leads them inevitably from authoritarianism into legalism, while the middle-class child's dynamism leads to the creative, active application of moral principles.

MIDDLE-CLASS DYNAMISM

Max Weber is probably the best known writer to suggest that this dynamic activism was precipitated by the protestant reformation and has since been characteristic of the middle classes. In essence he argued that the individualistic search for salvation, characteristic of the reformation, led to a transformation of society by the industrious, frugal puritans. The incidental accumulation of capital led to modern industrialization, but this was only a by-product of the moral dynamism of men who believed that the intelligent and sustained application of rationally derived principles could transform their world.

The middle classes, it is argued, are the inheritors of these traits. Consequently, as we shall see, they still assume that personal dynamism can master and transform the environment; that sustained application leads to success; that it is what a man *does* and *is* that ultimately matters; and therefore, lastly, that their ideal child is one who displays these personal qualities.

Obviously one's mastery of the environment is only achieved

through hard work. This is a fact to which any advanced scientific researcher will testify. For this reason some writers are now saying that the application of effort directed by the first protestants to establishing God's kingdom on earth, has now been replaced by our rational and scientific attempts to control the social and physical worlds. The cynic may even go further and argue that personal salvation is now indexed by an ascending line on a sales chart, but puritan devotion to work and unbounded confidence in the inevitable mastery of all hindrances to the good life, are still endemic to the middle classes. They believe that rational, active, individual effort is the hallmark of achievement. Harold Macmillan exemplified this ideal in a signed memorandum hung on the walls of both his private office and the cabinet room when he was Prime Minister. It simply read 'Quiet, calm, deliberation disentangles every knot' (3). It summed up the dynamism of the middle-class man of action.

Anthony Sampson confirmed that such people utilize the systems and amenities they create. He discovered that the divisions of class become increasingly identified as differences between those who know how to organize things to their advantage and those who do not. The middle classes, it seems, have become well versed in utilizing the welfare state which they helped to create. It is they who take advantage of the services and grants meant specifically for the working class. With these they build extra bathrooms, make inordinate demands on the health service, turn grammar schools and universities into middle-class enclaves, and insist on those environmental improvements which will enhance the value of their property.

This belief in the efficacy of sustained application, naturally becomes a character trait of the children in these families. Jackson and Marsden studied the educational attitudes of such families and found that this tough and optimistic outlook prevailed. Middle-class parents perpetually refused to accept that their children could not obtain any benefit from tertiary education. Such advantages, they believed, were within the grasp of even moderately talented children who applied themselves realistically and energetically to its challenge. Consequently, the writers conclude, such children 'have inherited their parents' spirit of self-help, their drive and many of their social sympathies, and on the whole they now pursue their professions with considerable vigour' (4).

Such children may consequently appear to be over-achievers. Strodtbeck, for example, found that these successful, confident children so utilized their educational environment that (with socio-economic status as the only variable) they always did better at school. These clearly represent the type of teenagers Barry Sugarman met in his research, who were convinced that they could and should master and utilize their educational environment, and so make the most of themselves. Of course, it may simply be that they are achievement orientated, but, as Rosen showed, such achievement motivation is correlated with social class.

In a chapter concerned with the dynamism of middle-class children it is inevitable that attention would thus be focused on their efficient exploitation of our educational system, but its implications range far more widely than this. Such dynamic characteristics, as have been enumerated, emerge in a host of different ways. These are naturally enhanced by social confidence, articulacy and the sustained expertise in cultural and sporting pursuits, which middle-class homes and schools inculcate in the young. Thus the analysis can be extended still further.

Such children appear also to develop a greater degree of open-mindedness, and sustain an intellectual receptivity to new ideas. They display considerable social competence, and appear to be at home under widely differing circumstances. Conversations with them are free, casual and well informed, and indicate that these children are familiar with abstract ideas and can readily turn to a consideration of the principles involved. Withal they disclose intellectual, as well as social resilience, and their creativity of mind discloses that from childhood they have been accustomed to conversing with intelligent adults who have listened to their views with interest and care. In any social crisis they side with authority, and indeed identify with it, yet still recognize that it is only a social tool. Thus when moral dilemmas arise, they tend to apply principles in a dynamic and creative way.

All of this contrasts starkly with the stereotyped working-class child who is characterized by the antitheses of these qualities. He is likely to be restricted and dogmatic in his opinions and his linguistic limitations will only enhance this deficiency. He will live by precedent and rules, even though this may be in the breach rather than the observance. In any conflict with the law he will be more likely either to passively accept it as an inevitable feature of life, or actively flout its requirements. His moral life will therefore be legalistic and conservative.

The only final point which needs to be re-affirmed is a simple one. These children are the product of the parental attitudes in their homes. The dynamic child cannot emerge from either the harsh authoritarian or the disorganized, haphazardly indulgent families described earlier as characteristic of the working classes. Klein has expressed this truth succinctly. 'Mothers who let their children run wild do not produce forceful, driving, socially successful children;

neither do indulgent and over-protective mothers; neither do the restrictive and over-concerned' (5).

Working-class Passivity

As already noted, studies of the working classes have been complicated by the inevitable demographic changes which follow a war. Originally it was possible to analyse this topographically compact and economically deprived stratum of society as a stable system. One of the best known of these investigations is that of Kerr in a slum area of Liverpool. Later, as such areas were cleared and the inhabitants moved to new towns, changes in traditional working-class life styles naturally occurred. Previously conditioned by close-knit-kinship systems, localized within a restricted area, they had to be re-formed under different conditions. The family was now scattered and the communal living of slum areas was replaced by the relative isolation of council estates. Willmott and Young are standard sources of information concerning the effects of such changes.

Now, finally the emergence of affluent workers has produced a further change. The possibility that such lower-status members of society are now aspiring to obtain a foothold in the middle classes, by a process of embourgeoisement, will be examined in the next chapter. The most recent source of information on this phenomenon is the report of Goldthorpe and his colleagues. Over a decade ago such a worker denied having any working-class allegiance. 'I'm working class only in the works, outside I am like anyone else' (6).

Yet despite these changes it is still possible to delineate the fundamental social negativism of such citizens once they step outside the kinship circle. Spinley vividly described her London slum-dwellers as those whose 'relations with other people was coloured by negativism'. Kerr supported this view by concluding that her comparable Liverpudlians were characterized by a basic 'retreat from sociability'. Even in Ashton, where strong bonds were forged between the miners, Dennis *et al.* found that social life was narrow and resistant to new experiences.

In all three cases negativism is apparently induced by similar circumstances. The deprivation and hardships of such under-privileged lives are hardly likely to produce a sustained carnival atmosphere; and constant economic pressures produce a high (if concealed) level of anxiety (7). All three, in fact, display standard reactions to anxiety and stress. Hence there is a reduction of exploratory behaviour, and genuine social interaction is kept to a minimum.

Even under less adverse conditions, this social negativism is still apparent. In Oxford, for example, Mogey found that most lower-status people spoke rejectingly of their neighbours, but it was their social isolationism which is relevant here. He noted a curious but significant phenomenon. The increased affluence of the workers was reflected by the abundance of toys possessed by the children. Yet they were mostly of such a kind that children *had to play with them inside the house.*

This privatization (see Chapter 10) appears to be a characteristic of affluent workers. In Woodford, for example, Willmott and Young record that it is the middle classes who joined the clubs: the workers stay at home (8). It is not, therefore, surprising to find that children reared in this milieu and emulating the attitudes of their parents, are resentful of the social competence and confident ease of manner they find amongst the middle classes. As Richard Hoggart observed, even the successful working-class scholarship child 'does not acquire the unconscious confidence of many a public school trained child of the middle classes'. Consequently if success eludes him he ascribes it to their 'character, ability to mix, and boldness' (9).

The anxiety, referred to earlier, also appears to account for another feature of working-class negativism. Lipset, for example, has shown that the political views of such men are characterized by an inflexible dogmatism which is apparently impervious to informed, reasoned discussion. It has long been realized that aggression (another lower-status trait), is related to anxiety, but now Alan Smithers has found that dogmatism, is also related to anxiety. He discovered that it was a *defence* erected against anxiety; but in the process the mind closed itself to both new worries and new information. Consequently dogmatism is characterized by a reluctance to receive new ideas.

Predictably dogmatic workers speak in stereotyped phrases (10) which endorse this intellectual inflexibility. Such language then also discloses itself to be a medium of communication inimical to the processes of abstract, conceptual thinking. It is not surprising that their children acquire the 'restricted code' of Bernstein and inherit all its limitations. Even their language it seems enhances the conservative negativism of their life-style and makes them more able to comprehend tangible rules and regulations rather than abstract moral principles.

Legalism and Moral Dynamism

Joseph Fletcher has recently drawn attention to the fact that 'There are at bottom only three alternative routes to follow in making moral decisions. They are the legalistic; the antinomian; and the situational' (11). It is the first and the last which concern us here. The legalistic system is constructed from a fabric of rules and regulations. Situational morality, which Fletcher then proceeds to advocate, has no such structure. It consists of the creative, situational, dynamic application of moral principles.

I have elsewhere argued that in an individual, the latter is the more mature form of morality (12), and Fletcher endorses this view. A notable example of the contrast between these two also appears in the cultural evolution of our society. Sir Richard Acland reports how during the English Commonwealth period, Parliament was presented with its first opportunity to apply the principles of jurisprudence and political science to contemporary problems. He records with dismay how they repeatedly teetered on the brink of actually doing so, but then lost their nerve and made recourse to established legal guides, notably the Great Charter of 1215.

This over-simplication of a complex parliamentary phase of development may function as a paradigm. Children can be sharply divided between those who live perpetually within a legalistic structure, and those who are willing to discern and then apply moral principles. And once again it is clear that this dichotomy follows a social-class pattern.

Social-class Differences

We have already seen that the intellectual, emotional, linguistic and personal development of lower-status children leads them to construe life in authoritarian terms, which soon passes into a legalist frame of mind. Baldwin found that autocratic authoritarian parental attitudes produced children who were passive and submissive. Rosenthal and his colleagues added their clinical findings that children reared in this way become not only submissive to authority but excessively 'rule-bound' in their attitudes. Kohn and Schooler also confirmed that working-class authoritarianism produced children who are extremely sensitive to externally imposed rules: in fact, such children were conditioned to actually need them.

Others have found that this also results not only from such authoritarianism but also from the *laissez-faire* environment of working-class children. Their childhood, as Miller observed, is characterized by long periods during which there is virtually no parental control. These children too, need rules for their guidance, even when they have passed beyond the developmental level of moral authoritarianism. Ford and his colleagues concluded the same. Discussing the correlation between social class and functional autonomy they reported that the working-class milieu is 'likely to produce behaviour which is best described as 'ruleful' (13).

This curious ambivalence which we have repeatedly noted, results from the fact that in a working-class home 'Parental approval can be expressed in a number of ways ranging from "you carry on, it's all right with me", to "if you don't I'll beat the living daylights out of you" (14).

Consequently all such working-class children were in a social situation where they both *acquired* and *required* a legal framework for their conduct (15). Thus they adhere to this entrenched mode of life, for not to do so would mean learning new modes of behaviour and having to cope with situations for which they have no previously determined pattern (16).

By contrast, middle-class families produce children whose incipient autonomy leads them beyond legalism. Baldwin showed that democratic families produced children willing to make fearless exploratory assaults on their environment. Strodtbeck confirmed this by concluding that in such families there was a greater disposition 'to believe that the world can be rationally mastered and that a son should risk separation from his family' (17).

It is therefore characteristic of such children that, unlike their lower-status peers, they seek not material possessions but personal worth. Lewis and Maude express this by tersely observing that the middle classes emerged 'not solely because they wanted to *have* but because they wanted to *be*' (18). Indeed Douvan goes even further than this and concludes that middle-class children ultimately seek personal achievement as an end in itself, rather than as the means of attaining some further reward. Thus the experience, reported by Kent and Davies, is foreign to them. They found that even aspiring lower-status parents made their personal affection and approval depend on the achievement of their children. This is not the case with middle-class children, consequently one finds such children in adulthood tending to view their work in terms of its expressive rather than its instrumental function. Naturally autonomy is also an essential element in this life-style. Describing such a boy, Spinley reports that although he is confidently certain of his later success, security and social status, one desire stands out beyond the others. 'He wants to exercise authority or at least not to be under the authority of someone else' (19).

This then, is the middle-class child. He is convinced that persistence, self-control, independence and autonomy will enable him to master his environment. Intelligent, perceptive, ambitious and conceptually sophisticated, he recognizes that legal systems are only social tools to be used for man's advantage. The diminution of dogmatism, which Lipset reported, makes him more tolerant of unconventional, political, religious and moral opinions. Thus he stands poised on the brink of moral maturity. The dynamism which leads him to apply his reason to everyday problems leads him also to apply principles to the resolution of moral dilemmas. As Weber and

Tawney have shown, these inheritors of the puritan ethic have no rest until they have resolved them.

One current spectacular illustration of this fact is the meteoric rise to prominence of Ralph Nader. His vigorous attacks on industrial and commercial exploitation in America simply reflect, he says, 'the Puritan Streak' in his essentially middle-class organization. A report on this phenomenon by Davie inadvertently highlights the dynamism of the members of this organization. One of Nader's aides has Abraham Lincoln's dictum above his desk: 'To sin by silence when they should protest, makes cowards of men.' Furthermore, the whole Nader enterprise is devoted to ensuring that the principles of public service and honest dealing will characterize American industry and commerce.

At a less spectacular level this dynamism may also be seen operating in any industrial dispute. There the labour force and the executive team tend to polarize in their approach to the problem. On the one hand the workers refer to the regulations enshrined in their union rule book. On the other hand the management, whose dynamism has promoted them to executive level, will try to reach a settlement on the basis of applied reason, which in ideal situations, would be expressed in the form of moral principles.

MORAL CREATIVITY

Basing his actions on the application of perpetually valid principles, rather than immutable codes, an individual is clearly involved in a creative process. Thus to Koestler's threefold analysis of bisociated creativity as artistic, scientific and humorous, one may now add moral creativity. To thus speak of moral creativity may lead one to be misunderstood. This does not mean that we can act as we like, after the manner of aberrant anarchists or existentialists. The matter is both simpler and more complex than this.

The truly moral man approaches every new situation with that total openness endowed by love and reason. These dynamic forces then act upon the raw material of any human encounter in a creative way. This spontaneous response, to people with love and to problems with reason, releases cultural and scientific forces of unimaginable power which then breach all our conventions. It therefore follows that fundamental moral principles compel us to behave positively and creatively. Such a bald statement needs to be elaborated and supported by evidence and arguments which are open to public inquiry.

As most educationalists will know, creativity is a current topic of interest and Lytton has swiftly applied this concept to educational problems and so placed it on a broader canvas. Such interest may partly reflect the fact that in a mass, urbanized society it is becoming increasingly difficult to exercise our personal uniqueness. One corollary of this may be the fact that in a cyberculture we want to emphasize the divergent, lateral and bisociative creative forms of thinking, which cannot yet be replicated by a computer. The reason may be less devious. It may simply be that our increased sophistication, in psychological measuring, has enabled us to handle this slippery concept with greater confidence.

Guilford was first led to a consideration of this when he found that even the most complex intelligence tests, catering for 120 intellectual abilities, still excluded some human mental activities. These he described as 'creative' since they were characterized by flexibility and divergence. Thus, although six years later he was still trying to clarify his terms and devise adequate tests, he did succeed in blazing a trail which both he and later psychologists have followed (20).

The moral connotations of creativity do not emerge from the fact that it is contrasted with destructiveness. It is more subtle than that. Creativity appears to be linked with the autonomy and flexible dynamism which we have already accepted as crucial determinants of mature morality. Such an assertion can be traced through the literature of this subject. Barron found that creative individuals refused to surrender their originality to the demands of society, and five years later added that such children were also characterized by flexibility of personality and dynamism of thought. Torrance maintains that creative children are characterized by 'searching for a purpose, having different values, being motivated by different rewards, and searching for uniqueness' (21). Finally, Getzels and Jackson conclude that when a child 'chooses the ethical rather than the expedient alternative' and 'holds to personal ideals transcending such qualities as appearance and social acceptability' (22) he is displaying creativity of mind.

Leach, in her review of the literature on rigidity as a limitation on creative thinking notes that despite the varying terminology of the different psychologists all agree on one thing. They speak of a child, who displays creative originality, as being flexible in his approach to life, receptive to environmental stimuli, and dynamic in his autonomous striving for personal expression.

Divergent and Lateral Thinking

Further evidence has recently been supplied by Liam Hudson whose work also attempts to provide a testable concept of identity (see Chapter 4). Rejecting the nomenclature of Getzels and Jackson as 'bound to mislead', he spoke of *divergence* instead of *creativity*.

Then having tested his hypothesis he showed that children could be divided into convergers and divergers. Convergers follow traditional routes to clearly identified goals; while divergers spread outwards in a creative search for new ideas, hypotheses and answers. He also argued that 'The arts offer more elbow room for individuality; the sciences less' (23). Consequently he concluded that convergers specialized in science and divergers in the arts.

This research report attracted a number of criticisms. It is, after all, natural for a creative scientist to resent being classified as a converger. He could point to the fact that our culture has advanced because of the findings of science, and that scientific inquiries had been characterized by ingenuity, inventiveness and originality. Furthermore, subsequent retests threw doubt on the validity and reliability of Hudson's testing techniques.

His second research report made it clear that he had noted these criticisms, and although the findings confirm his original conclusions, the categorical classifying no longer casts a shadow over his results. This change can be most vividly conveyed by simply comparing two of his statements. He began the first report by stating, 'The aim of this book is to delineate two types of clever schoolboys; the converger and the diverger' (24); and he ended the second by saying, 'even at the outset I was not pigeon-holing' (25). Between those two statements lies a mass of valuable material.

In the first volume he showed that convergers were clearly authoritarian in their attitudes; and is equally specific in the second research. 'Convergers', he writes, 'tend to hold authoritarian attitudes' (26). They disapproved of those who were too independent, and strongly approved of obedience. They willingly submitted themselves to authoritarian dicta; preferred a clear structure, within which to work; and readily accepted the advice of acknowledged experts. In the second volume, studying the degree to which children would yield to authority he found that respect for authority was most apparent amongst convergers who yielded most.

The relevance of this for the present study is immediately apparent. In the last analysis the personal qualities displayed by both the innovating, moral dynamist and the creative diverger appear to coincide. Hudson actually affirms quite definitely that the convergers are authority orientated and legalistic in their outlook. It is equally apparent that his divergers are basically morally creative. A contrast between the polarized positions within each conceptual structure makes this clear.

The legalist is not only sensitive and amenable to authority, he tends to assume that he must converge upon an accurate answer to his problem. He prefers to do this within a rigid frame of reference.

He is happiest when homing on to a single target within an accepted structure for it relieves him not only of uncertainty, but also of responsibility (27). He assumes that the law is the system within which he must conduct himself and in any dilemma he makes recourse to it, assuming that it will provide him with a closed-ended solution.

For the moral dynamist, on the other hand, morality consists of acting upon decisions reached by the situational application of moral principles. He is thus in an open-ended diverging situation in which he keeps all the options open. His conduct is prescribed not by law but by a consideration of all the factors involved. He does not converge upon a fixed moral fiat, but diverges into the realm where goodness becomes an amalgam of a host of possible actions.

Hudson appears to be right when he argues that such children ultimately study the humanities. Here their imagination and creative talent can be given full rein as they write, paint, sculpt, compose and behave morally. But he is wrong when he assumes that such activity is foreign to scientists. Both science and morality are ultimately creative when they are the milieux for conduct characterized by the open-ended application of principles to new situations — Magee has argued that 'the most important aspect of science is its moral creativity' (28).

Edward de Bono's conclusions are similar to Hudson's. The terminology is different, but the ideas are closely related. Hudson preferred to speak of divergent rather than creative thinking, and contrasted this with convergent thought. Now de Bono introduces the notion of lateral thinking, as a form of creative activity, and contrasts it with vertical thought.

The similarity is immediately apparent when one considers the conceptual structure de Bono presents. He argues that vertical thinking is a process whereby an individual attempts to solve a problem by abstracting those elements, which he believes will lead to a final, definitive solution by the process of logic. Lateral thinking, on the other hand retains all the available, apparently uncorrelated information and works on the permutations they provide. In this way a whole variety of valid solutions are reached, even when apparently unrelated elements of information are juxtaposed. The barrier of single-mindedness, which prevents this, he calls the 'arrogance clamp'. Then goes on to say, 'The *must be* mistake shuts out the possibility of a completely new point of view which has not yet been generated' (29). Like Arthur Koestler, he believes that creativity (for him the product of lateral thinking) is apparent in the insights of science, art and humour.

Again it is obvious that this analysis supports the views that vertical thinking converges upon a single solution while lateral thought diverges into a host of equally valid possibilities. After outlining his position in this way, de Bono made it perfectly clear that the distinction lay between the view that there was only one right answer, and the willingness to accept that there might be many. Thus he writes, 'Although the feeling of absolute rightness is characteristic of human thinking, there is only one place where it is justified. This is when one is working within a *closed* system' (30).

This need for 'absolute rightness' in a 'closed system' is characteristic of the legalist. He lives within the limitations of a legal system and looks to it for conclusive answers to his moral questions. In contrast the lateral thinker takes note of all the relevant situational factors, recognizes that there are any number of possible courses of action open to him, and then finds the one which he deems to be most appropriate in the circumstances. He thus lives in the 'open' system where numerous possibilities offer themselves as appropriate without being exclusively right.

This subject cannot be left without reference to the refreshingly stimulating work of Abraham Maslow. Some Christians curiously dismiss his humanistic psychology and sociology as though it threatened their faith, yet his description of the 'self-actualizing' man is one of the most vivid and accurate contemporary portrayals of what the New Testament calls the man 'in Christ'. The relevant point is that such a man is the creative, morally mature person of whom we have been talking.

Self-actualizing men are the epitome of autonomy, responsibility and moral maturity, yet their prime characteristic is that of creativity. Maslow found that their 'codes of ethics are individual rather than conventional. The unthinking observer might sometimes believe them to be unethical, since they can break down not only conventions but laws when the situation seems to demand it. However, the very opposite is the case. They are the most ethical of people even though their ethics are not the same as the people around them' (31).

As the report progresses, one grows increasingly conscious of the excellence of these men with their freshness, penetration, psychological health, easy recognition of the pseudo, impatience with the sham stereotype, and ease of perception. They need not, continues, Maslow, express their creativity in writing, composing, painting or any of the spectacular activities associated with the effortless superiority of this personality type. All his subjects simply behaved naturally, but did so in refreshingly original ways. All their maturity emerged as creativity, whether it was in helping a neighbour or making a major moral decision. Could such people, he argues, be more human, more representative of humanity at its highest? Are they closer to the species in its technical taxonomical sense? Are we in fact observing *real* human beings when we face creative moral agents? 'These people', concludes Maslow, 'seem to see the true and the real more easily. It is because of this that they seem, to other more limited men, creative' (32).

Social-class Differences in Creativity

From what had been said earlier one would expect to find that creativity was correlated with social class. Unfortunately, Getzels, Jackson and Hudson all used samples of highly intelligent children from middle-class backgrounds; and the only valid class distinctions they made are within this group. It could, of course, be argued that social class and intelligence are correlated; but how does one then explain the presence of a highly intelligent converger? Hudson gives a clue in his passing reference to the working-class origins of many scientists, and then commits himself by saying that, with the benefit of hindsight, he now realizes that he had been comparing 'two British sub-cultures' (33)—and we shall pursue this line.

If we eliminate the bizarre responses of the mentally sick, and sexual variations in the use of artefacts (34), we may return to a consideration of cultural factors as an explanation of creativity. Some cultures and sub-cultures are so rigid that rules hold undisputed sway: education in them consists of acknowledging the appropriate authorities and any attempt to deviate is met with harsh retribution. Other cultures allow wide ranges of latitude to their members and tolerate divergent patterns of conduct and thought. Clearly creativity is more likely to survive in the latter, and, as we have seen, this would correspond to the middle-class milieu.

Furthermore, the variations within this sub-culture (e.g. the intelligent convergers) could be explained in terms of personality differences. There is now an abundance of evidence indicating that an individual's willingness to discard the security of a closed system and thus expose himself to ambiguity depends upon a personality factor. Leach's 'rigid' child, Hudson's 'converger' and de Bono's 'vertical' thinker all have in common the fact that they cannot tolerate cognitive dissonance (35). Thus whereas the potentially creative lower-status child would be impeded by his environment (36) the higher-status child would not. Consequently a social-class correlation might emerge.

Miller argues that social circumstances today, in an alienated, urbanized situation, inevitably make it increasingly difficult for man to be original and creative. 'But for the mass of people', he says, 'it was previously hidden by severe deprivation, war or economic depression'. Conversely the conditions of a middle-class home, characterized by at least economic sufficiency and an absence of physical deprivation, would be an ideal environment in which to cultivate this creativity. Obviously there is also a positive element involved. It is not only the negative absence of deprivation which has this effect, it is the positive presence of other factors too. Toys which exercise the imagination; conversations which tax linguistic facility; opportunities to express opinions, ideas, modes of conduct and *recherché* ambitions are all contributory elements. As Miller observes, 'that children are able to be creative is obvious, provided that they are brought up in a reasonably good way; appropriately loved, fed and nurtured'. Such children clearly have the security which others seek in legalism.

Working in an institution where the different social classes mingle, in the course of pursuing various activities, highlights this difference in attitudes. The fundamentally middle-class professional or managerial staff use the system as a structure within which to work. By contrast the workers, whatever their function, tend to limit their activity to clearly specified areas and punctiliously end at a specified time (37).

IMPLICATIONS OF MORAL DYNAMISM

All that has been said above makes it clear that mature morality is only possible when the agent is an autonomous, dynamic, creative person. This is appropriate for life in society is characterized not by its neatness but by its complexity. There are rarely any simple solutions, any more than there are simple problems. Most of them are open-ended and present one with a multiple-choice situation. In such circumstances it is only the comprehension and application of general principles that is likely to be of any real value.

Since moral problems are also invariably characterized by the fact that they are amenable to many different solutions, creativity is even more necessary. Thus the moral agent should approach these not only as a responsible, autonomous human being, but as one who recognizes that it is the creative application of moral principles, and not a rigid subscription to regulations, which will solve them.

Only two final points need to be made here. A discussion of moral dynamism ought to lead into a consideration of the problem of motivation, since such moral dynamism might also imply the power to do what one knows ought to be done. I have discussed this complex question elsewhere (38) and argued that it is crucial to moral education, since such a process must produce children who do not merely *know* what they deem to be right but are also capable of *doing* it.

This, however, is a problem whose detailed consideration lies beyond the province of the present book (39).

The second consideration is as equally complex in a different way. It relates to the fact that if the conceptual structures associated with morality are essentially divergent, bisociative and creative, this may account for the fact that these cannot always be verbalized. Such structures are lateral in form while language, in its normal usage, is linear. The former weaves and wanders, connecting concepts, creating possible courses of action, linking, combining and associating apparently unrelated elements; while the latter, if used normally, passes with a steady, certain step from one logically connected point to another.

This raises a number of related points. Language, of course, need not be simply the logical tool implied in the preceding paragraph. It can be used poetically, metaphorically and allegorically, and in the context of morality, it can have a variety of valid usages (40).

For the moment, however, the important point to note is that many of the problems associated with morality may spring from the fact that it is not entirely amenable to linguistic forms. Thus despite the fact that the articulate middle-class child has an advantage in his ability to abstract and then apply moral principles, this does not mean that morality is restricted to the bounds of linguistic competence. It can and does often exceed them. There are times when all men must be able to say 'I just *feel* that this is the right thing to do'.

The articulate may subsequently be able to apply moral principles, discuss the validity of varying moral criteria, and so *appear* to have followed a rational course, but if morality is creative in form it must burst the bounds of language. This does not mean that the inarticulate child is moral. It simply means that morality in its highest form exceeds the confines of linguistic competence.

REFERENCES

1 Barber (1961), p. 108, and Lipset (1960), p. 111.
2 Willmott (1960) found little 'status-striving amongst the Dagenham working class. Dennis *et al.* (1956) describes how their miners suppressed any hint of refinement or sophistication by using banter of the 'my-we-are-posh' variety. Mogey (1956) reports how his young working-class families in Oxford had to suppress any aspirations beyond the life-style of their class. Ineichen (1971) notes that his conjugal respondents were ashamed of possessing occupational and social ambitions and concluded that 'ambition' appeared to be a new taboo. Indeed, beyond striving continuously for an adequate rising wage-packet and hoping that their children would do a little better than they, there was little evidence of any commitment to a dynamic life-style. In Hoggart's terse phrase the working classes are not the 'great doers of this world'. In all honesty one must add that the dynamic

achievement-orientated member of the middle class often uses his success to exploit rather than serve his fellows.

3 Egremont (1968), p. 170.
4 Jackson and Marsden (1965), p. 41.
5 Klein (1967), p. 604. Note yet again this working-class ambivalence.
6 Zweig (1961), p. 162.
7 Even where economic anxiety is temporarily relieved, the miners had other serious worries. One told Zweig (1948) 'Life in the pits is a hard struggle with certain defeat at the end'. He then went on to describe the difficulties of his work. Such pressures as these produce the working-class solidarity which Young and Willmott (1957) noted in Bethnal Green. But this could result from a need to feel secure, rather than warm social loyalties, as Coates and Silburn showed.
8 See Willmott and Young (1960). They also garner evidence from other areas.
9 Hoggart (1967), p. 247.
10 Zweig (1952) said that his workers could only express their views in 'popular sayings' (p. 216). Mogey (1956) found that his discussion groups for workers foundered because they were limited to 'fixed stereotyped phrases' (p. 46). Bennett (1971) investigating infertility provides a graphic example of this. One childless working-class father said that testing for infertility was 'degrading because if you can't reproduce you're not a man' (p. 9).
11 Fletcher (1966), p. 17.
12 See Kay (1968).
13 Ford *et al.* (1967), p. 377.
14 Rose (1968), p. 41.
15 Smithers (1970) compared the results of personality tests with measurements on the Rokeach dogmatism scale and found that dogmatic, legalistic young people were both happy and secure when they had clear regulations to guide their conduct.
16 Kerr (1958), p. 117.
17 Strodtbeck (1969), p. 343.
18 Zweig (1961) noted that it is characteristic of the working classes that they would rather work overtime than study to gain more qualifications. See pp. 75 ff and 100 ff.
19 Spinley (1954), p. 137.
20 Actually Woodworth first distinguished between convergent and divergent thinking in 1918 and Spearman isolated a related factor which he designated 'fluency' in 1927.
21 Torrance (1962), p. 124. Note that he still thinks that there is a 'need for rewarding creative thinking' (p. 12).
22 Getzels and Jackson (1962), p. 135.
23 Hudson (1966), pp. 37 and 139.
24 *op. cit.*, p. 1.
25 Hudson (1968), p. 91.
26 *op. cit.*, p. 7.
27 *op. cit.*, p. 72.
28 Magee (1965), p. 30.
29 de Bono (1971), p. 74.
30 *op. cit.*, p. 152.
31 Maslow (1970), p. 158.
32 *op. cit.*, p. 171. It should be noted, however, that Maslow's research techniques were unconventional. These resulted from the fact that he was precisely the kind of creative personality being discussed here.

33 Getzels and Jackson (1962) 'The greatest proportion come from middle- and upper-class families. Others occupy managerial and white-collar positions. Hudson (1968) admits that he had hitherto had little sociological interest in his sample. Here he describes it as 'overwhelmingly upper middle class, middle class and lower middle class' (p. 97). Consequently he had to distinguish between upper middle-class public schools and lower middle-class grammar schools (p. 14). See further p. 3.

34 An old joke illustrates this point. An irate husband, flecked with blood complained that his cut-throat razor was blunt. 'That's strange,' mused his sympathetic wife. 'It was sharp when I cut the lino yesterday.'

35 Festinger (1957) describes this as a state of conflict with no clear normative pattern as a guide. It is furthermore a conflict between belief and action, practice and precept because no dominant standard assures any rewards for conformity. Lipset (1960) indicates a class factor here noting that 'the lower strata are the least tolerant' (p. 103).

36 Jackson (1971) is eloquent on this point. Speaking of children threatened by authority he writes that they 'cannot develop or become creative for fear of disapproval' (p. 127).

37 Contrast the workers streaming from factory gates while the directors' lights stay on in their offices. It has also been observed that this distinguishes a wage from a salary since the latter indicates that the recipient does not limit himself to specified activities and hours.

38 See Kay (1968).

39 See May (1969), 'Dr Kay goes too far when he suggests that moral education would be effective only when children are enabled not only to think morally but also to act morally' (p. 124). I consider this to be an illegitimate transference from religious education to moral education. Clearly it is wrong to attempt to inculcate religious conduct, but (as I argue below) it is not only appropriate in moral education. It is also essential.

40 This has been discussed fully in Kay (1970) where a full treatment of Noam Chomsky's arguments will be found.

Bibliography

ACLAND, RICHARD, *We Teach Them Wrong* (Gollancz, 1963).

ARENDT, HANNAH, *On Violence* (Allen Lane, 1970).

BALDWIN, A. L., 'Socialization and Parent–Child Relationships', in *Child Development*, No. 19, 1948.

BARBER, B., 'Social-class Differences in Educational Life-chances', in *Teachers' College Record*, No. 63, 1961.

BARRON, F., 'The Psychology of Imagination', in *Scientific American*, No. 199, 1958.

BARRON, F., *Creativity and Psychological Health* (Van Nostrand, Princeton, 1963).

BENNET, J., 'What Would You Do if the Doctor Said You Couldn't Have Children?' in *Observer*, Suppl., 31 October 1971.

BERNSTEIN, BASIL, *Class, Codes and Control* (Routledge & Kegan Paul, 1971).

BONO, EDWARD DE, *Lateral Thinking: A Textbook of Creativity* (Ward Lock, 1970).

BONO, EDWARD DE, *Practical Thinking* (Jonathan Cape, 1971).

CHOMSKY, NOAM, *Syntactic Structures* (Humanities Press, 1957).

CHOMSKY, NOAM, *Cartesian Linguistics* (Harper & Row, 1966).

COATES, K. and SILBURN, R., *Poverty, Deprivation and Morale in a Nottingham Community: St. Annes* (Nottingham Univ. Press, 1967).

DAVIE, MICHAEL, 'Nader and His Raiders', in *Observer Review*, 24 October 1971.

DENNIS, N., HENRIQUES, F. and SLAUGHTER, C., *Coal is Our Life* (Eyre & Spottiswoode, 1956).

DOUVAN, E., 'Social Status and Success Striving', in *Journal of Abnormal and Social Psychology*, Vol. 52, 1956.

EGREMONT, LORD, *Wyndham and Children First* (Macmillan, 1968).

FESTINGER, L., *A Theory of Cognitive Dissonance* (Tavistock, 1957).

FLETCHER, J., *Situation Ethics* (Student Christian Movement, 1966).

FLETCHER, J., *Moral Responsibility* (Student Christian Movement, 1967).

FORD, J., YOUNG, D. and BOX, S., 'Functional Autonomy, Role Distance and Social Class', in *British Journal of Sociology*, Vol. 18, 1967.

GETZELS, J. W. and JACKSON, P. W., *Creativity and Intelligence* (John Wiley, 1962).

GOLDTHORPE, J. H., *The Affluent Worker in the Class Structure* (Cambridge Univ. Press, 1969).

GUILFORD, J. P., 'Creativity', in *American Psychologist*, No. 15, 1950.

GUILFORD, J. P., 'The Structure of Intellect', in *Psychological Bulletin*, No. 53, 1956.

GUILFORD, J. P., 'Three Faces of Intellect', in *American Psychologist*, No. 14, 1959.

HOGGART, R., *The Uses of Literacy* (Penguin, 1962).

HUDSON, LIAM, *Contrary Imaginations* (Methuen, 1966).

HUDSON, LIAM, *Frames of Mind* (Methuen, 1968).

INEICHEN, BERNARD, 'The New Taboo', in *New Society*, 21 October 1971.

JACKSON, B. and MARSDEN, D., *Education and the Working Class* (Routledge & Kegan Paul, 1965).

JACKSON, GEORGE, *Soledad Brother* (Penguin, 1971).

KAY, WILLIAM, *Moral Development* (Allen & Unwin, 1968).

KAY, WILLIAM and MATHISON, JANE, 'The Evolution of Consciousness', in *Teilhard Review*, Vol. 3, No. 2, 1969.

KAY, WILLIAM, 'A Teilhardian Resolution of the Naturalistic Fallacy', in *Teilhard Review*, Vol. 5, No. 1, 1970.

KENT, N. and DAVIES, D. R., 'Discipline in the Home and Intellectual Development', in *British Journal of Medical Psychology*, Vol. XXX, 1957.

KERR, M., *The People of Ship Street* (Routledge & Kegan Paul, 1958).

KLEIN, JOSEPHINE, *Samples from English Culture*, Vols I and II (Routledge & Kegan Paul, 1965).

KOESTLER, ARTHUR, *Act of Creation* (Hutchinson, 1964).

KOESTLER, ARTHUR, 'The Three Domains of Creativity', in J. F. T. Bugental (Ed.), *Challenges of Humanistic Psychology* (McGraw-Hill, 1967).

KOHN, M. L. and SCHOOLER, C., 'Class Occupation, and Orientation', in *American Sociological Review*, Vol. 34, October 1969.

LEACH, PENELOPE J., 'A Critical Study of the Literature Concerning Rigidity', in *British Journal of Social and Clinical Psychology*, No. 6, 1967.

LEWIS, R. and MAUDE, A., *The English Middle Classes* (Phoenix House, 1949).

LIPSET, S. M., *Political Man* (Heinemann, 1960).

LIPSET, S. M., *Political Man* (Doubleday, 1963).

LYTTON, H., *Creativity and Education* (Routledge & Kegan Paul, 1971).

MCCARRY, CHARLES, *Citizen Nader* (Cape, 1972).

MAGEE, BRYAN, *Towards 2,000* (MacDonald, 1965).

MASLOW, A. H., *Motivation and Personality* (Harper & Row, 1970).

MAY, PHILIP, 'Book Review', in *Spectrum*, Vol. 1, No. 3, 1969.

MILLER, DEREK, 'Youth and Creativity', in *New Society*, 13 February 1969.

MILLER, W. B., 'Lower-class Culture as a Generating Milieu for Gang Delin-quency', in *Journal of Sociological Issues*, Vol. 14, 1958.

MOGEY, J., *Family and Neighbourhood* (Oxford Univ. Press, 1956).

RAYNOR, JOHN, *The Middle Class* (Longmans, 1969).

ROKEACH, M., *Beliefs, Attitudes and Values* (Jossey-Bass, 1970).

ROSE, GORDON, *The Working Class* (Longmans, 1968).

ROSEN, B. C., 'The Achievement Syndrome', in *American Sociological Review*, Vol. XXI, 1956.

ROSENTHAL, M. J., *et al.* 'A Study of Mother–Child Relationships in the Emotional Disorders of Children', in *Genetic Psychology Monograph*, Vol. 60, No. 1, 1959.

SAMPSON, ANTHONY, *The New Anatomy of Britain* (Hodder & Stoughton, 1971).

SMITHERS, ALAN, 'Personality Patterns and Levels of Dogmatism', in *British Journal of Social and Clinical Psychology*, Vol. 9, 1970.

SPEARMAN, C. and JONES, L. W., *Human Ability: A Continuation of the Abilities of Man* (1927) (Macmillan, 1951).

SPINLEY, BETTY M., *The Deprived and the Privileged* (Routledge & Kegan Paul, 1953).

STRODTBECK, F. L., 'Family Interaction, Values and Achievement', in A. H. Halsey, J. Floud and C. A. Anderson (Eds), *Education, Economy and Society* (Collier-Macmillan, 1969).

SUGARMAN, BARRY, 'Teenage Boys at School', Unpublished Ph.D. thesis, Princeton, 1965.

TAWNEY, R. H., *Religion and the Rise of Capitalism* (Murray, 1948).

TORRANCE, E. P., *Guiding Creative Talent* (Prentice-Hall, 1962).

WEBER, MAX, *The Protestant Ethic and the Spirit of Capitalism* (Allen & Unwin, 1930).

WILLMOTT, PETER, *The Evolution of a Community* (Routledge & Kegan Paul, 1960).

WILLMOTT, PETER and YOUNG, M., *Family and Class in a London Suburb* (Routledge and Kegan Paul, 1960).

WOODWORTH, R. S., *Contemporary Schools of Psychology* (Ronald Press, 1931).

YOUNG, M. and WILLMOTT, P., *Family and Kinship in East London* (Rout-ledge & Kegan Paul, 1957).

ZWEIG, F., *Men in the Pits* (Gollancz, 1948).

ZWEIG, F., *The British Worker* (Gollancz, 1952).

ZWEIG, F., *The Worker in an Affluent Society* (Heinemann, 1961).

Chapter 10

Moral Embourgeoisement

The Privileged Bourgeoisie

The evidence supplied in the preceding six chapters could induce a violent reaction in the mind of an egalitarian reader for it may be interpreted as a eulogy of the middle classes at the expense of the working man and his family. However, it must be emphasized that the conclusions are based on irrefutable evidence, and it is just simply a fact, as Sugarman found in his study of teenagers, that high social status is correlated with a high moral reputation.

However, if any deduction is to be drawn, it is not that the middle classes are a superior breed. It is that the economic, educational, and cultural privileges which they enjoy should become the property of all. One does not need to be a saint to recognize that the harshness of economic deprivation can diminish the humanity of man. Nor does one need to become a Sister Theresa to recognize that poverty erodes that innate altruism which the privileged can display, because their lives are not circumscribed by the threat of unemployment, the fear of hire-purchase payments being defaulted, and the sense of inferiority they may feel before the self-confident, highly-educated, well-heeled, monied man of property.

This sense of harassment which the lower-status man feels is placed firmly in a sociological setting by two reputable researchers. Furstenburg in his discussion of the structural changes taking place in the working classes contrasts the process of embourgeoisement (whereby the working classes aspire to middle-class status (1)) with their debilitating experience of alienation—a state which Marx long ago described as being induced by the depersonalizing of men in industry whereby they become little more than economic and industrial commodities. This, Furstenburg continues, is made worse by the privatization, or withdrawal from social activities, characteristic of this social group. Runciman argues that social stratification is built on class, status (2), and power, and shows that the working man feels that he is deprived in each of these areas. Thus his alienation is exacerbated by this sense of isolation and impotence.

If the evidence points to any one overriding consideration it is surely that no country can be content with its political, industrial or educational system while some of its citizens live under those conditions of deprivation, which diminish their humanity and prevent the realization of their moral potential. Taken in this sense the evidence becomes more palatable. It points to the fact that our educational system should be engaged in introducing the best of our middle-class values to the whole community. This is not intended to be a patronizing implanting of 'grammar school values' so rightly derided by Jackson and Marsden, it is simply a recognition that the abundance of money, time, culture, concern and enlightened educative experiences, both in the home and the school, ought to be equitably distributed. At the moment it is mostly the privileged middle classes who enjoy them. They should, in the interests of morality if nothing else, be made available to all.

Vaizey argues, that:

> every child should have its own, separate well-heated bedroom; that it should have enough to eat; that it should have a certain degree of emotional security derived either from the presence of its parents, or from parent substitutes, who tend to be around in well-organized, moderately prosperous houses. Each child should be able to take part in intelligent and frank discourse, that the radio should occasionally be tuned to the music programme, that visits to the theatre and to the ballet and opera should be part of the normal activity of the household; that an annual holiday should be an event, but an expected event; that there should be books and newspapers lying around and a reasonable supply of well-cared-for pets; that the children should have access to gardens; that the parents should expect to be consulted about their child's progress at school, and that their own views, idiosyncratic though they may be, should be paid attention to by the schoolteachers and in particular by the headmistress and headmaster (3).

A critic might be tempted to dismiss it as an idealized picture, but it is difficult not to accept that it represents the democratic ideal to which most of us subscribe. Indeed one could go further and argue that the recent decision to raise the school leaving age, marks a further step in the direction of an ideal which includes tertiary education as a right for all and not a privilege for a minority. However, we must not lose sight of the fact that the process of moral embourgeoisement should not only bring an end to social inequity but also facilitate the dissemination of those values and attitudes which induce the growth of moral maturity. This immediately raises the question, 'Does our society display evidence of developing along the lines of embourgeoisement?' Are the working classes, in fact, slowly being assimilated into the middle classes?

Middle-class Wages for Workers

For almost twenty years now the work of Marsh, on social mobility, has made us aware of the fluidity of our social stratification in terms of occupation. More recently Davies has linked the notion of social mobility with changes in the political order of modern democracies and made us more aware both of this delicate interaction and of the complexity of such mobility. One cannot, he argues, speak of mobility in an unqualified sense. It must always be thought of in a wider context than that of occupation, for status and political change, are also relevant factors. However, whether one takes a simplistic or complex view of this phenomenon, it is clear that we live in a socially mobile society. If, as politicians in office would have us believe, we live in a society characterized by an expanding economy, we should expect this social mobility to follow an upward course. If then the process of embourgeoisement (4) can be crudely defined as one in which a working man enjoys a sustained middle-class income and by acquiring middle-class spending habits begins to feel that he is middle-class himself, then one would expect to find this as a feature of national life: and indeed it looks as if this may be so.

Wilson, discussing the possibility of a working-class culture existing in our technological society, concludes that 'it has been and is being abolished by the absorption of the working classes into the middle classes' (5). Thus although the fact of social mobility implies that it is possible either to rise or fall in the social scale it seems to be generally agreed that the present trend is an upward one, and hard empirical facts confirm this.

Roger Girod, for example, has recently investigated the dynamics of this phenomenon, and setting out to discover some of the little-known mechanics controlling it, he plotted status changes in the working lives of Genevans, on the basis of evidence supplied by the electoral roll. He found that status changes at the time of a first job, were invariably downwards, while those in mid-career were usually upwards. More important, however, was his discovery that while many working-class children rise, it is rare for a middle-class child to fall in status. He preferred not to generalize, since little is known about the mid-career changes, but he did commit himself to the view that increased educational facilities are responsible for this.

It is therefore not surprising to find that Abramson and Books discovered that those who were moving up the social scale believed that the barriers were disappearing, while the static or socially depressed respondents thought the opposite. Equally predictably they found that the former were satisfied with the social structure, while the latter were the malcontents, and formed the ranks from which social agitators emerged.

Enhanced educational opportunities augmented by mass media appear to give momentum to this apparent move towards classlessness, but other forces are also at work. Cyril Smith discovered that improved standards of living were accompanied by an urge for respectability. In addition Zweig found that the quality of working-class life was dramatically transformed when improved housing conditions were provided for workers. However, the case for embourgeoisement can perhaps be pleaded most strongly when working-class wages are considered.

Mayer is the strongest advocate of this view. He argues simply that the undoubted redistribution of income will lead inevitably to the workers attaining genuine middle-class status. His complex arguments, however, are distilled into his affirmation that 'the traditional dividing line between manual workers and white-collar employees no longer holds, because large segments of the working class now share a 'white-collar' style of life and many also accept middle-class values and beliefs' (6). Such is his thesis and quotations affirming that 'The proletarian wage-earners are becoming homogeneous with the white-collar workers and are joining the middle classes' (7) can be indefinitely duplicated from his work.

Mills also affirms that the narrowing of this income gap is blurring the class distinctions. His study of the white-collar workers led him to a colourful conclusion. He believed that a 'status-panic' will accompany the higher-status realization that this is happening. Then, he argued, they will 'seize upon minute distinctions as bases for status' (8). Less dramatic, but still supporting this view, Miller and Riesman agreed that as manual workers adopt a middle-class style of life the latter will change their behaviour and consumer patterns to retain a status differential.

Such arguments and evidence led Gavin Mackenzie to investigate the economic dimensions of embourgeoisement. Taking a 40% random sample from the 'one in a thousand' national sample based on the 1960 Census, he concluded that 'all differentials separating the blue- and white-collar groups have disappeared' (9). Hence on the basis of income alone it would seem that the top level of the working class is becoming commingled with the lowest level of the middle class. This point will be considered below when discussing the heterogeneous structure of the classes, but it thus looks as though a good case can be made in support of this argument.

However, as one would expect, there are critics of this view.

Richard Hamilton is possibly the most pungent advocate for the rejection of this thesis. In discussing the income difference between skilled and white-collared workers he has shown that the cleavage has been artificially enhanced. Then after making a more realistic assessment of the income difference between the blue- and white-collar workers, he concludes that 'The white-collar worker typically begins with a higher-income and this difference is maintained through to middle age' (10).

This too is the conclusion of Raynor, who approached the problem in a rather novel way. Discussing the middle-class lament over their alleged loss of status and income, and wryly observing that one of the most enduring myths about the middle class is the opinion that the differentials between them and the workers is narrowing, he appends some hard facts in the form of income tables. On the basis of these he comments 'Despite the myths, the middle classes, it would seem, have done quite well for themselves over the last fifty years' (11).

Hamilton's criticisms went further. He argued also that even if Mayer's calculations had been accurate it would still not have proved that the working classes were moving up the social scale. This point was taken further by Goldthorpe *et al.*, who in collaboration with Lockwood, argued that any change was merely an extension of the working class in an economically upward direction. This conclusion is also supported by Cohen who discovered that workers became more contented as they approached the middle-class level of income. Consequently, as they did not aspire to the middle-class norms which were not native to the work situation, this group displayed the least desire to encourage their children to go to college.

This point could also be emphasized by using the 'reference-group' as a tool. Runciman employed this to explain why the deprived workers, in the 1920s, did not revolt in England. The manual workers, he explained, only compared themselves economically with other workers. Thus the dissaffection which adverse comparison with the middle classes would have produced, did not emerge. While these reference groups remain, workers compare themselves with workers and are thus content.

To clinch this rebuttal of the embourgeoisement thesis reference can be made to the later research of Goldthorpe and his colleagues in Luton. Here, it was argued, was a community where the high wages paid to workers in the car industry, should blur the blue-collar and white-collar line of demarcation, but this study reached a simple but firm conclusion. Neither the work situation nor the social experience of the blue-collar worker could be regarded as middle class. As has already been noted above, the privatization of the manual group, which distinguishes them sharply from the middle-class group, was imposed by the limitations of the job. Shift work and long hours effectively prevent manual workers from following the traditional higher-status pursuits in organized clubs and associations.

The Heterogeneous Working Class

Such an apparent *impasse* can be resolved by reference to two possibilities. First, it seems that those who take income as the primary criterion affirm the process of embourgeoisement, while those who prefer to think of 'life-styles' do not. Second, the heteronomous nature of the working class could mean that the upper levels are entering the bourgeoisie only at a point of overlap.

Leaving the first consideration for a moment, we need to look more closely at the working class, for much of the embourgeoisement debate has revolved around the affluent, skilled craftsman, which immediately introduces the distinction between skilled and unskilled workers which Dahrendorf employed in his analysis of class conflict in industry. Consequently it is rightly said that 'It is foolish to generalize about the working class, treating it as a homogeneous lot' (12).

This basic dichotomy can be made more complex by adding further dimensions to it. Even Mayer, the ardent advocate of embourgeoisement admitted that 'we still have a sizable segment of workers who are not socially mobile, who live in a separate working-class culture' (13). Rose adds to this the view that while the upper levels of working men may be approximating to the higher-status style of life, the poorly paid are being further depressed. This was confirmed the following year by a 1969 survey of family expenditure, which showed that while the traditional middle classes became wealthier the earnings of low paid labourers lagged behind other manual workers. Consequently Rose extended this analysis and argued that the working class should be sub-divided into upper, middle, lower and deviant groups. When Gavin Mackenzie reviewed the class situation of manual workers he too had to conclude that 'Statements about *the* working class in post-capitalist societies are insufficiently precise. Indeed, there is evidence to suggest that, in some instances, differences *within* the blue-collar labour force may be greater than between segments of certain groups of white-collar workers' (14). All this, it should be noted, takes no cognisance of the ethnic factor which has long been a potent element in American working-class heteronomy and is fast becoming equally powerful in Britain (15). Leggett, for example, found that all his blue-collar workers were first or second generation immigrant stock; and Bennett Berger, arguing that the lowest socio-economic positions are occupied by immigrants, concludes, 'Our images of working-class life, are dominated by ethnic motifs' (16).

An Area of Overlap

The middle class is equally both socially and economically (17) heterogeneous. In a comprehensive academic appendix Josephine Klein draws together all the criteria for distinguishing the social classes and shows that there are at least seven categories in the middle class. As we shall see later, the lowest level here is made up of clerks who approximate to the highest working-class level. Hence it is upon this group that the embourgeoisement thesis concentrates.

Before turning to examine this possible area of overlap a further contributory factor appears to be promoting the process of embourgeoisement. This is simply that the lower levels of the middle classes appear to be increasingly socially depressed in their lifestyle. The Pahls, for example, despite the limited sample used, appear to be indicating a real trend in declining managerial and professional aspirations when they observe that 'What we may be describing is the beginning of a middle-class reaction against competition' (18). Some attribute this to the introduction of working-class graduates into the professions. Teaching and medicine, for example, now appear to reflect the methods of the workers, for it is there that the strike (the workers' ultimate weapon in negotiation (19)) has recently been used for the first time. This is what Leslie Davison had in mind when he concluded that 'working-class culture is spreading upwards through society' (20).

We saw in an earlier chapter that the deferred-gratification pattern was an essential personal quality in a mature moral agent. There the picture was painted as brightly as possible and the middle-class penchant for this was emphasized. Now a qualification must be added. Upwardly mobile members of the working class appear to have brought some present orientation with them.

If it is objected that the earlier argument, stressing that future orientation was essential to enable a child to pass successfully through the élitist educational system, contradicts this, Barry Sugarman presents some salutary evidence to the contrary. He hypothesized that one characteristic of the middle-class pupil role was deferred gratification. Whether his findings are disquieting or not depends upon one's ideology, but simply expressed he found that a contra-pupil role had replaced the traditional pupil role. Now even middle-class teenagers emphasized immediate gratification. This, says Sugarman, suggests that a youth culture is entrenched in society in which teenagers support each other in their rejection of the 'middle-class' school values. Thus a 'teenage' role appears to have replaced that of the 'pupil' role and inverted its values in the process, which necessarily leads to a consideration of the 'counter-culture' which will need to be discussed later.

Global explanations for this trend are not difficult to find. It may be ascribed to the hire-purchase economy, which inevitably emphasises present gratification. In his study of the young offender, West endorses this and confirms the argument linking present gratification with immorality by concluding that 'Increased crime in recent years is probably linked to the developing "openness" and casualness of our society and its emphasis upon 'have-now-pay-later' consumption' (21). Second, it may be argued, the Welfare State is sapping us of our sense of responsibility and, consequently, 'no one cares, no one saves, no one bothers' (22). The political orientation of this view was illuminated by John Davies, the Secretary of Trade and Industry, and formerly head of the CBI who proclaimed in the House of Commons, 'We believe the whole need of this country is to gear its policies to the great majority of the people who are not lame ducks, and do not need a hand, and who are quite capable of looking after their own interests. National decadence,' he continued, 'is a consequence of treating the whole country as though they were lame ducks' (23).

Thus in a welfare state, characterized by a hire-purchase economy, it is not surprising that present gratification characterizes some segments of the middle class, and also the teenage aspirants to it.

To support this view one can refer to Brian Inglis's study of public morality where he argues that the 'umclass' (i.e. the formal middle-class establishment) represents a value system which is becoming increasingly shrugged off. Thus our private lives are now characterized by gratification, hedonism, egocentricity and materialism. Since, for the sake of appearances, our public conduct attempts to conceal this, we have the unedifying spectacle of moral schizophrenia undermining our social life.

A recent study from Israel confirms this. In testing a series of hypotheses to explain the increase of delinquency amongst higher-status teenagers. Shoham and his colleagues, contrasted middle-class and working-class adolescents on probation. He found that both groups were characterized by a desire to seek the immediate fulfilment of their sensual desires. The only difference seemed to be that each desired those things which their sub-cultures valued most highly.

However, it is clear that the lower level of the middle classes is subtly changing. One mark of a profession, for example, was its abhorrence of strikes, yet now doctors, nurses and teachers have all displayed a taste for this activity. Again, it must be remembered that every social movement is complex, and this discontent could well arise from the lower-status entrants into the higher-status occupation. As Josephine Klein has noted 'one classic condition for anomie (is) a marked increase in income' (24). But this anomic condition of the new bourgeoisie, marked by individuation, could lead to corporate organized activity to alleviate this aspect of alienation.

Pahl is emerging as an undisputed authority on the structure of urban life, and in a penetrating survey of the interrelationships existing between income, work, status and housing in cities he has included a diagram which vividly displays this confluence of the two social classes. There, in answer to the question 'For whom are cities built?' he shows that the lower salaried white-collar worker has to make do with poor quality private housing, while the higher wage-earning skilled manual worker exerts pressure through his new increased spending power and enjoys the best of public housing. Thus the privatized affluent worker appears to be a new dominant figure in British social life; so much so that when Paul submitted his report, on contemporary Anglican Church life, he reminded the hierarchy that they had to take cognisance of this fact (25). Indeed, so self-conscious had these affluent workers become in Luton that Goldthorpe *et al.* found that they thought of themselves as a class situated roughly between the lower and higher levels. For these the old dichotomy of 'us' and 'them' had disappeared.

It thus seems that Runciman's reference group thesis has sharpened. The affluent worker sustains his status by reference to affluent workers, and if anything, detaches himself from the old working class. Privatization, however, prevents him from entering fully into higher-status social groups, for while clerks work thirty-eight hours a week, these workers needed to toil for over fifty hours to attain their level of income. 'Affluence', it seems, 'has been achieved only at a price' (26). This is made worse, as Shostak found, by the fact that most blue-collar workers are involved in what can only be called the corrosive humiliation of tedious, repetitive, meaningless tasks. This not only detracts from the high wages they supply, but necessarily leads them to take an instrumental rather than a (typical middle-class) expressive view of their work. In non-technical jargon this means that while artisans tend to view labour as little more than an instrument for obtaining money, professional men can so express themselves, through their occupations, that they feel society benefits from the application of their personal expertise.

Hence, despite pressure from ambitious wives, who are not subject to these erosions of time, simple logistics prevent many affluent workers from entering the middle class. Although, of course, many do, and the sociological problem presented by this fact is the need to explain precisely which societal pressures produce this change. However, light can be thrown on this by a consideration of the position of the lowest level of white-collar worker—the clerk. The area of overlap becomes highlighted here.

Gavin Mackenzie has shown that 'The similarities between clerks and craftsmen, especially those economically based, should outweigh the dissimilarities' (27). He qualifies this by arguing that the differences are rooted in the social structure; but even this criterion is disappearing.

Lockwood, who is an invaluable source of information on the lower middle class, claimed that clerical work was only distinguished from unskilled labour because of the training it demanded and the greater security it provided. However, Zweig reported that some affluent workers rued the fact that their sons were not strong enough to take up manual jobs and so had to resort to clerical work. Then, as Lockwood further found, the marriage ties of such men with working-class wives make it impossible to distinguish between the two classes. This was endorsed by his reference to the fact that of the men who began as clerks 40% entered the professional strata, while 30% reverted to manual work. The former, it emerged, displayed future orientation, married later and had clear middle-class aspirations. Thus the differences do appear to be *rooted in social structures*. The others, as Stacey suggested from her work in Banbury, form a 'lower frontier'. It is this area of overlap which, she said, could with equal justification be called 'lower middle class' or 'superior working class' (see figure 1).

Thus it seems clear that the economic commingling of clerks and craftsmen is more than the extension of the working class, as Rose supposed. It is much more likely to be a process of that 'normative convergence', i.e. the process whereby a new group adopts the new consensus as a norm, which Goldthorpe *et al.* confirmed. It must be remembered, however, that this is based almost entirely on the criterion of income, and not upon the 'life-style' displayed. Thus it is perfectly possible to argue that in this economic sense 'The term *mainstream* working class denotes a category of workers whose occupation is disproportionately white-collar' (28).

Differences in Life-style

If then income is the sole criterion, the hypothesis of embourgeoisement could be sustained and many manual workers would now be considered as at least having a foothold in the middle classes, but Goldthorpe and Lockwood destroyed the naïviety of this argument. Despite their view that normative convergence was a reality, they stressed that the two groups would remain distinct for, with the

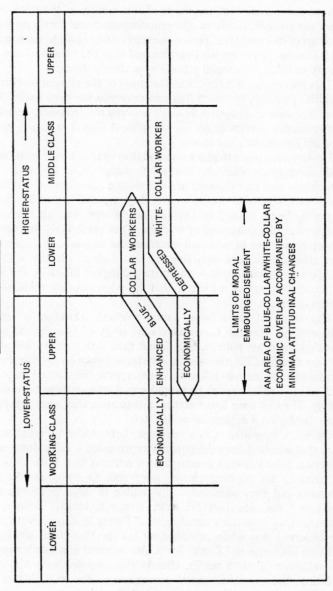

Figure 1. The boundaries of moral embourgeoisement

THE BOUNDARIES OF MORAL EMBOURGEOISEMENT

SOCIAL CLASS

LOWER-STATUS · HIGHER-STATUS

WORKING-CLASS · MIDDLE CLASS

LOWER · UPPER · LOWER · MIDDLE CLASS · UPPER

ECONOMICALLY ENHANCED · BLUE-COLLAR WORKERS

ECONOMICALLY DEPRESSED · WHITE-COLLAR WORKER

LIMITS OF MORAL EMBOURGEOISEMENT

AN AREA OF BLUE-COLLAR/WHITE-COLLAR ECONOMIC OVERLAP ACCOMPANIED BY MINIMAL ATTITUDINAL CHANGES elimination of income differentials, other more subtle factors emerge (29).

Such confirmation of the thesis of this section of the book overrides the considerations of the embourgeoisement thesis presented in terms of income alone. Hence one may return again to the research of Kohn and Schooler who emphasized that the value-systems and life-styles of the two social groups were clearly distinct.

This also comes out clearly in the study of the affluent worker, by Goldthorpe *et al.*, to which frequent reference has been made. *They show that once a distinction is made between the economic, relational and normative aspects of his life the affluent worker is clearly not an aspirant for middle-class status.*

He may earn more than a white-collar worker but he is relationally and normatively distinct. His relationships with his wife (30), workmates and management are not middle class, nor are his social relationships outside work, where they are still essentially lower status by being limited to kin and neighbours, and his friendship web is primarily composed of workers. Thus predictably he does not expect promotion or personal advancement at work. In conformity with this pattern, not only does he not seek to identify with the middle classes but displays an entirely different life-style, the most important feature of which is that he possesses few middle-class norms or values.

This study of the affluent Luton workers, however, is not an isolated case. Hannah Gavron's classic study of housebound wives revealed the same pattern. She found that, although working-class nuclear families (i.e. the new lower-status upwardly mobile home) were similar to their middle-class counterparts, they lacked the social and cultural skills needed to extend social relationships beyond the family. Thus by their lower-status privatization they were prevented from displaying a higher-status life-style.

David Downes also adds his evidence here. Although rejecting the view that working-class delinquency represented a sub-culture, as in America, he did discern one important relevant fact. With affluence, he argued, the working classes were able to enjoy middle-class pleasures but they were culturally unable to develop middle-class goals and the attendant life-style. Hence hedonistic delinquency resulted. One important conclusion of Farley is also relevant here. He observed that while privatization led the blue-collar worker to enhance his home and family life it also exposed him much more to the influence of mass media. Clearly this, coupled with his social isolation, has enormous moral consequences, for such citizens are forced into the anomic normlessness of alienation.

Returning to the affluent worker for a moment, Bennett Berger, like Goldthorpe studied affluent car workers. His sample was chosen because a large number of them moved, with a new factory, from Richmond, California, to the suburb of Milpitas. He showed clearly that the expected metamorphosis from a working-class to a middle-class life-style did not take place. Voting habits did not change (31). Privatization remained. There was no swing to religion and their sense of class-identity was unimpaired. They benefited economically but in terms of life-style there was no change. Yet a curious ambivalence remained. The privatized worker believed that class differences were diminishing. Lockwood's researches, for example, led him to conclude that 'Because of his social isolation he (the privatized affluent worker) may be more exposed to impersonal influences, and given his influence and privatization, the view that class differences are on the wane is a plausible one for him to maintain' (34).

This reference to voting patterns and religious activity is important here and both have been confirmed elsewhere. McKenzie and Silver, for example, studied working-class conservative voters in order to discover whether they formed a sub-culture within the working class. They found that they did not. By no criterion at all, income, age, sex, privatization, religious belief, or trade-union membership, were differences betwen the political left and right workers discernible. All displayed a lower-status life-style. Bechhofer (a contributor to Goldthorpe's work in Luton) says simply:

> I have no reason to change an earlier statement in the study, *The Affluent Worker*, that affluent workers retain 'important areas of common social experience which are still fairly distinctively working class; that *specifically middle-class norms are not widely followed nor middle-class life-styles consciously emulated* and that assimilation into middle-class society is neither in progress nor in the main, a desired objective' (33).

The term privatization is not intended to be a stigma, for, as has been shown, the attendant concentration on home life may be a practical advantage to society as a whole. One benefit which appears to accrue from it, is a renewed interest in child welfare. Toomey, for example, has found that working-class parents with high aspirations for their sons, tend also to be privatized. Thus their social isolation leads to a focus on familial conditions. However, this conflict with Cohen's findings, could perhaps be resolved by the Jackson and Marsden conclusion, reached when they studied working-class families with such educational aspirations. 'Were we looking', they mused, 'not so much at upper working-class homes, as sunken middle-class families? Families which had come down in the world seemed more ready to re-invest their energies in the education of their children' (34).

Thus in its crude economic form the embourgeoisement thesis must be rejected. Then the distinct life-styles of the two social groups confirm that the arguments presented in this section are still valid. Of course, the affluent workers constitute a new class, virtually living in a normless limbo inelegantly called a 'classless inegalitarianism' (35). With white-collar workers they share the same occupational and educational aspirations for their young. Companionate marriages, family-centredness and a sense of themselves as belonging neither to 'us' nor to 'them', are common to both groups. The possession of motor cars and well furnished homes, replete with labour-saving devices, obviously affect the lives people lead. All this evidence from the car workers in Luton must not be allowed to blur the educational implications of social stratification. Since the middle class ranges from clerks to executives, and the lower class rises from council labourers to affluent workers, there is bound to be some economic overlap, but as even futurologists now agree 'The working class would never disappear' (36). Thus the last word may be left with Marquand, who observed that in the light of twentieth-century social and political development, during which the gulf between the classes has narrowed considerably, 'The surprising thing is not the extent to which the gulf has narrowed, but the extent to which it has remained'.

Values as the Criteria of Embourgeoisement

Therefore it is clear that educational opportunities provide the means whereby a lower-status child becomes upwardly, socially mobile. Of course, many socio-economic traits remain unchanged in this process. Hoggart pointed to some of them when referring to the working-class scholarship-boy who rises into the professional middle classes. 'He is unhappy', says Hoggart, 'in a society in which the toffee-apples are not accurately given to those who work hardest nor even to the most intelligent; but in which disturbing imponderables like "character", "ability to mix" and "boldness" have a way of tipping the scales' (37). Nevertheless, lower-status children can rise in the social hierarchy for, as Anthony Sampson has recently shown, graduates now hold power in Britain, and graduate status produces an assured rapid, upward mobility for a low-status child.

Over a decade ago Young described a nightmare meritocracy in which clever children of every social class would be selected and segregated so effectively that the rest of society would be branded as inferior. All this was to be achieved without recourse to the bizarre techniques envisaged by Aldous Huxley. Thus, despite the religious and ethnic structural barriers to social mobility, which Merton has enumerated, it seems that this upheaval can take place without any overt signs of disturbance. Young and Willmott, for example, discovered this in their East London working-class families. 'Social ascent achieved by means of school does not raise any more of a barrier within the family than social ascent achieved by other means' (38). Indeed, they later observed that this social mobility only produces that concomitant geographical mobility necessary to follow high-status employment. Thus familial contact is maintained, provided, of course, that the children marry spouses from the same social class.

Naturally, such children came from homes which provided them with adequate motivation. Zweig, for example, found that his workers were ambitious for their children and said 'We want to give them a better chance than we had'. As one would expect, these homes were characterized by the warm, realistic relationships we observed earlier to be characteristic of higher-status families. Douvan and Adelson confirm this, and add that upwardly mobile boys were reared in a way which encouraged the growth of achievement and autonomy.

Such success stories, however, can have their flaws. Raymond Williams has graphically portrayed the most obvious one in his description of such social mobility as 'the ladder version of society'. The ladder, he says, offers a chance to climb, but you have to *climb it alone*. The autonomy required can easily become social isolation, and this is most apparent if the motivation to climb is augmented by a desire to escape from lower-status life. Thus, in their study of successful, upwardly mobile American business men, Warner and Abegglen found that they were 'characterized by an inability to form intimate relations and are consequently often socially isolated' (39).

Josephine Klein sums up this argument with characteristic succinctness by noting that 'If the child has learned persistence, self-control, independence and his own value as an individual, he has been successfully socialized for high achievement' (40). Those moral qualities which were outlined in the preceding chapters are also, it seems, a warranty of personal as well as moral, success. How Samuel Smiles would have loved to have learned this! However, the delicate balance which can lead a child either into autonomous success, or the lonely striving of an isolate, serve to remind us of the caution with which Girod approached this subject. But we may at least conclude that increased educational opportunities, allied with the home conditions which will enable a child to maximize on them, are the means whereby the *élite* of the working class may become absorbed into the middle classes. However, it does not follow that the process of embourgeoisement facilitates this. Before social assimilation ends the privatization and realizes the social aspirations of the rising blue-collar worker, parent–child relationships are basically unchanged. Privatization can intensify the relationships between them, since privatized families are compelled to increase their mutual emotional demands. At this stage basic values have not changed. Personal aspirations are still circumscribed by social-class limitations and the more intimate relationships between parents and children may do little more than perpetuate working-class values and attitudes.

Education and Mass Media

Improved educational opportunities thus appear to be one source of the notion that society is in the process of embourgeoisement, and these, it seems, are extending. Hitherto limited to the teenager, these opportunities are being increasingly seized by older working-class aspirants for graduate status. Every university now has a swelling number of mature undergraduates, whose low social status prevented them from graduating earlier.

The Open University was established deliberately to facilitate this and can now proudly report that 'More skilled workers are applying to join' (41). Equally, less mature under-achievers, are also going on to graduate. Sussex University, for example have a special entry scheme for unqualified early school-leavers, who display academic ability. When asked why they had not graduated earlier these young adults, from unskilled and semi-skilled homes said, 'My family needed the money', or 'Nobody at home expected me to stay at school' (42). Nevertheless this is just a tip of the iceberg. Floud *et al.* are amongst a host of researchers who have concluded that although educational opportunities are enhanced, it is invariably the middle classes, who by their attitudes rather than their talents, benefit from them, and Little and Westergaard confirmed this from their research. While showing that class differentials in the access to selective secondary schooling had diminished in the 'fifties they had to conclude that 'social inequalities in educational opportunity may even have widened in recent years, rather than narrowed'. Thus even now the number of undergraduates from working-class homes is disproportionate to their population size.

Because of this disappointing conclusion others have looked elsewhere to find an educative process inducing embourgeoisement, and claim to have found it in the influence of modern mass media. Just after the war Warner and Henry dismissed these as fantasy problem solvers, but they are taken more seriously today. Peck and

Havighurst, for example, conclude that 'they actually had the added function of repeating and reinforcing the conventional morals of middle-class America' (43). This view was concurrently endorsed by Lenski in his analysis of the religious factor in the appeal of mass media. The most powerful advocate of this process is Hoggart, who in his two volumes concerned with society and literature, like McLuhan, reveals a favourable impression of the media. Naturally guarding himself against the charge of not recognizing that philistinism and commercial interests can prostitute their function, he still sees mass media as the agents whereby the genuinely classless society can be realized. Thus he concluded that 'The mass media must, whether consciously or not, work towards a culturally classless society (44)'.

Of course, the subject is not so simple as such observations would suggest. Sampson suggests that our deeply divisive class structure is exacerbated by the tendency of national papers to polarize around either middle-class or working-class readers.

Embourgeoisement and Morality

This apparently ineradicable dichotomy of society has enormous implications for national life, covering political, industrial, social and educational areas of activity. Sampson, for example, believes that this continuing class division perpetuates the problem of involving workers and voters in the processes of government and administration. Apart from the phalanx of able local councillors, who may rise through the political hierarchy until they attain national eminence, the working classes are fundamentally apathetic. This is why Worsthorne goes to great lengths to destroy what he calls this 'socialist myth' of proletarist rule. Consequently he argues with considerable force that even the Labour Party is recognizing the political incorrigibility of the masses, who seem disposed to see no further than the next unrealistic pay-rise. Some may shy at his final conclusion that in order to realize socialist ideals the influence of the uninformed many must be offset by conferring more power on an educated *élite*. However, recent industrial unrest under a Labour Government make it difficult to fault him on his primary argument that class divisions baulk the means whereby their inequity may be ended.

Sampson's view that such an *impasse* results from having middle-class members of parliament who cannot communicate with the voting proletariat can also be extended to industry. Here one may argue that the social barriers between management and worker is a primary cause of unnecessary industrial unrest—a point which was elaborated in the previous chapter on moral dynamism. Sturmthal also adds his evidence that this is a problem in both capitalist and socialist states. Workers' Councils, he argues, are theoretically ideal, but they fail in practice. They fall down, quite simply, because they have to straddle two sub-cultures, and because they seek to protect workers' interests, while participating in management decisions, they are emasculated.

Such a dichotomy also appears in a society characterized by extended home ownership. As multiform private housing estates were erected it looked as though the social distinctions might become blurred. Orlans, for example, speaks gushingly of this trend in Stevenage as a revival of the village where different social strata lived together. Yet just after the war, in the era of the new towns, Glass observed that 'The mere shortening of the physical distance between different social groups can hardly bring them together, unless, at the same time, the social distance between them is also reduced (45).

Middle-class inhabitants of lower-priced private housing estates today must surely sympathize with this view. Social differences are not dissolved. As affluent workers move in, so middle-class inhabitants move out. As an ex-inhabitant of such an estate the writer can testify to the veracity of this view and subscribe entirely to Pahl's findings, in 'A Two Class Village'. No amount of social or conversational goodwill seems able to surmount the barriers erected by education, life-style, values and recreational activities. Such a phenomenon is now recognized to be world-wide in its ramification. Byrne, for example, has found that in Hawaii, India, Mexico and America it is still true that the more attitudes and values a stranger is seen to have in common with oneself the more attractive he is likely to appear. Hence it is more probable that a personal relationship will be established with him rather than with a compatriot whose life-style is different.

In the light of such experiences Mao Tse-tung seems excessively idealistic. He believes that socialism would saturate society through 'close contact with the masses' (46). The only effect proximity appears to have in the West is that of intensifying tension and hostility, or at least ossifying class consciousness. Consequently Pahl points out that since the war 'urban sociologists had to struggle against these ideologies' (47).

This is equally true of the school situation. Oppenheim's research led him to conclude that 'Middle-class and working-class children do not mix much with one another. They tend to form mutually exclusive cliques at school and the parents tend to encourage them in this, and to urge upon them a selection of friends who conform to their own class values.' This, as one would expect, produces tension for working-class children, for character reputations at school depend not so much on a child's social class as on the degree of his conformity to the middle-class mores of the school. The crucial point for any moral educator lies in the fact that relative affluence conceals these different life-styles. Thus while the basic moral dichotomy remains, the superficial distinctions (e.g. well-cut quality clothing, cigar smoking, wine drinking, continental holidays and the erosion of class accents) are being blurred by educational and financial advantages. Thus deceived, educators may be unaware of the fundamental moral differences existing within the same class-room filled with clean, well-nourished, neatly-clothed children from both social groups.

The educational task lying before us now will be discussed in the next section of the book. For the moment it only needs to be re-iterated that moral education may partly consist of ensuring that the middle-class values and life-style should be inculcated by the schools.

It is possible to parody this view, as does Klein when she suggests that the ideal personality is often 'thought of as the middle-class personality with all the disadvantages removed'. But as Lewis and Maude less wryly say of the middle class they studied, 'The moment a man rose into them, influences were at work to civilize and change (him) for service to the community as a whole' (48).

This ascent is clearly both desirable and possible. Hoggart is the most obvious example of such a transition, and his works contain a sensitive, documented account of this progress, but this educational task will be fraught with difficulty. Shoshak in his depressing account of the American worker's situation, highlights one facet of this. 'The working class', he concludes, 'makes the least best use of its life-enhancing possibilities' (49). Leaving aside considerations of intelligence, it is surely the task of moral education to ensure that this tendency is reversed. Then *both* social classes will not only enjoy the life-styles currently limited to higher-status families, but will also possess in a more mature form those moral traits outlined above.

REFERENCES

1 According to Goldthorpe and Lockwood (1963) there are three phases in the process: (1) privatization, i.e. isolation from other workers; (2) aspiration, i.e. attempting to adopt middle-class norms; (3) assimilation, i.e. acceptance by the middle classes. Goldthorpe *et al.* (1967) stress that until accepted such a worker is still essentially working class. Blondel (1963) made the point that many workers consider themselves to be middle class when they are not. And Mogey (1956) made the depressing observation that they have only moved from poverty and kinship into relative affluence and loneliness (p. 124).

2 It should be noted that 'status' and 'class' are not technically synonymous.

Watson (1964), for example, found that although miners were classified with comparatively well-paid occupations in some areas of Scotland it was a despised activity. Hence miners had lower status than their social class warranted. A similar standard example of this in reversed form, is the situation of a City Councillor who may be a lowly working man. Here his status is higher than his social class would suggest. This is discussed in Bendix and Lipset (1953).

3 Vaizey (1971), p. 787. But note that Jackson (1968) and Davies (1965) both plead for the retention of some working-class value to cement an egalitarian society.

4 Goldthorpe and Lockwood (1963) coined this term to describe the technical process whereby blue-collar workers were accepted into the existing middle classes.

5 Wilson (1964), p. 42.

6 Mayer (1963), p. 467.

7 Mayer (1956), p. 78.

8 Mills (1951), p. 72.

9 MCKENZIE (1967), p. 38; cf. Bugler (1970). 'Comparison of car workers and teachers is remarkable for the (financial) similarities it reveals, not the differences. The Coventry teachers run a kind of siege economy of the middle class' (p. 9).

10 Hamilton (1963), p. 369. Support for this is also supplied by Parsler (1970) who showed that even in egalitarian Australia the white-collar wage median was 16% above those of manual workers. For those who see only the affluence of workers Townsend (1958) and Coates and Silburn (1970) remind us that the half century of advance, since Rowntree (1922) studied the urban poor, has not eliminated squalor and deprivation from our society.

11 Raynor (1969), p. 58.

12 Leggett (1968), p. 3. This is the basic weakness of Shoshak (1969). Despite an early reference to the need to assess working-class skill (p. 37), he still generalizes without reference to this essential qualification.

13 Mayor (1963), p. 467.

14 MacKenzie (1970), p. 342. Hence religion can be a divisive factor, as in Northern Ireland where Catholic and Protestant working-class members are not only clearly distinct but also violently opposed to each other. And what Segal and Schaffner (1968) call the 'ethnic class problem' means that the middle-class Negro does not identify with the white bourgeoisie, even though racial assimilation is taking place. Note too that skilled men are turning to unskilled better-paid work as a homeostatic process.

15 That this is also true of Britain is indicated by the growth of 'Powellism', in which Enoch Powell, MP, advocates the repatriation of all recent immigrants before our working-class culture collapses.

16 Berger (1968), p. 95.

17 Parsler (1970), found that the median earnings of the professional and executive Australians were 71% above those of the white-collar workers. There is, it seems, disparity even in egalitarian societies.

18 Pahl and Pahl (1971), p. 262.

19 Raynor (1969) makes the point that middle-class unions do not have the same power to harm society, but growing militancy is changing this.

20 Davison (1969), p. 115.

21 West (1967), p. 83.

22 Boyson (1971), p. 146.

23 *Guardian,* 5 November 1970.

24 Klein (1967), p. 271.
25 Paul (1964), p. 48. 'A new and dominant figure in the social pattern is the young husband earning about £1,000 a year, saddled with a thirty year mortgage for the semi-detached he is buying, paying off weekly for his furniture, saving for a second-hand car and too preoccupied with painting the window frames and decorating the bathroom at week-ends to go to church.'
26 Goldthorpe *et al.* (1969), p. 58. 'In addition a considerable gap remains between the two occupational groups with regard to that traditionally middle-class pursuit—membership of voluntary associations. Excluding unions, over half of the manual group did not belong to a single club or association. This high level of privatization can be explained largely in terms of the limitations imposed by the nature of the jobs in which these people are involved. Shift work and long hours go a long way to precluding any effective form of social life on the middle class pattern.'
27 MacKenzie (1967), p. 41.
28 Leggett (1968), p. 15.
29 Rawin (1965) shows how income is the sole criterion in a socialist state. We do not know, as Reiss (1961) found, precisely how occupational prestige is related to social class. But on one point Pahl (1970) is emphatic. In a utopia of economic equality, 'different occupations are allocated different prestige *with distinct and separate styles of life*' (p. 56) (My italics.)
30 Bott (1964) found that marital roles were stylized, and Komarovsky (1962) added that after the birth of the first child there was marital role diffusion. Males became involved in work and sport, while wives became preoccupied with the trivia of household duties and rituals.
31 Goldthorpe (1968) rejected this political version of embourgeoisement when he found that neither affluence nor home ownership reduced the Luton workers' support for the Labour party.
32 Lockwood (1966).
33 Bechhofer (1971), p. 708. (My italics.)
34 Jackson and Marsden (1962), pp. 53 and 55.
35 Goldthorpe (1969), p. 172.
36 Davie (1971), p. 25.
37 Hoggart (1957), p. 247.
38 Young and Wilmott (1957), p. 153.
39 Warner and Abbegglen (1955), p. 194.
40 Klein (1967), p. 38.
41 *Guardian*, 18 August 1971.
42 Church (1970), p. 14.
43 Peck and Havighurst (1964), p. 25.
44 Hoggart (1970), Vol. 1, p. 273.
45 Glass (1948), p. 190.
46 Mao Tse-tung (1967), p. 179.
47 Pahl (1970), p. 119.
48 Klein (1967), p. 374.
49 Shoshak (1969), p. 290. Finding this social dichotomy in his research conclusions Oppenheim (1956) concluded that it was not sufficient to attribute specific attitudes, values and attitudes to one social class of school children. A definitive picture revealed that the seemingly unrelated attitudes and values did actually 'hang together' and form a coherent cluster in each sub-culture. This may account for the durability of life-styles reported by Willmott and Young (1960). When lower status families from Bethnal Green were rehoused in a suburb, little sub-cultural change occurred. The

life-style remained basically the same, except that the geographical isolation caused some disintegration of the working-class kinship web. A further change was induced by modified marital roles. It was found that the husband's supportive role became one of complementarity with the wife (cf. Bott (1964)) and this led to a restricted form of familial privatization.

Bibliography

ABRAMSON, P. R. and BOOKS, J. W., 'Social Mobility and Political Attitudes'. Paper delivered to 1969 Midwest Political Science Association (Reported in *New Society*, 19 June 1969, as 'Mobile Youth and the Open Society').

BAIN, G. S., *The Growth of White Collar Unionism* (Oxford Univ. Press, 1970).

BECHHOFER, FRANK, 'A Sociological Portrait: Income', in *New Society*, 14 October 1971.

BENDIX, R. and LIPSET, S. M., *Class, Status and Power* (Routledge & Kegan Paul, 1967).

BERGER, B. M., *Working Class Suburb* (Univ. California Press, 1968).

BLONDEL, J., *Voters, Parties and Leaders* (Penguin, 1963).

BOTT, ELIZABETH, *Family and Social Class* (Tavistock, 1964).

BOYSON, RHODES (Ed.), *Down With the Poor* (Churchill Book Club, 1971).

BROGAN, C., 'Nothing to Lose But Their Bourgeoisie', in *Daily Telegraph*, 16 January 1971.

BUGLER, JEREMY, 'The White Collar Poor', in *Observer*, 11 January 1970.

BYRNE, D., *et al.*, 'The Ubiquitous Relationships, Attitude, Similarity and Attraction Across Culture Study', in *Human Relations*, Vol. 24, No. 3, 1971.

CHURCH, MICHAEL, 'The Drop-Outs Who Went on to Graduate', in *Times Educational Suppl.*, 18 September 1970.

COATES, K. and SILBURN, R., *Poverty: The Forgotten Englishman* (Penguin, 1970).

COHEN, E. G., 'Parental Factors in Education Mobility'. Unpublished Ph.D. thesis, Harvard 1958.

DAHRENDORF, R., *Class and Class Conflict in Industrial Society* (Routledge & Kegan Paul, 1959).

DAVIE, MICHAEL, 'Futurology', in *Observer*, 3 January 1971.

DAVIES, HARRY, *Culture and the Grammar School* (Routledge & Kegan Paul, 1965).

DAVIES, I., *Social Mobility and Social Change* (Macmillan, 1970).

DAVISON, LESLIE, *Sender and Sent* (Epworth Press, 1969).

DOUVAN, E. and EDELSON, J., 'The Psycho-dynamics of Social Mobility in Adolescent Boys', in *Journal of Abnormal and Social Psychology*, Vol. LVI, 1958.

DOWNES, D. M., *The Delinquent Solution* (Routledge & Kegan Paul, 1966).

Family Benefits and Pensions (HMSO, 1971).

Family Expenditure Survey (HMSO, 1969).

FARLEY, RICHARD, 'Television and the Consumption Habits and Aspirations of a Selected Sample of Adolescents'. Unpublished M.Ed. thesis, Leicester 1969.

FLOUD, J., HALSEY, A. H. and MARTIN, F., *Social Class and Educational Opportunity* (Heinemann, 1956).

FURSTENBURG, FRIEDRICH, 'Structural Changes in the Working Class: A Situational Study of Workers in the West German Chemical Industry', in J. A. Jackson (Ed.), *Social Stratification* (Cambridge Univ. Press, 1968).

GAVRON, HANNAH, *The Captive Wife* (Routledge & Kegan Paul, 1966).

GIROD, ROGER, 'Mobilité Sequentielle', in *Revue Française de Sociologie*, Vol. 12, No. 1, 1971.

GLASS, R. (Ed.), *The Social Background of a Plan* (Routledge & Kegan Paul, 1948).

GOLDTHORPE, J. H. and LOCKWOOD, D., 'Affluence and the British Class Structure', in *Sociological Review*, Vol. 4, 1963.

GOLDTHORPE, J. H., *et al.* 'The Affluence Worker and the Thesis of Embourgeoisement', in *Sociology*, Vol. 1, No. 1, 1967.

GOLDTHORPE, J. H., *et al. The Affluent Worker: Political Attitudes and Behaviour* (Cambridge Univ. Press, 1968).

GOLDTHORPE, J. H., *et al., The Affluent Worker in the Class Structure* (Cambridge Univ. Press, 1969).

HAMILTON, RICHARD, 'The Income Difference Between Skilled and White Collar Workers', in *British Journal of Sociology*, Vol. 14, 1963.

HAVIGHURST, R. J. and TABA, H., *Adolescent Character and Personality* (John Wiley, 1963).

HOGGART, RICHARD, *Speaking to Each Other*, Vol. 1—*About Society*; Vol. 2—*About Literature* (Chatto & Windus, 1970).

HUXLEY, A. L., *Brave New World* (Chatto & Windus, 1932).

INGLIS, BRIAN, *Private Conscience: Public Morality* (André Deutsch, 1964).

JACKSON, BRIAN, *Working Class Community* (Routledge & Kegan Paul, 1968).

KLEIN, JOSEPHINE, *Samples of English Cultures*, 2 Vols (Routledge & Kegan Paul, 1967).

KOHN, M. L. and SCHOOLER, S., 'Class, Occupation and Orientation', in *American Sociological Review*, Vol. 34, No. 5, 1970.

KOMAROVSKY, MIRRS, *Blue-Collar Marriage* (Random House, 1962).

LEGGETT, J. C., *Class, Race and Labour* (Oxford Univ. Press, 1968).

LENSKI, GERHARD, *The Religious Factor* (Doubleday, New York, 1961).

LITTLE, ALAN and WESTERGAARD, J., 'The Trend of Class Differentials in Educational Opportunity in England and Wales', in *British Journal of Sociology*, Vol. 15, 1964.

LOCKWOOD, DAVID, 'Sources of Variation in Working-Class Images of Society', in *Sociological Review*, Vol. 14, 1966.

MACKENZIE, GAVIN, 'The Economic Dimensions of Embourgeoisement', in *British Journal of Sociology*, Vol. 18, 1967.

MACKENZIE, GAVIN, 'The Class Situation of Manual Workers', in *British Journal of Sociology*, Vol. 21, 1970.

MCKENZIE, R. T. and SILVER, A., *Angels in Marble: Working Class Conservatives in Urban England* (Heinemann, 1968).

MAO TSE-TUNG, *Quotations from Chairman Mao* (Bantam, 1967).

MARQUAND, DAVID, 'Less Equal Than Others', in *Observer*, 12 June 1966.

MARSH, D. (Ed.), *Social Mobility in Britain* (Routledge & Kegan Paul, 1954).

MARX, KARL, 'Alienated Labour', in E. Josephson and M. Josephson (Eds), *Man Alone* (Dell, 1966).

MAYER, K. B., 'Recent Changes in the Class Structure of the United States', in *Transactions of the Third Congress of Sociology*, Vol. III (London, International Sociological Association, London, 1956).

MAYER, K. B., 'Diminishing Class Differentials in the United States', in *Kyklos*, Vol. 12, 1959.

MAYER, K. B., 'The Changing Shape of the American Class Structure', in *Sociological Research*, Vol. 30, 1963.

MERTON, ROBERT, *Social Theory and Social Structure* (Free Press, Glencoe, Illinois, 1957).

MILLER, S. M. and RIESMAN, F., 'Are the Workers Middle Class?', in *Dissent*, Vol. 8, 1961.

MILLS, C. WRIGHT, *White Collars* (Oxford Univ. Press, 1951).

MOGEY, J. M., *Family and Neighbourhood* (Oxford Univ. Press, 1956).

OPPENHEIM, A. N., 'A Study of Social Attitudes of Adolescents', Unpublished Ph.D. thesis, London, 1956.

ORLANS, H., *Stevenage: A Sociological Study of a New Town* (Routledge & Kegan Paul, 1952).

PAHL, J. M. and PAHL, R. E., *Managers and Their Wives* (Allen Lane, 1971).

PAHL, R. E., 'The Two Class Village', in *New Society*, 27 February 1964.

PAHL, R. E., 'Whose City?', in *New Society*, 23 January 1969.

PAHL, R. E., *Patterns of Urban Life* (Longmans, 1970).

PARSLER, R., 'Some Economic Aspects of Embourgeoisement in Australia', in *Sociology*, Vol. 4, No. 2, 1970.

PAUL, L., *The Deployment and Payment of the Clergy* (Church Information Service, London, 1964).

PECK, R. F. and HAVIGHURST, R. J., *The Psychology of Character Development* (John Wiley, 1964).

RAWIN, S. J., 'Changes in Social Structure in Poland Under Conditions of Industrialization', Unpublished Ph.D. thesis, London, 1965.

RAYNOR, JOHN, *The Middle Classes* (Longmans, 1969).

REISS, ALBERT J. Jnr., *et al.*, *Occupation and Social Status* (Free Press, 1961).

ROSE, G., *The Working Class* (Longmans, 1968).

ROWNTREE, B. and SEEBOHM, M., *Poverty: A Study of Town Life* (Longmans, 1922).

RUNCIMAN, W. G., *Relative Deprivation and Social Justice* (Routledge & Kegan Paul, 1966).

RUNCIMAN, W. G., 'Class, Status and Power', in J. A. Jackson (Ed.), *Social Stratification* (Cambridge Univ. Press, 1968).

SAMPSON, ANTHONY, *The New Anatomy of Britain* (Hodder & Stoughton, 1971).

SEGAL, D. R. and SCHAFFNER, R., 'Status, Party and Negro Americans', in *Phylon*, Vol. XXIX, No. 3, 1968.

SHOHAM, SHLOMO, *et al.*, 'The Etiology of Middle Class Delinquency in Israel', in *Human Relations*, Vol. 24, No. 4, 1971.

SHOSTAK, A. B., *Blue Collar Life* (Random House, 1969).

SMILES, SAMUEL, *Self-Help: With Illustrations of Conduct and Perseverance* (Centenary Edition, J. Murray, 1958).

SMITH, CYRIL, *People in Need* (Allen & Unwin, 1957).

STACEY, M., *Tradition and Change* (Oxford Univ. Press, 1960).

STOTT, D. H., *Unsettled Children and Their Families* (Univ. London Press, 1956).

STURMTHAL, A., *Workers' Councils: A Study of Workplace Organisation on Both Sides of the Iron Curtain* (Harvard Univ. Press, 1964).

STURMTHAL, A. (Ed.), *White Collar Trade Unions* (Univ. Illinois Press, 1966).

SUGARMAN, BARRY, 'Teenage Boys at School', Unpublished Ph.D. thesis, Princeton, 1966.

SUSSMAN, M. B., 'The Help Pattern in the Middle-Class Family', in *American Sociological Review*, Vol. XVIII, 1953.

TOOMEY, D. M., 'Home-centred Working-class Parents' Attitudes Towards Their Sons' Education and Careers', *Sociology*, Vol. 3, No. 3, 1969.

TOWNSEND, P. B., *The Family Life of Old People* (Penguin, 1963).

VAIZEY, JOHN, 'Anti-Anti School', in *New Society*, 21 October 1971.

WARNER, W. L. and ABEGGLEN, J. C., *Big Business Leaders in America* (Harper, New York, 1955).

WARNER, W. L. and HENRY, W. E., 'Radio Daytime Serials', in *Genetic Psychological Monograph*, No. 37 (Massachusetts Province Journal Press, 1948).

WATSON, W., 'Social Mobility and Social Class in Industrial Communities', in M. Gluckman (Ed.), *Closed Systems and Open Minds* (Oliver & Boyd, 1964).

WEST, D. J., *The Young Offenders* (Duckworth, 1967).

WILLIAMS, RAYMOND, *Culture and Society* (Chatto & Windus, 1958).

WILLMOTT, P. and YOUNG, M., *Family and Class in a London Suburb* (Routledge & Kegan Paul, 1960).

WILSON, J. B., 'Education and Indoctrination', in T. B. H. Hollins (Ed.), *Aims in Education* (Manchester Univ. Press, 1964).

WORSTHORNE, P., *The Socialist Myth* (Cassell, 1971).

YOUNG, M., *The Rise of the Meritocracy* (Thames & Hudson, 1958).

YOUNG, M. and WILLMOTT, P., *Family and Kinship in East London* (Routledge & Kegan Paul, 1957).

ZWEIG, F., *The Worker in an Affluent Society* (Heinemann, 1961).

Part Two

The Moral Influence of the School

Chapter 11

The Contribution of the School

School as a Substitute Home

Leaving aside the fact that teachers may tend to purvey middle-class norms, and subscribe to the mores of the bourgeoisie, one can tentatively conclude that they have now become the agents of a deliberate attempt to socialize the next generation and impose their value system upon it. Whether this is an immoral abrogation of a familial function will be discussed below where it is argued that schools should become familial in form. However, many teachers do see their role still as that of missionaries saving children from the fate which the inequities of society have imposed on them. Musgrave, for example, says quite explicitly, 'Teachers see the schools as a rescue operation to save children from their parents and their social class' (1).

That this is a viable activity is clear from Barbara Wootton's view that institutions can take over parental functions without detriment to the child. She supports this view with an abundance of evidence and concludes that more 'good may be done by running the institutions better than by leaving the children in their homes' (2). Hence we now assume that parental *surrogates* are as efficacious as biological parents. To Bettelheim's Kibbutzim report and Wootton's analysis of maternal deprivation, both of which diminish the alleged influence of the family and enhance that of the school, one may add Duncan's comment that 'The large institutions that shaped me are more preferable to what I've seen of family life. Schools, hospitals, almost any residential institution seem to me preferable models to the one-family-house society' (3).

Perhaps it is relevant to observe at this point that the somewhat licentious propositions for communal living and sexual freedom, made by both Neville and Cooper, should not blind us to the value of organized communal life. Riesman has already made us aware of the fact that much of our conduct is socially determined. Hence we are already what he calls, 'other-directed' men and women. May it not be that the eastern emphasis on 'the masses' is entering the western hemisphere and that society, and its secondary institutions, may be taking over from the nuclear family as a dominant social control? This, at least, is what opponents of the bourgeois system are claiming.

HOME OR SCHOOL?

From a welter of conflicting evidence one may conclude that *both* home and school are potent forces in moulding a child's morality. This has been sufficiently affirmed by empirical research to stand as an axiom (4). It is therefore reasonable to suppose that when these two forces augment each other their influence could be irresistible. That, at least, is the conclusion to which most researchers have come (5).

This naturally leads to two related questions which can only be mentioned in passing. First, has one here a reflection of the nature/nurture controversy? If home influences are primarily genetic (6) and those of school are essentially environmental, it looks as though one may have this question raised in an acute form. Second, social-class factors must enter here. Obviously schools tend to purvey and subscribe to middle-class norms. With children coming from both lower- and higher-status homes it is inevitable that for some there will be a clash of values, while for others home norms will be reinforced. Amongst the plethora of evidence one may cite two cases. Mays, for example, argued that in the education of Liverpool children, working-class origins are a distinct disadvantage. Although he then elaborated the complexity of school-community relations, he did not modify his view that lower-status children suffer. Equally unequivocal is the report of Kathleen Cullen. After research in a small Irish town she concluded that children who behaved well at school were more likely to be higher on the socio-economic scale than those who behave badly. She ultimately ascribed this to parental interest. This, too, it seems, was correlated with social class, family size and personal aspirations.

Musgrove versus Fletcher

When one looks more closely at the contrast between the views of Musgrove and Fletcher it becomes apparent that this is not so much a conflict, as two different ways of looking at the some social phenomenon.

Musgrove argued that the family no longer has an educative function of any kind. Tracing this decline from the sixteenth to the twentieth century he argued that industrial, social and educational development have usurped the functions of the family. Thus from the nineteenth century onwards the family abdicated its educative responsibilities.

Such an argument can also be supported by Riesman who suggested that the family was dethroned in the realm of moral socialization when the period of 'transitional growth' into industrialization led to an urbanized period of incipient population decline. It was then that 'other-directed' conduct began to replace 'inner-directed' behaviour. The latter had required a 'psychic gyroscope' orientated by guilt mechanisms and value-goals acquired early in life. Thus psychologically and sociologically the parents, as goal setters and value arbiters, had dominated. Now the emergence of 'other-directed' behaviour meant the decline of parental influence. Thus to Musgrove's picture of children deserting the home, for the factory and school, must be added Riesman's argument that they now desert parents for peers.

Against this one may place the view of Fletcher who argues with equal conviction that the family is today reviving its educative functions. He compares nineteenth-century industrial man, living in hunger, fatigue, disease, squalor and depravity, with twentieth-century man reaping the harvests of industrialism and able to enjoy a stable, happy home-life with his family, with more time to devote to children and greater psychological health to enable love and companionship to characterize family life. Some may assert that the greater educative concern of parents is merely a compensation for their own lack of formal education. But his line of argument can be augmented by Gorer, Young and Willmott to show that parents are now taking their educative roles more seriously.

Thus from the apparently diametrically opposed views of Musgrove and Fletcher one can gain a clearer picture of familial influence. It is true that the state is usurping many functions of the family but these are what sociologists call the 'non-essential' functions relating to health, formal education and economic pursuits. Where 'essential' functions are concerned, the family fulfils them more adequately than ever before, simply because with more leisure, security, and money, the personal needs of each member can be satisfied.

It is therefore possible to argue that the family is still an educative agency. It has not abdicated its role as the agent of moral education. Yet it cannot function in isolation. One may conclude with Musgrove that the educative family has disappeared, or with Fletcher that it has been realized by working through the educational system. However, it is clear that *the family must co-operate with the school in producing mature moral agents*: and although many go further and insist that schools have arrogated the task of socialization, all would agree that emphasis should be placed on this co-operation.

Familial Co-operation

Clearly this complex interaction of parental and educational influences, cannot be finally teased out into a simple pattern. This may be why, although different emphases are placed on the home and school, most educators join in advocating that both should co-operate in the task of educating children.

Young and McGeeney express this truth in what they call the 'syllogism of parental participation', of which they say, 'A rise in the level of parental participation augments their children's performance at school. Teachers, by involving parents in the school, bring about a rise in the level of parental encouragement. Teachers, by involving parents in the school, augment the children's performance' (7). This conclusion contains many more elements than the one isolated here, but all are related, and further inquiry only reveals that the central element is confirmed.

This conclusion is not new. At the turn of the nineteenth century, Dewey advocated it in his study of the school and society, and since then it has become almost a shibboleth. While recognizing that such co-operation can be dysfunctional (8), Taylor supports this view in his contribution to a book of readings dealing with the problem of linking home and school. After the experts have made their contributions he still concludes that 'there is a very general acceptance of the desirability of forging links between home and school' (9). This too was the conclusion of Sharrock, who subscribed to the view that home influences are the most potent, and yet still concludes that 'it is essential for school and home to work together in the educational process' (10).

Parental Participation

The position of parents is obviously complex and the home is the most potent influence on children. Thus co-operation between the home and school is desirable. When this does not exist school achievement and moral behaviour are positively correlated with parental social class. This was the conclusion reached by both the Plowden and Newsom Reports. Therefore, in order to maximize on the educational system of this country, parents should be involved.

This does not seriously suggest that parents should be induced to become School Governors, although Watts made this proposition. However, if parental attitudes are more influential than school conditions, parental participation is essential if the educational system is to be fully effective. How may the potency of home background be placed at the service of education? We have heard much of 'pupil power'. May we not now hear more of 'parent power'? The most natural channel for this is the Parent–Teacher Association (PTA).

Here parents, wanting the best for their children, may learn how to augment school teaching by their conduct and conversation in the home. Teachers, involved with their children as persons will learn more from the parents than any record card could show.

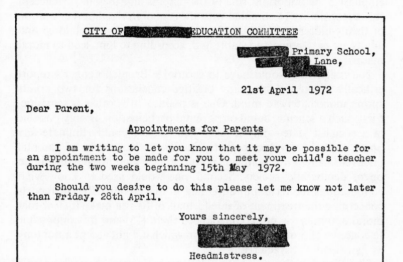

CITY OF ███████ EDUCATION COMMITTEE

█████ Primary School,
██████ Lane,

21st April 1972

Dear Parent,

Appointments for Parents

I am writing to let you know that it may be possible for an appointment to be made for you to meet your child's teacher during the two weeks beginning 15th May 1972.

Should you desire to do this please let me know not later than Friday, 28th April.

Yours sincerely,

████████

Headmistress.

Figure 2. Copy of a letter obviously intended as a deterrent to parent participation

Yet although official education reports advocate this system as a practical policy and recommend the forging of 'all existing links' (11), very little is done. There are a number of reasons for this. Musgrove suggests that teachers discourage the formation of such organizations as a way of protecting themselves from parental pressures, which as Becker has shown, is much more common in authority-orientated schools. Young and McGeeney show how subtle such pressures can be. They recorded that at the John Lilburne Primary School there was an annual, tea-less, open-day where parents could only speak publicly with the teachers. A more potent deterrent (12) would be difficult to devise! It has also been suggested that pupils are the prime obstacle, since they fear that a union of teachers and parents will be established in opposition to them (13): but it is difficult to believe that pupils could exert such influence!

However, one thing is certain. The formal association of parents and teachers is minimal in this country. Musgrave cites evidence showing that only 3% of British parents attended any PTA, while a comparable survey in America revealed that almost half of them were members (14). In contrast to this, Bronfenbrenner's comparative study shows how Russian parents take children to school and join in the celebrations with which each term opens. The schools emphasize the important role of the parents and they in turn accept the responsibility to combine with the school in the moral education of their children. As a result, the relationships between children and adults are easy-going and stable and, according to him, lead to moral maturity.

Naturally, one would have to scrutinize Bronfenbrenner's report critically before reaching any positive conclusions for two points spring immediately to mind. One is political; the other is semantic. First, such a scheme, based on parental participation, is only possible in a socialist state—only a 'class-less' society could eliminate any home and school value-conflict. Equally, such a degree of parental involvement requires political legislation of a kind not possible in an open, 'democratic' society. Second, one would need to know what connotations the term 'morality' had in this context. Recent reports concerning the treatment of intellectuals in Russia make it clear that moral autonomy is not countenanced there (15) and it is impossible to conceive of a mature moral system which did not accept autonomy as its essential characteristic.

The Plowden Report continually emphasizes what has been said above concerning home and school and urges co-operation between parents and teachers. For, teachers, it argues, are linked to parents by the children for whom they are responsible. The triangle should be completed and a more direct relationship established between teachers and parents (16). It then goes on to discuss morality, noting that 'schools should, as a minimum, cater for certain essential relationships' (17).

There is, however, a danger here that ought to be mentioned. Coles, for example, asks whether contemporary Caucasian children have been induced to lead protracted adolescent lives because the average (i.e. middle-class) family and school shelter them from adulthood. This at least is a refreshing criticism since it indicts the family and school for doing too much rather than not enough. However, many researchers have pointed to the importance of this home–school relationship in the sphere of moral development.

The literature on delinquency is so voluminous, that it would be tedious to cite even a selective sample, however, since the 1920s researchers, in this area, have agreed that children placed in a position of value-conflict are all delinquency risks. Such studies led naturally to 'the impression that the family is failing to supply adequate moral guidance' (18). Musgrove emphasizes that this was a false impression, and says that parents are increasingly 'making their views known to teachers and exerting pressures on the school to modify its procedures' (19).

Many other writers have highlighted this important value relationship between home and school. Hartshorne and May, although vulnerable to the criticism that they merely measured children's resistance to temptation, still showed conclusively that honesty in a child only became a consistent attitude when home and school mutually reinforced each other's values. Webb, although concerned primarily with younger children, still insisted that delinquent conduct, expressed through bullying, could only be eliminated by a change in the total atmosphere of home *and* school. Hence she advocated that teachers should make contact with the homes of such children to bring about value-environmental co-operation and harmony.

THE COLLECTIVE SOLUTION

It is not necessary to adopt extreme views and argue that the nuclear family may well be both morally impotent and non-viable in our modern, industrialized, mass society. Two important experiments in communal child rearing, where home and school co-operate, with none of the deficiencies and tensions of the 'hippie' commune, have resulted from more moderate, politically respectable views. The first is established in Russia; the second in Israel; and undoubtedly when the 'bamboo curtain' is finally lifted, supportive evidence will also be supplied from Chinese communes.

Attention has already been directed to the report of Bronfenbrenner eulogizing Russia as a nation which has succeeded in bridging this gap between home and school. Outlining the divisive nature of home–school relations in America he contrasted these with the stable, unifying relationship he found between home and school in Russia. This argument then reached its climax in a relevant quotation from the eminent Russian educator Anton Makarenko who insisted that 'Our family is not like the bourgeois family. It is an organic part of Soviet society' (20). This collectivism was a constant theme in his writings. Many years before, he had insisted that 'Real Soviet education can only be achieved when the entire collective of children, adolescents and teenagers regards itself as part of Soviet society' (21).

From this socialist ideal of a state commune, one may turn to consider a deliberate attempt to integrate familial and educational influences in communes established *within* the state. This is the Israeli kibbutzim experiment. In its ideal form a kibbutz could serve as a mirror reflecting the essential elements of social life and child-rearing practices. Its advocates claim that if only we would do this without preconceived prejudice, we would be better able to understand the advantages of communal living, and the social disabilities suffered by children reared in a brick box by a nuclear conjugal pair.

Bruno Bettelheim is probably the best known advocate of kibbutz life. It is not generally known, however, that a decade before him Spiro lived, as an observer participant, in a kibbutz and recorded his impressions. He noted that property was communally owned, money was abolished and child rearing was no longer a prerogative of the conjugal pair. Predictably, his most important conclusion was that as kibbutz children grew they lost interest in private property, and their social attitudes became culturally structured to the point where their acquisitive tendencies almost disappeared.

Bettelheim also lived in a kibbutz and recorded his impressions. Again a relevant and valuable conclusion emerged. He too reported that children were not reared by their biological parents, and confirmed Spiro's conclusion that kibbutz children became unconcerned with material possessions: but he also added an important dimension. Children reared by a succession of *metapeloth* (i.e. parental surrogates) developed a strong social sense. Deprived of parents they were thrown back on to the group. Consequently, 'life is truly with the group: the children are comrades not competitors' (22).

All, of course, is not sweetness and light. Honest and objective reports reveal that the kibbutz experiment is subject to considerable criticism. This cannot be dismissed as a displacement of anti-semitism, for many of the critics are Israelis. Directly because of this a recent Jewish symposium on children and families in Israel (23) is concerned more with rebuffing critics and eulogizing the kibbutzim, than with making a sociological assessment. Yet despite its propagandist theme this is a valuable volume. It shows how the Israelis responded to the challenge of building their nation and used the kibbutz as one basis for this venture. Furthermore, it adds considerable weight to the evidence of Bettelheim and Spiro, showing that many Israeli problems are being partially solved by an educational programme which integrates both home and school.

HOME/SCHOOL CO-OPERATION IN MORAL EDUCATION

Despite the emphasis which Craft *et al.* place on the complexity of interaction between home and school, it is possible to argue that their mutual co-operation is essential in the task of moral education. Reference has already been made to the difficulties which arise when home and school interact in a pluralist, democratic society. At the risk of tedious elaboration it must further be observed that at least one further complicating factor is present.

Schools not only have to prepare children to become members of a society with a particular moral ethos, but also one which is sustained by a particular economic system. This 'preparation of pupils for adult working life' is already established in Sweden where 'work experiences' are part of the normal educational process (24). This concept has also taken root in Russian education. Indeed, work in modern industry was Makarenko's principle vehicle of education and also the pivot around which the entire life of his pupils revolved.

To all this one only needs to add the dimension of social-class divisions, which lead into 'the conflicts experienced by the socially mobile child, who finds differences between what is expected of him at home and school' (25). This further dysfunctional aspect of the educational process also causes breaches within families and so makes home and school co-operation even harder. This co-operation is essential, for *powerful though home influences may be, they are more potent when home and school unite.*

There will naturally be social-class difficulties in the area of moral education, comparable to those which Bernstein and others have highlighted in the area of linguistic and conceptual development, but there are at least six ways in which these can be alleviated.

First, the current value-conflict may be eliminated. This could be accomplished by either eulogizing working-class values, in the fashion of Hoggart, Jackson and Davies, and so incorporating them into the educational system; or by establishing a 'commune' milieu for child rearing which Bettelheim claims 'demonstrates that children raised by educators in group homes fare considerably better than many children raised in poverty-stricken home, and better than quite a few raised at home by their middle-class parents' (26).

Failing this, the second solution is probably the ideal one. Teachers and parents should be enabled actually to co-operate with each other. This does not simply mean to imply that we should form better Parent–Teacher Associations. It is more long term than this. *It may well be that moral education will begin by educating the next generation of parents.* Thus to domestic science, sex-education and general literacy one would add competence in child rearing so that the pre-conditions of morality are established in the next generation. The psychological insights communicated might well then issue in greater co-operation between home and school. This could also have the side-effect of eliminating the more deleterious effects of value-conflict between sub-cultural norms. Such a programme of moral education may need to be a protracted one, with each succeeding generation becoming not only more adequate as parents but also increasingly more morally mature. Consequently, drastic policies might well be suggested in order to achieve rapid results.

Third, it may therefore be argued that schools should be elevated to the position of predominant influence. Hutchins refers to this as 'the triumph of the community, over the family' (27), citing pre-school nurseries as an illustration of this principle. As we have seen, Fletcher also argues obliquely for this in claiming that familial influence must be exerted through the school.

Fourth, there is the converse of this radical solution which is supported by such men as Illich and Reimer, advocates of the abolition of educational institutions and the establishment of what they call a 'de-schooled' society. They argue implicitly that this home/ school conflict can be resolved by eliminating or transforming the current system of education.

The fifth solution adopts a sociologically evolutionist point of view. It argues that both the family and school are changing institutions. We ought, therefore, not to place too much emphasis on the current conflict. All institutions change as society evolves, and in this process both society and its members adapt themselves to prevailing conditions. This could also be called the 'homeostatic' model (see Chapter 13). Schon pleads this case most plausibly. On the analogy of homeostasis in animal organisms, he argues that societies and institutions also make adaptations. Thus within them the component elements (either as cells, organs or persons) react to preserve their place in the whole, and the whole reacts to accommodate them within it. His argument assumes two things. First, that social stability depends on the belief that our actual institutions will survive; and second, our conviction that actions which lead to viable adaptation will dominate. In this he is most convincing. It could be concluded, therefore, that schools and homes will follow this homeostatic path and slowly accommodate themselves to each other.

The final solution is a practical development of this. It argues that we must accept schools and homes, in a class-ridden society, and work through them as they are. Tapper argues that school and home play different but complementary roles, located at varying points within the stratification of society. This model of socialization (28) distils down to three phases: in the first the home is all important; in the second, school and peer influence dominates; in the third, the individual emerges with roles, attitudes and functions appropriate to his position in the social hierarchy. Expressed thus, the system looks like an élitist caricature. However, this would be unfair to Tapper. We shall therefore, discuss his theories more fully in Chapter 15.

All these suggestions can coalesce into the proposition that moral education has the task of transforming society. At its simplest, this task requires competent teachers to educate the next generation of parents so that they can co-operate to produce morally educated children. However, outside this area there are few guide lines, and one often feels like an actor moving in a spot of light on a darkened stage; or an explorer in a clearing surrounded by impenetrable jungle. No wonder Sharrock concluded her research by gasping, 'At both primary and secondary level, it is clear that more information is needed about current practices' (29).

Two valuable affirmations can be made here. If the influence of family and parents predominates in the growth of child morality, then the parental role and the familial structure would seem to be most efficacious. This, it seems, implies that *teachers must become parental in their roles and schools should be familial in their structure.*

Obviously such a bald assertion must be qualified. Although it is officially recommended that teachers should act *in loco parentis* (30), this is only one of their roles. They may also be academic specialists. Hence while in the infant school the parental role should dominate, in a sixth form it would be subordinate to this academic function: but it ought still to be present as a sustained and potent influence.

There are some who would subscribe to Peters' view that 'The main function of the teacher is to train and instruct; it is not to help and cure' (31). There are others who go to distorted extremes with a caricature of progressive education, forgetting that the true teacher is one who loves both his children and his subject. The academic who only loves his subject is disloyal to his pupils; the teacher who only loves his pupils is a traitor to his subject. Through it all should shine the unwavering light of concern for children as persons.

As we shall see in Chapter 13, school structures vary. Nevertheless, all should still be characterized by familial and fraternal concern, whether it be expressed through personal tutors, counselling groups or school houses. If this view appears to be a fanciful pipe-dream, one only needs to refer again to Bronfenbrenner's account of Russian education. There he shows quite clearly that teachers are genuinely parental, and the schools familial, in their organization.

Obviously both the parentalism of the teacher and the familial structure of the school should reflect the qualities of an *ideal* parent and family. If only this could be done, what social transformation might be achieved? The kingdom of 'right' relationships could indeed be established on earth.

One final point at least is clear. Schools have a vital role to play in the reclamation of society and the cultural advancement of homo sapiens. Theirs is the privilege of playing a vital role in preparing each generation to move closer to the point where homo sapiens becomes homo moralis and inaugurates the neotimetic age (32). It is both a daunting task and a humbling responsibility, but if we can do this it will be our greatest educational triumph.

The arguments presented here, have been protracted in order to show not only that home and school should be partners in the moral education of children, but also to affirm that even without this support our schools may have a valid and essential contribution to make. We are not helpless when homes withhold or withdraw their support. Schools *do* have a contribution to make, and given the resources, they should be enabled to do so.

REFERENCES

1 Musgrave (1968), p. 227.
2 Wootton (1959), p. 155, but see Chapter 4.
3 Duncan (1972), p. 186.
4 McCandless (1969), pp. 2 ff. The Eppels (1966) finally conclude that 'the moral character is formed by the child's family experiences' (p. 162); but they do classify both parents and teachers as 'primary moral influences' (p. 48). Peck and Havighurst (1964), pp. 143–5, and Cullen (1969), p. 73, agree on this point.
5 Niskanen and Pihkanen (1971) have found this true of morally aberrant schizophrenic and paranoid, psychotic patients, who obtained institutional treatment while living at home.
6 Of course, home influence is also environmental and this can affect children in different ways. Allport (1963) observes shrewdly here that 'The same fire that melts the butter hardens the egg' (p. 72).
7 Young and McGeeney (1968), pp. 40–1.
8 It can, as Taylor (1968) found, 'separate the child from the family' (p. 235).
9 *op. cit.*, p. 227.
10 Sharrock (1970), p. 58. Cullen (1969) supports this view.
11 Newsom Report (1963), para. 204, *et al.* Plowden Report (1967), para. 110, *et al.*
12 See the facsimile of the deterrent received by the writer (Fig. 2). I was informed that 'it *may* be possible' for me to see my child's teacher. The remote possibility of 'Should you desire' was given a clear deadline. I most certainly intended to see my child's teacher, but I wondered what reactions were elicited in the working-class homes of the council estate where the school is situated.
13 ROSLA (1966), p. 29.
14 Musgrave (1968), p. 233.
15 Medvedev and Medvedev (1971).
16 Plowden Report (1967), para 107, *et al.*
17 *op. cit.*, para. 112, *et al.*
18 Musgrove (1966), p. 9.
19 *op. cit.*, p. 14.
20 Bronfenbrenner (1972), pp. 2–3.
21 Makarenko (1965), p. 15.
22 Bettelheim (1969), p. 89.
23 Jarus *et al.* (1970).
24 Newsom Report (1963), paras 295 and 222.
25 Oppenheim (1956), p. 285.

26 Bettelheim (1969), p. 281.
27 Hutchins (1968), p. 26.
28 Tapper (1971), p. 38.
29 Sharrock (170), p. 125.
30 Tomlinson (1961) constitutes an official statement on this point.
31 Peters (1964), p. 85.
32 The term 'neotimetic', like 'neolithic' is a neologism also coined from two Greek words, meaning 'new value'. The 'neotimetic age' is intended to stand in contrast to the 'neolithic age', for whereas the latter was characterized by man's mastery of the material order by the use of his cognitive powers the former may well be initiated by comparable mastery of the social order by man's moral powers. Consequently the terms homo sapiens and homo moralis appropriately describe the denizens of each cultural phase. This thesis is developed in the author's forthcoming *Evolution and Morality*.

Bibliography

ALLPORT, G. W., *Pattern and Growth in Personality* (Holt, Rinehart & Winston, 1963).

BECKER, H. S., 'The Teacher in the Authority System of the Public School', in A. Etzioni (Ed.), *Complex Organizations—a Sociological Reader* (Holt, Rinehart & Winston, 1965).

BERNSTEIN, B., *Class, Codes and Controls* (Routledge & Kegan Paul, 1971).

BETTELHEIM, B., *The Children of the Dream* (Thames & Hudson, 1969).

BRONFENBRENNER, U., *Two Worlds of Childhood* (Allen & Unwin, 1972).

CRAFT, M., RAYNOR, J. and COHEN, L., *Linking Home and School* (Longman, 1968).

COLES, R., *Children of Crisis: A Study of Courage and Fear* (Faber, 1968).

COOPER, D., *The Death of the Family* (Allen Lane, 1971).

CULLEN, K. C., *School and Family* (Gill & Macmillan, 1969).

DAVIES, H., *Culture and the Grammar School* (Routledge & Kegan Paul, 1965).

DEWEY, J., *The School and Society* (Univ. Chicago Press, 1956).

DUNCAN, B., 'Smother Love', in *New Society*, 27 January 1972.

EPPEL, E. M. and EPPEL, E., *Adolescents and Morality* (Routledge & Kegan Paul, 1966).

FLETCHER, R., *The Family and Marriage* (Penguin, 1962).

FLOUD, J. E., HALSEY, A. H. and MARTIN, F. M., *Social Class and Educational Opportunity* (Heinemann, 1956).

GORER, G., *Exploring English Character* (Cresset, 1955).

HARTSHORNE, H. and MAY, M. A., *Studies in the Nature of Character*, Vol. 1 —*Studies in Deceit* (Macmillan, New York, 1930).

HOGGART, R., *The Uses of Literacy* (Penguin, 1962).

HUTCHINS, R. H., *The Learning Society* (Pall Mall Press, 1968).

ILLICH, I., *Celebration of Awareness* (Calder & Boyars, 1969).

ILLICH, I., *Deschooling Society* (Calder & Boyars, 1972).

JACKSON, B., *Working Class Community* (Routledge & Kegan Paul, 1968).

JARUS, A., MARCUS, J., ROEN, J. and RAPAPORT, C., *Children and Families in Israel* (Gordon & Breach, 1970).

MCCANDLESS, B. R., *Children: Behaviour and Development* (Holt, Rinehart & Winston, 1969).

MAKARENKO, A. S., *Problems of Soviet School Education* (Progress Pubs., Moscow, 1965).

MAYS, J. B., *Education and the Urban Child* (Liverpool Univ. Press, 1962).

MEDVEDEV, Z. A. and MEDVEDEV, R. A., *A Question of Madness* (Macmillan, 1971).

MUSGRAVE, P. W., *The Sociology of Education* (Methuen, 1968).

MUSGROVE, F., 'Decline of the Educative Family', in *Universities Quarterly*, No. 14, 1960.

MUSGROVE, F., *The Family, Education and Society* (Routledge & Kegan Paul, 1966).

NEVILLE, R., *Play Power* (Cape, 1970).

NEWSOM REPORT, *Half Our Future* (HMSO, 1963).

NISKANEN, P. and PIHKANEN, T. A., 'A Comparative Study of Home Treatment and Hospital Care in the Treatment of Schizophrenia and Paranoid Psychotic Patients', in *Acta Psychiatrica Scandinavia*, Vol. 47, Fasc. 3, Munksgaard, Copenhagen, 1971.

OPPENHEIM, A. N., 'A Study of Social Attitudes of Adolescents', Unpublished Ph.D. thesis, London, 1956.

PETERS, R. S., 'Mental Health as an Educational Aim', in T. H. B. Hollins (Ed.), *Aims in Education* (Manchester Univ. Press, 1964).

PLOWDEN REPORT, *Children and Their Primary Schools* (HMSO, 1967).

Raising of the School Leaving Age (HMSO, 1966).

REIMER, E., *School is Dead* (Penguin, 1971).

RIESMAN, D., *et al.*, *The Lonely Crowd* (Yale Univ. Press, 1964).

SCHON, D. A., *Beyond the Stable State* (Temple Smith, 1971).

SHARROCK, A., *Home School Relations* (Longman, 1970).

SKINNER, B. F., *Walden Two* (Macmillan, 1962).

SPIRO, M. E., *Children of the Kibbutz* (Harvard Univ. Press, 1958).

TAPPER, T., *Young People and Society* (Faber, 1971).

TAYLOR, W., 'Family, School and Society', in M. Craft *et al.* (Eds), *Linking Home and School* (Longman, 1968).

TOMLINSON, G., *Citizens Growing Up*, Ministry of Education Pamphlet, No. 16 (HMSO, 1961).

WATTS, R., 'Parents in School', in *Bow Group Pamphlet*, September 1971.

WEBB, L., *Children with Special Needs in the Infants' School* (Collins, 1969).

WOOTTON, B., *Social Science and Social Pathology* (Allen & Unwin, 1959).

YOUNG, M. and MCGEENEY, P., *Learning Begins at Home* (Routledge & Kegan Paul, 1968).

YOUNG, M. and WILLMOTT, P., *Family and Kinship in East London* (Routledge & Kegan Paul, 1957).

Chapter 12

The School as a Social System

The preceding chapters not only made it clear that schools can contribute to the moral education of children, but have also tentatively indicated the nature of this task. This chapter will now suggest ways in which the school as an institution effects this process.

At first sight it is a daunting prospect. Not only do many standard sociological works omit any reference to the school (1), but this under-researched area is as we shall see, infinitely complex. Peter Mann comes to our aid here for he has shown that sociological inquiry either complicates or simplifies the problems being reviewed. With this invitation to act as a 'simplifier' rather than a 'complicator' one may adopt a simplistic approach without, it is hoped, being accused of naïvety.

As we have seen, the school does not exert its influence in isolation. On the one hand Kurzwell may argue that the influence of the family is waning and nothing is taking its place. On the other hand many may insist that the school cannot compensate for the demise of the home influence (2). John's finding that 'the family today is simply undergoing a process of change, whereby it is being adjusted to meet the demands of a highly complex industrial society', enables us to conclude again that home and school must co-operate in a new cultural milieu.

It is true, of course, that many parents 'are inadequate in the moral skills they transmit' (3), but this only emphasizes that the educational system must accept its responsibility as an agent of socialization (4). The view that schools should undertake this task can appear in moderate or extreme forms. Some are content if schools merely transmit a uniform culture, and produce good citizens (5). Others demand that schools should produce morally mature citizens and insist that they should examine 'the process by which men and societies develop and change the values by which they live' (6).

The Complexity of the Task

We have already seen that this is made complex by the nature of mature morality; but this is further complicated by the structure of our schools. In essence moral education consists of establishing and sustaining a child's identity, self-acceptance, paradigmatic experiences, a mature conscience and sustained social success as preconditions of morality. Upon these must be built the primary traits of moral judgement, future-orientation, personalism, moral flexibility and dynamism. Finally the primary moral attitudes of autonomy, rationality, altruism and responsibility must be assiduously nurtured. As we have also seen these three clusters are not only related, but within each, the individual components cohere, and from them should emerge the new moral quality of rational-altruism (7).

Precisely how such elements may be measured in order to assess the relative success of moral education, is not known (8). Clearly this is a task more appropriate to psychology than sociology. But the problem here is simply to discover whether these personal moral elements may be inculcated, formed and nurtured within the present school structures.

The Complexity of the School

Once it is accepted that one aim of education is to produce good citizens and not just scholars, the task seems to be simple. Schools must no longer exclusively purvey knowledge, they must be equally involved in inducing moral values, principles, norms and conduct.

One cannot just talk about 'schools' or 'the school'. This would be rather like talking about rocks or pebbles on the beach—a specific beach may be clearly defined, but each particular pebble is unique. Thus although we may speak of *the* educational system, its component parts are all distinct. A simple contrast makes this clear. By reference to 'the' school, does one mean a top preparatory school or an EPA primary? A top public school or a *Daily Mail* comprehensive? (9)

Yet despite the inherent uniqueness of each school it is still possible to classify them. They are either primary or secondary, public or state schools. These are then divided into boarding and day schools, which may be co-educational or mixed, with each one varying in size. The most recent divisive criterion now distinguishes comprehensive schools from separated ones. Then other variations appear. Some are streamed and others are not. Some employ a pastoral house system, others dispense with it. The curriculum and teaching techniques may differ in each. Finally consider the ethos and structure of the school; some may be authoritarian, others democratic and still more display a spirit of *laissez-faire*.

It is clear from this that one should not generalize. It is also equally clear that the relative efficacy of these different systems must be examined in the light of schools as agents of moral education. However, the problem can be simplified. We may study schools in terms of their institutional structure, teacher-influence, curricular content and technique and the peer-experiences they offer. The first is the prime concern of this and the following chapters. The rest will then follow.

From the welter of evidence I perused before writing this chapter, one clear conviction has emerged. *Genuine moral education is maximally effective only in a democratic system.* We have already spoken of the need for a secular equivalent of conversion, and for teachers to become the secular equivalent of pastors. If then the home is one of the most potent influences in the sphere of moral education, one may conclude also that schools must be familial in structure and teachers parental in practice, if moral education is to be conducted by the school; but here the terms *familial* and *parental* must be interpreted as expressions of ideal relationships.

SOCIETY DETERMINES CHARACTER

Before actually analysing schools as social systems, it is important to emphasize that the structure of these sub-cultures affects both the personality and conduct of its members. This is why De Cecco's prescription for the regeneration of schools builds on the assumption that the best way to change pupil behaviour is to change the schools of which they are members. What evidence is available to support this assertion?

Culture's Effect on Individual Character and Conduct
Gordon Allport begins his study of this theme by asserting that 'Everyone admits that culture is vastly important in shaping personality' (10). Sociologists and anthropologists, concerned to construct a general theory of social action, will acclaim this fact for it is now axiomatic that our personality is a prime determinant of our conduct (11).

Vivid examples of fascinating, cultural differences in conduct are not difficult to find. The typically Caucasian child whose competitiveness is encouraged, stands in contrast to children of different cultures, many of whom refuse to compete with each other no matter what the circumstances may be (12). This need not result, as Eysenck and others have suggested, from racial and genetic variations but solely from cultural differences (13). This, at least, was the view of Mead who almost half a century ago showed that amongst related New Guinean tribes one could find the typically friendly, honest Arapesh and the equally unfriendly, dishonest Mundugumur. More recently, Whyte has shown how the organized society produces the conforming 'organization man'. Such evidence could be indefinitely multiplied to show that even deviant and recreational behaviour are determined by the societies in which men live (14).

Hitherto such information has been unsystematized. Now Ossowska has examined it in the light of both philosophy and sociology. While recognizing the force of economic factors (15), she still maintains that moral values depend on social factors. Indeed she describes her work as a study of the 'social determinants of moral ideas'. However, it is clear that some cultures induce higher levels of morality, in their members, than do others.

Schools' Effect on Individual Character and Conduct

If this is true of cultures and sub-cultures it would seem necessarily to imply that it is also true of such sub-systems as schools. Here, too, 'we are what other people let us be' (16). One can see why this should be so. Socialization not only induces us to conform to the conventions of society but it also leads us to enact the roles prescribed by social expectations (17). Furthermore, this tendency is endorsed by the fact that such social 'sensitizing' results in group decisions being accepted by individuals even when they are contrary to the individual's normal beliefs and practices (18).

Sociologically sophisticated theories can be erected to account for this apparently obvious and normal fact. It is said that the group, rather than the individual, is the basic unit of society. Vierkandt, for example, argued that groups were organisms which acted like persons. Hence individuals were like organs of the body and were inevitably subservient to it (19). Less bizarre was Durkheim's view that the group is causally prior to the individual. This could be summed up simply by the Confucian aphorism that 'There was no man until there were two men'. It does, however, underwrite the view that societies are one of the prime determinants of individual character and conduct (20).

Such considerations as these lead inevitably to the view that every society has an innate value system which it imposes on individual members. Sprott expressed this succinctly by arguing that every human group 'has standards or norms of conduct incumbent upon its members to obey' (21). At its lowest this could result from man's unconscious participation in social ritual. At its highest it could express Mead's conclusion that both individuals and their morality are essentially social in origin.

Even when one has said that it still remains true that many of our societies are consciously structured, and that these structured forms affect us in different ways. The works of Lippitt, Lewin and White are classic demonstrations of this fact. Working singly, in pairs, or all together, they have demonstrated that in a teaching situation children behave according to the way in which the group is structured. When it is authoritarian, and arid legalistic procedures dominate, children withdraw into submissiveness. In a *laissez-faire* situation they become indifferent and irresponsible. In a democratic situation children co-operate in a responsible manner and emerge as individuals. Now research by Kathleen Evans and Kent and Davies has confirmed that such different types of classroom and home organization, respectively, affect the personality and behaviour of the children concerned.

It must, of course, be remembered that a child's personality orientation is a potent factor. Hence a democratic child may be happy with a democratic teacher, but an authoritarian child might not. Yet the fundamental thesis remains unchanged. A child's social environment has a fundamental influence on his personality and conduct.

That such research should culminate in a eulogy of democracy is not surprising, but this conclusion has been endorsed by many others who have shown that democratic procedures lead towards both autonomy and social co-operation (22). Whether this results from the integrative power of a freely shared value system, is problematic (23); but it seems unavoidable to conclude not only that school structures affect character and conduct, but that they are most morally efficacious when they take democratic forms.

It is true, of course, as Oppenheim found, that this school influence is largely informal. Brown is certainly correct when he affirms that little is known of the effect of different school structures on moral maturation, except that 'attitudes are formed by the social structure'. The point concerning democratic structures and their influence on personal autonomy is crucial to this discussion. Here then lies a paradox. The influence of the school society must be used to inculcate all the moral qualities enumerated above and then not merely tolerate, but actually inculcate autonomy in its members. Here is the sociological form of Teilhard's paradoxical anomaly that 'union differentiates'; by which he meant that we are only truly ourselves as individuals when we are fully integrated into a society.

Unfortunately most people find themselves frustrated by institutions (24), or merely adjust to them and become conformers. They do not so organically unite with them that they become truly themselves. The fault may lie with the system or with the individual, but, since we are concerned with the influence of school on character and conduct, it must be stressed that schools should be so organized that they produce autonomous, moral agents. When they do not, then they are dysfunctional (25) and, according to Argyris, ought immediately to be re-organized so that psychic energy can be released to allow the members to become self-actualizing, modifiers of their society (26).

That most schools are dysfunctional is a fact which has been repeatedly affirmed by the 'anti-school' writers (see Chapter 14). However, before any social system can be adequately renovated, its structure must be thoroughly comprehended. Thus it is not only because schools have such a potentially potent influence, but also because we want to harness that potency in the cause of moral education, that they must be analysed in sociological terms.

Now this is an extraordinarily difficult task. Not only are all schools unique in their organization but within them there appear to be very few identical aims and accepted roles. Even those aims and roles which do exist are often the cause of domestic debate. Thus this is a confused and confusing area of inquiry, and it is no comfort to be assured that the study of schools as organizations is still in its infancy.

Classical Sociologists

Since both compulsory education and sociology emerged contemporaneously in modern societies one would naturally expect early sociologists to comment on education. Indeed, this is the case, even though as with some later writers, the comments are usually peripheral.

No sociological study can afford to ignore Weber. His thesis that all sociological propositions must be confirmed by empirical facts, is crucial to our study. Consequently many early sociological studies of the educational system owe much to him.

His findings can be easily outlined. He claimed that legitimate norms in schools were established (as in the state) by submission to authority since they too were specialized bureaucracies (27). Thus the 'ideal' pupil had a 'bureaucratic personality' which enabled him to blend in with the system (28). Like Durkheim, another founding father of educational psychology, he was concerned to establish both the relationship between education and social change, and its manifestation in society (29). Thus for him schools were microcosms of a socially stratified society (30). Beyond that he did not progress.

Following this view, that schools must inculcate morality as their duty to society, came the work of Waller, best remembered for his aphorism 'school is a museum of virtue'. He showed clearly that 'The school is a closed system of social interaction which exists wherever and whenever teachers and students meet for the purpose of giving and receiving instruction' (31). In his major work the position is quite clear. He viewed a school as 'a social organism' and devoted the first chapter of that book to arguing that each school was a special culture worthy of analysis. For him this social organism (not to be viewed merely as an organization) served both society and the pupils. Hence although any organization is an arrangement for the satisfaction of human wishes, these wishes include the pupils' 'wish for response, wish for recognition, wish for new experience and wish for security' (32). Mead emphasized that such analyses were not merely to be used to enhance schooling processes. They must induce and prepare children for the realities of social change, evolving moral standards, and the value system of society at large.

During the subsequent war years Mannheim, then a refugee in England, added his voice to this proclamation. Shedding the Nazi induced despair which had engulfed him, and aware of the need to build a new post-war world, he turned his attention to this task. He did not doubt that schools were one of the most potent tools for this. He thus saw education as more than a teacher–pupil interaction. It was one means of changing society and thus had to be fully understood in order to be utilized. Some may be offended by his avowedly élitist proposals within a democratic structure, but his analysis of schools as the media to disseminate culture, without diluting it, is central to any concept of moral education.

Finally we turn to C. Wright Mills, who would no doubt have resisted any move to place him amongst the classical sociologists, for he was highly critical of contemporary sociology. However, since he has now been dead for more than a decade one may legitimately place him here. For him the task of sociology was simply that of challenging and changing social ideas and prejudices. Every institution was thus essentially political, and this for him included the school. Fascinated by the interaction of culture and personality he applied his fundamental pragmatism to every social problem. Accepting schools as centres of social influence he became convinced that radical change here would facilitate the emergence of the new society for which he yearned.

Valuable though these analyses are they hardly lead us forward. All agree that a school is a social system, with a specific responsibility to the state, which must therefore be subject to rigorous sociological analysis in order to ensure that society may benefit from their activities. But that is as far as they go.

Current Analyses of the School

Fallow decades passed after Waller's attempt to show how sociological analysis could assist schools in the task of education, and therefore today teachers and students are still only able to refer to half a dozen such works, each containing incomplete analyses. The most comprehensive of these provides much of the data for understanding the school as a system. Guarding himself against the charge that he is a structural-functionist (33) Lambert affirms that the school 'still operates as a social system in its own right' (34). He and his collaborators then make a thorough analysis of its structure, with a detailed investigation of the interaction of its component parts, and the roles played by each sub-group.

In contrast to this, Shipman clearly employs the structural functional model. The preface defines his two-fold objective as, first, describing schools as social organizations and, second, 'to introduce sociological concepts while analysing the working of schools'. Compared with Lambert his analysis is simplistic, but for students and teachers, this is most helpful. However, he does not avoid the many pitfalls in the path of such an investigator. Despite his obvious dependence on the work of Etzioni (35) he still confuses such concepts as 'goals', 'values', 'norms' and 'ends'. Nor does he discuss precisely what a structural-functional analysis implies. Finally he leaves open the question concerning any interaction and interrelationship between varying component elements in the school, e.g. curricular content, school mores and pupil ethos.

Musgrave's sociological analysis is augmented by two other publications. It is preceded by a volume which places the school in its social setting and then discusses the way in which it can enhance our national life by inducing social change and making maximum use of children as a nation's most valuable raw material. It is followed by an edited volume which adds an historical dimension and seeks 'to illustrate the reliance and possible practical results of a joint study of sociology and history' (36).

In the volume specifically devoted to a sociological analyses of the school Musgrave builds on his earlier work. There he had affirmed that schools are intended to maintain and rejuvenate society; and to facilitate our understanding of this process he enumerated five basic functions. Schools had to: (1) transmit the culture of society; (2) provide innovators; (3) sustain and augment government; (4) stratify society; and (5) sustain the economy (37).

Now he further clarifies his position. For him schools are servants of the state, but serve it best by realizing their own goals. He tends to assume too easily that each school can have a 'goal-consensus' for this conflicts with his delightfully delicate suggestion that such goals are affected by the quirks of headmaster, staff, curriculum and pupils. However, his overall ideal is clear. He wants schools to be effective in 'the move from an élitist to an egalitarian social system' (38).

In the course of this survey we are introduced to global notions concerning society. Hence Musgrave shows clearly how societies are bonded together by attraction, compulsion or internal cohesion. We are introduced to the minutiae of goal function and role within the society, and given a clear analysis of the instrumental versus expressive elements of school life (39). But no mention has yet been made of moral education. Musgrave remedies this, even though the references are tantalizingly brief. Throughout his book he makes it clear, in analysing the school as a system, that he wants also to discover how one may best assess its moral consequences. It is indeed a pity that such a wealth of material had to be compressed into so limited a space, for this theme needs to be developed.

We thus do not appear to have progressed much further. All these sociologists agree that schools must serve the needs of both society and their pupils. The moral element in this is most clear in Musgrave's work; but altogether these men do little more than analyse the school into its component parts and then discuss these in terms of function, role, interaction and goals. Some emphasize the interpersonal element; others the functional. But at least the picture is becoming clearer. If a school is an organism, in the sense of being both an organization and a system, it is an advantage to be able to analyse it into its component, distinctive and crucial elements (40).

Olive Banks and Others

Further information on this theme has been provided by a number of writers, either in papers and articles or chapters in sociological studies. They are presented here in the chronological order of their publication; except for the work of Banks which, despite its brevity, is a mine of valuable information and insights.

Relevant to a consideration of moral education is the sociological approach to schools which considers their role in the process of socialization. This studies the value system of the school; the sub-culture of adolescents; the selective function; and the elimination of dispensable children. Parsons made an early pioneering study in this area, and despite some ambiguities he is less open there to the charge that his inclusive generalities can lead to misunderstanding (41). He wrote clearly of 'the socialization function of the school' (42); developed the view that children will always be differentiated according to achievement, by school membership; and showed how the contra-school culture can become an alternative ground for achieving social success. However, through it all runs his conviction that schools must function to enable children to move from nurturant homes to competitive extra-school organizations.

Some may dismiss Parsons' work because he is concerned more specifically with the classroom than the school. This, however, is remedied by his contemporary, Schelsky, who dealt specifically with the school and almost echoed Parsons, by pointing out that the school system served as a social stabilizer. As such it reflected the stratification of society and thus conferred or withheld future economic and personal status, security and consumption. Hence, school is the prime determinant of a child's 'life-chances'. This, he concluded, resulted in tensions within the school community, ameliorated only by the tacit assumption that success was 'according to achievement' (43).

Ottaway is also of value since his contribution is embedded in a book which is virtually a panegyric of democracy. In his exposition of the theme that 'children are not yet members of society, and are at school partly for this purpose of being socialized' (44), he argues that democratic school procedures can inculcate responsibility and autonomy.

Webb sees schools as reservoirs of hostility, guilt and despair. This highlighting of the relational element is valuable but depressing. Thus although Webb argues that his is 'an attempt to set up a model which will perhaps shed light' his use of this conflict model provides little encouragement. Teachers caught between the hostility of their pupils and the guilt-displacement of their headmaster, and having to adopt what he calls the 'drill-sergeant' role with discipline, punishment and custodial routines as their weapons in a repressive system, may well wonder how moral education can be conducted in such a milieu.

Although Brembeck was criticized earlier for claiming to have made a cross-cultural study, when in fact he only deals with American schools, he is of value here. He argues that schools are microcosms of society and then goes on to show how the values, functions and structure of schools reflect this relationship. Hence he emphasizes the part that both social class and familial influence play in the process of education. A reflection of Webb's despondency then appeared in Hargreaves' report. He found that when pupils were divided, according to their school orientation, one had an 'academic' and a 'delinquent' stream. Thus while it was still true that school only confirmed the latter in their delinquency, the former not only became socialized but also derived vocational benefit from the system. He concluded, 'major reforms are necessary if pupils are to be adequately educated and drawn from delinquent values and behaviour' (45).

This emphasis on poor social relations within a school may thus lead to some concern, but it can also remind those educators, who do not actually have to deal with near-delinquent, physically powerful, teenagers that teaching 'Newsom' children can be a demanding and taxing task. However, this relational aspect must be stressed for, as Hirst reminds us, once we speak of organizations as having some purpose we must mean 'a body of *people* with a definite purpose'.

This is especially true when one notes that Cotgrove defines this purpose as 'the development of personal qualities including the inculcation of values and norms' (46).

An interesting and valuable contribution has also been made by the Shaftels. They argued that a school was an institution which was so organized that it could allocate a variety of roles to its members (47) which, they argue, is essential for moral growth. By the use of role playing, personal values could be inculcated in children, and by this means, it is said, they would be enabled to discover, and not merely be told, what was meant by generosity, altruism and loyalty.

Brief mention ought also to be made of a study which examines the influence of schools on the process of socialization. Morrison and McIntyre argue that attempts at moral education, conducted in ignorance of the psychology and sociology of attitude formation and change, are at best time wasting, and at worst positively disastrous (48). Their book deals with four themes: (1) social factors and academic achievement; (2) education and social conduct; (3) education and politics; and (4) education and vocational choice. Their thorough study of these themes makes it clear that the school system is a potent factor in preparing pupils for life in a society where they must earn a living, and live with others, and thus they discuss the ways in which schools 'seek by one means or another to form moral conduct and values in children' (49).

To continue with such evidence would be tedious. Suffice it to say that there are many more sociologists who have provided snippets of relevant information. Most of it may be classified as that which is intended to show 'how a sociologist views a school and how he sets about examining it' (50), in relation to the educational system.

The work of Banks has been left until now in order to emphasize its importance. Opening her book with the comment that 'The sociology of education is no more than the application of sociological perspectives to one of the major institutions of society', she is thus able to continue untrammelled by any need to explicate sociological strategy. Thus having established her vantage point she is free to concentrate on available empirical research. In this clear and concise survey she devotes two chapters to an analysis of the school, in the process of which she is also able to elicit cross-cultural references.

In these two chapters she deals first with the school as a formal organization and second as a social system. At first one is not aware of the value of this simple contribution to our study, but this dual analysis of the school as a social structure highlights an important point. The children in it are members of both a formally organized institution and also of a spontaneous web of relationships. The classic terms for these are *Gesellschaft* and *Gemeinschaft*, respectively, and emphasize that children are socially controlled by both the structured roles and also by the spontaneous grouping of the members.

Of these two, as in any other society, she believes that the most potent force is exerted through the informal social system. Thus she concludes, 'A school is much more than its formal structure; like all organizations it is also a social system involving a complex pattern of interaction' (51). Of course, it is this influence which is most potent in the formation of group norms and individual patterns of social conduct. For our purposes, however, her succinct analysis of democratic and autocratic procedures (52) is extremely important, for although she remains overtly uncommitted to either structure it is clear from her survey that the democratic process is greatly to be preferred, since it is this which is more conducive to social maturity.

The above material is virtually all that we have for our present purposes, and two conclusions follow naturally from it. First, the paucity facilitates one's acquaintance with the extant literature, and second the basic research has yet to be undertaken. We are, as it were, like astronomers before the first telescope was made. The conclusions of all the above writers can be rapidly distilled down to the view that schools reflect the society of which they are a part and that they must both socialize the pupils and also prepare them to function within this society. However, this leads to the paradoxical conclusion that such pupils must also act as catalysts of social change. Consequently, although the state's bureaucratic structure may be transposed to the school, the most beneficial system within them is built on the democratic procedures of an enlightened state. Finally, each school can be viewed as a formally organized *Gesellschaft* in which the nature of the institution, its members and their formalized curricula predominate; or as a spontaneous *Gemeinschaft* in which the social interreaction of teachers and peers predominate (see Table 1).

Table 1. *School as a system*

Expressive function	Instrumental function
Teachers as parental figures in a pastoral role	Teachers as academics
Curriculum providing opportunities for free inquiry	Curriculum defining academic aims
Pupils treated as persons	Pupils subordinate to the system
School preoccupied with personal deviations of children	School functioning primarily to provide society with workers
School forming a Gemeinschaft (informal organization)	School forming a Gesellschaft (formal organization)

Barry Sugarman

Now Sugarman has attempted to answer the question 'How do different ways of running schools influence their effectiveness at moral education?' (53). His first research project established the hypothesis that there existed a 'contra-pupil' role. Beginning with the assumption that the standard pupil role was related to the middle-class norms outlined above, he described it as characterized by future orientation, dynamism and individualism. His findings were predictable. He discovered that a 'contra-pupil' role was emerging, characterized by immediate gratification, passivity and group loyalty (54).

Then followed a study which continued this theme and investigated commitment to a youth culture and commitment to school. Here he found that high teenage commitment, measured by typical teenage activity, was positively correlated to unfavourable attitudes to school (55). He then went on to analyse the social organization of the school. At first the report reads rather like those enumerated above, but his contribution here consisted in arguing that the component elements in the school system can be analysed into three categories. First, there are the independent variables over which the school has no control. Then the intervening variables, consisting of permutations built upon the endorsed membership and structure of the school. Finally the dependent variables, resulting from the other two, which characterized the aims of moral education (56) (see Table 2).

He then developed his view that the formal structure of a school would have a profound effect on the moral education that took place within it (57). Here he argued that the formal structure would influence moral education through the media of school rules, reward systems, direct moral teaching and the schools relationship with society at large. This, of course, would be augmented by any pastoral system, interest groups, organized games, academic work, group projects, pupil responsibility and the exercise of control within the system. Thus teachers, the curriculum and pupil involvement in school policy would all be potent elements. Predictably, the informal social elements were then considered and it was concluded that role playing and social relationships were equally potent factors.

All of this may look like little more than an elaboration of the material already provided above, but its value lies in the fact that at every step Sugarman is fastidious in his desire to show how each element affects the development of moral maturity in children.

This study was rapidly followed by a much needed taxonomy of the data. Indeed Sugarman himself begins with the presupposition that 'we are very far from having a systematic general model for the

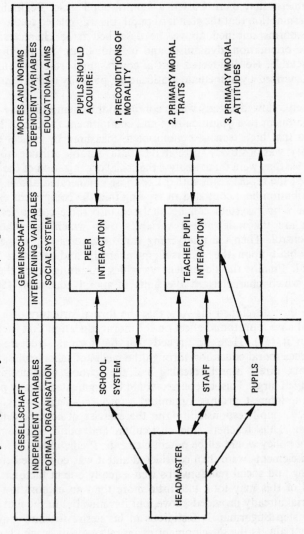

Table 2. *The flow of moral influence in schools (adapted from Sugarman)*

GESELLSCHAFT	GEMEINSCHAFT	MORES AND NORMS
INDEPENDENT VARIABLES	INTERVENING VARIABLES	DEPENDENT VARIABLES
FORMAL ORGANISATION	SOCIAL SYSTEM	EDUCATIONAL AIMS

PUPILS SHOULD ACQUIRE:

1. PRECONDITIONS OF MORALITY

2. PRIMARY MORAL TRAITS

3. PRIMARY MORAL ATTITUDES

PEER INTERACTION

TEACHER PUPIL INTERACTION

SCHOOL SYSTEM

STAFF

PUPILS

HEADMASTER

analysis of the school as a social system' (58). Here, although no new research is mentioned, Sugarman attempts to remedy the deficiency and proposes to use what can only be described as an 'economic' model, while doing so.

He sees the school embedded in society as a sub-system with clearly defined social delineations. Across these boundaries flow the 'input' material, which he had earlier called the independent variables. The organization and interior practices of the school, which he had called the intervening variables, then act on the available resources and produce the dependent variables. These then become the 'output' of knowledge and attitudes which flow into society as the individual pupils leave school as adult members of the community.

It is clear from this that the intervening variables are crucial. Just as no factory could produce goods if it damaged the raw material so no school can produce moral agents if the internal activities have an adverse effect on the pupils. Consequently, Sugarman draws attention not only to the mechanisms of social control and the nature of the existing norms, but also to the role of ritual, ceremony and authority.

Yet despite the meticulous nature of these papers he does not really advance on his predecessors. He does clarify our understanding of the elements which make up a school system, and he does show how they interact, but there is little to guide the moral educator. For example he echoes all those who precursed him by concluding that 'The school functions as an agency of transition between the family and society' (59). Unfortunately, he is sadly conservative in his view that schools should inculcate sensitivity to authority since pupils are destined to belong to an authoritarian society. However, he does stress the important distinction between positional and personal authority (60), although precisely how autonomy, as one prime ingredient of morality, can emerge from such a milieu is not very clear.

Cross-cultural Problems
Miller and Woock now introduce a most important element into the present discussion. Accepting the current American assumption that schools can solve many social and moral problems, they point out that America is currently faced with a welter of complex interacting difficulties. Therefore, it is argued, the educational solvent must be more subtle and complex than is generally supposed. Their analysis of this domestic problem is then developed. The point is this. They remind us that schools must be seen in their own cultural context, and that we cannot blandly accept evidence from one culture and

apply it elsewhere. This is one criticism that must be levelled at the 'anti-school' clutch of writers.

Bronfenbrenner also jolted this complacent assumption with his comparison of the school/society interaction in Russia and America. Although he eulogized the Russian system it is still true, as Rudman found, that there is a fundamentally healthy but highly complex interaction of school, state and the Party peculiar to Russia. Apparently, it is the lack of this which, some say, makes the American system so effete. Equally, as Ungoed-Thomas has shown, this interlocking forms a balance of power which is reflected only in the Russian school system, wherein 'democratic' procedures prevent any one individual or pressure group from affecting the policy of a school.

Of course, this is not a eulogy of Russian schools. It was observed above that such benefits accrue only to a system which deprives its members of autonomy, and it must be repeatedly asserted that morality cannot develop with this deprivation. However, Matthews has recently found that there appears to be as much bias against poor children in Russia, as there is in the U.S. or U.K. (61). Still the point is this: Miller and Woock remind us that the evidence elicited above can only rightly be applied to the culture from which it originates.

Interacting Variables

From the above data, it is clear that moral education will be affected by a number of interacting variables in the school system. Although Parsons is concerned primarily with role theory, these can easily be assimilated under his 'pattern variable' analysis. For he also describes them as 'pattern alternatives of value orientations' (62). His most valuable contribution here is, however, the view that social action is a dynamic response to varying polarities in the system. Children do not passively respond to the social influences acting upon them. Apparently they react dynamically to find what Parsons calls 'optimum gratification'.

In this process his polarities are clearly relevant to moral education. A child may react emotionally or rationally; he must adopt an individualistic or collective vantage point; he must choose between achievement-status and ascribed-status; he must decide whether to adopt a particularist or a universalist outlook; and finally he must resolve the conflict between the specificity of group and individual concerns and the diffuseness of mature morality (63). From all this it is clear that moral action also results from ideas and values—a point which Parsons repeatedly stressed.

This pattern-variable analysis has two distinct advantages over Sugarman's tripartite, variable structure. It not only absorbs his analysis of variables and discloses that the influence of a school system, on individual morality, is both inordinately complex and mutually reciprocal; it also reveals that any advantageous change in the system must affect every element. It is thus of little use having, say, a democratic school ethos if this does not affect all the other elements, including the teaching methods (64). However, as we shall see below, an analysis of school systems in terms of 'models' partly alleviates this problem.

In order to clarify the position, all this data has been represented diagrammatically (see fig. 3). Here it should be noted that any two of the component elements of a school system could be connected by a reciprocal flow-line, for the essence of these variables is that they are all interrelated. Furthermore such reciprocity reveals the dynamic interaction of the individuals embedded in the system.

Parsons has often been accused of thus structuring a falsely static system; a criticism which might well be directed at Sugarman, whose analysis implies that pupils are passively moulded by the other variables. However, it is this complex interaction which makes it so difficult to provide a simple answer to the question, 'How does the school affect moral growth?' The fact remains that we need to know precisely which interactive construct of these variables is most efficacious in the socialization of children. There is clearly a considerable amount of original research to be done here, but when this is accomplished we should be better equipped to assess how far the school as a social system can be used to inculcate, establish and perpetuate those moral preconditions, traits, attitudes, norms and roles which form the foundation of moral maturity.

REFERENCES

1 cf. Davis (1967), Madge (1963), Fletcher (1971), *et al*. This may result from a paucity of inadequate data, which, in turn, resulted from several related factors. Shaw (1966), for example, found that teachers were reluctant to allow themselves and their schools to be scrutinized. Researchers had no comprehensive strategy and procedure. There were no accepted criteria for discriminating between schools. Finally, new concepts were needed for this task. Clearly since depth research would be misleading under these circumstances, and simple descriptions would be inadequate, we have the present procedural impasse.

2 Bernstein (1970), pp. 344 ff. It should be noted, however, that this argument is built on the view that the school context is invariably middle class.

3 Bernstein (1971), p. 78.

4 Durkheim (1956), 'Education is the action exercised by the generation of adults on those which are not yet ready for social life' (p. 137), and education 'is the methodical socialization of the young generation' (p. 71).

5 'The interest of the State is to see that the nation's life may be retained in its integrity' (Spens Report, pp. 147–8). One should not forget, however,

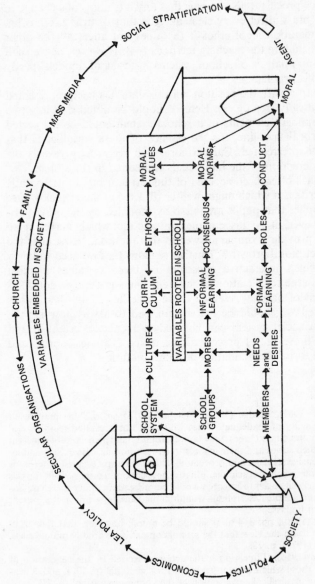

Figure 3. Variables in moral education (based on Parsons, 1951, pp. 101–12). N.B. Although Parsonian this diagram contains no polarities and does not imply that moral education is a process intended to induce social equilibrium. It is presented here to indicate the complexity and interaction of the relevant variables.

that such a uniformity may result from the presentation of a single sub-cultural ethos. At one extreme there is the ideal of leadership upheld by the public schools, and at the other the ideal of competent, honest industry in subservience to economic rulers, as preached in secondary modern schools. This knotty problem is eliminated by Clarke (1948), who sums up his thesis and opens his book by saying 'An educative society is one which accepts as its overmastering purpose the production of a given type of citizen'.

6 Vickers (1968), p. 74.

7 Moral maturity requires a man to make free *autonomous* decisions. These are based on *rational* considerations, and concern for the people involved issues in *altruistic* attitudes. Finally a sense of *responsibility* is needed to implement these decisions so that they take a behavioural form. The fact that this all resolves itself down to rational/altruism is developed in Chapter 19. This is actually the inchoate view of Cronbach (1954) and Peck and Havighurst (1964).

8 Wilson (1969) and Kay (1969) attempted this. No doubt the current surge of interest in related research may enable us ultimately to quantify these moral qualities, sanctions, attitudes and traits. Wilson (1973) has provided some guidance in this area.

9 From 13 to 17 March 1972 the *Daily Mail* published a series of 'startling revelations' about the 'chaos in our comprehensives'. The alleged teacher-informant found 'teachers fighting violence, vandalism, truancy and an almost total breakdown of discipline'.

10 Allport (1965), p. 165.

11 See Havighurst and Taba (1949), Peck and Havighurst (1964), and Levinson (1957, 1959) who all show the influence of personality on conduct in organizational and free situations.

12 The Hopi, Sioux and Zuni Indians, like the Australian aborigines, all co-operate in solving problems and will not give an answer to a problem when in the presence of one who does not know the answer. See Porteous (1931), Klineberg (1965) and Duncan (1972).

13 For example, Eysenck (1971), where he argues against the environmental hypothesis.

14 Mays (1963) found that the social structure determined the nature of crime and delinquency. Erikson (1969) concluded that personal problems result from cultural forces. Mercer (1972) has shown how our urban environment determines the nature of recreational activity. Schroden (1968) shows how drunken behaviour is socially determined. Ross (1939) argues that moral differences can be explained by reference to 'differences in the circumstances of differing societies' (p. 173). Wootton (1945) showed how even sub-cultural differences have an equally profound effect.

15 Ossowska (1971), 'I fully appreciate the role of economic class interests in the shaping of morality, yet I consider this to be only one factor among many others' (p. 97).

16 Pahl (1970), p. 78. He sums up the conclusion of Klein (1965), cf. Beatrice and John Whiting (1971), who show that rural and urban children differ profoundly in respect of their levels of altruism and egoism. Berger (1968) sums this up: 'We become that by which we are addressed' (p. 117).

17 Kay (1969) showed that the dominant sanctions of reciprocity and the ideal self both reflect social expectations.

18 Asch (1952), Sherif and Sherif (1956), Kelley and Woodruff (1956), Lewin (1947) and McDavid and Harari (1968) all showed the force of group pressure to induce subjects to accept arguments contrary to their norms

and mores. It was earlier argued that one's conscience may be an internal-ized *social* control (see Chapter 8). Durkheim (1953), pp. 35–46, and Mead (1934), pp. 173–8, discuss this point. Finally Davies (1971) makes a practical point. If pupils will not express opinions contrary to group norms it is 'difficult to find out what pupils really think on moral matters' (p. 52).

19 Vierkandt (1923) argued that the group, like the individual, was more than the sum of its parts. I possessed self-consciousness and acted as a person. This mystical idea is not original. St Paul spoke of all Christians as 'The body of Christ' (Eph. 4:12).

20 Durkheim's *Angelicism* affirms that 'the social group precedes and consti-tutes the individual, that it is the source of all higher values, and that social states and changes are not produced, affected or modified by the desires and volition of individuals'. Quoted from Barnes (1948, p. 499). Mead (1934) says 'The self is a social self . . . It is important to conceive of a self arising outside social experience' (p. 140). Thus from Vierkandt (1923), through Durkheim to Mead (1934) one traces a dilution of the notion.

21 Sprott (1958), pp. 11 ff. Ottaway (1962) develops this theme (pp. 148 ff), but Sumner (1904) long ago concluded 'The mores are social rituals in which we all participate unconsciously' (paras. 66–8, 80–3).

22 Lewin (1947) demonstrated that group discussion led to both greater freedom and social responsibility. Coughlin (1970) using Homans' criteria for *internal* and *external* systems activity, found that open democratic systems, as opposed to closed, authoritarianism, led to co-operation and autonomy rather than conflict and compliance. See Chapter 16 below for a discussion on the value of democratic systems, and Chapter 18 for a review of value-validation.

23 Giddens (1968) stresses that one should study the processes whereby value-systems are established, rather than follow Parson and Dahrendorf in drawing attention to the integrative function of a common value-system. Berger (1968) is perhaps of most value here. He reviews, as did Ossowska (1972), the use of violence and economic pressure to induce conformity, but concludes that the most potent is morality as a social system' (pp. 86–90).

24 Cooper (1971), like Karl Marx, argued that this is also true of the family. It prevented individuals from realizing their true potential (see Chapter 17). Hargreaves (1967) showed that this was also true of schools, which merely develop delinquent values in less able pupils (pp. 173–6, *et al.*).

25 Dysfunction is an unintended consequence which both runs counter to the avowed function of the system and simultaneously threatens its stability and effectiveness.

26 Argyris (1964), pp. 82–6, 110–12. Note that this is a reciprocal activity. Berger (1968) says 'human dignity is a matter of social permission' (p. 121). Golding (1954) crisply adds 'The shape of a society depends on the ethical nature of the individual' (p. 189).

27 Spencer (1970), pp. 123 ff.

28 Gordon (1971), pp. 60 ff.

29 Bidwell (1969), pp. 1241 ff.

30 Tumin (1969) distinguishes between the Weberian and Marxist view of social mobility. Bottomore (1970) develops the argument and shows that Weber was the first to present a comprehensive alternative to the Marxist view, by arguing that one should distinguish between stratification by class and stratification by social prestige (pp. 25 ff).

31 Waller (1967), p. 6.

32 *op. cit.*, pp. 6, 134, 135.

33 i.e. one who views a social organization in mechanical terms, and interprets all internal events as being conducive to internal stability (see Chapter 13).

34 Lambert (1970), p. 14.

35 Etzioni (1964). He defined social organizations as 'social units that pursue specific goals which they are structured to serve' (p. 4).

36 Musgrave (1970). Introduction.

37 Musgrave (1968), (pp. 123–4).

38 Musgrave (1968), Chapter 2. This is one of his four counter-poised, i.e. (1) religion, (2) élitism versus egalitarianism, (3) education and economy, (4) independence and the control of schools.

39 Musgrave (1968) presents this in diagrammatic form (p. 47). Parsons (1967) stresses that the *expressive*, personal element should dominate with infant children and so facilitate their transfer from home to school; while the *instrumental*, impersonal element should dominate with school leavers to facilitate their entry into adult society. Johns (1965) develops this theme (p. 134). See Diagram C.

40 Hargreaves' (1972) emphasis on the relationships of school members is of value here. It is a valuable corrective to Lambert (1970) whose colleagues stress the system rather than the members.

41 See the spirited defence of Mitchell (1967), 'Parsons elaborated a *framework* to study action; not a theory of action' (p. 38). 'Parsons has provided a general theory of action' (pp. 68–9).

42 Parsons (1959), p. 442.

43 Schelsky (1959), pp. 414–19.

44 Ottaway (1962), p. 167.

45 Hargreaves (1967), p. 192.

46 Hirst and Peters (1970), p. 106. Cotgrove (1968), pp. 78–9.

47 Role-allocation is a crucial concept because: (1) it is a central element linking the disciplines of both psychology and sociology, and thereby emphasizing both a system and its members; and (2) every social structure can be regarded as a configuration of interlocking social roles.

48 Argued earlier by Kay (1968), pp. 253 ff.

49 Morrison and McIntyre (1971), p. 85. Heavy reliance on current developmental theories diminishes the sociological value of this book.

50 Mays (1967), p. IX. See also Brim (1958), Hoyle (1965), Bidwell (1965) and Morrish (1972).

51 Banks (1971), p. 182.

52 *op. cit.*, pp. 183–7.

53 Sugarman (1968), p. 17. The manuscript of his major work *The School, Social Learning and Moral Education* is currently lodged with the NFER (September 1972) but other publications make his position clear.

54 Sugarman (1966).

55 Sugarman (1967).

56 Sugarman (1968a).

57 Sugarman (1968b).

58 Sugarman (1969), p. 15.

59 *op. cit.*, p. 31.

60 Bernstein (1969) distinguishes between positional (role) and personal (status) authority. Note that this reflects the Marxian view of class-status and the Weberian notion of prestige-status.

61 The Marxian view that social stratification was based only on class was ousted by the Weberian view that prestige stratification was equally important. This is now supported by prestige conflict amongst leaders of communist states. Guthrie *et al.* (1971) and Hertzog *et al.* (1972) provide evidence

of this disparity in the political and educational systems of democratic states.

62 Parsons (1951), pp. 46 ff and 58 ff.

63 One dimension of moral maturity reaches from 'specificity' to 'diffusiveness'. The former is determined by circumstances and not principles. The latter by principles and not circumstances.

64 These do not include those variables determined by society, of which schools are but one element of a sub-cultural kind. Thus the tension between school and society at large adds a further dimension. For, as Beals and Siegel (1967) observe, strain emerges when members of an organization attempt to resolve, in terms of their values and beliefs, problems which arise from interaction with external conditions emanating from the social environment.

Bibliography

ALLPORT, GORDON W., *Pattern and Growth in Personality* (Holt, Rinehart & Winston, 1965).

ARGYRIS, C., *Integrating the Individual and the Organization* (John Wiley. 1964).

ASCH, S. E., *Social Psychology* (Prentice Hall, 1952).

BANKS, OLIVE, *The Sociology of Education* (Batsford, 1971).

BARNARD, CHESTER I., 'Organizations as Systems of Co-operation', in A. Etzioni (Ed.), *Complex Organizations* (Holt, Rinehart & Winston, 1965).

BARNES, H. E. (Ed.), *An Introduction to the History of Sociology* (Univ. Chicago Press, 1948).

BEALS, A. R. and SIEGEL, B. J., *Divisiveness and Social Conflict* (Stanford Univ. Press, 1967).

BERGER, PETER L., *Invitation to Sociology* (Pelican, 1968).

BERNSTEIN, BASIL, 'A Socio-linguistic Approach to Socialization', in J. Gumberz and P. Hynes (Ed.), *Directions in Socio-linguistics* (Holt, Rinehart & Winston, 1969).

BERNSTEIN, BASIL, 'Education Cannot Compensate for Society', in *New Society*, No. 387, 1970.

BERNSTEIN, BASIL, *Class, Codes and Control* (Routledge & Kegan Paul, 1971).

BIDWELL, CHARLES, 'The School as a Formal Organization', in J. G. March (Ed.), *Handbook of Organizations* (Rand McNally, 1965).

BIDWELL, CHARLES, 'Sociology of Education', in *Encyclopaedia of Educational Research* (Collier-Macmillan, 1969).

BOTTOMORE, T. B., *Classes in Modern Society* (Allen & Unwin, 1970).

BREMBER, C. S., *Social Foundations of Education* (John Wiley, 1966).

BRIM, O. G., *Sociology and the Field of Education* (Russell Sage Foundation, New York, 1958).

BRONFENBRENNER, URIE, *The Two Worlds of Childhood* (Allen & Unwin, 1972).

CLARKE, F., *Freedom in the Educative Society* (Univ. London Press, 1948).

COOPER, O., *The Death of the Family* (Allen Lane, 1971).

COTGROVE, S., *The Sociology of Education* (Methuen, 1968).

COUGHLIN, R. J., 'Social Structure in Relatively Closed and Open Systems', in *Educational Administration Quarterly*, Vol. 6, No. 2, 1970.

CRONBACH, L., *Educational Psychology* (Harcourt Brace: New York, 1954).

DAHRENDORF, R., *Class and Class Conflict in Industrial Society* (Routledge & Kegan Paul, 1959).

DAVIES, J., 'The Effects of Group Pressure Upon the Expression of Moral Belief', in *Journal of Moral Education*, Vol. 1, No. 1, 1971.

DAVIS, KINGSLEY, *Human Society* (Macmillan, 1967).

DE CECCO, JOHN P., *The Regeneration of the Schools* (Holt, Rinehart & Winston, 1972).

DUNCAN, B., 'Smother Love', in *New Society*, No. 487, 1972.

DURKHEIM, EMILE, *Sociology and Philosophy* (Free Press, Glencoe, 1953).

DURKHEIM, EMILE, *Education and Sociology* (Free Press, Glencoe, 1956).

ERIKSON, ERIK H., *Childhood and Society* (Penguin, 1969).

ETZIONI, AMITAI, *Modern Organizations* (Prentice Hall, 1964).

EVANS, K. M., *Sociometry and Education* (Routledge & Kegan Paul, 1961).

EYSENCK, HANS, *Race, Intelligence and Education* (Temple Smith, 1971).

FLETCHER, RONALD, *The Making of Sociology*, Vols 1 and 2 (Michael Joseph, 1971).

GIDDENS, ANTHONY, 'Power in the Recent Writings of Talcott Parsons', in *Sociology*, Vol. 2, No. 3, 1968.

GILBERT, D. and LEVINSON, D. J., 'Ideology and Personality in Mental Hospital Aides', in D. Greenblatt *et al.* (Eds), *The Patient at the Mental Hospital* (Free Press, Glencoe, 1957).

GOLDING, WILLIAM, *Lord of the Flies* (Faber, 1954).

GORDON, L. V., 'Weber in the Classroom', in *Journal of Educational Psychology*, No. 62, 1971.

GUTHRIE, J. W., KLEINDORFER, G. B., LEVIN, H. M. and STOUT, R. T., *Schools and Inequality* (MIT Press, 1971).

HARGREAVES, DAVID H., *Social Relations in a Secondary School* (Routledge & Kegan Paul, 1967).

HARGREAVES, DAVID H., *Interpersonal Relations and Education* (Routledge & Kegan Paul, 1972).

HERTZOG, E., NEWCOMB, C. and CISIN, I. H., 'But Some are More Equal than Others', in *Journal of Orthopsychiatry*, Vol. 42, No. 1, 1972.

HIRST, P., 'Philosophy of Education', in *British Journal of Educational Sociology*, Vol. XVIII, No. 2, 1970.

HIRST, P. and PETERS, R. S., *The Logic of Education* (Routledge & Kegan Paul, 1970).

HOMANS, G. C., *The Human Group* (Routledge & Kegan Paul, 1957).

HOYLE, E., 'Organizational Analysis in Education', in *Educational Research*, November 1965.

JOHNS, E. A., *The Social Structure of Modern Britain* (Pergamon, 1965).

KAY, WILLIAM, *Moral Development* (Allen & Unwin, 1968).

KAY, WILLIAM, 'An Investigation into the Moral Attitudes of Primary and Secondary School Children', Unpublished thesis, Nottingham 1969.

KAY, WILLIAM, 'The Self Concept as a Moral Control', in *Journal of Moral Education*, Vol. 2, No. 1, 1972.

KELLEY, H. H. and WOODRUFF, C. L., 'Members' Reactions to Apparent Group Approval of a Counter-norm Communication', in *Journal of Abnormal and Social Psychology*, No. 52, 1956.

KENT, N. and DAVIES, D. R., 'Discipline in the Home and Intellectual Development', in *British Journal of Medicine and Psychology*, Vol. XXX, 1957.

KLEIN, JOSEPHINE, *Samples of English Culture*, Vols 1 and 2 (Routledge & Kegan Paul, 1965).

KLEIN, JOSEPHINE, *Working in Groups* (Hutchinson, 1968).

KLINEBERG, OTTO, *Race and Psychology* (UNESCO, 1965).

KURZWELL, Z. E., *Anxiety and Education* (W. H. Allen, 1969).

LAMBERT, ROYSTON et al. *A Manual to the Sociology of the School* (Weidenfeld & Nicolson, 1970).

LEVINSON, D. J., 'Role, Personality and Social Structure in the Organizational Setting', in *Journal of Abnormal and Social Psychology*, Vol. 58, 1959.

LEWIN, KURT, 'Group Decision and Social Change', in Newcomb and Hartley (Eds), *Readings in Social Psychology* (Holt, Rinehart & Winston, 1947).

LIPPITT, R., LEWIN, K. and WHITE, R., 'The Social Climate of Children's Groups', in Barker, Kovnin and Wright (Eds), *Child Behaviour and Development* (McGraw-Hill, 1943).

LIPPITT, R. and WHITE, R. K., 'An Experimental Study of Leadership and Group Life', in Maccoby, Newcomb and Hartley (Eds), *Readings in Social Psychology* (Methuen, 1959).

MCDAVID, JOHN W. and HARARI, HERBERT, *Social Psychology* (Harper, 1968).

MADGE, JOHN, *Scientific Sociology* (Tavistock, 1963).

MANN, PETER, *Methods of Sociological Enquiry* (Blackwell, Oxford, 1968).

MANNHEIM, KARL, *Diagnosis of Our Time* (Routledge & Kegan Paul, 1943).

MAYS, J. B., *Crime and the Social Structure* (Faber, 1963).

MAYS, J. B., *The School in Its Social Setting* (London Univ. Press, 1967).

MEAD, G. H., *Mind, Self and Society* (Univ. Chicago Press, 1934).

MEAD, G. H., *The Philosophy of the Act* (Univ. Chicago Press, 1938).

MEAD, MARGARET, *Sex and Temperament in Three Primitive Societies* (Routledge & Kegan Paul, 1932).

MERCER, DAVID, 'Discretionary Travel Behaviour and the Urban Mental Map', in *Australian Geographical Studies*, Vol. IX, No. 2, 1971.

MILLS, C. WRIGHT, *Sociology and Pragmatism* (published posthumously—Oxford Univ. Press, 1967).

MITCHELL, W. C., *Sociological Analysis and Politics* (Prentice Hall, 1967).

MORRISH, IVOR, *Disciplines of Education* (Allen & Unwin, 1967).

MORRISH, IVOR, *The Sociology of Education* (Allen & Unwin, 1972).

MORRISON, A. and MCINTYRE, D., *Schools and Socialization* (Penguin, 1971).

MUSGRAVE, P. W., *The Sociology of Education* (Methuen, 1965).

MUSGRAVE, P. W., *The School as an Organization* (Macmillan, 1968).

MUSGRAVE, P. W. (Ed.), *Sociology, History and Education* (Methuen, 1970).

OPPENHEIM, A. N., 'A Study of Social Attitudes of Adolescents', Unpublished Ph.D. thesis, London, 1956.

OSSOWSKA, MARIA, *Social Determinants of Moral Ideas* (Routledge & Kegan Paul, 1972).

OTTAWAY, A. K. C., *Education and Society* (Routledge & Kegan Paul, 1962).

PAHL, R. E., *Patterns of Urban Life* (Longmans, 1970).

PARSONS, TALCOTT, 'The School Class as a Social System', in A. H. Halsey, J. Floud and C. A. Anderson (Eds), *Education, Economy and Society* (Collier-Macmillan, 1959).

PARSONS, TALCOTT, *The Social System* (Routledge & Kegan Paul, 1967).

PECK, R. F. and HAVIGHURST, R. J., *The Psychology of Character Development* (John Wiley, 1964).

PORTEOUS, S. D., *The Psychology of a Primitive People* (Arnold, 1931).

ROSS, W. D., *Foundations of Ethics* (Clarendon Press, 1939).

RUDMAN, H. C., *The School and the State in the U.S.S.R.* (Collier-Macmillan, 1967).

SCHELSKY, H., *Schule, Und Erziehung, der industriehlen gesellschaft* (Werbund-Verlag, 1962).

SCHELSKY, M., *Anpassung oder Widerstand?* *Soziologische Bedenken zur Schulreform* (Quelle & Meyer, 1963).

SHAFTEL, F. R. and SHAFTEL, G., *Role Playing for Social Values* (Prentice Hall, 1967).

SHAW, K. E., 'Why No Sociology of Schools?', in *Education for Teaching*, No. 69, 1966.

SHERIF, M. and SHERIF, C. W., *An Outline of Social Psychology* (Harper, 1956).

SHIPMAN, M., *The Sociology of the School* (Longmans, 1968).

SPENCER, E. MARTIN, 'Weber on Legitimate Norms and Authority', in *British Journal of Sociology*, Vol. 21, 1970.

SPENS REPORT, *Secondary Education* (HMSO, 1959).

SPROTT, W. J. H., *Human Groups* (Penguin, 1958).

SUGARMAN, B., 'Teenage Boys at School', Unpublished Ph.D. thesis, Princeton, 1966.

SUGARMAN, B., 'Involvement in Youth Culture and Conformity in School', in *British Journal of Sociology*, Vol. XVIII, 1967.

SUGARMAN, B., 'The Social Organization of the School', in *Problems of Research in Moral Education* (Farmington Trust Research Unit, Oxford, 1968a).

SUGARMAN, B., 'Moral Education and the Social Structure of the School', in *Journal of Curriculum Studies*, Vol. 1, No. 1, 1968b.

SUGARMAN, B., 'The School as a Social System', in *Moral Education*, Vol. 1, No. 2, 1969.

SUMNER, WILLIAM G., *Folkways* (Grimm, 1904).

TEILHARD, PIERRE DE CHARDIN, *The Phenomenon of Man* (Collins, 1960).

UNGOED-THOMAS, J. R., 'The Soviet School as a Formal Organization', in *Moral Education*, Vol. 1, No. 2, 1969.

VICKERS, GEOFFREY, *Value Systems and Social Process* (Tavistock, 1968).

VIERKANDT, A., *Gesellschaftslehre: Hauptprobleme de Philosophischen Soziologie* (Enke, Stuttgart, 1923).

WALLER, WILLARD, *The Sociology of Teaching* (John Wiley, 1967).

WEBB, JOHN, 'The Sociology of a School', in *British Journal of Sociology*, Vol. 13, 1962.

WEBER, MAX, *The Protestant Ethic and the Spirit of Capitalism* (Allen & Unwin, 1930).

WHITING, B. and WHITING, J., *Field for a Study of Socialization* (John Wiley, 1971).

WHITE, R. K. and LIPPITT, R., 'Leader Behaviour and Member Reaction in Three Social Climates', in D. Cartwright and A. Zander (Eds), *Group Dynamics, Research and Theory* (Tavistock, 1968).

WHYTE, W. H., *The Organization Man* (Jonathan Cape, 1957).

WILSON, JOHN, *Moral Education and the Curriculum* (Pergamon, 1969).

WILSON, JOHN, *The Assessment of Morality* (NFER, 1973).

WOOTTON, B., 'Public and Private Honesty', in *Political Quarterly*, July/September 1945.

WOOTTON, B., *Social Science and Social Pathology* (Allen & Unwin, 1959).

Chapter 13

Some Models of School Organization

The evidence provided above can also be couched in the complementary form of models which are intended to both enhance our understanding of complex organization, and also to disclose the nature of all the cohering component parts. The logical classification of these is easy. They begin with mechanical models naturally indigenous to an industrial society and end with conflict models native to a society torn by cultural strife.

Mechanical Models

A number of mechanical models have been used. Mey, for example, speaks of social systems in the terminology of physics and mathematics. Here children are like molecules in a chemical compound, or ciphers in an equation. Theodore Mills made recourse to a cybernetic model to explain change and growth in a social group. King felt compelled to use the model of mechanical solidarity in order to understand why some pupils rejected moral values and norms, while others accepted them. Sugarman used an 'economics' model to analyse the effect of his school variables on moral education (1).

Organismic Models

When schools are viewed as social organizations, and not as rigidly structured institutions, a new model has to be used. This stresses the dynamism of the personal component. Thus one passes from mechanical to organic solidarity. At its lowest, it can be concerned with personal reactions to situations (2). At its highest it is concerned with dyadic interaction (3), but throughout, it treats the individuals as though they were elements in an organic, rather than a mechanical whole. Hence they are like organs in the body, rather than cogs in a machine. It should be noted, however, that such homeostatic structures, unlike equilibrium systems, do not reach a condition of staticity.

Equilibrium Models

Just as organs in the body's homeostatic system tend to retain some form of equilibrium, so organizations and their members are deemed to preserve social equilibrium. They do this, argues Schon, by the members reacting to preserve social stability. It is this interpersonal feedback, differentiation of roles and homeostatic responses which, say Katz and Kahn, characterize the equilibrium model of an open-system society. One can naturally find some bizarre expressions of this view (4), but in essence it seeks to emphasize that life in schools can be viewed as a homeostatic process leading towards social stability. Hence values and norms are socially integrative if they are conducive to this end.

The Structural–Functional Model
Buckley has recently argued that all the mechanical and organismic models are outmoded. Thus one has next to consider the 'structural–functional' model used by Parsons and employed by Shipman in his analysis of the school. It develops the analysis of the previous equilibrium models very simply. The first emphasized that societies are organic wholes. The second, that individual members in it could initiate actions leading to some form of social equilibrium. Now, Parsons' 'pattern variables', not only interact one on the other, but also emerge as sub-systems whose function is primarily to sustain social equilibrium.

In essence the 'structural–functional' model can explain how schools sustain their social life even with a turnover of membership by suggesting that continuity is provided because social structures emerge to satisfy the social needs of each individual. Furthermore, it shows how equilibrium models can eliminate the notion of dysfunction. With the polarization of pattern variables, one of the opposite values may appear to be dysfunctional, yet can, in fact, be an ultimately stabilizing element (5).

This is essentially a model which implies that social integration results from social consensus, since a society becomes morally stable when all share a common value system. Therefore the prime emphasis, here, is on a society and the interrelationship of its sub-systems, rather than on the individual members. It can, of course, be criticized for thus attaching too much importance to the institution and not enough to the individual; one consequence of which is the assumption that moral education will be a technique employed to achieve and then sustain social equilibrium. It also fails to take account of the fact that most societies are dynamic, in the sense that values, roles and functions are always changing. Hence a dynamic society cannot be defined in terms of consensus and equilibrium. It therefore follows that the structural–functional model is inadequate. Hence many prefer to use the 'conflict' model.

The Conflict Model

Such critics prefer to use this because it is more attuned to the social facts of life in an organization. Those who do so (6) dismiss the Parsonian model as unrealistic. It is an illusion, they say, to believe that societies can achieve stability, and that all internal activity is exclusively directed towards this end. Every social system is a conflict situation, and in a school, say Beals and Siegel, the strife between the generations and social classes is made worse by tensions resulting from the interaction of the school and the neighbourhood.

However, Lambert used this model in his sociological analysis of the school. While recognizing in a lyrical paragraph that conflict can transform any society for both good or ill, he still concluded, 'It is in this perspective of in-built conflict that the chief elements of a school as an organization should be viewed' (7). The ardour of such an affirmation must, however, be cooled by the observation that he, like Shipman, had to resort to the structural–functionalist model as well as the conflict model.

Obviously every model has some value, in that each stress different elements in the system. However, a rapid abdication of their theoretical structure, by proponents of the 'conflict' model, makes it clear that they are not entirely committed to this view of the school system. Musgrave's blunt words are relevant here. Observing that such conflict-induced dysfunction may be beneficial in certain situations, he concludes that as a result of this conflict, 'the school class must usually be working below full efficiency' (8).

It is legitimate to note at this point that both the structural–functional and the conflict model complement each other. Just as the former is inadequate since it tries to disregard the inherent conflict in any social situation, so too the latter disregards the innate drive of every society to attain balance and stability.

So far no single model has provided insight into the structure of a school as a socializing agent. If any moral values, attitudes and norms are created they appear to be little more than ethical epiphenomena. Members of the organization, it seems, think and behave as they do merely in order to sustain social equilibrium or canalize conflict into creative channels. Thus to the above models we must add two which appear to throw light on the socializing process in school. These are the familial model and the therapeutic model.

The Familial Model

If schools are organized in terms of a familial model then teachers can function in a parental role, within an institution bearing the marks of family life; both of which, as we have seen, are crucial components in moral education. Teachers already adopt this role as being *in loco parentis*, and many enlightened schools already operate on a familial basis. Of course the term 'familial' must be clearly defined since families vary from the mutually hostile, uncharitable occupants of a slum dwelling to the stereotype middle-class home characterized by security, physical well-being and an abundance of love. For this model therefore we must refer to an ideal extended-type family, i.e. a multi-age, multi-ability, emotionally secure unit with a web of friendship and kin networks penetrating the community towards which they feel some sense of responsibility (9). Thus a familial school would be one in which the relationships were familial, the teachers were parental, the pupils were granted ascribed status, the school was involved in neighbourhood life, and the system was based on a democratic, fraternal, benevolent power structure.

Naturally there are dangers in a system which can so easily lend itself to dysfunctional activities (10), and one must ask whether children can pass easily from the nuclear family of their homes, into the extended-type family of a school, and, ultimately, into a world society based on fraternalism and democratic procedures. However, actual experiments, in which the school approximated to the familial model, reveal how successful it can be.

Some saw education in such personal terms and viewed the aim of education as the inculcation of autonomy in the pupils concerned. Thus the process was one in which the individual became 'self-actualizing'; and then proceeded to develop as such in the free environment of a familial structure where unconditional love and acceptance were the norm (11). Others emphasize responsibility and service to the community, and have found that a familial school structure facilitates this (12). Finally, as a reply to Greene's argument that academic standards would suffer in the process, one may point out that academic, as well as personal standards rose when children worked in a school which provided such 'a secure family structure', and that all the emotional and educative needs of the children were met (13).

The Therapeutic Model

From the evidence presented so far it is clear that the concepts of moral maturity and mental health are closely linked. It is therefore legitimate to assume that a school, in which effective moral education is taking place, could be classified as a therapeutic community. Conceptually structured by this model a school would then be deemed to engage in therapy of some kind; and consequently the teachers would be therapists.

Again, there are obvious dangers here. The roles of teacher and therapist can be so confused that neither is effective (14). It is difficult not to conclude that schools can have a therapeutic function to perform, for even remedial academic work qualifies as such (15). When teachers are actively involved in helping pupils with their personal problems, they are inevitably involved as therapists. Consequently we can apply pastoral terminology to this process. When pupils are morally and spiritually sick, we say simply that it is the teacher's task to provide a cure. (16).

Of interest here is Sugarman's analysis of a therapeutic community, and his application of this model to the school. With consummate skill and sociological expertise he shows how all the benefits of a therapeutic community could accrue to anti-social pupils, regardless of whether their difficulties originate in personal maladjustment or sheer boredom. The only point to emphasize here is a simple one. The transformation of schools into therapeutic communities, or even the incorporation of a therapy unit into the school, could alarm many. Thus he argues that we might try 'the use of various approaches implied in the therapeutic community model in a somewhat diluted form throughout the school' (17).

Such reports make it abundantly clear that the matrix of these societies is love and discipline. These terms, however, have to be understood aright, before any conclusions can be drawn. Love here means disciplined love, and discipline means compassionate authority (18). In fact one is compelled to resort to the concept of rational altruism (see Chapter 19), to describe the qualities required, for both must be present. As Peck and Havighurst concluded 'Such love and such discipline are *both* essential, joint determinants of good character' (19).

It could be argued that this model is too idealistic. The idea of institutions based on discipline is familiar enough, but to extend this and argue that they can also be based on love, could savour of naïvety. Such critics may well refer to Bowlby's thesis that the love which is necessary for psychic health, is primarily maternal. This is not the case. First, 'it is not a matter of *which* parent but what *kind* of parent' (20); and, second, Barbara Wootton has extended the argument further, claiming that the love necessary for moral and mental health can be provided by parental *surrogates* in an institutional setting. In this shifting emphasis one thus reaches the point where it is now accepted that institutions can provide that form of love which was earlier thought to be a maternal prerogative. Hence it can be concluded that schools can provide not only the discipline, but also love, which together form the most powerful determinants of moral development.

The Validity of Sociological Analysis
Before concluding this chapter two related questions have to be raised. The first arises because the partially incoherent data may result from the fact that schools are not genuine social systems. Perhaps the appeal of, say, the 'conflict' model arises from this. However, because of such doubts the query must be pursued—can schools be analysed in sociological terms?

There are three relevant points. First, they can be, and have been, subjected to valid analysis as social structures. From this it has emerged that they are clearly integral sub-systems of society and can therefore be subjected to the same form of analysis (21). Second, it may be that it is too early to erect global, all-embracing theories. We may still be at the pre-systematic confused 'wonder' stage of investigation (22), making hesitant forages into the stage of 'utility' where 'many of us will live to see the social sciences become the primary means by which we seek to determine social policies' (23). Lastly, *structuralism* suggests that once we recognize a group to be a society (in much the same way as Chomsky argues we can recognize language) it is amenable to investigation.

Simply expressed, *structuralism* argues that the societies of man are determined by the innate 'structuring' capacity of the human mind. Consequently the sociological analysis of any 'society' is natural and legitimate since all social and mental structures result from the same innate capacity to formulate both knowledge and experience (24). Such a view will be familiar to many working in diverse disciplines while some may be tempted to dismiss it as a new form of subjective idealism. If the above points are accepted it is clear that social analysis can be applied to the school. But this raises the second question—can this be done objectively?

Value-laden Sociological Analysis
There seems to be a simple conflict between those who consider value-laden judgements to be valid and those who do not. However, the matter is more complex than this. Objectivity can mean two things. It either means objective as opposed to subjective data; or it refers to that same objective data unaffected by the observer. Hence since data cannot be known until it is perceived it is difficult to find some way of making a sociological value-free judgement.

The notion of value-free judgements originated with Weber, who wished to place sociological investigation on terms of parity with other sciences. Musgrave has recently followed this line of thought and concluded. 'A science should contain no prejudice. Therefore a sociology of education must give a neutral analysis' (25). This accurately reflects Weber's term *Weitfreiheit*, which means not indifference to man's difficulties, but an objective and reasoned approach to their solution.

Yet value-laden sociological assessments must intrude, despite the laudable desire to retain total objectivity of judgement, and while Lazarsfeld claimed to have 'value-neutrality' he still had to conclude that 'value-laden biologists and physicists are not limited in the scope of their work' (26). Even when Myrdal begins his book by referring to 'The search for objective truth' he still has to concede that sociological value-premises must be stated. This too is Peters' position. He argues that the study of man can never be value free, even though it ought (27).

However, Runciman has now shown that Weber did not really mean that sociology can be value-free. His reappraisal of Weber's work shows that in it one finds three methodological assumptions. First, there is always the possibility that value-judgements will intrude. Second, social action is invariably subjective in nature. Third, 'because cultural evolution is subjective the social scientist cannot frame his explanations without implicit dependence upon presuppositions of a value-relevant kind' (28).

Value-laden judgements, it seems, are therefore legitimate. Numerous contemporary exponents of this can be found. Perhaps the most lucid is Alastair MacIntyre. He argued that all social theory is ideological, because it must be understood in a social context, and since all social institutions are reciprocal functions of the beliefs which their members have about them, they must also be value-laden. Consequently, 'the individual object or action is identifiable only in the context of the totality; the totality is only identifiable as a set of relationships between individuals' (29). The fervour with which he pursues this argument is apparent from his indictment of Lipset, who, he claims, pretends to be morally neutral when he is not; and of Hare who protests that morality can be studied out of its sociological context but does not do so. His position, however, can be neatly summarized. He rejects the assumption that values and facts can be separated. What experience has joined, he argues, let no man put asunder!

However, the less philosophically minded might prefer the argument of Norman. He believed simply that sociologists must shed their value-free armour because they carry the responsibility of helping to awake mankind to its plight (30). Whichever view one takes, in approaching the school, one must necessarily approach with preconceptions about the nature of man, society and morality. Not to do so would be as anomalous as measuring the validity of historical documents with litmus paper, or the potency of a chemical by the mellifluity of its name.

The Dual Role of the School

We can now outline the dual role of the school. It must serve both its pupils and society at large. The former will consist of establishing and perpetuating the moral preconditions, traits and attitudes outlined above. This, however, need not be an élitist process even though these moral qualities will aproximate more to higher- than lower-status moral norms. When dealing with moral embourgeoisement for example, it was stressed that the emotional, political, economic and moral privileges at present possessed by the former, must become the prerogative of all.

To attain this level of parity, however, official moral education must inevitably be involved in promoting those policies which will ensure that all children are thus privileged, or at least that none are deprived. We have seen that this influence will include both service and reformation, for schools have a duty to improve society, herein lies one serious difficulty. Emergent morally-mature young people may be destined for a society not yet prepared for them.

We may agree on the nature of moral maturity. Society may want schools to produce such young adults, but some politicians seem to prefer citizens who will not look too rationally at their arguments. Industry does not appear to want autonomous men: advertisers want gullible consumers: even the organized church and unions appear to prefer members who are not independently responsible. Thus, in many walks of life autonomy is a distinct disadvantage. When to this one adds the fact that the moral educator has to fight against the norms of a hire-purchase, privatized, alienated, mass-media dominated society, it seems that little can be done until society is radically and fundamentally changed. Thus, in the light of the analyses in this chapter the question must now be asked, 'How then can schools be better equipped to morally educate the young and so transform society for good?'

WHICH MODEL TO USE?

This can be put more sharply since the sociological analyses of Chapter 12 disclosed the nature and interaction of the variables; and the various models, presented here, disclosed the different overall systematic structure (31). In the light of this we may ask, 'Which model of the school system will most effectively utilize the sociological variables in order to advance moral education?'

A brief critical survey (32) may lead to an answer. The mechanical model is inadequate because moral agents have wills of their own. The organismic takes no account of the fact that individuals are not

entirely subordinate to their social system. Homeostatic and equilibrium models cannot be accommodated to the exploratory and
creative element in moral conduct, and the structural–functional
models stress social rather than personal needs. The most damning
indictment of all is the fact that moral values and norms are thereby
deemed to be merely the means of achieving an harmonious, stable,
integrated society, and moral values become little more than utilitarian epiphenomena.

It could also be claimed that the static nature of these models
disqualifies them from functioning in a moral milieu, for it is here
that the conflict model emerges as having much to commend it since
it caters for the strife and conflict endemic to any healthy society.
Again, this must be disqualified since it places too little stress on
the socially integrating power of moral principles. Thus we are left
with the familial and therapeutic models of the school system: i.e.
we must consider whether all the variables, outlined above, are most
effective when organized systematically within a familial or therapeutic structure.

The Appropriate Familial Model

The suggestion that schools should be organized on a familial model
is open to serious criticism. Psychologists can remark ruefully that
it facilitates a flight to the nurturant, maternal protector when the
responsibilities of adulthood loom nearer. Practising teachers can
dismiss it as unrealistic and cite evidence to support their case. In
many schools pupils and teachers are antagonists caught in a web
of violence and hostility. Democracy is praised; but autocracy is
practised. Aiming to unite society, schools seem to foster division and
discontent. Consequently teachers become resentful when hostility
to them is then indexed by the level of their underpaid, under-
privileged status. Sociologists can cite exchange theories to highlight
the lack of disinterested motivation in social bonding. Thus they
could refer to Blau's theory of exchange and power in which he
argued that all relationships are motivated by the privileges, benefits
or power they are expected to bring.

All this may be true. To modify the concept, one may argue that
no model, like Weber's 'ideal type', approximates to reality, since
no society is ideal. We merely seek the closest approximation. Or it
could be argued that schools are like this because they have yet to
be organized on a familial basis.

However, the familial model does seem best. It incorporates the
qualities found in all the other models. As an 'extended' family it
has less of the deficiencies of a 'nuclear' family, and it can also
incorporate the advantages of the therapeutic model for both of

these are based on disciplined love and responsibility. Thus if subsumed under the pattern of an 'extended' (33) family, with the benign authority structure now known to be essential to its stability, a familial school is a viable educational possibility.

Such a familial structure is one within which children can also develop into autonomous, responsible, altruistic moral agents. Obviously altruism cannot survive in a society based on conflict. The popular structural–functional form of sustaining the stability of a school community restricts the growth of moral autonomy. Thus it is only in a familial society that genuine social responsibility can flourish (34).

Furthermore, such a familial environment is required to facilitate both the emergence and cultivation of the preconditions of morality. Only in such a social setting can children experience the love and acceptance which enables them to stabilize these foundations of morality. In its rich social environment they can develop a sense of their own identity. The easy, reciprocal, familial relationships will enable every child to both realistically assess and then accept his own nature. Such a community will abound with those moral paradigms which will canalize each child's 'identification' energy into conduct acceptable to the community. Finally, since status within a family is ascribed by the group, rather than earned by the member, the experience of success is assured (35). Naturally, this may extend from little more than the success associated with being an accepted member of the family, up to the success which would otherwise confer status, if it were not already ascribed. In every case, however, the familial group would ensure that no child experienced the indignity of failure and rejection, despite the opprobrium of personal inadequacy.

Schools should therefore, it seems, become familial organizations, with a structure approximating more to the extended family, which earlier characterized tribal or folk society. In this sense they would be the lay equivalent of the family and disclose three moral advantages not now possessed by them. As 'families' they would enjoy that potency of influence in moral education, which is one prerogative of families. They would fill a gap in social life left by the church, and so assume the social and moral roles abdicated by that other essentially familial and therapeutic system, and they would form a bridge between home and society (36).

The Bridge Between Home and School

When sociologists turn their attention to the school as a system in relation to other social systems, it is usual for them to locate all the points of conflict, friction and dysfunction. It ought to be emphasized here, therefore, that in the form of extended families such schools would introduce a measure of social stability by acting as a natural bridge between home and society.

The observation that extended familes approximated to some forms of society, has recently been elaborated by those who claim that even urban man is essentially a villager (37). It is said that he there builds up a sub-group in which relations are more guarded than in primary groups, but more intimate than in secondary groups. A familial school would be such a system but it would enjoy an advantage of supreme value to moral education. Both the ascribed status natural to home life, and the achieved status demanded in society, would be available in school. Hence the open acceptance involved in ascribing status and the success and achievement implicit in achieving status (appropriate to one's ability) both facilitate moral growth. The former because loving acceptance is a fundamental precondition of morality. The latter because this positive reinforcement encourages continual growth.

In this process children are also prepared for entry into adult life without having to negotiate the problems associated with passing from one value-system to another. Then, as they cross this bridge into society, children may increasingly affect its *mores*. Coming from familial schools they may help to create a fraternal society, and, if this is also to be considered as a valid aim of moral education, all humanistic teachers, regardless of their ideological or political commitment, can then join in this exciting venture.

Implications for the School

It has been repeatedly noted that an authoritarian, non-familial school structure not only prevents moral development but also induces moral immaturity (38). By reflecting a familial structure *all* schools could be immediately organized so that both they, and the constituent school classes, were multi-age and multi-ability units.

Within that comprehensive structure all teachers would be parental counsellors and all activities familial and therapeutic. Viewed formally such a school would foster the preconditions of morality through the therapeutic ethos of the organization. Familial school classes would not only facilitate the establishment of the preconditions of morality, they would also provide opportunities for autonomy, altruism and responsibility to flourish. Then the curriculum content could inculcate rationality and the moral traits of judgement, deferred gratification, flexibility and dynamism (39).

This could also be viewed in another way. We spoke earlier of the need for a secular form of conversion to enable children to do what they knew they *should* do. This analogy can now be carried further.

Teachers would become secular pastors and the school could be viewed as a secular church. Then school assemblies and other rituals could be the secular rites of this secularized institution (40). Consequently, just as the whole administrative and procedural life of the church is focused on the salvation of each individual, so the administration and procedure of school life would focus on a child's total maturation.

Holt and the whole anti-school group, are undeniably right in their assertion that in the last analysis only our children and their relationships matter. Thus under the familial model we see that it is persons, and contact between person and person as *persons*, that ultimately matters.

Dewey long ago observed that academic work had 'taken over our schools', and we have seen this tendency swell, for our competitive society over-values the intellect and under-values personal worth. In it the clever fraud who makes a fortune is elevated as a paradigm. The moral man seeking neither fame nor fortune for himself, is derided. Of course they may accrue to him as a result of his efforts, but when they do he holds them lightly, preferring to serve, rather than exploit, his fellows.

This academic pressure felt more fully in the secondary school and less so in the primary school, probably militates against the effectiveness of secondary moral education. It is true that like any family a school should accommodate itself to children as they grow. It will facilitate this by sustaining primary school home ties with an active PTA, and establishing contact with society by means of an 'out-going' year in the secondary school. However, the point is this. Such a model places the emphasis firmly on moral and personal qualities; not on intellectual expertise, no matter how scintillating it may be.

In schools we have been given the supreme privilege and opportunity to form the values and attitudes of each generation, and from this process it is hoped that morally mature young men and women will emerge.

Our task is to develop the human potential of children, and not merely to produce literate and numerate citizens. If we succeed then our children will become the mature self-actualizing ideals of Rousseau, Froebel, Tolstoy, Dewey, Allport, Rogers and Maslow, etc.

At the moment almost all educational endeavour is devoted to academic excellence. Consequently most moral education occurs incidentally—although fortunately this situation is now changing. Why should the process not be reversed? Should we not at least experiment with the suggestion that the situation should be inverted so that all educational endeavour is devoted towards the moral and personal development of children; with academic learning almost incidental to the process?

This is not educationally naïve. In a controlled experiment it was found that 'in societies without schools, instruction within families is seldom deliberate but occurs in the course of ordinary work and in play and games' (41). In a familial school such learning would, it seems, continue. One does not even have to be as radical as this. Obviously schools must teach pupils on the basis of formal curricula to prepare them for a working career, but it seems perfectly clear, from all the evidence, that even if the focal point was moved from academic to personal attainment, much would be achieved. They will not then be inefficiently producing the competitive, materialistic, consumers so rightly disparaged by the anti-school writers. Instead the scientists, technologists, doctors, teachers, administrators, artisans and labourers who emerge will be dedicated not to aggressive divisiveness but to conciliatory union. Consequently our society will be built upon unifying altruism, instead of the competitive greed which leads to industrial, economic and cultural strife.

Plowden's hopes that homes could be changed by schools has been proved unrealistic. If the home is one of the most potent factors in moral education, what then can be done? The answer, it seems, is to create familial schools. Herein lies our hope. While we can do little to affect the homes from which our children come, we can modify the schools to which they go. If these can be re-organized on the familial model, employing the variables which research discloses as being most effective, we may yet begin to implement the 1944 *Education Act*, which insisted that 'It shall be the duty of the Local Education Authority for every area to contribute towards the spiritual, moral, mental and physical development of the community'.

REFERENCES

1 Spiegelman (1968) used a benefit/cost model to calculate the expense of eliminating delinquency. Consequently Richmond (1969) warns that the educator 'must be aware of the extent to which his outlook is conditioned by industrial ways of living' (p. 16). Sennett (1971) observes, 'We have confused a machine-using society with a vision of society as a machine itself' (p. 86).

2 This is Hargreaves' (1972) basic model. He calls it 'symbolic interactionism' (pp. 21 ff).

3 This is the face-to-face interaction, the life-long preoccupation of Goffman (1970).

4 Morris (1969) calls education a painful *rite de passage* into adulthood (pp. 203 ff). Musgrave (1968) claims that 'rituals are used to transmit values to pupils' (p. 82). Lacey (1970) describes this as 'sub-cultural forma-

tion' (p. 73). Wakeford (1969) saw 'pupil-adaptation' in terms of élitist accommodation (p. 48). Tronc (1967) deemed this to be 'characteristic of 'bureaucratic structures' (p. 137). But all are models of the homeostatic trends of a stratified society.

5 Parsons (1967) defines polarized variables as: affectivity versus affective neutrality; self-orientation versus collectivity orientation; universalistic standard versus particularistic standard; evaluating people by ascriptive criteria versus achievement criteria; a specific social response versus a diffused response (see pp. 60, 62–6). He claims that these five dichotomies may interact and provide thirty-two complex variables (p. 47). It is thus possible to accept that apparent dysfunctions may become functional in such a polarized model of society. Religious and political organizations illustrate this. Initially disrupting society they finally contribute to its cultural evolution.

6 Coser (1956, 1967), Dahrendorf (1959), Galtung (1959) and Smelser (1962) all accept 'Conflict as a way of Life' (Galtung, 1969, p. 590). Dahrendorf (1959) and Rex (1965) could have strengthened their opposition by claiming that Parsons is too utilitarian to make any contribution to our understanding of social cohesion. Even his terms disclose this, for 'functionalism' implies that moral values and norms have no intrinsic validity. Their contribution lies solely in their ability to function as catalysts of social integration.

7 Lambert (1970), p. 15. The participant–observer report of Richardson (1967) and Johnson (1970) support this. Sennett (1971) argues that conflict is creative. Leigh (1971) found that a 'disorganized' team worked better than a 'managed' group.

8 Musgrave (1968), p. 250.

9 Britten and Britten (1970).

10 Greene (1967) showed how schools can too easily become merely instruments of social activity in the neighbourhood. Hagstrom (1968) shows how 'in societies without schools, instruction within families is seldom *deliberate* but occurs in the course of work, play and games'. Thus familial schools need not abdicate their educational functions in affective activities.

11 e.g. Hobart (1968).

12 Britten and Britten (1970) stress that genuine education has this social outreach. Bronfenbrenner (1971) shows how the Russian familial education system leads to a highly developed sense of social responsibility.

13 Kidd and Kidd (1968) reporting on the 'Head-start Project'.

14 Wilson (1968) and Bantock (1967) agree that teachers should be therapists but argue that the respective teacher roles must be clearly distinguished. On the other hand, Peters (1964) says bluntly 'The main function of the teacher is to train and instruct; it is not to help or cure' (p. 85). This point is also made by Yarlott (1972). Clearly the introduction of school counsellors (Lytton 1968) and school intergroup relations specialists (Blumenberg 1968) would ease the situation.

15 Ashlock and Stephens (1966) describe the work they report as 'educational therapy'. Witty (1967) stresses that deprived children need to be healed.

16 Webb (1967) speaks of her work as 'salvage and first aid'. Wilson (1968) describes his as 'educational therapy'. Stratta (1970) insists that even borstal institutions should become therapeutic to 'realize the human potential of the individual'.

17 Sugarman (1970), p. 88.

18 Peck and Havighurst (1964), pp. 124 and 181; Sugarman (1970), pp. 80 and 82; and Sackerman (1971), pp. 36 and 55.

19 Peck and Havighurst (1964), p. 182, cf. p. 125.

20 *op. cit.*, p. 121.

21 See Hoyle (1965) and Anderson (1970).

22 Nunn (1947). Every subject goes through the stages of 'wonder', 'utility', and 'systems' (pp. 268 ff).

23 Douglas (1970), Introduction. Compare Kohn (1959) insisting that social action must be based on the scientific formulation of social change.

24 Lane (1970) presents the three principles of structuralism as: (1) all patterns of social behaviour are codes, like languages; (2) man has an innate structuring capacity which determines the structure of all social phenomena; and (3) relations can be reduced to binary oppositions. This clearly absorbs a number of other systems. Innate language (Chomsky), disclosure situations (Lévi-Strauss), polarities (Parsons) and related phenomena all belong here because both mental and social structures result from the structural nature of the human mind. This view has impeccable credentials. Madge (1964) spoke of the 'society of the mind'. Halbwachs (1958) argued that social stratification originated as much in the process of conceptualizing as in the actual social dynamics of a given situation. Bruner (1966) believed that any experience of the phenomenal world only had validity because it reflected human mental structures. Merleau-Ponty (1969) argued that 'The world is something we create' (p. 11). Gurvitch (1971) insisted that the actual structure of social forms must be inherently united with the sociology of knowledge. All of the above-mentioned writers stress the inherent unity of an individual's knowledge and the social object of that knowledge. In this complex area Runciman (1971) is an excellent guide.

25 Musgrave (1965), p. 11.

26 Lazarsfeld (1968), pp. 709 and 798.

27 Peters (1969) discussing 'the possibility of a value-free concept of man' says, 'The trouble about most existing concepts of man is that they themselves covertly incorporate ethical evaluations' (pp. 232–4). Hirst (1970) makes recourse to 'truth criteria' but this does not extricate one from the dilemma since such criteria have to be selected on some predetermined criterion (p. 213).

28 Runciman (1972), p. 73; but compare Runciman (1971) 'Sociology cannot be an autonomous subject with laws of its own' (p. 44).

29 MacIntyre (1971) thus supports the structuralist view (p. 83).

30 Mills (1967) claimed that sociologists should be socially committed. Indeed they should direct their work to 'urgent public issues and insistent human troubles' (1970, p. 28).

31 Hills (1967) defined research as 'the search for system, or order, in experience'.

32 There are many others. Nelson and Besag (1970) used four models: the administrative, social-class influence, the institutional and the cultural. Hersom (1970) derived models from the activities of production, maintenance, adaptations, environmental interaction and administration. McLeish (1969) makes reference to the dialectic (Marx), functionalist (Malinowski), psychoanalytical (Freud) and social action-change (Parsons).

33 Fletcher (162) provides a brief but detailed review of family structures (Chapter 2).

34 Hendon (1970) argues this in a wider context.

35 See Linton (1947) for familial ascription versus economic achievement; Parsons (1951) for ascriptive versus contingent status; Eisenstadt (1956) for kinship orientation versus achievement orientation.

36 Dewey (1940) argued that the separation of intellectual and moral training,

and the failure of the latter, could only be remedied when 'the school is an embryonic typical community' (p. 15).

37 cf. Gans (1962). Young and Willmott (1970) found this true of Bethnal Green (p. 116).

38 See Peck and Havighurst (1964), pp. 152, 185, 191–3; Kay (1968), pp. 132–9. Hence when Schucking (1970) eulogizes Puritan education thus: 'It may well be asked whether more recent generations have yet devised as effective a system of moral training for the young' (p. 170), one must observe that this was a system of social control not moral education.

39 This need not exclude healthy competitiveness. Phillips and D'Amico (1956) found that while interpersonal relationships blossomed under conditions of co-operativeness, competition did not harm them.

40 cf. North (1972) with his survey of psychiatrists as secular priests.

41 Hagstrom (1968), p. 24.

Bibliography

ALLPORT, GORDON W., *Pattern and Growth in Personality* (Holt, Rinehart & Winston, 1963).

ANDERSON, C. A., 'Sociology of Education in a Comparative Perspective', in *International Review of Education*, Vol XVI, No. 2, 1970.

ASHLOCK, P. and STEPHEN, A., *Educational Therapy in the Elementary School* (Charles C. Thomas, Springfield, Illinois, 1966).

BANTOCK, G. H., *Education, Culture and the Emotions* (Faber, 1967).

BEALS, A. R. and SIEGEL, B. J., *Divisiveness and Social Conflict* (Stanford Univ. Press, 1967).

BERGER, P. L., *Invitation to Sociology* (Pelican, 1968).

BLAU, P. M., *Exchange and Power in Social Life* (Wiley, 1964).

BLUMENBERG, ELEANOR, 'The School Inter-group Relations Specialist', in *Sociology of Education*, Vol. 41, No. 2, 1968.

BOWLBY, JOHN, *Maternal Care and Mental Health* (WHO, 1952).

BRITTEN, J. O. and BRITTEN, J. H., 'Schools Serving the Total Family and Community', in *Family Co-ordination*, Vol. 19, No. 4, 1970.

BRONFENBRENNER, URIE, *The Two Worlds of Childhood* (Allen & Unwin, 1971).

BROWN, J. A. C., *Techniques of Persuasion* (Pelican, 1963).

BRUNER, J. S., *et al.*, *Studies of Cognitive Growth* (Wiley, 1966).

BUCKLEY, WALTER, *Sociology and Modern Systems Theory* (Prentice Hall, 1967).

CHOMSKY, NOAM, *Syntactic Structures* (Humanities Press, 1957).

CHOMSKY, NOAM, *Cartesian Linguistics* (Harper & Row, 1966).

COSER, LEWIS, *The Functions of Social Conflict* (Free Press, 1956).

COSER, LEWIS, *Continuities in the Study of Social Conflict* (Free Press, 1967).

DAHRENDORF, ROLF, *Class and Class Conflict in Industrial Society* (Stanford Univ. Press, 1959).

DEWEY, JOHN, *Moral Principles in Education* (Philosophical Library, New York, 1959).

DOUGLAS, J. D. (Ed.), *The Impact of Sociology* (Appleton Century Crofts, 1970).

EISENSTADT, S. N., *From Generation to Generation* (Routledge & Kegan Paul, 1956).

ETZIONI, AMITAI, *Complex Organizations* (Holt, Rinehart & Winston, 1961).

FLETCHER, RONALD, *The Family and Marriage* (Penguin, 1962).

GALTUNG, JOHAN, 'Pacifism from a Sociological Point of View', in *Journal of Social Issues*, Vol. 3, 1959.

GALTUNG, JOHAN, 'Conflict as a Way of Life', in *New Society*, 16 October 1969.

GANS, H. J., *The Urban Villagers* (Free Press, Glencoe, 1962).

GOFFMAN, ERVING, *Strategic Interaction* (Blackwell, 1970).

GREENE, MAXINE, 'Morals, Ideology and the Schools', in *Educational Theory*, Vol. 17, No. 4, 1967.

GURVITCH, GEORGES, *The Social Frameworks of Knowledge* (Blackwell 1971).

HAGSTROM, WARREN O., 'Deliberate Instruction Within Family Units', in A. M. Kazamias and E. H. Epstein (Eds), *Schools in Transition: Essays in Comparative Education* (Allyn & Bacon, Boston, 1968).

HAGSTROM, WARREN O., 'Deliberate Instruction Within Family Units', in A. M. Kazamias and E. H. Epstein (Eds), *Schools in Transition* (Allyn & Bacon, Boston, 1968).

HALBWACKS, MAURICE, *The Psychology of Social Classes* (Heinemann, 1958).

HALSEY, A. H., 'The Sociology of Moral Education', in W. R. Niblett (Ed.), *Moral Education in a Changing Society* (Faber, 1963).

HARE, R. M., *The Language of Morals* (Oxford Univ. Press, 1964).

HARGREAVES, DAVID H., *Interpersonal Relations and Education* (Routledge & Kegan Paul, 1972).

HENDON, J., *et al.*, *Education for Tomorrow's World* (Grosvenor Books, 1970).

HERSOM, NAOMI, 'Organizational Dimensions of School', in *Alberta Journal of Educational Research*, Vol. XVI, No. 2, 1970.

HILLS, R. JEAN, *The Concept of System* (Centre for the Advanced Study of Educational Administration: Eugene, Oregon, 1967).

HIRST, P. H. and PETERS, R. S., *The Logic of Education* (Routledge & Kegan Paul, 1970).

HOBART, CHARLES W., 'Freedom and the School', in *Canadian Education and Research Digest*, Vol. 8, No. 3, 1968.

HOLT, JOHN, *How Children Fail* (Pitman, 1964).

HOLT, JOHN, *The Under-achieving School* (Pitman, 1970).

HOYLE, E., 'Organizational Analysis in the Field of Education', in *Educational Research*, Vol. VII, No. 2, 1965.

JOHNSON, DAVID, *The Social Psychology of Education* (Holt, Rinehart & Winston, 1970).

KAHN, ALFRED J. (Ed.), *Issues in American Social Work* (Columbia Univ. Press, 1959).

KATZ, D. and KAHN, R. L., *The Social Psychology of Organizations* (John Wiley, 1966).

KAY, WILLIAM, *Moral Development* (Allen & Unwin, 1968).

KAY, WILLIAM, 'Ontology and Values', in *Teilhard Review*, Vol. 5, No. 1, 1970.

KIDD, A. H. and KIDD, R. M., 'The Head Start Classroom as a Therapeutic Environment', in *Young Children*, Vol. XXIII, No. 3, 1968.

KING, RONALD, *Values and Involvement in a Grammar School* (Routledge & Kegan Paul, 1969).

KNIGHT, M., *Morals Without Religion* (Dobson, 1960).

LACEY, C., *Hightown Grammar* (Manchester Univ. Press, 1970).

LAMBERT, ROYSTON *et al.*, *A Manual To The Sociology of the School* (Weidenfeld & Nicolson, 1970).

LANE, MICHAEL, *Structuralism: A Reader* (Jonathan Cape, 1970).

LAZARSFELD, P. F. *et al.*, *The Uses of Sociology* (Weidenfeld & Nicolson, 1968).

LEIGH, ANDREW, 'You Too Can Be Dynamic', in *Observer*, 20 June, 1971.

LEVI-STRAUSS, CLAUDE, *The Savage Mind.*

LINTON, RALPH, *Cultural Background of Personality* (Routledge & Kegan Paul, 1947).

LIPSET, S. M., *Political Man: The Social Bases of Politics* (Heinemann, 1960).

LYTTON, HUGH, *School Counselling and Counsellor Education in the United States* (NFER, 1968).

MACINTYRE, ALISDAIR, *Against the Self Images of the Age* (Duckworth, 1971).

MADGE, CHARLES, *Society in the Mind* (Faber, 1964).

MASLOW, A. H., *Motivation and Personality* (Harper & Row, 1970).

MCLEISH, J., *The Theory of Social Change: Four Views Considered* (Routledge & Kegan Paul, 1969).

MEY, HAROLD, *Field Theory—A Study of its Application in the Social Sciences* (Routledge & Kegan Paul, 1972).

MERLEAU-PONTY, M., 'What is Phenomenology', in J. D. Betts (Ed.), *Phenomenology of Religion* (Student Christian Movement, 1969).

MILLS, C. WRIGHT, *Sociology and Pragmatism* (Oxford Univ. Press, 1967).

MILLS, C. WRIGHT, *The Sociological Imagination* (Pelican, 1970).

MILLS, T. M., *The Sociology of Small Groups* (Prentice-Hall, 1967).

MORRIS, DESMOND, *The Human Zoo* (Jonathan Cape, 1969).

MUSGRAVE, P. W., *The School as an Organization* (Macmillan, 1968a).

MUSGRAVE, P. W., *The Sociology of Education* (Methuen, 1968b).

MYRDAL, GUNNAR, *Objectivity in Social Research* (Duckworth, 1970).

NELSON, J. L. and BESAG, F. P., *Sociological Perspectives in Education—Models for Analysis* (Pitman, 1970).

NORMAN, C. M., 'Role of sociologists in race relations', in *Phylon*, Vol. 32, No. 2, 1971.

NORTH, MARTIN, *The Secular Priests* (Allen & Unwin, 1972).

NUNN, PERCY, *Education, its Data and First Principles* (Edward Arnold, 1947).

PARSONS, TALCOTT, *The Social System* (Routledge & Kegan Paul, 1951).

PECK, R. F. and HAVIGHURST, R. J., *The Psychology of Character Development* (John Wiley, 1964).

PETERS, R. S., 'Mental Health as an Educational Aim', in T. H. B. Hollins (Ed.), *Aims in Education* (Manchester Univ. Press, 1964).

PETERS, R. S., *Ethics and Education* (Allen & Unwin, 1969).

PHILLIPS, B. and D'AMICO, L. A., 'Effects of Co-operation and Competition on the Cohesiveness of Small Face-to-Face Groups', in *Journal of Educational Psychology*, No. 47, 1956.

PIAGET, JEAN, *Structuralism* (Routledge & Kegan Paul, 1971).

PLOWDEN REPORT, *Children and Their Primary Schools* (HMSO, 1967).

REX, JOHN, *Key Problems of Sociological Theory* (Routledge & Kegan Paul, 1965).

RICHARDSON, ELIZABETH, *The Environment of Learning: Conflict and Understanding in the Secondary School* (Nelson, 1967).

RICHMOND, W. K., *The Education Industry* (Methuen, 1969).

ROGERS, CARL R., *On Becoming a Person* (Houghton, Mifflin, 1961).

RUNCIMAN, W. G., 'What is Structuralism?' in *Sociology in its Place* (Cambridge Univ. Press, 1970).

RUNCIMAN, W. G., *A Critique of Max Weber's Philosophy of Social Science* (Cambridge Univ. Press, 1972).

SACKERMAN, HENRY, *The Westbank Group* (Sphere Books, 1971).

SCHON, DONAL, *Beyond the Stable State* (Temple Smith, 1971).

SCHUCKING, L. L., *The Puritan Family* (Routledge & Kegan Paul, 1970).

SENNETT, RICHARD, *The Uses of Disorder* (Allen Lane, 1971).

SHIPMAN, M., *The Sociology of the School* (Longmans, 1968).

SHIPMAN, M. D., *Education and Modernization* (Faber, 1971).

SMELSER, M. J., *Theory of Collective Behaviour* (Routledge & Kegan Paul, 1962).

SPIEGELMAN, ROBERT G., 'A Benefit/Cost Model to Evaluate Educational Programs', in *Socio-Economic Planning Sciences*, Vol. 1, Pt. 4, 1968.

STRATTA, ERICA, *The Education of Borstal Boys* (Routledge & Kegan Paul, 1970).

SUGARMAN, B., 'The School as a Social System', in *Moral Education*, Vol. 1, No. 2, 1969.

SUGARMAN, B., 'The Therapeutic Community and the School', in *Interchange*, Vol. 1, No. 2, 1970.

TEILHARD, PIERRE DE CHARDIN, *The Phenomenon of Man* (Collins, 1960).

TRONC, K. E., 'A Conceptual Model for the Study of the Communication of Authority in a Bureaucratic Education System', in *Journal of Educational Administration*, Vol. V, No. 2, 1967.

WAKEFORD, J., *The Cloistered Elite* (Macmillan, 1969).

WEBB, LESLEY, *Children with Special Needs in the Infant School* (Colin Smyth, 1967).

WEBER, MAX, *The Protestant Ethic and the Spirit of Capitalism* (Allen & Unwin, 1930).

WILLOWER, D. J., EIDELL, T. L. and HOY, W. K., *The School and Pupil-control Ideology* (Administrative Committee on Research, Pennsylvania State Univ., 1967).

WILSON, T. R., 'The Defiant and Disruptive Student', in *Education and Urban Society*, Vol. 1, No. 1, 1968.

WILSON, J. B., *Education and the Concept of Mental Health* (Routledge & Kegan Paul, 1968).

WILSON, T. R., 'The Defiant and Disruptive Student', in *Education and Urban Society*, Vol. 1, No. 1, 1968.

WITTY, PAUL A. (Ed.), *The Educational Retarded and Disadvantaged* (Chicago Univ. Press, 1967).

WOOTTON, BARBARA, *Social Science and Social Pathology* (Allen & Unwin, 1959).

YARLOTT, G., *Education and Children's Emotions* (Weidenfeld & Nicolson, 1972).

YOUNG, M. and WILLMOTT, P., *Family and Kinship in East London* (Penguin, 1970).

Chapter 14

School Organizations and Ideologies

When one has surveyed the various sociological analyses of the school it is clear that such theorizing is too nebulous to be of solid value. As was said earlier, each school is unique. However, despite this it is still possible to classify the *types* of school currently in existence. They may be either private or public, secondary or primary; and the permutations of that simple analysis can be further multiplied. Thus although sociological analyses clarify both the nature and the interaction of the component elements in a school, they cannot take cognisance of such variations as these.

As a natural consequence of moving now into the second century of compulsory education the public are acquainted with the general structure of primary and secondary education. The teacher and student interested in moral education and wishing to have less ephemeral sources of information have recently been well served. Banks, for example, has described different types of schools in order to shed 'light on the social function of the various forms of secondary education' (1). Gibberd provided a parallel series of school case-studies to show that school can effectively combat the growing rate of delinquency. Others have shown how potent are the various elements of school life which help children to develop their values and attitudes (2).

PRIMARY SCHOOLS

Despite the publication of the Plowden Report in 1967, and the interest stimulated by the subsequent controversy, there is curiously little hard current data about our primary schools. Perhaps we shall have to wait patiently for pupil-power to reach that level and then hope that any resultant ferment will throw such information to the surface.

Thus, apart from the comprehensive historical survey of Whitbread there is little resource material (3). Her competent survey of the work of progressive child-centred teachers, like Montessori and Isaacs, is most helpful but in her spirited defence of nursery schools she beats the air. Successive Ministers of Education have shown an outmoded reluctance to increase these facilities, which in view of what has been said concerning the crucial importance of establishing the preconditions of morality seems to be a wholly irresponsible attitude. However, Education Ministers are politicians and must bow to the dictate of economics rather than to educational principles. Blackstone's view enables one to be more charitable, for she stressed that one effect of the Plowden Report was to emphasize parental influence (4). It could thus be argued that economic effort here might be little more than battering at an open door.

State Schools

However, British primary schools are now noted for their child-centred approach. It would be surprising had they been otherwise. The advocates of such an educational policy have been both numerous and vociferous. Fortunately, the earlier excesses of some enthusiasts, unacquainted with the rigour of Dewey's theories, have subsided. Of course parodies of progressive education may still be found, but they are usually traced to lyrical headmistresses who argue emotively and assume that when left to themselves children will spontaneously blossom. Consequently such strictures as those of Peters and his colleagues are necessary. He argued that child-centred education was not a free-for-all. We must, he argued, stop producing teachers 'who practise something approximating to a free day without keeping a careful check on what in fact each child has learnt' (5).

Thus we find, on the whole, healthy communities in which children learn to accept themselves and each other, and develop their reason, curiosity and self-confidence. Although written by a thoroughgoing Deweyan, Atkinson's account of such a community, where purpose and interest are so brought into the process of education that children reveal creativeness of mind and willingness to co-operate, is not merely a eulogy of an ideal. A visit to a good primary school of this kind soon reveals that they are already geared to attain the goals of moral education.

Furthermore, a recent trend has enhanced this influence. As Victorian structures are being replaced by modern buildings these schools are increasingly adopting the 'open-plan' system (6). Gardiner has described them and shown how they answer many of the questions posed by progressive teachers in 'closed-system' schools. Obviously if children are to be free to explore their environment, by what Postman and Weingartner call the 'inquiry method', they must have access not only to books but to each other too. Thus in this way moral education will be facilitated, for it encourages individuality of purpose and inter-age contacts. Children in this environment then become more responsible and self-reliant. Yet they still have the class group to provide them with the all important security they need.

Progressive education in an open-plan school, obviously poses some problems. Noise is inevitable, and acquaintance with young children reveals that as noise levels rise they simply shout louder. Then again questions about academic standards must be asked. If children have increased associations with each other, what happens to the all important adult–child relationship? Thus permutations based on academic and disciplinary problems can be duplicated until one is forced to observe that this might only work with highly motivated well-behaved children under a teacher who is an amalgam of Piaget and Dewey. Yet when all this is said the fact remains that such schools facilitate the development of the moral qualities, traits and attitudes enumerated earlier.

Private Schools

Of course this eulogy need not apply to the private sector of primary education. Those acquainted with life in a preparatory school will know that not only are the buildings invariably inadequate, and the staff less competent (7) but also that the whole ethos is geared towards the passing of the common entrance examination. Such children may imbibe the standard bourgeois conventions of conduct but they may ultimately emerge as competitive-minded, clamant-demanders of privilege and status. This does not mean, of course, that no moral pupils can emerge from such schools but only that when they do it is in *spite* of the school and not *because* of it.

It is thus not surprising to find one headmaster addressing a gathering of such teachers with withering scorn. While advocating progressive education and open-plan schools he said, 'I see our only hope in the new thinking in primary schools' (8). Those who have hitherto found comfort in the fact that every inquiry revealed that the private were superior to the state primary schools must face the report of Davie, Butler and Goldstein. They reveal predictably that they found private school children to be well ahead of state school children in reading and arithmetic, but when allowance was made for social class these differences were considerably reduced; and extensive analysis shows that if there are any differences, they are only marginal.

STANDARD SECONDARY SCHOOLS

In turning to the secondary phase of education one must not assume that this is a progression from schools concerned with personal development to those which ought to be primarily concerned with academic criteria. This is where children are given a second chance to develop personally. In his study of sexual and drug abuses Miller points out that these problems spring from the fact that all adolescents pass through 'identification and self-realization' crises. What then are we to make of a society which places such young people in schools which vary from privileged security to educationally deprived squalor?

The Secondary Modern School

Again there is very little available data from which to draw conclusions. In his analysis, Dent long ago argued that since these schools catered for the vast majority of children they should transmit all the personal and scholastic benefits normally bestowed by other schools to the privileged few. Hence such schools early became focal points of that social idealism which looked to them for help to found a better society. However, Dent concluded that, 'The number and range of problems confronting the Secondary Modern School are almost infinite (9).

Soon after this Taylor looked again at what he called 'the idealistic view' that such schools could produce a society in which 'motives higher than those of profit and personal gain would direct human endeavour' (10). Almost a decade earlier Banks had shown that parity and prestige between secondary schools could not be established while grammar schools were invested with social supremacy. It is this conclusion which Taylor, like Loukes, developed when he showed that the secondary modern school has tended to re-enter the academic race as a contestant intending to prepare its pupils for upward social mobility. Now the introduction of CSE examinations has confirmed his views. Thus, instead of attaining parity of esteem by *parallel* criteria it has abdicated its moral role and succumbed to public pressure to become another educational agent of social ascent (11).

Then the inevitable storm-clouds gathered. The selection process sent children into the secondary modern school convinced that they were failures, and this, as Hargreaves later showed, affected the social climate of these schools. For although the abler pupils responded with higher academic aspirations, most merely became hardened in their discontent. Thus he concluded his research with the comment that 'major reforms are necessary if the school is to be a force which draws children from delinquent values and behaviour' (12).

It is therefore not surprising to find Partridge continuing in this vein. Reporting on a school which is described as 'the pride of the local education authority' he reported that authoritarianism and corporal punishment permeated the whole structure of the school. In the light of such information Webb's depressing account of schools characterized by hostility and animosity becomes wholly credible.

The fact that it is the academically orientated boy who succeeds here, is an indictment of the system. As Hannah Gavron showed, grammar schools are clearly intended to purvey the administrative, professional ethos which they inherited from the public schools. For while secondary modern schools are intended to be vocationally minded, it is neither clear what these vocations are, nor how they ought to set about the task. It is thus no surprise to find research showing clearly that non-academic attainment is employed by pupils to gain status and dignity. Start, found that this hunger for identity and prestige was satisfied most completely by athletic performance, although more recently writers have shown that knowledgeability in the world of 'pop' is an equally satisfying substitute.

One may shrug off these unpalatable truths and relegate such pupils to the faceless masses of industrial unrest, but these pupils form more than half of our school-age society. It is this fact which the Newsom Report repeatedly stressed. Yet despite the disquieting nature of this report one still finds, years later, that subsequent Ministers of Education do little to replace the myriad of Boer War semi-slum buildings which house the bulk of the next generation of citizens (13).

Thus deprived and made to feel inferior the delinquency and smouldering resentment of such children is understandable. When adolescents realize that they are the deprived, dispensable, manipulated inferior fodder of a wealthy nation we may well have a civil war of such bitterness and intensity that our culture could collapse.

Clearly a massive rebuilding campaign should be initiated immediately. But that is not enough. Viable moral education must be introduced. A school-leaver was once asked what he thought of the new buildings. 'It could all be marble sir,' he replied, 'but it would still be a bloody school' (14). It is not alarmist to observe that unless some radical changes are made it could soon be a bloody revolution too.

The Grammar School
Despite the egalitarian idealism, to which reference has been made, it is clear that grammar schools enjoy greater prestige and status. With selective entrance and sharp competition for teaching posts it could not be otherwise. One would therefore expect to find more data in this sector, as indeed is the case. A number of writers have surveyed the area in general terms (15) and still more have reported on specific schools (16). Such schools are academic forcing houses

which have increasingly and sometimes reluctantly, opened their doors to the clever lower-status child. Indeed their repeated references to university places and old boys who made good, can leave one in no doubt as to the academic and élitist aims of many such schools (17).

If one should hesitantly ask how working-class children fare in such an atmosphere, Jackson and Marsden are swift to reply that mostly they just do not manage to adjust. Indeed these authors conclude with the sweeping comment that 'The history and achievement of the grammar school is a fine one. It has spread secondary education through middle and lower middle classes, breeding able and cultivated men and women. Only in our time it has foundered on a rock; the working class' (18). Sweetness and light, it seems, are not for working-class children. They are not only educationally blind but also have deficient academic taste-buds. It is therefore no wonder that such an eminent ex-grammar-school headmaster as Harry Davies should enter the lists with a resounding riposte to this claim and conclude by saying that the ethos of such schools would benefit by an injection of the best working-class values (19).

Yet even the most defensive of men must consider this fact carefully. Dale and Griffith found that failure in a grammar school was correlated with social class. Precisely which social elements predispose working-class children towards underachievement is not clear, but this is what it does. When to this one adds Lacey's finding that a sociological analysis of the grammar school discloses that the working-class sub-group is the least successful when striving for academic excellence, the indictment seems to be complete.

The advocates of comprehensive education thus find their protagonists supplying them with lethal weapons, and so the tables are turned. Whereas Harry Davies rightly argued that working-class children have much of value to offer the grammar school, we now have a *volte face*. Writers like Hewitson, sensing the demise of educational privilege in the state sector, now argue that we must strive to ensure that the 'essence of the grammar school' is incorporated into the comprehensive system. Nowhere does he precisely define the nature of this essence, but his meaning is clear. High standards of academic attainment, personal success, and social maturation must not die with the grammar school system.

However, grammar schools are far from dead. What then do we know of their moral influence? Very little it seems, and that which is available for public scrutiny is often contradictory. Take a simple case. In a comparative study Wragg found that a grammar school child was characterized by a higher level of emotional security, than that found in secondary modern pupils. This sounds reasonable for such pupils mostly come from stable, moderately wealthy homes: but in the light of this what is one to make of Musgrove's findings? He concluded that a grammar school 'systematically humiliates its pupils, reduces their self-esteem, promotes uncertainties, ambiguities and conflicts in social relationships' (20) and thereby not only subjects them to more stress, than their modern school counterparts, but also defers their personal maturation by inducing neurotic anxiety.

What, in fact, do grammar schools accomplish? Does their influence retard or advance the personal and moral maturity of their pupils?

It is a relief to turn to research which acknowledges the complexity of this question. In his superb study King investigated the factors affecting the honesty, truthfulness, tolerance, cultural interests and general social values of grammar school pupils. All the research took place in one pseudonymous London school, and the researcher admitted that 'the methodological problems of measuring values and value changes, are immense' (21). As one would expect, he found the school ethos saturated, with middle-class values. Consequently, middle-class children, especially second-generation grammar school pupils, fared much better than the working-class or first-generation child.

Despite succumbing to the temptation to observe that values are 'caught not taught', the primary worth of his study lay in disclosing the complexity of these influences. In addition to social-class factors, he concluded, one must take cognisance of a pupil's age, status, peer group, academic competence and personality. Indeed at one point he argues that pupil interaction and standards of conduct depend more on the school's social structure and internal organization, than on the status of the home; thus confirming the findings of Herriot and his colleagues in America. Hence the thesis of this book could be inverted. We are arguing that schools should conduct that form of moral education which inculcates the preconditions, traits and attitudes of morality. King found that it was the possession of these which affected the efficacy of the process. Increased moral maturity, like wealth, appears to accrue to those who already possess some.

The Public School (22)

Interest in our public schools probably arises spontaneously in the breast of every class-conscious Englishmen. Wearers of the old school tie naturally want to eulogize the source of their privilege; while others, brought up on a diet of public-school based school yarns, find the subject fascinating. Equally antagonists investigate both with a beady eye cocked to locate a further abuse which can enhance their advocacy for the establishing of a democratic republic, with a new social structure. Unfortunately one can find an abundance of evidence most of which is written by old boys who are naturally concerned about the future of their schools in a welfare state where privilege is being slowly eroded (23).

Such whistling in the dark, however, can grate on the ears of EPA teachers. McConnell blandly assumes that Etonians have inalienable rights as a privileged élite and to assure us that this is fit and proper he gives three supportive reasons: the 'old boy network' works efficiently; the school recruits very selectively; and the education provided is superb. Hard on his heels come two Wykehamists who applaud the fact that the excellence of their old school leads to 'over-representation' of a public school élite in the higher echelons of status and power. Although they do acknowledge that such schools perpetuate inequality of opportunity and so observe that today 'the problem is not the over-privilege of a few, but the under-privilege of the many' (24).

It thus seems that there are three lanes in the educational process. The secondary modern school directs its pupils into the deprivileged mass of our labour force during their mid-teens, where they mostly smoulder with resentment. The grammar school usually sends its pupils on to tertiary education, where they are absorbed in middle-management or lower professional occupations. The public school leads to Oxbridge and the top jobs. It can, of course, be argued that such a pupil 'will probably receive his due reward' (25) but The Public Schools Commission were therefore justified in deeming that such an educational system divided our society, and, as Abrams and Spinley have shown, our population is composed of the educationally deprived and the educationally privileged (26).

Boarding Schools

Before passing on, it ought to be noted that public schools are characterized by two other features. First, they are mostly residential; and, second, they are usually single-sex schools. The implication of the latter fact, for moral education, is discussed below (see Chapter 15). But what of the effect which residence in school has on a child's moral development?

Little is known of the relative effects of both residential and non-residential school experience. Clearly it cannot be discussed in isolation from two related elements affecting morality, viz. the consequent diminished family influence, and the accentuated peer-group pressures, but there is some evidence to suggest that boarding school experience facilitates moral growth.

Bronfenbrenner, for example, in investigating American and Russian educational practices found that boarding-school pupils were much more resistant to anti-social behaviour than day-school children. A similar, but more generalized conclusion was also reached by Fraser. His comprehensive survey of boarding education focused on Makarenko's view that the collective influence was the more potent on morality, and such an influence was most powerful in a boarding school. Consequently he concluded from his evidence that moral education was much more successful in boarding than day schools. To this one may add the parallel work of Rees who also concluded that moral and religious influences were more potent in these schools.

Lambert's compilation of residential pupils' despairing and apathetic accounts of their lot, in such schools, make such conclusions sound strange—but they are impeccably acceptable. Residence transforms a school into a truly familial system. Consequently all the potency of home influence is brought to bear on such pupils. Inglis records the force of this. 'By the end of the first term', he writes, 'the school code had been instilled; at the beginning of the second I was ready to enforce it on the new boys' (27).

However, since residential education for all is clearly not economically viable, it cannot be recommended as an aid to moral education. It can, however, be asserted that this evidence suggests once more that the most effective model for a school engaged in deliberate moral education, is that based on the extended family.

THE ÉLITIST SYSTEM

Despite the above indictment of the public school system, many leap to the defence of its élitist principles. We shall now consider two of these; one from Scotland and one from England. Highet argues that if Scotsmen have the means to do so they should be allowed to provide this education for their children. He argues that there is an increased demand for places; that the education received is better; and finally that middle-class families want to spend money on education, while their working-class counterparts prefer to spend it on hair-dos and bingo. By this device he is able to avoid concluding that the sociological function of public schools is to serve and perpetuate the élitist norms and goals of a privileged class. It need hardly be said that such crass manipulation of sociological data makes one suspect his arguments.

A contemporary English argument came from Howarth, the ex-High Master of St Paul's School. Committed to an élitist social principle, he argues that egalitarianism is responsible for most of our current social, economic and political ills. Thus his targets range from the permissive society to the American high school; each of which he hits in turn with both accuracy and force. Once in his stride he ridicules the Newsom Commission which proposed extending the public school facilities to state-aided children, and then goes on to censure the present campaign to establish parity of esteem for all schools. Then while accurately analysing much that is wrong with comprehensive schools he suddenly shudders to a halt. He ought, logically, to go on and explicate the middle-class values which are threatened by the new comprehensive schools, after all he does call them 'dysfunctional systems', but he does not. Thus, it is clear at this point that he does not rightly understand what is meant by 'equality of opportunity'.

Hence in this way two eulogies of the middle classes and their values are presented and sustained; and it is explicitly argued that public schools will ensure their survival. Such arguments have a long history. Plato's élitist proposals were proposed again in Mannheim's suggestion that there should be one form of education for society's potential leaders and another for the masses. It cannot be overlooked that the university system is also essentially élitist (28).

It can, of course, be argued that public schoolboys are morally superior. They are, it is alleged, generally honest, responsible, reliable and committed to the tenets of fair-play (29)—but insiders see behind their uncritical acceptance of stereotyped values. Wilson, himself a Wykehamist, says of public schoolboys, 'they are not critical, and one could hardly say that they are filled with a love of reform or humanitarian feeling' (30).

An apparent anomaly must be clarified here. This castigation of public school boys is not entirely incompatible with the earlier eulogizing of the middle classes (see Chapters 5–9). Two possible explanations come readily to mind to account for this apparent clash of evidence. First, the superior moral qualities of future orientation, moral flexibility, moral dynamism and moral creativity, can all prepare an individual to exploit as well as serve his fellows. This is particularly true if he has benefited from an exclusive, élitist form of education. Second, it can induce such a boy to sub-scribe to élitist norms. Then in passing from educational superiority to personal pride, such upper middle-class boys may emerge as arrogant, selfish and irresponsible.

One could build on close acquaintance and be more trenchant than that. The urbane manner and ready smile of the confident *élite* do not conceal the underlying arrogance of what continentals call the 'hypocrite class'. Working men, to them, are inferior persons ripe for exploitation: even successful, graduate, grammar school boys are patronized. When one lives in this ethos of anti-democratic, twisted values it is extremely hard not to ask intermittently, 'How can morally mature men and women emerge from such a morally inverted milieu?' One can only assume that parents perpetuate this expensive system because its moral dysfunctioning within a distorted educational system is thereby concealed. Hence the academic orientation of most public schools prepares men and women for tertiary education and then the top jobs (31).

An Élite of Service

It is now axiomatic that the modern English public school system was initiated in the nineteenth century to train young men to administer our colonies with justice and probity. Based on this assumption even the barbaric modes of discipline, adopted in these schools, were seen as necessary training for such arduous responsibilities. Now, instead of training young men for responsible service to the state, they appear to be preparing young men and women for lives of privilege (32).

It must be remembered, however, that the middle-class personality characteristics (see Chapters 4–10), outlined above as essential for mature morality, are displayed by many public school pupils. From this one can only conclude that the system is wrong. Consequently when morally mature young men and women emerge from these schools it is *in spite* of the system and not *because* of it.

There are some signs that the public school system is changing. Weinberg, an ardent advocate of the public school system, concludes that this will result from contacts with the business world. With curricular changes financed by business interests, these schools will produce men and women who 'carry into business the pristine norms of gentlemanly behaviour and leadership they have internalized at their public schools' (33). Weinberg then went on to produce the first sociological study of the English public schools; a document which eulogized the system dedicated to 'function as the custodian of élite values and norms' (34).

It is a pity that such erudition is so vulnerable to criticism. The aim was laudable enough. He wanted to relate such schools to society at large, but in the process he makes confident generalizations and errors. He inflates the authority of the headmasters and high masters, and nowhere does he define precisely what he means by an 'élite', nor the relationship between this group and the social classes in our complex social structure. Since his book is defined as 'the sociology of élite education' this omission is rather remiss.

However, embedded in this confusion, is one valuable conclusion. He argues that these encroaching business interests will erode the institutional form of public school organization and so lead to its modification. However, moral educators cannot be satisfied with change in itself—we want changes which will advance moral education. Obviously there must be an élite of some kind. Our societies function in this manner. In political, economic, academic and aesthetic areas of national life, we must have leaders. It is self-evident that we must have consultant surgeons, psychiatrists, architects and sanitary engineers to ensure that society and its members are protected from the ravages of incompetent enthusiasts (35). Although many public schoolboys worthily fill the ranks of these professions, this does not justify the privilege such schools have of providing a disproportionate number of such men (36).

If then, there is to be an élite, moral educators must surely argue that it ought to be an élite based not on *privilege* but on *service* to the community. This was the original intention of the modern public school, and it should be the ideal of every school. The only élitism which is acceptable to the morally mature man is that based on service to his fellows. If, as seems to be the case, we must have this élite, let it be an aristocracy of service and not privilege (37). In that way all children from all strands of our tripartite system can belong to an élitist group. The corporation worker, artisan, brain surgeon, academic and business man will then all serve society by applying their particular expertise to the tasks in hand; not with the single aim of gain, but with the morally laudable intention of serving others.

Contemporary unrest is disclosing that our society cannot survive while based on crass competitive greed. Such rampant materialism has led to a pagan worship of the physical, and religion it seems has lost its moral potency. This is the void moral educators have to fill. If it is left empty the moral disintegration of our culture seems to be inevitable.

THE ANTI-SCHOOL TREND

In the light of the above evidence it seems legitimate to conclude that the moral influence of our schools is more harmful than beneficial. It produces an élitist, and quasi-élitist class based on privilege and merit. This then not only induces present educational disparity, but also later economic inequity.

Such disenchantment with schools can be found as a common theme in a number of contemporary books. In effect they say simply that schools are dysfunctional. Taking this stance they could have been used to strengthen the arguments of those who lay stress on the influence of the home. Their introduction has been deferred until now since they are more rightly appropriate to a discussion on the influence of the school as a social institution.

Ivan Illich

The leading protagonist here is Ivan Illich; a turbulent Catholic priest, whose swingeing attacks on contemporary morality have earned him the opprobrium of both state and church. Heralded by its blurb and with reviewers competing to outdo each other in aphoristic eulogies, one could be excused for being initially sceptical. Yet on reading his *Deschooling Society* it becomes clear that he has many relevant and trenchant observations to make.

In an earlier work he establishes the breadth of his terms of reference. 'By school,' he writes, 'I do not mean all organized formal education. I use the terms "school" and "schooling" to designate a form of child care and a *rite de passage* which we take for granted' (38). Arguing that education, under political and economic pressures, arose as a parallel system to military and governmental systems he concludes that this was done by moulding them into an all-embracing ideological structure. Then comes his barbed and cutting conclusion. 'This restraint on healthy productive and potentially independent human beings,' he says, 'is performed by schools with an economy which only labour camps could rival' (39). His position is thus that of an opponent to the ideological, economic and political systems of which the school is an essential part.

His denunciation continues in this vein in the later work, when he argues that current astronomic expenditure on education should not be indulged by the wealthy countries while more than half the world is underdeveloped. Furthermore, this process perpetuates a materialistic hierarchy which reinforces the values of privileged acquisitive societies. Hence education is seen as the path to wealth and not to service. Yet, he continues, the process is both expensive and inefficient. Prolonged schooling usually only equips many men to do work for which a few years of training are adequate. Thus he dismisses the school's aim.

Schools themselves are then criticized. These he calls 'manipulative institutions' and argues that they merely process children in the way that prisons process prisoners. In this function teachers are little more than custodians. Even the dedicated schoolmaster, it seems, cannot encourage his pupils to relate to 'real' social problems, in this milieu. Nor can he establish those viable social relationships with them, without which it is impossible to enable them to realize their potential as human beings.

His ideal is then inevitably that of democratic, humanistic, resistance to urbanized, technological society. Schools ought, he continues, to be places where young people experience a true understanding of the nature of society, of their own humanity, and of the interaction between the two. It is inevitable that he should then conclude,

'Fundamental social change must begin with a change of consciousness about institutions' (40).

Heard in isolation his voice would command attention, but the tones become compelling when we hear them echoed elsewhere in the work of equally concerned and competent educators. It would be tedious to repeat the themes already heard in Illich. Suffice it to say that the titles of their books sound like a dirge sung over the corpse of the school (41).

Everett Reimer

However, Reimer's work can illustrate this point since he most clearly reflects the views of Illich. He too observes that 'A function of schools more directly in conflict with their educational aims than custodial care, is the sorting of the young into the social slots they will occupy in life' (42). However, all is not bitter and dark. Reimer affirms that the central thesis of his book 'is that people can become aware of their bad institutional habits and can change them' (43).

Finally, to this, one need only add the view of Postman and Weingartner who affirm that schools should inculcate autonomy; and Holt's view that schools have such an artificially structured form that they must necessarily teach children to be hypocritical and deceptive if they are to succeed—a practice which he says serves children well later on.

Schools as Dysfunctional Systems

A purely sociological point can be interjected here, since this denigration of schools is also a denunciation of society. Thus one ought also to consider the literature currently disseminating the claims of 'an alternative society'. Amongst the more moderate writers one could perhaps place Atkinson. He claims, simply, that all existing sociological frameworks are dysfunctional because they are too deterministic. None of the 'anti-school' writers make this point, but it is a potently valid one. Schools are self-perpetuating dysfunctional systems of consumer values (44).

Such publications appear to have been prompted by recent legislation in Great Britain, to raise the school leaving age, for such a potentially dangerous decision has forced us back to primary considerations. All these writers thus deal with fundamental educational questions. Does schooling destroy creativity and originality? Do schools repress individual development? Should schooling not lead to autonomy? Would more schooling vitiate the educational processes? Are schools necessary? These, and many more, are the questions being asked and, for moral educators, whose only hope lies in better moral education in the schools, an answer *must* be found.

It would be fatally easy to point out that almost all these writers speak more of the American situation than the British. It is true that both cultures have fundamentally different social and political problems to solve, but this cannot be used to dismiss the arguments themselves. For despite this it is difficult not to agree that they all remind us that our society is sick, and in so far as schools reflect some facets of society, they too are sick (45).

Transforming the school

Since Illich is the most radical of these writers his work could be dismembered and emerge discredited. For example one might highlight his educational naïvety. He has an optimistic but unrealistic view of what children would do if left to themselves. This lack of realism extends to an almost total ignorance of developmental psychology. Such lacunae in his knowledge readily lead him to conclude that schoolmasters are dispensable. In addition he refuses to admit that teachers can provide vision; that schools can be centres of free inquiry; and that only the highly intelligent child will benefit from his suggestions. In this way he could be damned with faint praise or dismissed as a man whose mind is a chaos of brilliance.

This, however, does not mean that we should dismiss him. It ought rather to lead us to consider carefully what he says and then re-examine the education system in the light of his strictures. Seen then against his wider backcloth we may listen more carefully to men like Stephens. Attempting to analyse the processes which lead to the establishment of educational systems and schools, he sets his findings against the background of cultural evolution. Such cogent arguments as he then presents are a sufficient corrective to the anti-school writers. He believes that schools were founded in the context of evolutionary survival, and they thus ensure the quasi-stability of values and norms. It is naturally impossible to do justice to his complex and profound work in a sentence or two. Suffice it to say that the author's refusal to tear schools from the society in which they are rooted enables him to show that schools are an essential and inherent element in civilized societies.

Thus rooted in society schools can be accepted as an integral element—but this does not mean that they are perfect. The 'anti-school' writers have much to commend them. Schools are palpably not as we would desire them to be. However, if any social instrument of man's purpose is dysfunctional, one merely gets it to work properly. These writers have shown us that schools do not function properly; but such work must not be dismissed as the latest cottage-industry dedicated to deriding the educational system, for they do offer valid alternatives. We *must* heed their warning but in a rather different way than they would expect. After all if one's car will not start, it is not taken as a signal to muster followers and proclaim a crusade for the abolition of cars. One merely gets it mended so that it works properly. It is the same with schools.

Privilege and Morality

Finally an abrasive point must be stressed while clarifying an apparent anomaly. In the previous section the middle classes were eulogized. Here, particularly with reference to the public school system, they are denigrated. This is not a contradiction. It must be remembered that only a small proportion of the middle classes patronize the public schools, and those who do so are not necessarily raging examples of rampant greed. Their scions have honoured our country in many ways and varying circumstances, often displaying commendable integrity and self-sacrifice, but it is still tragically true that all who subscribe to this élitist system must inevitably be tainted, in varying degrees, with that sense of privilege and superiority, endemic to the public school system.

Morality is a flower which can barely survive in the arid wastes of élitism and privilege for all privileges imply the existence of the under-privileged; and every élite is detached from the masses. It is this élitism and privilege which has been condemned. And when the middle classes seek to purchase this for their children they must either ensure that privilege is always accompanied by responsibility, or be condemned as saboteurs of national morality.

REFERENCES

1 Banks (1955), p. 12.
2 cf. Collier (1959), Chapter 7.
3 See Bassett (1970), the Grudgeons (1971) and Probert and Jarman (1971).
4 This is supported by The Government Social Survey, The National Child Development Study and The Manchester Institute of Education Report, all of whom were commissioned by the Plowden Committee.
5 Peters (1969), p. 20.
6 *The Harvard Educational Review*, Vol. 39, No. 4 (1969), and the British *Report on Education*, No. 66 (1970), are both devoted to this theme. Kohl (1971) has shown that such architecture requires a non-authoritarian approach to teaching.
7 Robinson (1972) surveyed the staff of our 3,000 private schools and found that less than half were recognized by the DES as possessing 'reasonably qualified staff'.
8 Charles Batham addressing the eightieth annual conference of the Incorporated Association of Preparatory Schools in Cambridge (6 September 1970).
9 Dent (1958), p. 200.

10 Taylor (1963), p. 137.
11 Although *The Schools Council Bulletin* (1971) and Bruce (1969) try to rationalize the British examination system on the basis of the American pattern, they still reveal that grammar school criteria are invading the secondary modern school.
12 Hargreaves (1967), p. 192.
13 van der Eyken has been particularly scathing on this point. See *Observer*, 5 September 1971.
14 Newson Report (1963), p. 2.
15 Whitfield (1957), Campbell (1957) and Vincent (1969).
16 Lawson (1963), Graham and Phythian (1965), Fox (1967), Blishen (1970) and Lacey (1970).
17 But note Mays (1967) 'It is always dangerous to generalize about schools and grammar schools are probably much less homogeneous than most other kinds' (p. 61). To which one might perhaps add that all generalizations are false, including this one!
18 Jackson and Marsden (1962), p. 215.
19 See Davies (1965), p. 163, and Ali (1972).
20 Musgrove (1964), p. 106.
21 King (1969), p. 160.
22 In America this is called a private school.
23 Thus Kalton (1966) commissioned by the Headmasters' Conference, possibly prompted by the Public Schools Commission, told the Headmasters that all was well. Then Weinberg (1967) further assured them that public schools would be a source of élite values and norms for many years to come. Bamford (1967) authoritatively disclosed that public school élitism resulted not from the alleged excellence of the schools, but from the excellence of the pupils who came from good stock and belonged already to wealthy and influential families. One can only ascribe to the schools, he continues, the perpetuation of that ridiculous amateurism which, in the past, has heaped ridicule on our political and civil service systems. He does concede that many public school educated state officials have improved our national educational system. But that was in spite of rather than because of their own education.
24 Bishop and Wilkinson (1967), p. 241.
25 Bamford (1967), p. 312: but he does admit that 'the provision is lavish' (p. 330) and does not mention the point made by Kalton (1966) that there are only a sprinkling of pupils in public schools with less than 100 IQ.
26 This tripartism is reflected in the American Academy, Schoolhouse and City School. See Mead (1965), p. 421 ff.
27 Inglis in *Spectator*, 17 November 1961.
28 Niblett (1969) argues that English universities identify an intellectual élite while American universities aim to train a professional élite. One suspects, however, that these conflate. The élite of each country are able to express themselves *through* their work. The majority have to do this *in spite* of it.
29 Wakeford (1969) contains an abundance of partisan evidence here.
30 Wilson (1962), p. 113.
31 But this can be dysfunctional. Wakeford (1969) records boys rejecting schools' goals and substituting alternative aims (pp. 157 ff). McConnell (1967) refers to an Etonian who 'wants to beat the system which is restraining him' (p. 50). Hollis (1960) argues that the excellence of grammar schools will end this. But Abrams (1951) concludes that the system of privilege will be perpetuated by public school offspring of state-educated parents.
32 Wilson (1962) thinks that even if public schools are integrated into the

state system 'the pupils will be as privileged as before—perhaps more so' (p. 123). Tawney (1930) showed how this occurred with another élite—the property owners.

33 Weinberg (1966). We tend to forget that they produced Flashman as well as Tom Brown.

34 Weinberg (1967), p. 172.

35 Human equality is a vexed subject. Reid (1957) cautiously observes that there 'is much confusion about human equality and inequality' (p. 62). Young (1958) dryly notes that 'equality of opportunity means having the opportunity not to be equal'. But each complex culture needs an élite. Current élitist schools in Russia, Germany (Troger, 1968) and Kenya (Olson, 1972) confirms this, even though they are all attempts to introduce an élite training in a democratic system.

36 Ottley (1966), 'Over half our army officers come from public schools'. Rubinstein (1970) 'a disproportionate number of public school boys obtain positions of privilege and power'. Indeed the schools of our bishops and cabinet ministers virtually constitute *The Public and Preparatory Schools Year Book*. Hence Wilson shrewdly (1962) observes 'The social function of public school is to support a particular social class' (p. 113).

37 Troger (1968) functionally defines élites by achievement, power and status. To this should now be added a service-élite. Niblett (1969) says this is accepted in America, cf. Jesus 'Whoever wants to be greatest must become the servant of all' (Matthew 20:27).

38 Illich (1971a), p. 132. cf. Morris (1969) who compares education with a *rite de passage* (pp. 235 ff). Aronson and Mills (1959) found a positive correlation between the severity of initiation and subsequent attachment to the group.

39 Illich (1971a), pp. 86, 94, 171.

40 Illich (1971b), p. 163.

41 *Compulsory Miseducation* (Goodman), *School is Dead* (Reimer), *Teaching as a Subversive Activity* (Postman and Weingartner), *How Children Fail* (Holt), *The Underachieving School* (Holt). 'School is an Interruption of a Child's Education' (McCluhan repeating Shaw's Comment, *Times Educational Suppl.*, 11 September 1970).

42 Reimer (1971), p. 25.

43 *op. cit.*, p. 10.

44 Reimer (1971b), 'Consumer-pupils are taught to make their desires conform to marketable values' (p. 41). 'School is the advertising agency which makes you believe you need the society as it is' (p. 113 *et al.*). Atkinson (1971) and Hampden-Turner (1971) plead with equal cogency that *free* man must interact *freely* with his fellows if he is to be truly *free*.

45 It is not, of course, as simple as this. Eggleston (1967) reaffirmed the view of Dewey (1956) that although schools are moulded by society they also modify it.

Bibliography

ABRAMS, MARK, *Social Surveys and Social Action* (Heinemann, 1951).

ALI, TARIQ, *Coming British Revolution* (Cape, 1972).

ARONSON, E. and MILLS, J., 'The Effect of Severity of Initiation on Liking for the Group', in *Journal of Abnormal and Social Psychology*, Vol. 59, 1959.

ATKINSON, D., *Junior School Community* (Longman, 1962).

ATKINSON, D., *Orthodox Consensus and Radical Alternative* (Heinemann, 1971).

BAMFORD, T. W., *The Rise of the Public Schools* (Nelson, 1967).

BANKS, OLIVE, *Parity and Prestige in English Secondary Education* (Routledge & Kegan Paul, 1955).

BASSETT, G. W., *Innovation in Primary Education* (Wiley Interscience, 1970).

BLACKSTONE, T., 'The Plowden Report', in *British Journal of Sociology*, Vol. 18, 1967.

BLISHEN, EDWARD, 'Heads Down for Oxbridge', in *Times Literary Suppl.* (29 May 1970).

BRONFENBRENNER, URIE, *Two Worlds of Childhood* (Allen & Unwin, 1972).

BRUCE, GEORGE, *Secondary School Examinations: Facts and Commentary* (Pergamon, 1969).

CAMPBELL, A., *Eleven-Plus and All That* (Watts, 1957).

COLLIER, K. G., *The Social Purposes of Education* (Routledge & Kegan Paul, 1959).

DALE, R. R. and GRIFFITHS, S., *Down-stream: Failure in a Grammar School* (Routledge & Kegan Paul, 1965).

DAVIE, R., BUTLER, N., and GOLDSTEIN, H., *From Birth to Seven* (Longmans, 1972).

DAVIES, H., *Culture and the Grammar School* (Routledge & Kegan Paul, 1965).

DENT, H. C., *Secondary Modern Schools* (Routledge & Kegan Paul, 1958).

DEWEY, J., *School and Society* (Univ. Chicago Press, 1956).

EGGLESTON, S. J., 'Going Comprehensive', in *New Society*, No. 221, 1966.

EGGLESTON, S. J., *The Social Context of the School* (Routledge & Kegan Paul, 1967).

FLEMING, DAVID P., *The Public Schools and the General Education System* (HMSO, 1942).

FOX, L., *A County Grammar School* (Oxford Univ. Press, 1967).

FRASER, W. R., *Residential Education* (Pergamon, 1968).

GARDINER, S., 'Open-plan Discoveries at School', in *Observer*, 7 November, 1971.

GAVRON, H., *The Captive Wife* (Routledge & Kegan Paul, 1966).

GIBBERD, K., *No Place Like School* (Michael Joseph, 1962).

GOODMAN, P., *Compulsory Miseducation* (Penguin, 1971).

GRAHAM, J. A. and PHYTHIAN, B. A., *Manchester Grammar School* (Manchester Univ. Press, 1965).

GRUDGEON, D. and GRUDGEON, E., *An Infant School* (Macmillan, 1971).

HAMPDEN-TURNER, C., *Radical Man* (Duckworth, 1971).

HARGREAVES, D. H., *Social Relations in a Secondary School* (Routledge & Kegan Paul, 1967).

HERRIOT, P., *Language and Teaching* (Methuen, 1971).

HEWITSON, J. N., *The Grammar School Tradition in a Comprehensive World* (Routledge & Kegan Paul, 1969).

HIGHET, J., *A School of One's Choice* (Blackie, 1969).

HOLLIS, C., *Eton* (Hollis & Carter, 1960).

HOLT, J., *How Children Fail* (Pitman, 1964).

HOLT, J., *The Underachieving School* (Pitman, 1970).

HOWARTH, T. E. B., *Culture, Anarchy and the Public Schools* (Cassell, 1969).

ILLICH, I. D., *Celebration of Awareness* (Calder & Boyars, 1971a).

ILLICH, I. D., *Deschooling Society* (Calder & Boyars, 1971b).

ISAACS, S., *Social Development in Young Children* (Routledge & Kegan Paul, 1961).

JACKSON, B. and MARSDEN, D., *Education and the Working Classes* (Routledge & Kegan Paul, 1962).

JAMES REPORT, *Teacher Training*, Vols I–V (HMSO, 1970).

KALTON, G., *The Public Schools: A Factual Survey* (Longmans, 1966).

KING, R., *Values and Involvement in a Grammar School* (1969).

KOHL, H. R., *The Open Classroom* (Methuen, 1971).

LACEY, C., *Hightown Grammar—The School as a Social System* (Manchester Univ. Press, 1970).

LAMBERT, R., *The State and Boarding Education* (Methuen, 1966).

LAMBERT, R., 'The Public School: A Sociological Introduction', in Graham Katton (Ed.), *The Public Schools* (Longmans, 1967).

LAMBERT, R., *The Hothouse Society* (Weidenfeld & Nicolson, 1968).

LAWSON, J., *A Town Grammar School Through Six Centuries* (Univ. Hull Press, 1963).

LOUKES, H., *Secondary Modern* (Harrap, 1956).

MCCONNELL, J. D. R., *Eton—How it Works* (Faber, 1967).

MAKARENKO, A., *Problems of Soviet School Education* (Progress Publishers, Moscow, 1965).

MANNHEIM, K., *Diagnosis of Our Time* (Routledge & Kegan Paul, 1954).

MAYS, J. B., *The School in its Social Setting* (Longmans, 1967).

MAYS, J. B., *et al.*, *School of Tomorrow* (Longmans, 1968).

MEAD, M., 'The School in American Culture', in Halsey, Floud and Anderson (Eds), *Education, Economy and Society* (Free Press, 1965).

MILLER, D., 'Sexual Conflict and Drug Abuse', in *New Society*, 16 September 1971.

MORRIS, D., *The Naked Ape* (Corgi Books, 1969).

MUSGROVE, F., *Youth and the Social Order* (Routledge & Kegan Paul, 1964).

NEWSOM REPORT, *Half Our Future* (HMSO, 1963).

NIBLETT, W. R., 'Classification of Results in Degree Examinations in England and the United States', in *The World Year Book of Education* (Evans Bros, 1969).

OLSEN, J. B., 'Big City Schoolhouse', in *Educational Forum*, Vol. 35, May 1971.

OTLEY, C. B., 'Public School and Army', in *New Society*, No. 216, 1966.

PARSONS, T., *The Social System* (Routledge & Kegan Paul, 1951).

PARTRIDGE, J., *Life in a Secondary Modern School* (Penguin, 1968).

PETERS, R. S. (Ed.), *Perspectives on Plowden* (Routledge & Kegan Paul, 1969).

PLATO, *The Republic* (Clarendon, 1955).

PLOWDEN REPORT, *Children and Their Primary School* (HMSO, 1967).

POSTMAN, N. and WEINGARTNER, C., *Teaching as a Subversive Activity* (Penguin, 1971).

PROBERT, H. and JARMAN, C., *A Junior School* (Macmillan, 1971).

PUBLIC SCHOOLS COMMISSION, Vol I—*First Report* (HMSO, 1968). Vol. II *Second Report* (HMSO, 1970).

REES, R. J., *Background and Belief* (Student Christian Movement, 1967).

REID L. A., 'Equality and Inequality', in *British Journal of Educational Sociology*, Vol. VI, No. 1, 1957.

REIMER, E., *School is Dead* (Penguin, 1971).

RIESMAN, D., 'An Essay on Education and Equality', in *Daedalus*, Vol. 96, No. 3, 1967.

ROBINSON, G., *Private Schools and Public Policy*, Monograph No. 1 (Loughborough Univ. Tech, Dept. Social Sciences and Economics, 1972).

RUBINSTEIN, D., 'The Public Schools', in D. Rubinstein and C. Stoneman (Eds), *Education for Democracy* (Penguin, 1970a).

RUBINSTEIN, D. and STONEMAN C., *Education for Democracy* (Penguin, 1970).

SPINLEY, B. M., *The Deprived and the Privileged* (Routledge & Kegan Paul, 1953).

START, K. B., 'Substitution of Games Performance for Academic Achievement as a Means of Achieving Status Among Secondary School Children', in *British Journal of Sociology*, Vol. 17, 1966.

STEPHENS, J. M., *The Process of Schooling* (Holt, Rinehart & Winston, 1967).

STEVENS, F., *The New Inheritors* (Hutchinson, 1970).

STEVENS, F., *The Living Tradition* (Hutchinson, 1972).

TAWNEY, R. H., *The Acquisitive Society* (Bell, 1930).

TAYLOR, W., *The Secondary Modern School* (Faber, 1963).

TROGER, WALTER, *Elitenbildung: Uberlegungen Schulreform in Der Demokratischen Gesellschaft* (Ernst Reinhardt, Munchen, 1968).

VINCENT, W. A. L., *The Grammar Schools* (Murray, 1969).

WAKEFORD, J., *The Cloistered Elite: A Sociological Analysis of the English Public Boarding School* (Macmillan, 1969).

WEBB, J., 'The Sociology of a School', in *British Journal of Sociology*, Vol. 13, 1962.

WEINBERG, I., 'The Occupational Aspirations of British Public Schoolboys', in *School Review*, Vol. 74, No. 3, 1966.

WEINBERG, I., *The English Public School* (Atherton Press, 1967).

WHITBREAD, N., *The Evolution of the Nursery–Infant School* (Routledge & Kegan Paul, 1972).

WHITFIELD, G., 'The Grammar School Through Half a Century', in *British Journal of Educational Sociology*, Vol. V, No. 2, 1957.

WILCE, H., 'Infants in Industry', in *New Society*, 22 June 1972.

WILSON, J. B., *Public Schools and Private Practice* (Allen & Unwin, 1962).

WRAGG, M., 'A Test of the Emotional Maturity of Boys and Girls in Certain Grammar, Comprehensive and Modern Secondary Schools', in *Durham Research Review*, Vol. 5, No. 21, 1968.

YOUNG, M., *The Rise of the Meritocracy* (Thames & Hudson, 1958).

Chapter 15

The Comprehensive Solution

TWO POSSIBLE CORRECTIVES

From the evidence produced in the previous chapters, it is clear that an élitist system of education is inimical to moral development and therefore needs to be radically modified. Two efforts have been made to facilitate this. The first attempts to deal with 'the under-privilege of the many' by disseminating the 'over-privilege of the few' (1). This is done by the simple expedient of extending public school facilities to the population at large. The second tries to overcome this disparity by ending all privilege (and thus all under-privilege) by making all education a comprehensive system. Both are essentially sociological experiments, and both have had to weather sociological storms.

Extending Public School Facilities

Sustaining the thesis that the privileges of the few should, as far as is possible, be extended to all, we may turn to the experiments intended to do just that. Numerous reports and writers have suggested that the public schools (2) should be integrated into the state system, and many political and educational credos have been erected on the basis of this plausible proposal. Both Lambert, who was commissioned to undertake the research, and also the report of the Public Schools Commission, affirmed that there was a vast unsatisfied demand for such education. This, however, has been subsequently refuted (3). Even had there been such a demand, it would have foundered on a sociological rock. Hollis reported first, that LEA help with boarding school education was not accepted by parents, and second, that this was also because intelligent pupils dreaded becoming subsequent rejected misfits.

In a controlled research project Hipkin also showed that lower-status state school pupils found it impossible to adjust to the public school ethos, although their higher-status counterparts managed to do so with ease. This was also reported by Wakeford who found, first, that the intake was predominantly middle class, and, second, that the working-class boys were 'tearful and frightened' because they said nobody would believe that 'we are not on the telephone at home (and) living in a house that was not even semi-detached' (4).

As always when privileges are in jeopardy the privileged closed their ranks. It was claimed that this policy was initiated because 'Left-wing opinion has consistently seen the public schools as an affront to social justice', (5) and that working-class parents prefer to spend their money on 'cars and drinks and smoking and hair-do's and betting and bingo and so on' (6). It has been blandly added that those who wish to benefit are free to pay for this service (7). Finally it is argued that the public schools already approximate to a 'comprehensive system' (8). Public Schools, it seems, need not resort to immoral means to retain their privileges. Like all 'successful' schools they are embedded in society as self-perpetuating systems.

Comprehensive Schools and Moral Education

The second alternative is obviously to offer the same educational opportunities within the same schools for all the children in a specific area. It is not generally recognized that the 1944 *Education Act* sanctioned both a separatist *and* a comprehensive system, but since then, those committed to moving from an élitist to an egalitarian social system have tried to implement the latter. Acknowledging that the pursuit of equality is futile, they have nevertheless persistently proclaimed that equality of opportunity is essential in a democratic state.

Such idealism meets with frustrating difficulties. It was not generally recognized, as Rubinstein and Stoneman have shown, that education and politics are inextricably linked. We observed above that this must be so since moral education should change not only individuals but also their society. Soon the real political difficulties became apparent. A simplistic diagnosis can equate Tory policies with separatist education, and socialist principles with comprehensive policies, but it is more complex than that. Suffice it to say that local politics often appear to override educational principles (9). Consequently, initially sound schemes can emerge distorted, and thus vitiate the system. Corbett, for example, surveyed those implemented by hard-core uncooperating authorities and there found many enlarged secondary schools described as comprehensive. Multi-site schools are also all too familiar: and a high rate of teacher turnover, with a critical shortage of specialist staff, enervates even those schemes which are implemented (10).

Before continuing with this account it ought to be emphasized that this egalitarian movement is not unique to Britain. Sweden too has experimented with this appropriately democratic system of education (11). In Britain, however, there is an abundance of evidence which outlines both the ideals and the difficulties associated with the implementation of what many see as the only suitable educational system in a socialist state.

Naturally some reports have been sponsored by official bodies (12) from which one can obtain a sober account of the development of comprehensive schooling. Here too, one finds a clear picture of the organization and administration, teacher attitudes and qualifications, curricular opportunities, streaming techniques, school size and architecture. They also review and investigate the achievement level of children, their intelligence, the degree to which comprehensive schools can compensate for any academic disadvantage and the ease with which different kinds of children can successfully learn in a multi-choice time-table. Finally social-class, extra-curricular activities and school neighbourhood contacts are all explored: *but nowhere is there any specific reference to moral growth.* The orientation is almost totally academic for even practical subjects are elevated to this status.

One cannot avoid concluding from this that it is implicitly assumed that *comprehensives are intended to offer a grammar school education to all*, which is curiously tragic. When the aftermath of the second world war left growing delinquency and a value-vacuum in its train, the newly instituted comprehensive schools had an unparalleled opportunity to cope with these problems. Yet they too were caught in the manic, technology frenzy of making bigger things go further and faster, and so missed the opportunity of enhancing our culture, by ennobling its members.

As one would expect, individuals also contribute to our knowledge. Pedley's superb survey covers every aspect of a problem up until 1963 in which, he says 'quality is geared to the needs of a liberal democratic society' (13), and thereby discloses his egalitarian preferences. Rubinstein and Simon trace the history of comprehensive education from the mid-twenties, in a passionate apologia from advocates of comprehensive education and therefore contains sparse measured appraisal. Consequently they condemn early educators for imposing an educational system which necessarily mirrored class stratification; and then refute the advocates of grammar schools for their élitist policies.

Conway also outlines the political ideas and social attitudes which have led to the formation of the comprehensive movement. Burgess has produced a popular account which assumes that 'secondary education in England and Wales will become increasingly comprehensive' (14). Hence he ranges widely to sustain the theme that the rate of educational innovation is thus increasing. Yet once again one finds no evidence of this new educational system triumphantly seizing its chance to produce morally mature citizens.

Then to these general accounts one may add a further source of information. All are written with varying degrees of partisan commitment, but they do add more details to the picture already painted. These are mostly reports of the progress of individual schools (15), or groups of comprehensive schools (16), and make it abundantly clear that the generic term 'comprehensive' covers a wide variety of school systems. One study, by Moore, is concerned with the personal problems of the pupils yet it too falls far short of advocating that personal guidance in school which is essential to moral development.

Hence, once again, the moral educator has to turn from this material virtually empty-handed. However, it does become increasingly clear that the consensus of opinion supports the view that comprehensive education *qua* education is the most suitable milieu within which moral education can take place, even though opinion concerning the general value of these schools is divided.

How effective are Comprehensives?

In addition to the data provided above much more has been supplied by researchers dealing with specific issues. Taking the evidence concerned with academic standards first, there is little to add to Rubinstein and Simon's lyrical promotion of the unstreamed comprehensive as an educational promised land. Conway, however, provides a list of examination results which, he argues, ought to encourage the diminishing number of pessimists who fear for academic standards in comprehensive education. Beyond that there is little hard evidence (17).

The most immediately obvious non-academic advantage of this system is its elimination of a selective examination which ensures that no child need feel rejected. Since self-acceptance is correlated with both this experience and also with moral growth, this is a crucial factor. On the positive side this acceptance means that 'each individual has the opportunity to develop to her fullest extent' (18). Furthermore the size of such schools enables them to sustain a house system, which enables links to be forged with both primary schools and families and introduces pastoral care into this familial system (19). This, naturally, ameliorates the stress of transition to a secondary school.

A little-known research report, published over a decade ago, adds to this eulogy. There Miller presented data for concluding that comprehensive schools are preferable in every respect. They induce greater cultural unity; improve general cultural standards; establish parity of esteem; induce greater social cohesion; and encourage boys to stay at school longer. Since that time a considerable amount of research has confirmed these opinions (20).

This conclusion, however, is opposed by Stevens who is a redoubtable protagonist of the grammar school. She persistently presses the cause of separatist education and roundly criticizes the comprehensive system in the process. Yet when her hard evidence is studied it is clear that the only conclusion one may legitimately reach is the predictable, mediating view that in the comprehensive school lower-status children are likely to be demoted or have their academic potential unrealized: and the equally predictable fact that higher-status children still benefit.

The pleas of writers, like Howarth, who argue that this system will destroy middle-class values, can also be ignored for two reasons. First there is no empirical evidence to support it; and second, there is a considerable weight of evidence to show that class barriers remain. Oppenheim's earlier finding, that the different social classes did not mix at school, was confirmed by Musgrave who reviewed the evidence later and concluded that 'the case for social cohesion through this type of school is not as yet proved' (21). Ford, Holly, Marsden and Stevens have now provided considerable evidence to show that these social differences are still sustained within the school. This may well explain why some researchers have reported the existence of embittered working-class groups, in comprehensive schools, who fantasize their way through confusions and glamourize their depressed role in a system which had promised so much (22). Consequently critics can cite the evidence of King, Taylor and Urwin to argue that comprehensive schools have less integrative social value than is usually thought.

Such diverse conclusions again suggest that a mediating view is nearer the truth. This was the conclusion of Futcher. Studying the moral attitudes and personality traits of comprehensive school pupils he reached this simple conclusion. 'Where differences were significant it appeared that the comprehensive school was advantageous to lower modern stream boys, but not to upper stream grammar boys'. This conclusion, too, has received considerable support much of which has emphasized the important fact of social class.

The work of Julienne Ford

It is clear from such indecisive evidence that few firm conclusions can be reached. This at least was the view of Ford. With dispassionate clarity she presented the evidence to show that the comprehensive schools have failed. Yet despite this, she argues, we still need them, for the system we have is a chimera—a political gesture. Therefore the present, meritocratic, class-ridden, inadequate comprehensives must be replaced by genuinely egalitarian schools. We still need to establish a system which will enable children to realize their personal and intellectual potential regardless of social-class impediments.

Her report raises two important points. First, it is still problematic whether we have yet established a system of comprehensive education: second, it is far from certain that such a system could survive in our present form of society.

Non-comprehensive Comprehensives

By definition a comprehensive school should be all-inclusive. Consequently it should cater for *all* the children in a conveniently defined catchment area which can provide a balanced intake and offer an education designed to satisfy the personal and academic needs of all the pupils (23). Clearly these do not exist. Most are single-sex schools and many do not receive their share of the able students, who are creamed off by the grammar schools and public schools, and even removed by otherwise ideologically sympathetic high-status parents. Consequently Newsom-type children then preponderate in them, with sixth-form colleges, it is said, exacerbating the situation by removing the stabilizing social influence of young adults from the school society. Thus the indictment could continue. Many areas have no such school and, as Stevens has repeatedly argued, when they do exist it is often within a 'one-class' catchment area (24).

Because of such evidence many argue that a comprehensive school will only survive if the grammar school ethos can be implanted there. Hewitson, for example, argues that unless this is done, we shall have taken an educationally retrograde step (25). Even this, however, can be a divisive policy, for as Marsden has shown, such schools can already be classified as 'egalitarian' or 'meritocratic'. The former offer unstreamed progressive, non-specialized teaching and give weight to the needs of the less able. The latter employs streaming, to facilitate early specialization, and tends to concentrate on the abler pupils.

Obviously the needs of both slow-learners and gifted children must be met, and this may well be a thorny problem in a truly comprehensive system of education. However, that is essentially an academic problem, and we are concerned with social and moral development— it is clear from all the evidence adduced earlier that the truly comprehensive school, at both primary and secondary levels, is needed if children are to live together on an egalitarian basis of altruistic concern.

It seems then that only one conclusion can be drawn here. *We need comprehensive schools, but we have yet to establish them.* Perhaps the conflicting research evidence quoted above results from this fact. There is ground for some hope for although the triumphant cries from advocates of comprehensive education, have to be augmented by sober qualified research data (26), such evidence does suggest that comprehensive schools are possibilities even in our competitive, socially-stratified society. It will mean the end of church, voluntary, maintained and independent schools, but the moral gain will out-weigh this ideological loss.

Morally speaking the tripartite system of education made it clear that educators had not only lost their way, but had also lost the map. Though far from ideal, the present comprehensive system, with all its faults, has at least provided us with a map. The terrain has yet to be charted with care, and until this is done much of what passes for moral education will necessarily be of the *ad hoc* kind currently being disseminated by compilers of school textbooks who appear to be unaware of the fundamental problems. At least we have started, and in the present century of modern education we have made some progress. Now the really hard work has to be done. We must not only establish such comprehensive schools but also structure them in the service of moral education.

VARIATIONS WITHIN COMPREHENSIVES

School Size

This is the first and most obvious crucial internal variation in comprehensive schools. The commonly accepted ideal figure is 1,500 pupils, but now the chairman of the Comprehensive School Com-mittee has suggested the figure of 300 pupils (27). Research evidence here is again sparse and inconclusive. One finds not only extreme conclusions but also mediating views presented. This is not surprising, since there are, as we have seen, very few genuinely comprehensive schools. For example, Ross commended large schools because they could provide better curricular and pastoral facilities; but Cohen found that at this size they became so bureaucratized that inter-personal relationships were adversely affected (28). Furthermore others have shown that size is not necessarily correlated with either teacher of pupil attitudes to school or each other, and consequently have suggested that purely academic criteria should determine school size (29).

At first sight it would seem that all the advantages lie with the small community. Vivich and Bensman, for example, found that the small rural community was the stronghold of social virtue, and protagonists of small schools are legion. Marklund discovered that Swedish children realized their personal potential more fully in them. They were, according to Wicker, most able to enhance moral responsibility, moral dynamism and cognitive complexity in children. Baird claimed that levels of pupil-participation and non-academic attainments and accomplishments were higher in a small school. And Armstrong concluded 'Small schools do not, of course, guarantee stronger personal contacts, but a school in which everyone can be on nodding acquaintance with everyone else starts off at a great advantage' (30).

Such evidence cannot end the discussion. Size is a complex issue because schools must cater for both academic and moral education, and it may well be that the optimum sizes for each are negatively correlated. Indeed the advantages of each have been repeatedly confirmed. Barker and Gump isolated size as a factor in determining the social environment of an American High School and reached the conclusion that 'Large schools offer more facilities' but 'as schools get larger students become superfluous and redundant. Consequently a school should be sufficiently small that all of its students are needed for its enterprises' (31).

Campbell's superb review of the then current research made it clear that the primary difference between large and small schools was that pupils were *exposed* to a greater number of activities in the former, but actually *participated* more in the latter. This difference was significant over the whole range of both academic and interpersonal activities. This finding is also embedded in the report of Barker and Gump for they too stressed that although larger schools had more facilities these did not increase proportionately to the number of pupils. Hence more interpersonal activities were *accessible* but *participation* in them was less in the large school. Taylor too has summed up the situation by arguing bluntly that small schools are in a position to provide personal familial care, but that larger schools can maintain systems which support personal tutors and house masters.

It would seem then that the ideal comprehensive school should be sufficiently large to provide a wide range of curricular subjects with competent academic specialists, and yet small enough to ensure that healthy social relationships are sufficiently established to mould pupils' character and transmit moral values. Clearly this was in the mind of Armstrong when he suggested that comprehensive schools ought to cater for 300 pupils but be grouped into larger units to share academic and teaching resources and provide a sixth form and specialist teachers.

This points to the need for large schools containing smaller units, such as houses. These would then incorporate the social advantages of both large and small schools. Children could thus belong to a large community, approximating to the society for which they are destined; and also to a small society, similar in nature to the families from which they come. Moreover the house system would introduce many teachers in a pastoral role, within a familial group.

Such a system could only work if it satisfied a number of criteria. The new schools must be genuinely comprehensive by gathering into a multi-ability, multi-social-class system, all pupils currently attending grammar schools and independent schools. They must also have the services of the many able teachers at present working in these areas; and they must ensure that both specifically academic and also personal aims are realized in this system. It ought to be unnecessary to add that educational principles rather than political policies should determine the nature of our educational system, but unfortunately this is not so. Political rancour appears to be a prime ingredient in the present reorganization of our secondary schools.

However, the solid facts remain. Small units within a larger system (32) would facilitate both the academic and the moral achievement of the pupils concerned, by inheriting the educational advantages of both large and small schools.

Streaming or Non-streaming

At first glance the case for streaming children, according to academic ability in schools, appears to be unanswerable, for each school class or group can apparently thereby be taught, and enabled to advance together at an appropriate level and rate. This commonsense view, supported by entrenched teacher conservatism and currently discredited research, has resulted in the establishment of streaming as an integral element of school life today. Yet the simple facts are that the practice of streaming may merely confirm the hypothesis which supports its implementation (33); and at the same time fail to enhance the potential of the pupils involved (34). Both facts, of course, are related, but both join in a condemnation of this divisive system.

It is possible to refute such facts with research evidence. Douglas, for example, found that with streaming the higher group improved while the lower deteriorated. Many could then plausibly argue that we should retain and implement this system because it enhances the academic quality of the best children and wastes no time in putting an educational gloss on the worst. But clearly moral educators should hesitate to do this. Such élitism not only fragments the school community but also advances the few by the deprivation of many.

However, streaming may be rejected on academic grounds, but the indictment becomes even more savage when the moral and social consequences are considered. Even Douglas, who provided the above evidence to support streaming, concluded that its abolition would result in a growth in co-operation between the teachers and pupils concerned. The problem, as he sees it, is that advocates of streaming tend to 'think almost always in individual rather than social terms' and so stress the academic rather than the moral consequences of the system (35). Clearly this controversy originates in diverse views of our educational aims, and if the divisive, élitist streaming system is ultimately abolished we must be involved in the substitution of different educational aims and philosophies. These, it is to be hoped, will give primary emphasis to children as moral agents and not merely as empty, academic receptacles, waiting to be filled (36).

Under some such system the increased co-operation, mentioned by Douglas, would be augmented by greater altruism, empathy and responsibility generated amongst multi-ability pupils who co-operate with each other in every facet of school life. Evidence for this assumption abounds, but one in particular is relevant here. In Chapter 9 it was argued that one primary quality of morality is the open-minded, divergent and creative thinking which rejects legalism in favour of the situational application of valid moral principles, characterized by concern for people. Ferri, for example, found that it is precisely this kind of mentality which the non-streamed situation facilitates.

In sharp contrast to this generous co-operative spirit, one finds both successful and unsuccessful streamed pupils, 'competitive, acquisitive and philistine' (37). Furthermore, as Lacey found, such children suffer from the social isolation which is an inevitable corollary of dividing peer groups on the basis of impersonal academic criteria. And this incipient alienation survived, as Marris found, in tertiary levels of education.

It was argued earlier that if schools are to accept some responsibility for the moral education of their pupils, this is best done in a familial setting: and, clearly streaming militates against this. Discrimination on the basis of intelligence is inimical to family life. It should be equally true of schools. Of course it must not be forgotten, as Reid and Young remind us, that we are not all equal: but this merely stresses the need we have of each other. Society, like families, should be built on the basis of that mutual co-operation which is commensurate with our individual abilities. It should be so in schools too. Hence children who help each other in the process of learning, will be prepared to live in the greater society which it is hoped will then be built not on competitive greed, but upon mutual co-operation. As Mellor pointed out in her study of streaming in infant schools, 'The advantages of family grouping have long been appreciated' (38).

It must be stressed that schools should be both comprehensive and unstreamed. Clearly comprehensive schools, which eliminate the tripartite streaming of schools, should not perpetuate the same divisive system within their own structure: but this consistency is not always sustained. Despite the growing advocacy of non-streaming in comprehensive schools, Marsden and Ford both found 'merito-cratic' comprehensives which favoured rigid streaming. Conse-quently, argued Marsden, they are socially selective, and damaging to the pupils' morale. Ford added that such a system retained an iniquitous socially divisive discrimination against lower-status children. Clearly such schools reject children as ruthlessly as do streamed grammar schools and brand them as traumatically as the worst selective systems of the past. Consequently any moral educa-tion, based on acceptance and personal achievement, shrivels in such a morally moribund environment.

Of course, as Lunn has made perfectly clear to even the most entrenched protagonist on either side, streaming is an extraordinarily complex issue, with its ramifications rooted in the most unlikely places. In its most innocuous form it still 'rigidly defines relationships between individuals' (39) and thereby atrophies any free intercourse between children as individuals. At its worst, it produces the rampant, élitist, competitiveness which is the antithesis of that democratic, altruistic co-operation upon which mature morality is built. Hence, by the abolition of streaming, schools may more easily unite pupils, without either exclusivism or élitist structures, and so enable them also to feel wanted, successful and accepted.

Middle Schools and Sixth Form Colleges
Secondary education in England is also currently characterized by the establishment of both middle schools and sixth form colleges. There is very little available evidence upon which to base an assessment of a middle school, catering for the nine- to fourteen-year-olds which Edwards clinically describes as an 'educational hybrid'. Nicholson's detailed account of a purpose-built school paints a glowing picture of the ease with which it can surmount many of the educational and personal problems currently endemic in that age range. This view is also reflected elsewhere in both England and America (40).

One can see why this should be so. The emphasis on the *expressive* element in education is thereby perpetuated into adolescence and so sustains a young adolescent's confidence in his own identity and integrity. This then enhances his sensitivity towards people and develops his 'personalism'. Equally the progressive-type education of the primary schools is continued into adolescence and so sustains the creative, open-minded inquiring attitude which is so essential for the formulation of moral principles. Specific curricular material of this kind has yet to be devised, but Culling's first attempt presents an encouraging spectacle of education which, although ostensibly academic, nevertheless caters for the affective aspects of personality and the expressive element of school life.

The establishment of sixth form colleges has evolved from two contemporary educational trends. The first is the move towards comprehensive education: and the second a growing tendency for adolescents to defer leaving school in order to obtain the qualifications increasingly demanded by employers (41). Linked with the lowered age of maturation today the case for having separate educational establishments for pupils of fifteen to eighteen years of age seems to be irrefutable. When one adds the fact that this phase coincides with specific academic preparation for GCE and CSE examinations it is clear that this trend was unavoidable (42).

Other reasons for advocating the establishment of sixth form colleges abound. Some claim that the fifteen to eighteen year age-range forms a natural, third stage in educational development (43). Others that it would be a more economical deployment of specialist teachers and plant. Yet more argue that the facilities of all sections of the tripartite secondary system of education, should be gathered together once pupils have passed the statutory school-leaving age (44). If Edward Short's suggestion that the school-leaving age should be raised to eighteen by 1980 is adopted this would become a viable proposition, extending as it does, the principle of total comprehensive education into late adolescence. Furthermore those who want the grammar school tradition preserved would be mollified by this compromise expedient.

However, it is when one considers the moral consequences of this that the proposition becomes exciting. King elaborates the view that the psychological justification for establishing such schools or colleges lies in the fact that there pupils will be treated as adults who will be required to display initiative and enterprise. Thus co-operation and social responsibility would be nourished and a measure of autonomy would emerge. The wider range of interests catered for would also dilute the academic emphasis and enable the personal and expressive elements to flourish in school groups. This in turn would both cater for the non-academic interests of such adolescents and simultaneously eliminate the small intensive sixth form, which many have argued is a dysfunctional unit (45).

Thus in some such way as this both the 'willing' and 'allergic' adolescent pupils, identified by Warburton and Sumner, would have their personal, rather than their academic, interests fostered, during an extended, enforced stay in schools. This at least is partially the view of Marris who provides an abundance of factual information to answer affirmatively the question, 'Will such colleges be more attractive than merely staying on at school?'

Nursery Schools

Running parallel to these movements is the present demand for pre-school or nursery school provision. Despite governmental reluctance to increase educational expenditure, it now seems certain that nursery education will be extended. There are a few critics of the scheme (46) but the overwhelming weight of evidence is in favour of some organized pre-school educational provision. The reasons for this vary. Some merely think of it as a device to relieve the pressure on working mothers. Others claim that the system will ensure that the talent of deprived children is not wasted. When analysed carefully it is clear that this ground swell of opinion resolves itself down to the view that nursery schools will enhance the later moral development of children.

Some argue that it can counterbalance the social disturbance of deprived children and so enable all infants to begin the process of socialization on equal terms (47). Others suggest that nursery schools prepare children for the transition to a larger school society. Some stress that identity-growth and social success are characteristic experiences in this structured situation which will enable both the preconditions and also the basic attitudes of morality to emerge. Finally it has been repeatedly shown that the value-integration, natural to all adjusted personalities, and basic to moral understanding, is facilitated by nursery school experience, and so produces compliant, co-operative, self-reliant children who internalize their moral values and thus ensure later moral development (48). All of which is little more than a sophisticated version of the alleged Jesuit Maxim which could be translated thus, 'The pattern in secondary school is largely determined in the junior school which in turn depends on the pattern in the earliest years' (49).

Since such a costly intention is enervated by simple economic considerations, successive ministers of education have announced that for a start, they will promote nursery education in 'areas of special social need' (50). Current governmental determination to resolve this problem has been revived by Halsey's report on EPA schools (51). There he shows that the EPA is a viable educational unit; that nursery schools are the most effective and economic forms of counteracting deleterious home influences; that community schools regenerate the community concerned; that home and school can work together; that such schools can initiate a comprehensive social movement; and lastly, that gains made in the early years are maintained in the junior school. Perhaps the recommendation most likely to affect moral education concerns the training and employment of *Educational Visitors*. These are intended to improve the school's influence, in working-class districts, where educational opportunity is adversely affected by social conditions. At least in this way the 'preconditions of morality' (see Chap. 3) may be more firmly and rightly established.

Information reaching England from America provides qualified support and Pines' report of the education of under-privileged children there is a mine of such information. She is most helpful in her account of the American 'Head Start' project which is intended to compensate for inadequacies in the home life of infant children. This has met with some criticism; the most trenchant of which is that the project does no lasting good. At first all seems well, but the initial advantages (unlike the Halsey EPA benefits) appear to be so inadequate that the primary schools are unable to reinforce them. For some such reasons the American Moyniham Report blames home life for delinquency and the prodigal squandering of personal potential now characterizing American education. But the research report of Mentzer makes it abundantly clear that 'Head-Start' children are better equipped for first-grade experiences and once there are socialized much more readily.

A final snippet of evidence slots all this data neatly into place. Sarah and Moshe Smilansky have now described their ten-year programme of research into kindergarten provisions for infants. They concluded that a comprehensive nursery school, with a heterogeneous population, run by a multi-disciplinary staff, is most effective in enabling socially disadvantaged children to acquire personal stability, an iternalized value-system, motivation to succeed and positive attitudes to both society and school.

Clearly the establishment of both middle schools and sixth form colleges will have a profound influence on the constitution of any comprehensive school. The former would have three beneficial results. First, it would eliminate the current educational shock associated with passing from a primary to a secondary school. Second, it would cater for a third instead of a half of the school community, and so enable any comprehensive system to be composed of more manageable units. Third, it would allow the senior schools to retain the morally stabilizing influence of sixth forms. All this would naturally be augmented by the establishment of sixth form colleges, for the educational system would then have primary, middle and secondary schools each of which would be enabled to further the moral maturation of their pupils by catering for their developmental needs.

Furthermore, when one adds to this the fact that both primary and nursery schools would of necessity be truly comprehensive, the resultant system would be consistently egalitarian, while moulding the character of a child from infancy to adulthood. Moreover, this would not jeopardize any academic work, for this could all be done in the senior school where young adults would be more amenable to its disciplines and be appropriately treated with the concern and courtesy usually reserved for adults.

Community Schools

There is, however, one further major educational innovation which would affect the nature of any comprehensive. These are the proposed community schools, the nature of which needs to be meticulously defined. Gillett's analysis of four types of 'community school' is invaluable here. The first simply caters for all the children in one area. The second opens its buildings to adult groups in evenings and at week-ends. The third utilizes its environs as curricular material. The last as Gillett avers 'sets out to serve the community in addition to the community serving them'. Clearly only the last qualifies as a valid definition; a point which numerous writers have established elsewhere. Furthermore a cursory reading of research reports and surveys makes it clear that community schools must be viewed in the light of familial or therapeutic models. They must be an integral element in the immediate society and have the prime function of enhancing its social and corporate life. As such they are inevitably involved in moral education (52).

It can be argued that the desire for community schools is politically motivated. Levin's symposium discloses how complex this can be. The contributory writers show how the protagonists and opponents of the scheme reflect their views of political community autonomy and how they see such a movement in terms of political power. Others see in this trend a reflection of some teacher/parent conflict, with each wanting to gain ascendancy in deciding school policy. Some even see the movement, in Negro-dominated areas, as an attempt by black Americans to determine the future of their offspring (53).

The overwhelming impression, however, is that community schools are intended to facilitate community regeneration. This emerges clearly in the work of Fantini and his colleagues, who found that community schools were invariably established as a result of American campaigns to eradicate poverty and distribute local power more equitably. Inevitably this leads to a consideration of their therapeutic and remedial role, for, as Woock has argued, since other schemes have failed, compensatory education may be facilitated by this means.

The problems facing disadvantaged children have been admirably analysed by both Deutsch and Hellmuth; but it is precisely these deficiencies in linguistic, conceptual and social development which a truly community school could remedy, since it functions as an extension of the family and encourages parental participation. Furthermore, Jeffree and Cashdan have recently discovered that the handicapped, as distinct from the disadvantaged, child is twice deprived by having no access to a community school. Not only do their home-bound, limited social lives lack richness but they are also deprived of the normal extra-home experiences which bring contact with other children and adults in a wider range of activities. It is such handicaps as these which a therapeutic and familial community school could rightly remedy most effectively in the EPA situation (54). Thus functioning in this way community schools could also finally be able to establish parity of opportunity and esteem between the rich and the poor segments of society (55).

Further support for community schools can be adduced from studies comparing children in rural and urban schools. Once the opponents of both types have been considered (56) the evidence suggests that rural schools are more effective in moral education. The Whitings, for example, found that rural school children scored higher than urban children in measures of responsibility and altruism. Light too, supported these findings and showed that country children were more sensitive to moral issues. It is true that they are also more susceptible to the mores of family, church and peers; and displayed a higher degree of subservience to authoritarian dicta, while being less influenced by the new morality. But this is to be expected in a folk society.

What does seem clear, however, is that since rural schools are more orientated towards the community, such benefits as accrue in them may also be garnered by urban community schools. Thus it seems that effective moral education is enhanced in schools organically linked with the surrounding community (57).

There are, however, two difficulties here. Such community schools are most needed in EPAs. But these are staffed by middle-class teachers living in more salubrious environs. Thus one may have the spectacle of teachers trying to impart skills, values and moral sense to children amongst whom they do not live, and with whom they share no common culture.

However, the system does appear to work and Rogers' eulogy of the Leicestershire plan provides some comfort, but there is a further endemic problem. It was observed above that in order to ensure that the comprehensive nature of a school is not nullified by drawing pupils from a single social class, an 'octopus' catchment area may be required. This clearly militates against the establishment of a genuine community school. Thus in EPA situations, for example, community and comprehensive schools may be mutually exclusive concepts.

Single-sex or Co-educational

This final internal school variation needs to be considered since it too affects moral education. Commonsense demands that since all children are destined for life in heterosexual societies, co-educational schools should be the norm. Not only does research support this but the world-wide trend towards co-education substantiates it. (58).

A cursory glance at some evidence might suggest that the need for co-education is not now clamant. Rowland, for example, compared the standards of behaviour between pupils in single-sex and co-educational schools and found parity of concern for co-operation, politeness and non-aggression in all of them. The only difference Douglas and Ross found was that single-sex schools were more academically successful than co-educational ones; presumably because energy normally canalized into social activities was re-directed into academic pursuits (59). The overwhelming weight of evidence, indicating that moral education is advanced by co-educational schools, comes from the pen of one man—R. R. Dale.

During the last decade Dale has provided a plethora of this evidence. He first showed that teachers favoured co-educational schools for social and moral reasons (60); and then found that co-educational pupils were unanimous in their support of a system which enhanced social life and even (especially for the girls) improved staff–pupil relations (61). At this point he drew his existing findings together and published them as the first volume of a proposed tetralogy. With more room for argument he proceeded to demonstrate that the bland assumptions of the post-war government (e.g. that 'the balance of advantage may be held to lie on the side of the single-sex school') were palpably false. Here one finds an abundance of evidence to indicate that when educated together boys and girls behave better as individuals and groups, and display more concern when interacting with both teachers and peers (62). Simultaneously he then released more accumulated research which showed that social attitudes were healthier in a co-educational school; that the pupils were infinitely happier; and that all had a 'healthier attitude towards sex' (63).

Thus one comes to his second volume in the proposed tetralogy. Here he augments his earlier thesis. This was that educational policies in this area must be determined not so much by research findings as by society's attitude to the sexes in every aspect of their interaction. Now he affirms that groups in which the sexes are either allowed to commingle or are scrupulously separated, are sociologically distinct communities. However, this volume adds a plethora of evidence supporting the view that co-educational establishments are necessary if moral education is to be a viable and effective aspect of school life.

In this volume Dale examines specific aspects of social relationships in school. With a wealth of evidence from the children concerned he proceeds to show that in a co-educational school bullying is almost eliminated. Vicious quarrels among girls were less frequent. The atmosphere was relaxed and happy, and each sex tended to evoke more concern and compassion in the other. Finally there was 'less depraved sex talk', than in single-sex schools. Then to stress his central thesis he argued that both Russian and Nazi pre-war governments turned from co-education to single-sex schools because a militaristic spirit and aggressive attitude could be inculcated in this milieu. For, in the final analysis, Dale argues that co-education could be a force for peace in a war-weary world.

Conclusion

From the above evidence a picture of the school most effectively equipped to facilitate moral development, now begins to emerge. It must be a co-educational, genuinely comprehensive school. It should be sufficiently large to offer opportunities for the exercise of moral traits and attitudes, in work and play, and yet be small enough to sustain a community spirit. The process should last from three to nineteen years, with clearly defined and separate stages. This not only provides smaller units within which pastoral oversight can be exercised, but also caters for developmentally homogeneous groups.

The divisiveness of streaming should be eliminated, and the division, between school and community, dissolved. During the nursery, primary and middle phases the curricular emphasis could be devoted to refining personal relationships and affective, expressive roles. While the final secondary school phase could concentrate on academic work, and include studies of the cognitive element of morality. In this way the malevolent influence of disadvantaged homes can be offset and the benevolent influence of privileged homes can be augmented, by familial schools and parental teachers.

Currently many might find themselves in an educational dilemma. On the one hand they may reject the principle but applaud the practice of the British public and American private schools; and simultaneously feel compelled to applaud the principle but criticize the practice of comprehensive schools. However, it is difficult to refute the view that the latter is infinitely better for moral education.

It may now reflect a stratified society, yet will eventually become one means of eliminating the divisiveness of social class. This cannot but commend itself to religious and atheistic socialists alike, for it subscribes to their ethic of fraternalism.

Furthermore the comprehensive school could be truly democratic in that it reflects and accepts the variety of personal abilities found in society and could thus prepare its pupils for life in a 'Great Society' which should be characterized by concern and service. Its teachers can be parental and familial, since such diverse qualities amongst the pupils require them to step outside the cherished role of academic expert and assume the mantle of counsellor and friend. Cultivation of personal independence in the young would enable such pupils to pass from the pupil-centred primary school, to the autonomy of undergraduate life without smouldering with discontent in their teens or abusing their freedom at college and university.

However, such eulogies must be rooted in fact rather than fancy, and Ross, Bunton, Evisen and Robertson have provided an abundance of relevant facts. Their most recent and most thorough review of comprehensive schools repeatedly affirms two points which mark the system's success. First these schools have made it abundantly clear that success can no longer be based on academic criteria alone. It is the personal development of pupils which matters. They are people, not disembodied and dispassionate intellects. Thus we can now affirm that educational success necessarily implies moral maturity and social competence. Second they have shown that despite the attendant disadvantages in a school which must take children covering the whole spectrum of ability from every social class, academic success does now follow. Such children display a hitherto unknown resilience and tough-mindedness. They want to derive every possible benefit from education and proceed to do so by remaining on after the statutory school-leaving age. Alexander of Macedon may have discredited Plato's eulogy of the Philosopher-King, but we still need citizens who are both wise and good. If comprehensive schools fail to provide them the experiment ought rightly to be closed and filed alongside the histories of other failures: but all the evidence suggests that they have every hope of succeeding in this crucial task.

REFERENCES

1 See p. 246 above.
2 In America these are private schools.
3 King (1967) pointed to the confusion concerning such terms as 'public-school' and 'boarding-school' and 'wants' and 'needs'. Note Wakeford (1969) 'Much of the methodology of the research is clearly inadequate' (p. 181).

4 Wakeford (1969), pp. 180 and 186.

5 Collins (1969), p. 301.

6 Highet (1969), p. 173.

7 Crichton-Miller (1954). 'If the Welfare State, or any citizen in it, has some money to spend much can be done to help young people on these lines at individual schools' (p. 16).

8 Dancy (1966), p. 165.

9 Eggleston (1966), Corbett (1968) and Benn (1971) give detailed accounts of such fighting. Batley *et al.* (1971) record the decision-making procedure when comprehensives were established at Darlington and Gateshead, and clearly show the difficulties faced when local interests must be considered.

10 See Burgess (1972) and Howarth (1969).

11 Husen and Henrysson (1959) survey this and other European systems. Cunningham and Ross (1967) add information from Australia.

12 See IAAM (1967), DES (1967), NFER (Monks 1968a, b; Cox 1969).

13 Pedley (1963), p. 137.

14 Burgess (1970), p. 167.

15 See Chetwynd (1960), Holmes (1967), Berg (1968), Mays *et al.* (1968), Miles (1968), and Simmons and Morgan (1969).

16 NUT (1958), ILEA (1967), Halsall (1970) and Moore (1970).

17 cf. Mays *et al.* (1968). The comprehensive school 'succeeds in saving talent otherwise lost' (p. 107).

18 See Stevens (1970), Chapter 4, supported by Futcher (1960), Holly (1965) and Conant (1967).

19 Miles (1968), p. 64.

20 Udy (1969).

21 Musgrave (1968), p. 134.

22 Tapper (1971), Ford (1969) and Currie (1962).

23 Cole (1964). A comprehensive school must 'be called upon to provide a full range of courses and cannot in the long run be combined with the existence of a grammar school or any other distinct type of school'. Aberrant forms are listed by Judges (1953), p. 3.

24 It is claimed that 'octopus' catchment areas and LEA transport will ameliorate this.

25 Hewitson (1969) 'we will have stepped more steps behind than bears thinking on' (p. 127). Judges (1953) the essential requirements (pp. 17–18).

26 Even the superbly balanced report of Benn and Simon (1970) begins 'Comprehensive schools are no longer an experiment; they represent what will shortly be the standard pattern of secondary education' (p. v). They then conclude 'Comprehensive education is now securely established in Britain' (p. 347).

27 Crowther Report (1959), para. 37, stipulates 1,500, assuming the amalgamation of grammar, technical and secondary modern schools. Armstrong (1970) rejects this assumption and so advocates 300 pupils as the ideal size.

28 See Kaufman (1965), Cohen (1970) and Ross (1972), especially pp. 557ff.

29 Davies' (1971) academic arguments led him to suggest schools of 1,000 pupils. The social factors were rejected by Ross (1972), 'We found no relationship between pupil views and school size' (p. 558). Fraser (1970) too found few interpersonal relationships affected by size and advocates 'schools of the middle level of organizational complexity' (p. 385). Rowan (1972), using the same data, found that 'the relationship is significant at the 5% level' (p. 640).

30 Armstrong (1970), p. 101.

31 Barker and Gump (1964), Chapter 12. They also stress that the small school provides pupils with more opportunities to hold responsible positions.

32 This refers to the house system and not the class units, but class size is a problem. Burgess (1972) reports that the NUT want 'a declared objective of a maximum class size of 30' (p. 545), Gibbs (1951), and Taylor and Faust (1952) support this from research showing that small groups are more creatively active than large ones. Little *et al.* (1971) concluded 'Paradoxically our evidence showed that reduction of class size might be linked with lower performance and this finding is consistent with previous research' (p. 771). Oakley (1970) found that class size did not affect the teacher–pupil pattern of conduct, disciplinary problems, pupil activities or pupil–pupil interaction; except, of course, in extreme cases.

33 Musgrave (1968): 'Streaming acts as a self-fulfilling prophecy' (p. 166). Simon (1970): 'Streaming is a self-verifying hypothesis' (p. 219). Pidgeon (1970): Pupils normally attain the level of teacher expectation and 'it is under the circumstance of streaming that this effect is most likely to become apparent' (p. 47). Rowe (1970) 'Pupils live up to or down to the labels of their school streams' (p. 89).

34 Daniels (1961): 'When junior schools adopt the policy of non-streaming the result is, on average, an improvement' (p. 73). Musgrave (1968) 'The selection process lessens the capability available to this country' (p. 177). Marsden (1969) and Ford (1969) both found that streamed comprehensives neither led to a greater development of talent nor provided equal opportunity to pupils of comparable ability. Finally Ferri (1971) found no significant difference in academic attainment between pupils from streamed and non-streamed schools.

35 Jackson (1964), p. 79.

36 Simon (1970), p. 146. Armstrong (1970) supports this with his 'child-centred image of education' (p. 101).

37 Rowe (1970), p. 88.

38 Mellor (1970), p. 34.

39 King (1969), p. 159. This view is then developed with a wealth of evidence.

40 Popper (1967) 'the human condition at the onset of adolescence calls for a period of schooling which is neither elementary nor secondary but a distinctive phase between the two' (p. 93).

41 Edwards (1970) has charted the four-stage history of the sixth form and shown the complexity of factors affecting this. He sees this development reaching a natural climax in 'a completely separate sixth form college' (p. 102).

42 King (1968), Shield (1970) and Prust (1970) all provide factual accounts of this process.

43 See Spolton (1967); Peterson (1972) presents measured and balanced evidence which firmly indicates this conclusion.

44 See Burgess (1970).

45 cf. Davies (1971), 'the argument against the small sixth form is more concerned with the frustration of pupils than it is with economics' (p. 17).

46 e.g. Burgess (1972): 'Since the most powerful influence on a child's life is the home, can we plausibly seek to mitigate disadvantage by providing nursery schools? Should we not be seeking ways of operating directly on the home?' (p. 649). Tizard (1971): 'nursery education is seen as a potential threat to the family, whose fundamental role is the socialization of the young' (p. 176).

47 Short (1971): 'It must be a first priority if social disadvantage is ever to be

neutralized' (p. 63). Blackstone (1971): 'It will improve their chances of a fair start' (p. 72).

48 See Wildmer (1966), Platoff (1966), Redl (1968) and Scott (1969, 1970).

49 Peaker (1971), p. 163.

50 Lord Belstead (*Observer*, 8 November 1970). Short (1971): 'nursery education would be a first priority to the socially disadvantaged'. The Fabian Group (1970) and Getzels (1966) stress this. Finally, after this chapter was written the Government White Paper (1972) affirmed that 'Pre-schooling is the outstandingly economical and effective device in the general approach to raising educational standards in educational priority areas'. Consequently, 'The Government have decided to launch a new policy for the education of children under five' (para. 13).

51 Goldman (1969) contains a review of the original Plowden suggestions.

52 Cook (1941) argued long ago that we must accept 'as the chief measure of the school's work its ability to improve the area's way of living'. Britten and Britten (1970): 'The task of the school is defined as solving problems of importance to the families of that area.' Marsden (1971): 'Community schools introduce teaching methods and relationships with the outside world which will bring about a new ethos.' Poster (1971): 'no community school can fail to bring social service within its curriculum.' Midwinter (1972): 'The community school is a throughgoing device to identify school and community in every aspect for the better health of both.' Yates (1971): 'society generally would benefit from the arrangement. It could conceivably enable the children of this country to attain parity of esteem.'

53 Levin (1970). See the contributions by Fein, Gittell, Moskow and Levin, respectively. Fantini (1970) supports Lewin on this last point.

54 Ashlock and Stephen (1966) support this therapeutic view, but the concept of 'handicapped' must be widened. DES (1965) deals with social handicap; but many are now saying that intellectual brilliance ought to be treated in this way. The handicap here, they say, is that such children are so intellectually mature that they are rarely allowed to behave as children and feed on the emotional sustenance naturally supplied to them. Thus deprived, their social and emotional maturity is placed in jeopardy.

55 Wise (1968): 'I begin this study with the realization that the states of our nation do not now provide equality of educational opportunity to the residents.' Coons *et al.* (1970) suggests that American Federal distribution of finances with full community control of schools would end this disparity. Taylor and Ayres (1970) have highlighted the inequities of the British state system of education. Here the most subtle form of privilege is exercised by the wealthy parent who can afford to move to the area of the best local school. Bronfenbrenner (1972) and Ungoed-Thomas (1969) have also shown that there are similar disparities in Russia.

56 Strom (1966) found such poverty, underprivilege and discrimination so rife with urban pupils that it resulted in 'poor intellectual capacity and hostile attitudes to school' Lohman (1967): we see 'youth trapped within the urban ghetto and find schools unsympathetic and alien places'. But Griffiths (1968) found that rural subsistence standards of living, poor public amenities, social deprivation and submission to hierarchical authority all 'enervated the influence of rural schools'. Clearly, such evidence would lend itself to different interpretations with socio-economic status as a variable.

57 Such community schools may, in fact, appropriate existing integrated sub-communities: see Gans (1962).

58 UNESCO (1969).

59 See Douglas (1964), Douglas and Ross (1966) and Douglas *et al.* (1968).
  Wakeford (1969) records the lengths to which single-sex boarding school
  boys go to obtain feminine company (pp. 144 ff, *et al.*).
60 Dale (1965).
61 Dale (1966a, b, respectively).
62 Dale (1969a).
63 Dale (1969b).

Bibliography

ARMSTRONG, M., 'The Case for Small Comprehensive Schools', in *Where*,
  July 1970.
ASHLOCK, P. and STEPHEN, A., *Educational Therapy in the Elementary School*
  (Charles Thomas, Springfield, Illinois, 1966).
BAIRD, L. L., 'Big School, Small School: A Critical Examination of the
  Thesis', in *Journal of Educational Psychology*, Vol. 60, No. 4, 1969.
BARKER, R. G. and GUMP, P. V., *Big School, Small School* (Oxford Univ.
  Press, 1964).
BATLEY, B., O'BRIEN, O. and PARRIS, H., *Going Comprehensive* (Routledge &
  Kegan Paul, 1971).
BENN, C. and SIM, B., *Half-Way There* (McGraw-Hill, 1970).
BENN, C., 'School Style and Staying On', in *New Society* 17 (546) 1971.
BERG, L., *Risinghill: Death of a Comprehensive School* (Penguin, 1968).
BIRLEY, D. and DUFTON, A., *An Equal Chance* (Routledge & Kegan Paul,
  1971).
BLACKSTONE, T., *A Fair Start: Provision of Preschool Education* (Penguin,
  1971).
BRITTEN, J. O. and BRITTEN, J. H., 'Schools Serving the Total Family and
  Community', in *Family Co-ordinator*, Vol. 19, No. 4, 1970.
BRONFENBRENNER, U., *Two Worlds of Childhood* (Allen & Unwin, 1972).
BURGESS, T., 'The Further Education Option', in J. W. Tibble (Ed.), *The
  Extra Year* (Routledge & Kegan Paul, 1970a).
BURGESS, T., *Inside Comprehensive Schools* (HMSO, 1970b).
BURGESS, T., 'Education', in *New Society*, 9 March 1972; 16 March 1972;
  and 30 March 1972.
CAMPBELL, W. J., 'School Size: Its Influence on Pupils', in *Educational
  Administration*, No. 3, Pt. 1, 1965.
CHETWYND, H. R., *Comprehensive School* (Routledge & Kegan Paul, 1960).
CLEGG, A. B., *The Role of the School* (Educational Pamphlet: Councils of
  Education Press, 1963).
COHEN, L., 'School Size and Head Teachers' Bureaucratic Role Conception',
  in *Educational Review*, No. 23, Pt. 1, 1970.
COLE, R., *Comprehensive Schools in Action* (Oldbourne Press, 1964).
Comprehensive Education in Action (NFER, 1970).
CONANT, J. B., *The Comprehensive High School* (McGraw-Hill, 1967).
COOK, LLOYD, *Community Action and the School* (Ohio State Univ. Press,
  1941).
COONS, J. E., CLUNE, W. H. and SUGARMAN, S. D., *Private Wealth and Public
  Education* (Oxford Univ. Press, 1970).
COLLINS, J. M., 'The Labour Party and the Public Schools', in *British Journal
  of Educational Sociology*, Vol. 17, 1969.
CONWAY, E. S., *Going Comprehensive* (Harrap, 1970).
CORBETT, A.. 'A Long Way from Comprehensive', in *New Society*, 12 (302)
  1968.

COX, M., *One School for All* (NFER, 1969).

CRICHTON-MILLER, D., 'The Public Schools and the Welfare State', in *British Journal of Educational Sociology*, Vol. III, No. 1, 1954.

CROWTHER REPORT, *Fifteen to Eighteen* (HMSO, 1959).

CULLING, G., *Projects for the Middle School* (Lutterworth, 1972).

CUNNINGHAM, K. S. and ROSS, D. J., *An Australian School At Work* (Australian Council for Educational Research, 1967).

DALE, R. R., 'Co-Education: The Verdict of Experience', in *British Journal of Educational Sociology*, Vol. 35, No. 2, 1965.

DALE, R. R., 'The Happiness of Pupils in Co-educational and Single-sex Grammar Schools', in *British Journal of Educational Psychology*, Vol. XXXVI, Pt. 1, 1966a.

DALE, R. R., 'Pupil–Teacher Relationships in Co-educational and Single-sex Grammar Schools', in *British Journal of Educational Psychology*, Vol. XXXVI, Pt. 3, 1966b.

DALE, R. R., *Mixed or Single-sexed School?* Vol. I (Routledge & Kegan Paul, 1969a).

DALE, R. R., 'Co-Education in Secondary Schools', in *Trends in Education*, No. 14, 1969b.

DALE, R. R., *Mixed or Single-sexed Schools* (Routledge & Kegan Paul, 1971).

DANCY, J. C., *The Public Schools and the Future* (Faber, 1963).

DANIELS, J. C., 'The Effects of Streaming in the Primary School', in *British Journal of Educational Psychology*, February and June 1961.

DAVIES, T. I., 'The Minimum Size of a School', in *Trends in Education*, No. 23, 1971.

Decent Relations in 'Grapevine', in *New Society*, 2 March 1972.

DES REPORT ON EDUCATION, *Education under Social Handicap*, No. 20, 1965.

DES REPORTS ON EDUCATION, *Trends in School Design*, No. 66, 1970.

DES REPORTS ON EDUCATION, *Class Size in Primary Schools*, No. 70, 1971.

DES REPORTS ON EDUCATION, *Educational Priority*, No. 71, 1972a.

DES REPORTS ON EDUCATION, *Trends in Education*, No. 72, 1972b.

DEUTSCH, M., *et al.*, *The Disadvantaged Child* (Basic Books, 1967).

DOUGLAS, J. W. B., *The Home and the School* (McGibbon & Kee, 1964).

DOUGLAS, J. W. B. and ROSS, J., 'Single Sex or Co-ed? The Academic Consequences', in *Where*, No. 25, May 1966.

DOUGLAS, J. W. B., ROSS, J. and SIMPSON, H. R., *All Our Future* (Davies, 1968).

EDWARDS, A. D., *The Changing Sixth Form in the Twentieth Century* (Routledge & Kegan Paul, 1970).

EDWARDS, R., *The Middle School Experiment* (Routledge & Kegan Paul, 1972).

EGGLESTON, S. J., 'Going Comprehensive', in *New Society*, No. 221, 1966.

FABIAN GROUP, *The Planning for Education in 1980* (Fabian Soc., 1970).

FANTINI, M., MAGAT, R. and GITTELL, M., *Community Control and the Urban School* (Pall Mall Press, 1970).

FERRI, E., *Streaming: Two Years Later* (NFER, 1971).

FORD, J., *Social Class and the Comprehensive School* (Routledge & Kegan Paul, 1969).

FRASER, G. S., 'Organizational Properties and Teacher Reaction', in *Comparative Education Review*, No. XIV, pt. 1, 1970.

FUTCHER, W. G. A., 'A Comparative Study of Attitudes and Personality Traits of Children in Certain Comprehensive, Grammar and Modern Schools in London', Unpublished M.A. thesis, London, 1960.

GANS, H. J., *The Urban Villagers* (Collier–Macmillan, 1962).

GETZELS, J. W., 'Pre-school Education', in *Teachers College Record*, Vol. LXVIII, No. 3, 1966.

GIBB, J. R., 'The Effect of Group Size and of Threat Reduction upon Creativity in a Problem-solving Situation', in *American Psychologist*, Vol. 6, No. 324, 1951.

GILLETT, A. N., 'Teachers for Community Schools', in W. Taylor (Ed.), *Towards a Policy for Teacher Education* (Butterworth, 1968).

GOLDMAN, R. J., 'Reaction to Plowden's Educational Priority Areas', in *Education and Social Science*, Vol. 1, No. 1, 1969.

GOODMAN, P., *Compulsory Miseducation* (Penguin, 1971).

GRIFFITHS, V. L., *The Problems of Rural Education* (UNESCO, 1968).

HALSALL, E. (Ed.), *Becoming Comprehensive* (Pergamon Press, 1970).

Harvard Educational Review, 'Architecture and Education', Vol. 39, No. 4, 1969.

HELLMUTH, J. (Ed.), *Disadvantaged Children* (Washington Special Child Publications, 1967).

HERRIOT, R. E. and HOYT, ST J. N., *Social Class and the Urban School* (John Wiley, 1966).

HEWITSON, J. N., *The Grammar School Tradition in a Comprehensive World* (Routledge & Kegan Paul, 1969).

HIGHET, J., *A School of One's Own Choice* (Blackie, 1969).

HIPKIN, J., 'The Outsiders inside the Public School', in *New Society*, 12 (303) 1968.

HOLLIS, C., *Eton* (Hollis, 1960).

HOLLY, D. N., 'Profiting from a Comprehensive School: Class, Sex and Ability', in *British Journal of Sociology*, Vol. 16, 1965.

HOLMES, M., *The Comprehensive School* (Longmans Green, 1967).

HOWARTH, T. E. D., *Culture, Anarchy and the Public Schools* (Cassell, 1969).

HUSEN, T. and HENRYSSON, S. (Eds), *Differentiation and Guidance in the Comprehensive School* (Almqvist & Wiksell, Stockholm, 1959).

IAAM, *Teaching in Comprehensive Schools* (Cambridge Univ. Press, 1967).

ILEA, *London Comprehensive Schools* (1967).

JACKSON, B., *Streaming: An Education System in Miniature* (Routledge & Kegan Paul, 1964).

JEFREE, D. M. and CASHDAN, A., 'Home Background of Severely Subnormal Children', in *British Journal of Medical Psychology*, Vol. 44, No. 1, p. 27, 1971.

JUDGES, A. V., 'Tradition and the Comprehensive School', in *British Journal of Sociology*, Vol. II, No. 1, 1953.

KAUFMAN, B., *Up the Down Staircase* (Arthur Barker, London, 1965).

KING, J., TAYLORD, G. and URWIN, K. F., 'Comprehensives: A Dossier of New Evidence on Secondary Education', in *New Society*, 144 (14–17) 1965.

KING, R., 'State Boarding and the Future of the Public Schools', in *New Society*, 10 (250), 1967.

KING, R., *The English Sixth Form College* (Pergamon, 1968).

LABOUR PARTY, *Signpost for the Sixties* (Labour Party, London, 1961).

LACEY, C., 'Some Sociological Concomitants of Academic Streaming in a Grammar School', in *British Journal of Sociology*, Vol. 17, No. 3, 1966.

LAMBERT, R., *The Hothouse Society* (Weidenfeld & Nicolson, 1968).

LEVIN, H. M. (Ed.), *Community Control of Schools* (Washington Brookings Institution, 1970).

LIGHT, H. K., 'Attitudes of Rural and Urban Adolescent Girls Towards Selected Concepts', in *Family Co-ordinator*, Vol. 19, No. 3, 1970.

LITTLE, A., MABEY, C. and RUSSELL, J., 'Do Small Classes Help a Child?', in *New Society*, No. 473, 21 October 1971.

LOHMAN, J. D., *Cultural Patterns in Urban Schools* (Univ. California Press, 1967).

LOWNDES, G. A., *The Silent Social Revolution* (Oxford Univ. Press, 1937).

LUNN, J. C. B., *Streaming in the Primary Schools* (NFER, 1970).

MARKLUND, S., 'School Organization, School Location and Student Achievement', in *International Review of Education*, Vol. XV, No. 3, 1969.

MARSDEN, D., 'Which Comprehensive Principle?', in *Comprehensive Education*, No. 13, Autumn 1969.

MARSDEN, D., *Politics, Equality and Comprehensives* (Fabian Society, 1971).

MARRIS, P., *The Experience of Higher Education* (Routledge & Kegan Paul, 1964).

MAYS, J., *Education and the Urban Child* (Univ. Liverpool Press, 1962).

MAYS, J., QUINE, W. and PICKETT, K., *School of Tomorrow* (Longmans Green, 1968).

MELLOR, E., *Education Through Experience in the Infant School Years* (Blackwell, 1970).

MENTZER, R. T., 'Head Start', in *Young Children*, Vol. XXIII, No. 5, 1968.

MIDWINTER, E., *Projections* (Ward Lock Educational, 1972).

MILES, M., *Comprehensive Schooling: Problems and Perspectives* (Longmans Green, 1968).

MONKS, T. G., *Comprehensive Schools Research*, Reports on Education No. 36 (DES, 1967).

MONKS, T. G., *Comprehensive Education in England and Wales* (NFER, 1968a).

MONKS, T. G., 'Comprehensive Education', in H. J. Butcher (Ed.), *Educational Research in Britain* (Univ. London Press, 1968b).

MOORE, B. M., *Guidance in Comprehensive Schools* (NFER, 1970).

MUSGRAVE, P. W., *The Sociology of Education* (Methuen, 1970).

NEWSOM REPORT, *Half Our Future* (HMSO, 1963).

NICHOLSON, J. S., 'Delf Hill Middle School: Bradford', in E. Halsey (Ed.), *Becoming Comprehensive* (Pergamon, 1970).

NUT, *Inside the Comprehensive School* (Schoolmasters Pub. Co., 1958).

OPPENHEIM, A. N., 'A Study of the Social Attitudes of Adolescents', Unpublished Ph.D. thesis, London, 1956.

PAULSTON, R. G., *Educational Change in Sweden: Planning and Accepting the Comprehensive School Reforms* (Teachers College Press, New York, 1968).

PLATOFF, J., 'Pre-school Prototype: An Integrated Semi-cooperative Nursery School', in *Young Children*, Vol. XXI, No. 4, 1966.

PEAKER, G., *Plowden Children Four Years Later* (NFER, 1971).

PEDLEY, R., *The Comprehensive School* (Penguin, 1963).

PETERSON, A. D. C., *The Future of the Sixth Form* (Routledge & Kegan Paul, 1972).

PIDGEON, D. A., *Expectation and Pupil Performance* (NFER, 1970).

PINES, M., *Revolution in Learning* (Allen Lane, 1969).

POPPER, S. H., *The American Middle School* (Blaisdell, 1967).

POSTER, C., *The School and the Community* (Macmillan, 1971).

PRUST, A. and SHIELD, G. W., 'The Sixth Form College', in E. Halsall (Ed.), *Becoming Comprehensive* (Pergamon, 1970).

PUBLIC SCHOOLS COMMISSION, *First Report*, Vol. 1 (HMSO, 1968).

REDL, H. B., 'The Young Child in the Soviet Union', in *Young Children*, Vol. XXIV, No. 2, 1968.

ROGERS, T., *School for the Community* (Routledge & Kegan Paul, 1972).

ROSS, J. M., 'Does School Size Matter?—The Research', in *New Society*, Vol. 20, No. 501, 15 June 1972.

ROSS, J. M., BUNTON, W. J., EVISON, P. and ROBERTSON, T. S., *A Critical Appraisal of Comprehensive Education* (NFER, 1972).

ROWAN, J., 'School Size', in *New Society*, 22 June, 1972.

ROWE, A., 'A Headmaster's Point of View', in J. W. Tibble (Ed.), *The Extra Year* (Routledge & Kegan Paul, 1970).

ROWLAND, B. E., 'An Inquiry into the Standards of Behaviour of Boys and Girls Towards Each Other', Unpublished M.A. thesis, London, 1955.

RUBINSTEIN, D. and SIMON, B., *The Evolution of the Comprehensive School* (Routledge & Kegan Paul, 1969).

RUBINSTEIN, D. and STONEMAN, C. (Eds), *Education for Democracy* (Routledge & Kegan Paul, 1969).

SCHOOLS COUNCIL, *A Common System of Examining* (Evans/Methuen Educ., 1971).

SCOTT, E., 'The Influence of Nursery School Experience in Social Value Acquisition in Pre-school Aged Children' (No. 1), in *Educational Review*, Vol. 21, No. 3, 1969a.

SCOTT, E., 'Social Value Acquisition in Pre-school Aged Children' (No. 2), in *Sociological Quarterly*, Vol. 10, No. 4, 1969b.

SCOTT, E., 'Social Value Acquisition in Pre-school Aged Children' (No. 3), in *Sociological Quarterly*, Vol. 11, No. 1, 1970.

SHIELDS, J. B., *The Gifted Child* (NFER, 1968).

SHORT, E., *Education in a Changing World* (Pitman, 1971).

SIMMONS, H. W. and MORGAN, R., *Inside a Comprehensive School* (Clifton Books, 1969).

SIMON, B., 'Streaming and Unstreaming in the Secondary School', in D. Rubinstein and C. Stoneman (Eds), *Education for Democracy* (Penguin, 1970).

SMILANSKY, S. and SMILANSKY, M., 'The Role and Program of Pre-school Education for Socially Disadvantaged Children', in *International Review of Education*, Vol. XVI, No. 1, 1970.

SPOLTON, L., *The Upper Secondary School* (Pergamon, 1967).

STEVENS, F., *The New Inheritors* (Hutchinson, 1970).

STEVENS, F., *The Living Tradition* (Hutchinson, 1972).

STROM, R. D., *The Inner City Classroom* (Chas. E. Merrill Books, 1966).

SUMNER, R. and WARBURTON, F. W., *Achievement in Secondary Schools* (NFER, 1972).

SWAIN, H., 'Building for Education', in *Forum*, Vol. 12, No. 1, 1969.

TAPPER, T., 'Comprehensive Education and Pupil Aspiration', in *New Society*, 13 (346), 1969.

TAPPER, T., *Young People and Society* (Faber, 1971).

TAYLOR, D. W. and FAUST, W. L., 'Twenty Questions: Efficiency in Problem Solving as a Function of Group Size', in *Journal Experimental Psychology*, 44, 1952.

TAYLOR, G. G. and AYRES, N., *Born and Bred Unequal* (Longmans, 1970).

TAYLOR, W., *Heading for Change* (Harlech Television Publications, 1970).

TIZARD, J., *Community Services for Mentally Handicapped* (Oxford Univ. Press, 1964).

UDY, J., 'The House System in a Comprehenisve School', in *Education and Social Science*, Vol. 1, No. 1, 1969.

UNESCO Chronicle, 'World Trends Towards Co-education', Vol. XV, No. 5, 1969.

UNGOED-THOMAS, J., 'The Soviet School as a Formal Organization', in *Moral Education*, Vol. 1, No. 2, 1969.

VIDICH, A. J. and BENSMAN, J., *Small Town in Mass Society* (Oxford Univ. Press, 1958).

VINCENT, W. S., 'Class Size', in R. L. Ebel (Ed.), *Encyclopaedia of Education* (Collier Macmillan, 1969).

WAKEFORD, J., *The Cloistered Elite* (Macmillan, 1969).

WARBURTON, F. W. and SUMNER, R., *Achievement in Secondary Schools* (NFER, 1972).

WEST, E. G., *Education and the State* (Institute of Economic Affairs, 1965).

WHITE PAPER, *Education: A Framework for Expansion* (HMSO, 1972).

WHITING, B. and WHITING, J., *Field for a Study of Socialisation* (John Wiley, 1971).

WICKER, A., 'Cognitive Complexity, School Size and Participation in School Behaviour Settings: A Test of the Frequency of Interaction Hypothesis', in *Journal of Educational Psychology*, Vol. 60, No. 3, 1969.

WILDMER, E. L., 'Why Kindergarten?', in *Young Children*, Vol. XXI, No. 5, 1966.

WILSON, J., *Private Schools and Public Practice* (Allen & Unwin, 1962).

WISE, A. E., *Rich Schools: Poor Schools* (Univ. Chicago Press, 1968).

WOOCK, R. R., 'Community Operated Schools—A Way Out', in *Urban Education*, Vol. 3, No. 3, 1968.

YATES, A., *The Organization of Schooling* (Routledge & Kegan Paul, 1971).

Chapter 16

Democratic Schools and Socialization

The above eulogy of comprehensive education, as the one system most likely to enable moral education to become a viable aspect of educational activity, leads to a further consideration. If comprehensive educational policies are to be implemented it follows that such schools should be characterized by democratic forms and procedures. As we shall see below, the matter is more complex than this implies, but without this, moral education will become a structured form of social control instead of the liberating, human experience that it ought to be.

Dysfunctional Authority

It is generally recognized, in sociological analyses, that there are four basic kinds of community. Those bonded together by inter-active conflict; societies stabilized by internal attraction, whether it be for mutual advantage or service; unstable groups held together by compulsion, usually expressed through an authoritarian, hier-archical structure; and lastly sub-systems which cohere spontan-eously, through the expression of, and striving after, common interests. Of these, the last two are relevant since the former describes an authoritarian school, and the latter a school based on democratic procedures.

In a democracy one would naturally expect to find democratic schools, but such expectations are rarely realized. Since the time of Waller, observing over forty years ago, that schools are invariably 'despotisms on the verge of collapse', innumerable researchers have reported that schools are rarely democratic. A recent, potent comment of this kind has emerged as a symposium appropriately called *Education for Democracy* (1). It was published as a furious counter-offensive to the Black Papers, but in fact can be seen to contain moderate and closely argued theses. These advocated comprehensive education, discovery-learning, and comradeship between pupils and teachers. It then toppled the pillars of hierarchical élitism by attacking rigid streaming and traditional examinations. However, throughout its arguments it sustains one major theme: our educational system must be thoroughly democratized, if it is to function properly today. Consequently authoritarianism must be eliminated: it is now completely out of phase with social development; it must not be given a foothold in schools again.

One can see why this system should be condemned. It induces and sustains an infantile form of moral conduct (2). It generates hostility and animosity, for children say 'It is a place where *they* make you go and where *they* tell you to do things and where *they* try to make your life unpleasant if you don't do them or don't do them right' (3). The most damning indictment lies in the fact that an authoritarian institution stultifies that growth of autonomy without which no child can become morally mature. Such a condemnation can be augmented by Neill's view that the improvement of anything by authority, is wrong. It stands condemned on all counts as the antithesis of moral maturity: and yet if authority is rejected, something must be put in its place. It is not enough to enumerate the deficiencies of autocratic and regimented systems, for a school would still stand condemned if it ousted these but did not use its freedom to prepare children to be responsible members of society.

The Idealization of Democratic Schools
It is inevitable that democratic educational procedures should ultimately take root in democracies, for autocratic practices and policies are destined to be both exposed and replaced by them (4). This was what Graham found when she came to analyse the major sources of values common to American schools and thus had to head the list with 'democratic ideals'. The process is reciprocal, for a prime function of democratized schools in American is deemed to be the transmission of the norms and values necessary to sustain a stable democratic political system (5). This interaction is now being disclosed by pupil demands to be consulted at the decision-making stage of school life, and Katz's analysis of democratic 'hearing' procedures in school disciplinary cases has further elaborated the view that schools need democratic parental teachers. Furthermore, it is becoming increasingly common for parents to expect democratic forms of school life. In assessing the worth of a school they place increasing emphasis on the degree of democratization displayed. Even the trend towards open-plan schools facilitates this process for, as Kohl has shown, the non-authoritarian approach is essential under such circumstances.

The implications of all this for moral education have recently been highlighted by Bronfenbrenner's report of Russian children in school. There he found that the entrenched egalitarianism, in schools, inculcated two moral qualities in the children concerned. Compared with their American peers, they were not only infinitely more resistant to antisocial conduct but also took more initiative and responsibility for developing this attitude in others. The point, noted earlier, that such a process does not lead towards moral maturity in a state which prefers conformity to autonomy, is not relevant here. The system may be sound despite its abuse. There is one important clue embedded in this evidence: Russian egalitarianism, has a clearly defined power structure, and it is this which is required in any democratic system.

Genuine Democracy

It is very easy to ridicule democratic procedures. Not only is the achievement of decision by consensus a harrowing experience, but majority decisions can be determined by incompetent minorities. Imagine a situation where a society of 100 people had two totally inadequate members who subscribed to each other's whims, and was further equally divided on some crucial issue. The two inept members would obviously cast the deciding votes. For such reasons Churchill once observed with some asperity that democracy was the worst form of government, apart from all the rest. Democratic failure invariably results from misunderstanding the nature of this fragile socio-political structure.

This was highlighted years ago by the work of Lippett *et al*. In order to investigate the most efficacious class-room social climate they tested structured authoritarian, democratic and *laissez-faire* situations. The results were entirely predictable. Both social and academic advance was most marked in a democratic situation, under the guidance of a democratic teacher. It is often overlooked, however, that the *laissez-faire* group structure was as socially disruptive as the authoritarian. Consequently loose references to democratic forms of organization tend to be coloured by the unstructured system of *laissez-faire*. Yet a *laissez-faire* social system is more akin to authoritarianism than to democracy. This results from the dynamics of social control. It has, for example, been shown repeatedly that the non-democratic working-class milieu leads naturally to either extreme. The process appears to be as follows. Present orientation leads to an indulgent 'anything for a quiet life' permissiveness (6), but when this fails, oppressive authoritarianism is used to achieve the same end.

The findings of an extremely important inquiry are relevant here. Willower *et al*. applied the concepts of 'custodial' and 'humanistic' control to schools, since these had previously been used to study the techniques whereby mental nurses dealt with their patients. The custodial model uses sanctions, stresses impersonal relationships, and emphasizes status distinctions, while power and communication flow downwards. The humanistic model stresses interpersonal interaction and encourages two-way communication between teachers and pupils. It was discovered that in the authoritarian custodial system, children tended to be irresponsible and undisciplined: but in the democratic, humanistic system they practised self-discipline.

One final point, relevant to the thesis of the previous section of this book, concerned the characteristics of the teachers concerned. Using the Rokeach concept of closed and open-mindedness it was found that testing by Rokeach's Dogmatism Scale revealed that custodial teachers were invariably dogmatic and close-minded, while humanistic teachers had that flexible, openness of mind which is essential for the comprehension of moral concepts and principles. Again, it should be noted that humanistic forms of control were clearly structured and not *laissez-faire*.

One can see why democratic forms must have a clear power structure. The permissive, progressive system of leaving children to themselves, ostensibly to avoid frustration, is emotionally dangerous. Such children lose the assurance provided by simple regulations, and are left feeling that no adults care sufficiently to protect them even from their own tempestuous vagaries and tantrums. It is equally psychically dangerous, for we now know that children need a buffer of discipline as a protection against stultifying anxieties and fears.

Such views have considerable research support. Harris reported on a longitudinal study which examined adult character and child home experiences. It was found that democratic homes, characterized by consistent discipline and parental leadership, produced decisive, self-confident adults with a high level of self-acceptance. While children of permissive, *laissez-faire*, child-centred homes were indecisive, alienated, under-achievers. Schuham's findings are also relevant here. He discovered that an egalitarian pattern of familial life resulted in pathological, disturbed personalities amongst the children. Thus he suggested that the best family would be mildly authoritarian. Finally, in his participant observer report on the Daytop therapeutic community for drug addicts, Sugarman reported that even in such a familial group, 'There must be some clear authority structure' (7).

From evidence of this kind Davies' serious doubts 'about the possibility of reconciling the prefect system with a more democratic school organization' (8) can be allayed. If they are not, then logically every other related authority structure should be removed. If the analogy is pressed to its limits a case can be presented for eliminating all games, which require the submission of one boy to another; and all activities in which individuals are needed to take the initiative.

Surely it is more in accord with the evidence to accept the closely reasoned argument of Robson. He approved of the prefectorial system because it induced a sense of responsibility in the older boys and provided a secure framework for the younger.

It may be argued that such a structuring does not take cognizance of children as ebullient, creative, individualistic centres of activity; thus denying Holbrook's assertion that 'children are going concerns' (9). Any idyllic, naturalistic individualist view of children is only half true. Campbell and Lawton found that school children could remain as individuals while still being clearly aware of the spheres of authority and responsibility within their school. Subsequent discussion disclosed that they were willing to participate in decision making within the limits of such a structure.

Again, opponents of democratic school systems may point to the débâcle of Risinghill Comprehensive School as an example of the failure of non-authoritarian control systems in a large school, but this would not be just. Leila Berg's account of the incident makes it perfectly clear that the major cause of the school's collapse was the lack of staff involvement, who had neither the ability nor the desire to implement the headmaster's policy. Thus one is again forced back to the basic fact. Such a system needed a structured flow of decision and implementation with all members partaking responsibly in both.

There is one final point to make here relating to social class. The typical middle-class boy is usually future-orientated, convinced that he can affect decisions by participation, and personally individualistic. In contrast the working-class boy is present-orientated, passive and dependent. Consequently the former fits snugly into a truly democratic system, while the latter does not. This is because genuine democracy is akin neither to oppressive authoritarianism nor to unstructured *laissez-faire* practices. It requires responsible individuals to operate within a structured situation. It is thus not so much egalitarian as humanistic. As Maslow pithily observes, 'all self-actualizing persons may be said to be democratic people in the deepest possible sense' (10). Like the autonomous, individualistic higher-status pupils they are invariably able to fit into a system, but are always essentially themselves.

Before proceeding a logical fallacy must be noted. Because morally and personally mature persons emerge from a democratic society with a clear power structure, it does not follow that such systems will inevitably produce such people. To assume this would be to go beyond both the evidence, and the limits, of the arguments. It is only legitimate to say that since such morally mature people invariably emerge from these social systems, it is probable that such systems will produce these personality types! But even this is only a statistical probability for personality differences may induce unexpected results amongst individuals.

Comprehensives and Democracy

In her survey of the comprehensive school Ford reaches one firm conclusion. This system should democratize its pupils, but while it selects individuals for occupations in an hierarchical, social and economic structure the basis of class privilege will remain. Yet when Hughes condemned selective education for similar reasons, he showed conclusively that the comprehensive system and the democratic form of educational procedure rightly belong together. Why then is it that genuinely democratic comprehensive schools have yet to emerge? Is democracy untenable as a system? Is the familial model of school life unrealistic? Or has the alienation endemic to urban life already fractured those school communities which attempt to live on the basis of altruistic parity? (11).

Such questions can be endlessly multiplied, but one simple answer seems to be that there has not yet been a concerted attempt to implement such a policy. Teachers who, rightly or wrongly, fear the demands which such a system will make upon their personal and moral resources, may have resisted it. Pupil power, organized under the aegis of the National Union of School Students, may now be promoting it, but hitherto only isolated experiments have been conducted, and these have invariably foundered when indigenous difficulties were disclosed in the process.

Schools and Society

Yet there is one explanation which yet again emphasizes the fact which has been repeatedly asserted above. It may be that the familial comprehensive educational system must necessarily be democratic in form, *but such schools cannot exist in a society alien to these values.*

Comprehensive, democratic reforms are sterile in a class-ridden society based on privilege and hierarchical status. While social inequities are allowed, the implementation of a 'comprehensive' form of education is little more than cant (12). If, in fact, such schools stop short at changing society, then they are truly dysfunctional for their function is to change society, and not merely reflect it.

Thus again we find moral education and politics inextricably linked. When the educational system is vigorous and flexible enough to produce democratic citizens, we may begin to assume the characteristics of a democracy. Here morality and democracy intermingle for both refer to a cultural norm in which values and beliefs, operating within an institutional form, lead its members into freedom, autonomy, responsibility, courage, honesty, reason and love. Any society fed with such a supply of citizens cannot fail to eliminate the cankers of greed which have hitherto marred it.

Such a school ought presumably to reflect society by being multi-class. This has hitherto been the doctrine of planners who argue that people in a new town or estate, ought to form a multi-class unit. They will thus, it seems, be persuaded to live like urban villagers enjoying all the attendant richness of cultural and recreational life. Carey and Mapes have argued the contrary. On the basis of their findings, they showed that only families with similar social backgrounds readily intermingle (13). Hence they argued that housing estates should be planned to juxtapose such people; the simplest device being the congregation of similar houses.

Comprehensives and Morality

This planning problem is surely a failure of educational egalitarianism, and if schools based their policies on such failures the educational system vitiates itself. Schools must initiate change. Gans accepted that social homogeneity was to be expected in the primary groups, but that social intermingling should take place in school. Consequently he argued that schools ought to reflect the 'greater society' in their class structure. That is, they ought to display democratic rather than demographic homogeneity.

Sadly, this is still not the situation. It was observed earlier that many English comprehensives do not have a comprehensive population. Even in the egalitarian, democratic United States a recent survey of the comprehensive schools revealed that 'it is the school whose student body reaches from the highest class to lowest in just about the same proportions as in the country as a whole, that turns out to be the exception' (14). Such a school is essential if moral education is to become fully effective. Only the familial, therapeutic, egalitarian, anti-élitist, unitary force of such an institution can heal our social disorders. Animosity does not belong in a family. Arrogance has no place amongst equals. Snobbery is eliminated for one cannot disdain those one serves. Aberrant conduct becomes tawdry when all are mutually seeking to heal the distress and despair which attends so many lives. Furthermore only in such a school as this can those small, democratic, non-academic, flexible groups be established, which may be necessary for formal lessons in moral education. Thus we *must* have democratic schools if we are to have moral education (15) and these schools *must* function in a democratic society.

Only one last point needs to be made, which reaches back to the preconditions of morality. It is of little value to observe that middle-class children have greater facility in living autonomously. What does matter is that they have developed the independence of mind which leads to autonomy. As Maslow said so succinctly, 'The best technique for getting to this point of relative independence is to have been given plenty of love and respect in the past' (16).

REFERENCES

1 Rubinstein and Stoneman (1970).
2 Kay (1968) p. 132 ff develops this point.
3 Holt (1964) p. 37.
4 If these democratic procedures in moral education do establish a genuine, democratic social system there will inevitably be many political overtones. Every political form now familiar to us will be transformed. The autocratic, egalitarianism of communist countries and the bureaucratic socialism of democracies, will both be replaced by a genuine democracy. Of course this may not be realized for the democracy envisaged will enshrine the *ideals* of such a system; whereas the political democratic forms are compounded of compromises between anarchy and totalitarianism. Furthermore the sociological form may advocate a non-élitist, non-hierarchical class system instead of the classless society of egalitarianism.
5 Zeigler and Peak (1970), pp. 115 ff.
6 Klein (1965), pp. 455 ff, discusses this point, as do Chapters 14 and 15.
7 Sugarman (1970), p. 80.
8 Davies (1965), p. 91.
9 Holbrook (1969), p. 23.
10 Maslow (1970), p. 167.
11 See Sennett (1970).
12 Hewitson (1969): 'To be genuinely and completely successful a comprehensive school must be in the middle of a comprehensive community' (p. 158). Hook (1946): 'Education is the maturation of every man's natural powers within a democratic context and for a democratic society' (p. 74). Hemming (1969): 'We must have a democratic society for any moral growth' (pp. 196 ff)—but democracy does not imply classlessness. MacRae's (1972) claim that 'there is an odd pre-occupation of sociologists with social class' (p. 208) points to the apparently ineradicable tendency of all societies to form structured and tiered units. It is not class that we must eliminate, but the deprivation which is associated with specific socio-economic groups.
13 This was most pronounced with housewives with children who belonged to the same age groups (see Chapter 16).
14 Ramsey (1967): but Monks (1968) like Oppenheim (1956) found that the different social classes did not mix even in a comprehensive school. However, Maykovich (1972) found that racially mixed schools did tend to eliminate racial prejudice.
15 Ungoed-Thomas (1972) is a handbook to guide secondary school teachers intending to establish a democratic school.
16 Maslow (1970), p. 162.

Bibliography
BERG, L., *Risinghill: Death of a Comprehensive School* (Penguin, 1968).
BRONFENBRENNER, U., *Two Worlds of Childhood* (Allen & Unwin, 1972).
CAMPBELL, R. J. and LAWTON, D., 'How Children See Society', in *New Society*, 16 (425), 1970.

CAREY, L. and MAPES, R., *The Sociology of Planning* (Batsford, 1972).

DAVIES, H., *Culture and the Grammar School* (Routledge & Kegan Paul, 1965).

FORD, J., *Social Class and the Comprehensive School* (Routledge & Kegan Paul, 1969).

GANS, H. J., *The Livittowners* (Penguin, 1967).

GRAHAM, G., *The Public School in the New Society* (Harper & Row, 1969).

HARRIS, D. B., 'The Climate of Achievement', in *Child Development*, Vol. 39, 1958.

HEMMING, J., *Individual Morality* (Nelson, 1969).

HEWITSON, J. N., *The Grammar School Traditions in a Comprehensive World* (Routledge & Kegan Paul, 1969).

HOLBROOK, D., 'The Wizard and the Critical Flame', in *Moral Education*, Vol. 1, No. 1, 1969.

HOLT, J., *How Children Fail* (Pitman, 1964).

HOOK, S., *Education for Modern Man* (Dial Press, New York, 1946).

HUGHES, A. G., *Education and the Democratic Ideal* (Longmans, 1956).

KATZ, J. W., 'The Opportunity to be Heard in Public School Disciplinary Hearings', in *Urban Education*, Vol. IV, No. 4, 1970.

KAY, W., *Moral Development* (Allen & Unwin, 1968).

KLEIN, J., *Samples from English Culture*, Vols I and II (Routledge & Kegan Paul, 1965).

KOHL, H. R., *The Open Class Room* (Methuen, 1971).

LEWIN, K., 'Group Decision and Social Change', in Newcomb and Hartley (Eds), *Readings in Social Psychology* (Holt, Rinehart & Winston, 1947).

LIPPETT, R. and WHITE, R., 'The Social Climate of Children's Groups' in Barber, Kounin and Wright (Eds), *Child Behaviour and Development* (McGraw-Hill, 1943).

LIPPETT, R., LEWIN, K. and WHITE, R. K., 'The Social Climate of Children's Groups' in Barker, Kounin and Wright (Eds), *Child Behaviour and Development* (McGraw-Hill, 1943).

LIPPETT, R. and WHITE, R. M., 'An Experimental Study of Leadership and Group Life', in Maccoby, Newcomb and Hartley (Eds), *Readings in Social Psychology* (Methuen, 1959).

MACRAE, D. G., 'Classlessness', in *New Society*, 26 October 1972.

MASLOW, A. H., *Motivation and Personality* (Harper & Row, 1970).

MONKS, T. G., *Comprehensive Education in England and Wales* (NFER, 1968).

NEILL, A. S., *Summerhill* (Gollancz, 1962).

RAMSEY, N. R., 'The Clientele of Comprehensive Secondary Schools in the United States', in *Social Objectives in Educational Planning* (Organization for Economic Co-operation and Development, Paris, 1967).

ROBSON, W. A., 'Education and Democracy', in *Political Quarterly*, Vol. XXX, No. 1, 1959.

ROKEACH, M., *Beliefs, Attitudes and Values* (Jossey-Bass, 1970).

RUBINSTEIN, D. and STONEMAN, C. (Eds), *Education for Democracy* (Penguin, 1970).

SCHUHAM, A. I., 'Power Relations in Emotionally Disturbed and Normal Family Triads', in *Journal of Abnormal Psychology*, Vol. 75, No. 1, 1970.

SENNETT, R., *The Uses of Disorder* (Allen Lane, 1970).

SUGARMAN, B., 'The Therapeutic Community and the School', in *Interchange*, Vol. 1, No. 2, 1970.

UNGOED-THOMAS, J. R., *Our School* (Longmans, 1972).

WALLER, W., *The Sociology of Teaching* (Wiley, 1967).
WILLOWER, D. J., EIDELL, T. L. and HOY, W. K., *The School and Pupil Control Ideology* (Pennsylvania State Univ, 1967).
ZEIGLER, H. and PEAK, W., 'The Political Functions of the Education System', in *Sociology of Education*, Vol. 43, No. 2, 1970.

Chapter 17

Teacher–Pupil Interaction

TEACHERS AS MORAL EDUCATORS

It is fortunate that amongst an abundance of relevant published works one can trace a line of conceptual development. This thread runs from Waller who considered that 'Teachers are paid agents of cultural diffusion . . . hired to carry light into dark places' (1) and currently ends with Hargreaves who, basing his work on the 'symbolic interactionist' theory, impelled teachers, as communicators, into the centre of our cultural arena by asserting that 'Both human nature and the social order are products of communication' (2). Each affirmation obviously underwrites the view that teachers must accept that they are moral educators, whether this influence operates subtly through the ethos of the school, or overtly in a moral education lesson.

It may therefore be an occasion of some surprise to learn that the effectiveness of teachers as moral educators can be seriously questioned. They appear to possess all the advantages for fulfilling this role effectively. Apart from their status and role in the formal peer community of the school, theirs is the determinative influence which affects almost every area of school life. Yet in fact the evidence suggests that they can primarily only augment and modify existing moral attitudes—they cannot create them.

An optimistic assessment of the teacher's importance finds considerable support in the work of Castle. Basing his view on the century-old affirmation that 'in the manhood and womanhood of the teacher lies the very soul of the true method of moral instruction', he accepts without question that teachers are required 'to communicate the accepted morality of the community they serve' (3), and are, presumably, competent to do so.

To modify this optimistic view does not imply that one rejects it. It merely stresses that *in the school situation* the teacher is the most powerful determinant. Numerous researchers agree on this point. It needs no empirical confirmation to be convinced that a teacher cannot avoid affecting the conduct of his pupils. Official reports throughout the present century confirm this view. They all sustain the 1904 (4) view that teachers:

can endeavour by example and influence to implant in the children habits of industry, self-control and courageous perseverance in the face of difficulties; they can teach them to reverence what is noble, to be ready for self-sacrifice, and strive their utmost after purity and truth; they can foster a strong sense of duty and instil in them that consideration and respect for others which must be the foundation of unselfishness and the true basis of all good manners.

The Conflict of Values

At first glance the alleged conflict between parental standards and age-group norms would seem to support this. Children estranged from parents would presumably turn to their teachers. Such optimistic idealism, however, must face harsh facts. Teachers too are caught in a web of value conflict: they try to inculcate specific beliefs, values and attitudes only to discover that these stand in complete and bewildering contrast with those of the outside world. Some say that this is because much moral education is based on sporting codes vigorously transmitted by athletic middle-class masters. Those who agree with this argue that many teachers actually try to enforce middle-class values on the working-class children. Embourgeoisement may end this conflict, and it may also emerge that more teachers than we realize are increasingly coming from lower-status homes, which may then bridge the gap between the ethos of comprehensive schools and working-class homes. Failing this, some way must be devised to terminate the process whereby middle-class teachers alienate the working-class children placed in their care.

The Role of the Teacher

Attention has recently been focused again on the teacher's role. This probably results from two related facts. First, many say that teaching is too diverse to qualify as a profession. Thus the amorphous teaching body can never satisfy what Jackson and Elliott have disclosed as complex qualifying criteria. Second, the growing importance of such sociological notions as 'role definition', 'role expectancy' and 'situational role enactment', have drawn attention to this feature of interpersonal life. Hence attention has moved from considering whether teaching is a profession, and has become concerned with defining a teacher's role (5).

By concentrating on school-teachers the task of definition can be simplified, for the roles of such teachers are defined in relation to schools. Consequently, different models of the school will affect the teacher's role.

The most obvious model today is that which has survived for three millennia of formal teaching. A school is simply a school. It is a centre wherein trained personnel transmit a corpus of knowledge so that each generation can understand its past and so guide its future. Even as agents of social change, teachers function *qua* teachers— they simply teach. This is why Yarlott in his superb account of children's emotional education still insists that a teacher is not a therapist. He is simply a teacher. Such a view has many powerful advocates. Waller's more evangelical model is related to this. He sees the school in terms of a nineteenth-century missionary station bringing both a cultural heritage and an offer of civilized salvation to the uncultured, uncivilized masses.

The models presented in Chapter 13 cause teacher roles to proliferate. In the economic model teachers are managers, directors, or salesmen of an indeterminate commodity (6). Within the mechanical model one finds teachers functioning as graduate greasers, whose task is simply to keep the machinery of administration moving with education occurring as an incidental by-product. As centres of social equilibrium such schools contain teachers who strive to create law-abiding socially acceptable, honest workmen, and well mannered, economic housewives. Their ideal school is a secular monastery from which emanate waves of political, social and economic tranquility. Within the structural–functionalist model the task is more complex. Here a teacher sees his role as that of consciously equalizing opportunities for all the children. As such he becomes a potent democratic organizer whose primary role is that of social selection, and is more akin to an industrial relations officer in that he is concerned not with a product but with relations within the group, but his decisions can affect the socio-economic future of his pupils.

In turning to the therapeutic model we come to the heart of this problem. In an earlier chapter it was stressed that schools must be organized on a familial basis if they are to be effective agents of moral education. Consequently one primary role of a teacher is that of pastor. Obviously he must also be a 'teacher' and the delicate balance between the two roles must be adjusted at every stage. Infant children, for example, need a teacher who is preponderantly parental and minimally pedagogic. While on the other hand, sixth formers need a teacher who is both tutor and parent, with the stress laid on the former. Once the centrality of the parental role is accepted other related roles cluster round it. Such a teacher must also, for example, act as a secular equivalent of the priest (7).

For simplicity one can thus conflate the tasks of parent, priest and doctor and speak of a parental role, for they all share that quality of *personalism* to which reference was made above. All are stereotypes of the ideal relationship wherein *persons* deal with *persons* as *persons*. This does not mean that teachers should resort to mere affectivity, for such a teacher can function as an academic specialist yet still treat his pupils in this way. Indeed such a diffuse role will make teaching even more demanding than it is now. However, if moral education is to be effective then teachers must occupy these personal and parental roles (8).

Teacher Personality

Although the roles of a teacher make it inevitable that he will be either a willing or unwilling moral educator, the force of this influence will presumably be correlated with a series of variables. The two most obvious are personality and teaching techniques.

Before examining the influence of teacher personality on moral development it must be noted that there is contemporary concern over the quality of teachers as people. They have been described as neurotic, unenterprising security-seekers. Others note that less academically gifted children are more interested in teaching as a career, while the gifted seem to just drift into it. It is therefore no surprise to find that many teachers are not enthusiastic about their work. It can furthermore be argued, from available data, that teachers, clergy and doctors are often inadequate personalities. They can range from the genuine maladjusted 'do-gooder' to the pathological introvert. All three 'professions' carry a certain amount of power, have clear stereotypes, well-defined roles, and offer instant relationships with people, which make little personal demand. Clearly, uninformed and extravagant comments can be made at this point but when official reports also speak in these terms one must look again at this accusation, particularly since teachers are responsible for the vitally important task of moral education. This is also a problem concerned with status and emoluments, and a ground swell of writers are currently arguing that the glare of vocational idealism must not blind the public to the hard personal and economic facts facing the majority of teachers.

Many studies have shown that a teacher's personality is the most potent environmental force in the classroom. For example, it has been found that with pupils of contrasting academic competence the significant variable was not individual intelligence but differences between teachers. Clearly variations in technique apply here, but research reports constantly point to a high degree of correlation between teacher personality and class response. Indeed personality patterns observable in teachers are frequently replicated in pupils. How far this can be equated with 'identification' is not known but Staines makes the point that teachers change a pupil's 'self-picture' and it is this which affects his moral attitudes impinging as it does on 'identity' and 'acceptance'.

Since this is an interpersonal situation such features can be couched in homely terms. The greatest influence for good is apparently exercised by teachers who care for their children. After watching a number of successful lessons Loukes observed, 'These teachers, I began to feel, really cared. These men and women looked and sounded as if they cared, cared not only for the subject they taught but the children they taught it to' (9). It is this human warmth which matters, for children and adolescents respond to teachers who are felt to be human beings themselves.

Such human warmth and responsiveness, however, need not be accompanied by inefficiency. One team found that warm and friendly primary school teachers were also efficient; while such teachers in secondary schools were not more likely to be inefficient than those who were cold and aloof.

It is also generally agreed that teachers must be men and women of conviction, yet able to resist the temptation to evangelize. The Eppels wisely add here that precept and practice must go together, and confirm that teachers who have no deep convictions of their own form the stereotype of ineffectiveness. Thus the effective moral educator is one who can speak as a mature integrated *person* to less mature *persons*. It is in this way that the teacher's status as *loco parentis* is fulfilled. His status thus becomes parental and his class becomes familial, regardless of the orientation of his ideology. For this reason many Christian teachers can echo the words of the cleric Dr Micklem who wrote, 'I would rather my boys were taught by a reverent agnostic deeply conscious of the mystery of things than by an enthusiastic dogmatist who had all the answers pat'. Those who subscribe to this view will welcome the fact that most findings confirm that the character of the teacher is clearly the most potent element in moral education. It must not however, be forgotten that teachers can be moulded by the class ethos.

Teacher Techniques

Teaching techniques and the social environment of the classroom cannot be wholly separated from the teacher's personality, and some might argue that the teacher's contribution needs to be systematically evaluated before we assign any importance to specific kinds of teaching. Yet we know that the social structure of the class affects children, and the reports of Lippitt *et al.* show how children's behaviour is affected by the type of teacher-control exercised.

All that we know concerning formal peer group influence is also relevant here, and, since the teacher can control this element in the classroom, attention must be re-directed to it. Obviously such teachers must be masters of classroom sociometry, not only because children work best in accepted peer groups but because the isolates who usually form one tenth of the class community (and are delinquency risks because of this peer rejection) can thus be included in the groups. Furthermore, the structuring of these groups in middle schools can compensate for the absence of a sixth form, by the teacher himself becoming a group member. This could then help to bridge the gap between teacher and pupil cultures.

Therefore, just as the teacher can use the peer group to help disturbed, amoral children, so he can employ it to foster moral insight in normal children by drawing them into class discussions on personal and group problems. This is the function which teacher/pupil groups can perform, but it is one which is increasingly difficult in a dynamic society. As Mead noted 'the teacher of twenty years' experience may face her class less confidently than the teacher with only two' (10). This is because the latter is culturally closer to her pupils. However it is relevant to observe here that because traditional education is essentially a process of transmitting and consolidating knowledge, it is inevitably a conservative process, not only accepting innovations cautiously and discriminately, but perhaps antagonizing the fresh, creative minds of intelligent pupils.

It has already been argued that the teacher's influence should be exercised to produce a democratic social structure in the classroom. Ideally, he should therefore have an integrative, democratic personality and at least uphold the democratic ideal, for the acceptance of group goals and total pupil involvement necessitate the establishment of such a social structure. Thus even while manipulating the group, teachers must not be autocratic. Their influence must be exerted through the sanction of the group, because they are one of its members. In this context must be placed the maxim of Spens that 'the function of the staff in the corporate life of a school is one of guidance, not one of control' (11), thus teachers should ensure that pupils share in school and classroom organization as much as possible and so participate in a democratic procedure.

Such an idea *must* be central to education. This is not merely because very few teachers and pupils are now willing to subscribe to authority. It is both because the development of mature morality is stifled by authority, and also because children must be prepared for life in a democratic community. The moral educator must take the 'rootless and rudderless modern man' of Fromm and prepare him for autonomous, democratic living. It is clear that all this moral preparation cannot be accomplished by the inflexibility of personality which is thought to mark the teacher, but by the warm, human, involved person who is genuinely *in loco parentis* and who has broken down 'the thin but impenetrable veil that comes between the teacher and all other human beings' (12).

Teacher–Pupil Relations

The teacher–pupil relationship is thus clearly crucial. This is the teacher's most important social relationship, for moral education is clearly dependent upon the attitude of the teacher to his pupils. It is therefore natural to insist that we must investigate the attitudes and expectations of the teacher towards his pupils.

At the moment little of value can be said of this. Numerous reports show that social-class factors affect this mutual interaction. It is known, for example, that most teachers are upwardly socially mobile. They therefore react against children who do not display the ambition, future orientation and industry which they themselves are supposed to possess. Amongst many others there is one further complicating class factor from the side of the pupils. Some have shown that the *rapprochement* between higher-status children and teachers is enhanced by the middle-class child's normal acceptance of authority by virtue of professional status. Hence the conflict between teachers and lower-status children is further exacerbated, but even the *rapprochement* of teachers and middle-class children appears to be weakening. There was a time when members of a common sub-culture could bridge the generation-gap. Yet evidence is increasingly confirming that this generation-gap is now a cultural-gap, for various youth cultures appear to be consciously established in opposition to the mores of the bourgeois adult world.

Some may deride this idea of a youth culture as the creation of middle-age malcontents regretting their lost youth, but the facts indicate otherwise. Youth cultures share many common features. They stress sexuality, freedom, long hair, bizarre clothing, bohemian life-styles and economic independence. Such not only irritate the respectable citizen but make it clear that these sub-cultures have nothing in common with the increasingly impotent, balding, white-collar worker who must conform because he is committed to a twenty-year mortgage.

All the available evidence makes it clear that this fracturing of adult and child relationships is also occurring in the classroom. No longer can the British teacher deceive himself into believing that his pupils, in middle-class suburbia, are really polite, asexual, subservient, future-orientated miniatures of the ideal law-abiding citizen. Equally it is becoming increasingly clear that ideal American children are becoming an extinct species. The stereotype, whose frank and friendly extraversion enables him to display a maximum exposure of personal knowledge and opinions to any patient adult, is dying. Such children no longer exist as a significant group either in society or the classroom. Toffler has established this fact as beyond doubt in America, and numerous reports from Britain make it clear that we too are in the wake of this trend; a trend which is accelerated by the process of urbanization.

These factors can obviously limit teacher influence and may thus indicate why when asked which adults had influenced them most, only morally mature pupils repeatedly tended to name teachers. A contemporary study of importance in this context is that of Dale. Two thousand student teachers were asked 'Do you consider that any one (or several) of your teachers had a powerful influence for good in the development of your personality?' Even here, while dealing with upwardly mobile students, who were destined for the teaching profession, it was clear that such influence, although present, was peripheral. When perused with care, the clutch of reports, relevant to this aspect of a teacher's moral influence, make it clear that negative reactions such as these invariably spring from memories of teachers who were autocratic, detached or derisory.

Moral Educators
It is clear that more research is needed to evaluate the teacher's contribution in terms of his personality; the relative value of different teaching techniques; the nature of the teacher–pupil relationship; and the social climate of the classroom. Furthermore, this work not only depends on sustained contact between teachers and small groups of pupils over several years, but the necessary conflation of theology, psychology, sociology, ethics, politics and philosophy makes life preparation a difficult task for teachers and schools. Nevertheless, Fraser's review of education in the UK, the USA and the USSR leads one to conclude that however well teachers try to disguise their practice they do accept responsibility for the moral welfare and future of their children.

It would be naïve to assume that a personal ideology can be completely discounted, for personal value judgements must be rooted deeper than commitment to a cultural climate. In the words of the Crowther Report: 'the teacher is a man who has honestly fought his way through to a philosophy of life which he would like his pupils to share' (13). However, this must be achieved through that democratic sharing which will help each child to construct his own value system and provide him with personal moral stability in a dynamic society. In essence this philosophy may emerge as a greater faith in spiritual and moral, as opposed to material values: but this will be primarily a commitment to persons, rather than subscription to ideological dogmata. In such a process of humanization, people and their relationships will be the prime priority, and in this situation teachers may realize their vocational goal, as with sensitivity, altriusm and concern for truth, they play midwife to the birth of persons, whom they conceived as pupils.

The empirical evidence may be incontrovertible. 'The family lays the foundation for good character development. If the family fails the other institutions which deal with the child face a tremendous, *usually impossible, handicap*' (14), and the passing of over two decades has not changed that conclusion. But as King shows, our schools and teachers are changing. The democratizing of the state system of education has opened the way for the establishment of familial schools with parental teachers. As we shall see this permissiveness has also introduced expected and explicable deleterious elements; although this is true of much human cultural progress—the conditions which facilitate advance also lend themselves to abuse. Yet even enlightened moral education could inadvertently produce authoritarian or libertine adults, instead of the autonomous and responsible agents envisaged. If teachers can arrogate familial functions they may so influence the character and morality of the young that they will stand in the vanguard of those who are safeguarding the future of our species.

This is a difficult path to walk, but in taking this lonely, unglamorous path such a teacher will cease to be one who merely tells things to children and will instead become a spearhead of the moral and cultural advance of mankind.

PEER GROUPS

At an immature stage of moral development the dominant pupil attitude is one of conformity to his social group. For such children this conformity provides psychic and social security, and school life naturally accommodates itself to this need. In school one finds a peer society which exists in informal as well as formal groups, and simple sociometric tests can easily lay bare informal peer group structure.

As we shall see, this must be related to an emerging youth culture. National variations prevent one from adequately defining its nature. One thing is clear, however, this peer culture stands in sharp contrast to the values and attitudes of the adult members of the school community. Furthermore, there is evidence that peer influence is increasing. Sugarman found nearly ten years ago in Britain that the amount of support a schoolboy can obtain from his peers, for rejecting school values, is steadily increasing. It should therefore not surprise us that pupils and students today look more to their peers for moral guidance than they do to their teachers.

Parental Dominance

With this growth in potency acting on children who are not only susceptible to social pressure but also compelled by law to be educated in peer groups, it would seem that peer influence must dominate in the creation of moral attitudes at this stage of moral development. If this is so, then educational policy should take cognizance of this, and allow children to try and settle their own problems in an egalitarian situation.

One way of deciding whether children derive their moral values and attitudes from parents or from peers would be to identify any values held by the peers, which were not held by their parents. In the twenty-year-old research of Havighurst and Taba, the peer group was only credited with originating moral values if this was so; but they concluded, that 'was not found to be the case to any important degree'.

The truth lies between these two extremes. Children enter peer groups with a socially determined behavioural pattern already established. Therefore, they tend to enter peer groups of a particular kind, with social class as the dominant criterion. It has been generally assumed that primary school children are unaware of both social-class and ethnic differences, but Jahoda has refuted this. Children, it seems, are well aware of social-class differences. This is not immediately obvious simply because they have yet to learn the roles associated with them. Indeed Connell has identified three stages in developing class-consciousness. First, young children recognize differences in life-style. Then they correlate inequity of wealth with that of status. Finally, exposure to the socio-economic industrial system leads them to locate themselves in this hierarchical structure.

Consequently Oppenheim found that 'middle-class and working-class children do not mix much with one another. They tend to form mutually exclusive cliques at school, and the parents tend to encourage them in this, and to urge upon them a selection of friends who conform to their own class values' (15). This also happens without parental intervention. 'The kind of friends he is most likely to pick will themselves tend strongly to approve of him for behaviour his parents would think good. Hence moral behaviour and friendship cliques in adolescence are alike reflections of the way Johnny's parents have reared him' (16). Furthermore, Oppenheim found that the impression of inflexible artificiality, conveyed by this rigid grouping, was false. The distinction is much more consistent, than would at first appear, because the moral values and attitudes of each social class cohere and form a structured whole.

Thus it is not so much a matter of relative influence as of inter-action. Peer group and adult influences interact with each other with the result that although peer influence may dominate it can only modify or develop *existing moral values*. Perhaps the one area where peer group influence is unquestionably dominant is that of social group experience, particularly, as Teevan has shown, in sexual conduct, although even here peer group experience depends upon the values each child brings to the group. Thus interpersonal conduct amongst peers reveals that the moral attitude systems of children are related to those of their own adult society. Even 'conforming' children derive little of their moral values from peers. Thus one must be perpetually circumspect when drawing conclusions about the degree of peer influence.

There is here an interplay of interrelated factors. It could be the case that even the conformer goes to a group which will accept him. Then just as he naturally reflects its moral stereotype so in the first instance he unconsciously realized that the group mirrored his. In such a case the focus of his identification experience moves from the family to the peer group—but it is the family which originally determined which kind of peer group would be most attractive to him.

Peck and Havighurst thus succinctly concluded over a decade ago that 'The peer group appears to be less an originator than a reinforcer of moral values and behaviour patterns developed in the family. Adolescents as a whole, prove to admire respect and reward very much the same moral behaviour as do the respectable members of adult society. In fact the patterns of family experience prove to be prognostic of adjustment and acceptance in the adolescent society to a highly significant degree.' A current research report by Larson, however, appears to confirm the trend towards pupil autonomy. When asked to make a moral judgement in a hypothetical situation, most adolescents did so without reference to either parents or peers. Heteronomous replies showed clearly that even such pupils complied with parental rather than peer standards. And Morris too has found that (in a conflict situation against adults) young people do not resort to peer guidance: instead they subscribe to parental norms.

Thus the surprising conclusion is that even at the stage of greatest social sensitivity peers do not dominate in the creation and modification of moral attitudes. Just how far an emerging 'youth culture' will change this remains to be seen. At the moment the empirical evidence indicates that even the most powerful peer influence does little more than reinforce the existing value-system. However, numerous surveys and research reports have shown the enormous power possessed by groups in the process of attitude change. Hence attention must be given to the influence exerted by peers, even though groups are determined by parental norms.

Variations in Peer Interaction

This evidence must not therefore be taken to mean that peer influence is negligible. It is not. It only suggests that this influence cannot be exerted independently of the attitude clusters each individual brings to group. However, there are three variations, in this peer influence, which must be stressed. These are the social, sexual and psychological differences.

Of the first, it has been noted that there seemed to be differences between grammar school and secondary modern school pupils in attitudes to peer-group conformity. The differences were not entirely clear but there was a tendency for the grammar school pupils to show less conformity to friends (17). This can clearly be construed as a social-class difference for Sugarman later found that higher- and lower-status children could be distinguished in terms of personal individualism as distinct from a tendency to depend on parents or peers. Of the second, it has already been repeatedly noted that girls are more confused in their attitudes than their brothers or father; also that their peer groups are invariably unstable. Third, the greatest deviation appears to be between the different personality types (18). Adaptive personalities are successful conformists and have popular social reputations because they adjust to their peers and adopt appropriate conduct to facilitate that adjustment. They take on the beliefs and principles of their social environment readily without much question and without much inner commitment. Peer influence on the conformer is also likely to be powerful. Peck and Havighurst for example, record the answer of such a teenager to a research question. 'I don't really know what people think of me', she replied, 'It's not something you go around asking everybody. We mostly do the same things. I do what everybody else does, so I guess they probably think the same of me'.

The Value of Peer Influence

Probably the gravest deficiency of such an influence is that it tends to give pre-eminence to social approval and so elevates social conformity to the level of moral excellence. The memory of Christ, Socrates and other martyrs ought, however, to remind us that the social approval of one's contemporaries is not the *imprimatur* of morality.

On the positive side two things may be said which underline the value of peer influence. First, it can be used to enable severely deprived or anti-social children to become more morally mature. In the case of children from chaotic and unloving families the peer group can be used, under the skilful guidance of interested parental teachers, as a therapeutic, stabilizing agency. It can even help to augment a deficiency in the experience of identification, for peers are more often acceptable models and guides for adolescents (especially hostile, rebellious ones) than are adults.

Second by the careful utilization of peer relationships it should be possible to place personal relationships at the centre of the educational system, and so lead to the development of personalism. Then vigorous, spontaneous morality may emanate from these personal relationships; and maturity and vitality could then characterize the life of the school. Such pupils would regard persons as more important than things. Work would be approached with an awareness of its effect on attitudes, feelings and personal growth, and they could ultimately express their concern for personal values in industry, commerce or the professions and so sweeten and cleanse a national life which is too often based on materialism and blind rampant greed.

This is not an educational pipe-dream. Drew and Astin analysed the results from 250,000 respondents and showed that performance in every aspect of school and college life was determined by the levels of peer aspiration. Bronfenbrenner has made it clear that such an aim is not unrealizable idealism. His report on Russian education shows clearly the success with which peer groups are used to impose a communist ideology, enhance educational performance, and induce socially mature conduct in the pupils. Eaton, too, has shown how adult Israeli agencies have successfully co-opted peer groups to transmit integrative social values, with a minimum of resistance from the youths involved. It must, however, proceed towards an autonomous stage, otherwise the limitations, mentioned above, will disqualify it as an integral part of moral education.

Youth Culture
Despite the vestigial dominance of parental influence, peer groups appear to coalesce into a distinct sub-culture with norms at variance with the adult world. During the last two decades, first in America and then in Britain, we have thus witnessed the emergence of a youth culture. Coleman was one of the first to define this adolescent society over a decade ago, and has consequently drawn considerable opprobrium to himself. The difficulty of such an analysis springs from the nature of these sub-cultures. Occupied by adolescents for a short span of their lives, they are necessarily transient and ephemeral, presenting the bewildered adult observer with a kaleidoscope of changing fashions in manners, speech, dress and group activity. Consequently there is little hard evidence available which is not soon demolished by critics, and that which survives is soon dated and irrelevant. However, despite these difficulties, one may speak of a

youth-culture, itself complicated by social-class factors, but characterized by norms and goals which are inimical to adult life. Of
course, pop culture also attracts the no longer youthful and retains
its adherents as they grow older. However, the term 'youth culture'
is here intended to describe the values, interests and life-style of
adolescents.

The Origin of Youth Cultures

Varying explanations of the origin of youth cultures can be provided
by psychology, sociology and anthropology. While pupils are
sensitive to social approval, it is inevitable that they will conform,
in order to be accepted. Consequently they will then erect a sub-
cultural edifice to assure them of social security. Such cliques soon
become reference groups which not only confer instant identity but
also proffer stereotyped life-styles, subscription to which ensures
social acceptance. Such activities are doubly effective for the behaviour and appearance required to consolidate the group also antagon-
izes adults and thus makes this dimension of their alienation wholly
explicable. Consequently the influence of peers inevitably grows
stronger.

This view can be augmented by anthropological considerations.
Long ago Margaret Mead introduced us to the fact that adolescence,
in Samoan and New Guinean primitive societies, was a tranquil
phase of transition from childhood to adulthood. Later work stressed
that this resulted from a *rite de passage* which facilitated the transition. Some adults argue that extended schooling should operate in
this way, and support for recommendations that school leaving
should be delayed until legal adulthood indicates the strength and
popularity of this view.

Desmond Morris has propounded this theory in typically satirical
terms. Primitive initiation ceremonies consist of grouping children
away from their parents, under the control of selected elders, forcing
them to undergo structured ordeals, instructing them in the history
and rites of the tribe and only then admitting them to adult status.
The parallel is exact, he cries. This is precisely the function of schools.

Unfortunately, the system clearly does not operate as such. School
leavers are not treated as adults. During this protracted phase, and
immediately afterwards, earlier maturing adolescents are physically
adult but emotionally undeveloped. Consequently they strive for
adult status but are not accorded it. It is here that much antagonism
is engendered. Assuming that they have left childhood behind, a
mutual hostility springs from the fact that adults are made indignant
by their premature assumptions of maturity with no attendant
sense of responsibility. This may be because adults resent mature

pretensions in adolescents, but it may also spring from envy since few adults today enjoyed an adolescence marked by such economic, psychical, sexual and social freedom. Such reactions only cause adolescents to close ranks.

Others argue that consignment to such a social limbo exacerbates adolescent alienation, endemic in modern society. Feeling isolated and impotent in an anomic society, wherein the generation gap, even in the most integrated, privatized nuclear families, is widened by increasing educational opportunities, this estrangement is alleviated by the egalitarianism of a youth culture bereft of mature dominant males. Dandurand describes this as 'cultural retreat', a process which inevitably weakens their adherence to the values and norms of adult society.

Such factors have always characterized some social elements in the post-medieval world. Alternating permissiveness and puritanism have merely stressed this. Nor can it be a post-Victorian and post-Freudian liberation from social and sexual taboos, for this has always been a feature of adolescence in the modern age. Consequently many agree that the economic independence during an historically unique phase of individual development, is the new element. It is this, they say, which explains the uninhibited life-style of the young. They now have not only the leisure, social cohesion and youthful zest but also the resources to exploit the nascent hedonism in us all; and with earlier maturation the lower-age limit of this culture is perpetually falling, making adults even more envious and insecure.

Inevitably such a clash of sub-cultures will stress sexuality, for youth have this in abundance while many adults are past their prime. Consequently the trends towards pornography and permissiveness may originate with the envious middle-aged and then, for economic reasons, be imposed on this new adolescent market. They are constantly sexually stimulated by profit-hungry pornographers and advertisers. Cosmetic products are pressed upon them both as aphrodisiacs and charms, both reputed to gain a sexual partner and so secure their gender-identity. It is then that the inevitable divorce of sex and love is accomplished; a divorce which is psychically and socially damaging, because it places people in what Morris calls a 'subhuman frame of reference'. It is thus possible that a youth culture may be fostered by the adult economic manipulation of a profitable teenage market, and so justify those who claim that this image of a tawdry teenage culture is an adult creation.

However, there is an abundance of evidence which suggests that the teenage culture creates and satisfies its own demands. Indeed most beneficiaries are youthful, from teenage pop-idols through adolescent boutique managers to the clientele themselves.

Pupil Power

It is inevitable that such a youth culture results in pupil militancy; the twin sides of which are pupil-power and pupil-violence. The former first emerged in the form of a strike. Undoubtedly encouraged by teachers' strikes, pupils were reported, during May 1972, to have planned and executed a successful strike. In London police and pupils clashed as the latter were prevented from holding a rally in Trafalgar Square; and further unsavoury incidents occurred as frustrated pupils marched on London's County Hall. The pupil leader was then arrested and charged with obstructing the police.

Encouraged by a spate of journals and books, ranging from Berg's responsible and positive guidance to irresponsible anarchic incitement (see figure 4), pupils reacted in a predictable fashion.

CHILDREN'S RIGHTS

THIS MAGAZINE IS URGENT

Editorial board: Paul Adams (USA), Leila Berg, Nan Berger, Vivian Berger, Michael Duane, John Holt (USA), A.S. Neill, Robert Ollendorff

Repression and violence are increasing. The backlash daily grows stronger. The violence of authority breeds the violence of anti-authority, which then becomes the pretext for further repression, for calls for 'tougher measures' etc.–i.e. more violence. Children are conditioned in families and schools to accept and perpetuate the sickness of a society in which fear, hatred and coercion are the ruling agents from infancy onwards. The recently published book 'Children's Rights' (Elek, £2.50) has shown that our only real hope of creating a humane society; run not on these but on love, lies in radical change in child upbringing and education. We must work for this now, while there's still time.

How can a magazine do this? By being practical as never before. By providing for parents, teachers, students and children:

A National Information and Ideas Pool Who knows where to find all the projects, campaigns, free schools, groups working with kids, etc., etc.? Often they don't even know about each other. We'll tell you everything that's happening, and how to make it happen yourself. Let us know what you're doing: we'll publish it.

Children's Rights Adviser Service Parents, teachers, students, kids, your problems answered with genuine, non-mystifying advice by the editorial board and other experts. Personal replies to all who enclose a stamped, addressed envelope. Practical help given, and services organized, wherever possible.

Open Forum A dialogue across the generation gap, and a place to exchange ideas, experiences and difficulties. This is *your* magazine: reader participation is its essence. Participate.

News, Pictures, Cartoons As with the sacking of the young teacher, Christopher Searle, for publishing 'Stepney Words', the national press occasionally reveals the tip of the iceberg. We're going to reveal the rest.

The Most Advanced Thinking Ideas that can really come to something–by leading workers in the field. Some of these are on the editorial board (including the six authors of the book 'Children's Rights') and we are certain of a formidable array of distinguished contributors. Early contributions include John Holt on Oz and deschooling society, Michael Duane on Summerhill and on Risinghill case histories, Leila Berg on children's reading problems, Dr Robert Ollendorff on sex and the teenager, 'Starting a Free School' from the Scotland Road Trust, and a report for 1971 from Action Space.

What Can YOU Do? Use the magazine. Write to it, tell your friends about it. Most important of all at this stage if you want to do something valuable and effective, help get it off the ground by taking a year's subscription (12 monthly issues) at the bargain rate of £2 post free. Issue no. 1 will be on sale early in November 1971, price 18p.

If You Sympathise Subscribe Now

Figure 4. Facsimile of pupil-power publicity. Despite the laudable motives and profession of acceptable ideals it is difficult to accept the above without reserve. One writer urged discontented pupils to play truant, disobey teachers and disrupt the school. One more responsible publication discussed the legality of school systems and practices. Even the co-authors John Holt and Michael Duane produced an article sub-titled 'Fighting the System'. It is sad to note that much talent seems to be directed towards inducing antagonism between those who should co-operate.

They established the National Union of School Students, and so made it clear that pupils could no longer be ignored in educational decision making. The policy of the union is surprisingly mature, and gratifyingly confirms the views of the present book. Of course such aims are not new. The welcome innovation is the establishment of a serious pupil organization to propagate them (see figure 5).

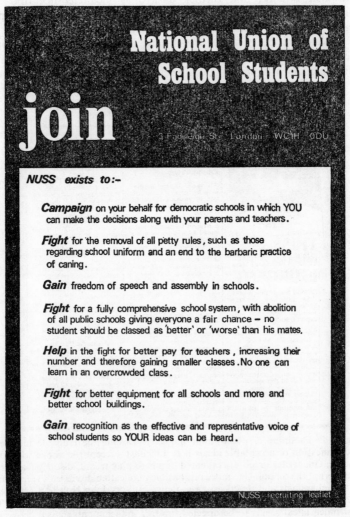

Figure 5. Facsimile of NUSS publicity literature

Already there is evidence that the autocracy of teachers and school governors is being challenged. Pupils are already infiltrating both committees and, with no economic security to preserve, are stating their views in an uncomprising manner. By such means the democratization of schools is assured. The only real danger, it seems, are the 'moral panics' to which Cohen refers. These result from over-hasty reactions, by advocates of law and order, to the gauche and bizarre manifestations of youthful autonomy.

Pupil Violence

There is, however, a darker side to this picture. Although not exclusively so, the evidence suggests that this youth culture leads to the responsible exercise of pupil-power amongst the middle classes, but to violent hostility amongst working-class children. This is sometimes explained by observing that lower-status sub-groups share a penchant for using aggression, rather than reason, to express their views. Unfortunately a decade of exposure to audio-visual evidence of violence in Vietnam and Northern Ireland, is blurring the social-class delineations of this phenomenon.

Those who wish to indict the working class refer to the increased hooliganism in the neighbourhood of their schools. Their unsettled and unsupervised lives at home, it seems, promotes delinquency. The new aggressiveness of hitherto politically impotent workers, aggravates this. Irresponsibility fostered here by the welfare state, leads to parental apathy. Skills then acquired can be tested by the disruption of public sporting activities and vandalism on public vehicles used to transport fans to and from sports matches. Since it has also been found recently that vandalism and theft are a working-class protest against middle-class norms, such a teenager is now ready to take crimes of violence on to the streets. This, it is argued, is the genesis of the recent wave of muggings.

Others, however, see this new wave of violence as a symptom of genuine delinquency, always an epiphenomenon of life in socially stratified urban cultures, and when this includes bourgeois teenagers it can indicate the collapse of traditional morality. In a Reith Lecture the speaker, referring to the vicissitudes of adolescence observed that, 'Popular morality is now a wasteland littered with the debris of broken convictions. Concepts such as honour or even honesty have an old fashioned sound; but nothing has taken their place' (19). Steel may show conclusively that although the general crime rate has risen, crimes of violence have declined. This is not true of adolescents, they are increasingly involved in criminal violence, and teachers in Britain and America claim that this is now entering the schools.

Over a decade ago British teachers smiled grimly at the reports on America's 'blackboard jungle'. They were then roused from complacency by the report of a British pupil's broken-bottle assault on a teacher. Since then similar attacks have become commonplace. After one headmaster was knocked out by a twelve-year-old pupil, teachers demanded to be protected from such violence. Margaret Thatcher, the Minister of Education, admitted that teachers were ill-equipped to deal with such situations. Finally, a judge ruled that teachers had a right to defend themselves, against such assaults.

In America the scene has not changed. Last year the *Log of Untoward Incidents*, kept by the New York Board of Education revealed that teachers are still being assaulted. It makes morbid reading. Even though many refuse to bring charges against their pupil assailants, there are numerous reports of staff being kicked, punched, bludgeoned, knifed, and even raped. Consequently, many women are refusing to work unprotected.

Violence is also evident between pupils. Derby City Education Committee have recently investigated reports of extortion, mugging and stabbing amongst the pupils of the city's oldest school. Staff, petrified by teenagers with knives and razors, are reluctant to intervene. In Lincoln a systematic process of violent intimidation was employed to extort money from fellow pupils. So helpless were the staff in this case that the rota of 'beatings', in the system, was chalked on a blackboard.

Both in British and American schools it seems certain that violence may soon become a greater problem than drugs and sex. Protestations to the contrary, have been silenced by the National Association of Schoolmasters. At successive annual conferences they had referred to the increase of pupil truancy, theft and vandalism. Now their major survey into school violence (20) has disclosed the seriousness of the situation, and suggested tentative remedial measures. But it must never be forgotten that this violence is only a symptom of a more serious malady afflicting society today. The remedy must therefore be radical and involve one in the transformation of the educational system.

At the NUT Young Teacher Conference in Nottingham, during September 1972, a resolution proposed by the Newham representatives dealt with the problem of violence. It suggested five ways of helping to ameliorate the problem: (1) pupils, as well as staff and parents should be involved in determining school policy; (2) class size should be reduced; (3) the staff should be helped to function in pastoral and supportive roles; (4) teachers with difficult classes should have their teaching loads reduced; (5) there should be a thorough reappraisal of school policies such as streaming, examinations and corporal punishment, which create antagonism between pupils and staff. Clearly all hinges on the first proposition. If teachers, parents and pupils were allowed some genuine participation in decision making, then the rest might well follow; but the image of a democratic, pastoral and familial school, outlined above, clearly elicits the approval of practising teachers.

Only two concluding points need to be made. Under circumstances of this kind the conflict model of the school (see Chapter 13) is tragically relevant, and the raising of the school-leaving age for British adolescents, who are annually maturing earlier, may intensify the problem until it reaches crisis proportions. One curious recent development of this is called 'lesson refusal'. Mostly confined to female urban school leavers, it consists of fulfilling the legal requirement of being present in school, but implacably refusing to join in any school activity—including lessons.

The Culture Conflict

Our pupils are thus caught in a culture conflict. They have to choose between the pupil role and the youth role. At the moment these are mutually exclusive. The former stresses deferred gratification and deference to adults. The latter emphasizes spontaneous hedonism and personal independence. Such a role-decision can be built on tortuous motives. Just as non-academic and non-athletic pupils have always sought to compensate by excelling as athletes and scholars, respectively, so now pop-art and school culture become centres of displacement activity for the less competent. School failures seek to become pop-art experts; and many inhibited, shy adolescents, in retreat from the youth role, seek haven in the pupil role.

In this conflict the youth culture dominates. Not only is it consolidated by the attendant sub-cultural social bonds, but the pupil role is rejected as a bourgeois tool. Its stress on academic values, frugality, honesty, regularity, industry and obedience are derided. Here an implicit paradox can be resolved. If parents are such powerful influences why do their children invert their values? Why are adults so rigorous in their condemnation of this process? It cannot all be attributed to that envy engendered when adolescents display those desirable qualities denied to adults by virtue of their age.

Reference to Jung's psychology offers a partial solution. According to him the self has two aspects; the *persona* which we present to others, and the hidden *shadow-self* of which we are ashamed. It is now known that the shadow-self cannot be hidden from one's offspring. Consequently, under both pathological and normal conditions, this may be the parental-self with which they actually identify. Consequently they not only emerge from the process of identification, with personalities diametrically opposed to those of their parents, but their values and friends (both determined by the parental shadow-self) are then disliked by parents who see their shameful selves mirrored in them.

Utilizing the Youth Culture

This youth culture cannot be toppled from its dominant position by punitive or patronizing teachers. Discipline, too is becoming ineffective as more children resent corporal punishment or the imposition of trivial school rules. Futile attempts to control male pupil hair length has made this clear. The only sensible resolution of this quandary is the utilization of the youth culture.

It could at first appear to be too dangerous to attempt. Teachers will undoubtedly find themselves faced with pupils who are increasingly vicious and self-assertive, but both traits may well spring from a pupil desire to affirm that democratic and personal dignity, which is conferred by their sub-culture. Hence youth cultures may well be sources of moral potency which we could profitably tap. It is true that they spawn mass pop concerts, characterized by uninhibited, flagrantly hedonistic conduct—but they also organize mass demonstrations against war, racism and inequity of every kind. Both have rowdy elements, but the moral force of the latter cannot be denied.

Such a delinquency spectrum is usually taken to indicate that adolescent rebellion can be malignant or benign. This analogy with cancerous body cells highlights the essential point. Although some adolescent delinquency may be so malignant that it might destroy the body of any society, some is clearly benign. It is this which can be bent to the task of moral education.

We have already observed that such social experiences can confirm and develop the preconditions of morality, even though they may appear to be contrary to adult values. This peer culture *can* be used with even more effect and so be welcomed by moral educators, as an aid to their task. Not only can it enable schools to utilize the autonomous, democratic, impulses nurtured by a youth culture, but the exercise of such pupil-power can cultivate moral responsibility and rationality. Furthermore it enables schools to perform their sociological function of role-allocation; a process which is known to foster moral development, and also identify and nurture the untapped moral talents of the children concerned.

Hitherto, schools had been limited to allocating roles indigenous to club activities. These were doubtless beneficial for they could inculcate empathy and respect for accepted rules, but there was still an unbridged gulf between them and the traditional pupil-role, based as it was on both moral and scholastic criteria. By canalizing a pupil's penchant for role playing this gulf may be bridged, and in the process schools may well find that the personal involvement required compensates for the almost total lack of emotional demands in the standard school curriculum.

This conflation of the pupil and youth roles will be a difficult task. Many autocratic senior teachers will bridle at the prospect of discussing important school policy with pupils. Equally, enthusiastic pupils must be reminded that most teachers are not only older but also wiser than they. Many rearguard actions will undoubtedly be fought over the question of school rules, but these must be faced if pupils are to feel that they are members of a community, for whose triumphs and failures they share a serious responsibility. This will also prepare them for life in a society which may be morally transformed by their influence.

Teacher–Pupil Co-operation
The co-operation, necessary for this utilizing of the youth culture, need not be too difficult to achieve. The manifesto of the National Union of Student Scholars (see page 314) makes it clear that pupil aims need not conflict with those of enlightened teachers. In addition to this it is clear that both teachers and pupils want moral education as a source of personal guidance for adolescents. McPhail, May and a School's Council inquiry (21) have all shown that about three-quarters of the adolescent population of British schools desire this. More recently an investigation by the author on three triennial occasions has shown that teachers are not only adamant, concerning the need for moral education, but are increasingly detaching it from religious education (22). Moreover, surveys and opinion polls during the last decade have made it abundantly clear that parents not only desire moral education for their children, but are looking increasingly to teachers, rather than clergymen, to meet this demand. Research and writing in the last decade is apparently assuring them that moral education is a viable school subject.

One thing must be clear. By its nature moral education cannot consist of adults instructing children, no matter how sophisticated they may be in concealing this activity. Moral maturity is indexed by responsible pupil participation in reaching and implementing, moral decisions. Hence from the start, democratic autonomy must be a characteristic of such lessons. Consequently, pupils should acquire democratic values rather than an expertise in democratic techniques, and then express them in behaviour rather than debate. Success here will be self-perpetuating, for such pupils can only enhance that democratization of schools which is so necessary for effective moral education.

REFERENCES

1 Waller (1965), p. 40. First published in 1932.
2 Hargreaves (1972), p. 15.
3 Castle (1958), p. 284.
4 See 1904 Board of Education *Handbook of Suggestions.*
5 See Hoyle (1969) and Musgrove and Taylor (1969). Johnson (1972) opposes 'functionalist' criteria and speaks of 'occupational control' (p. 45), and 'occupational cohesion' (p. 47). In either case teaching cannot qualify as a profession.
6 See Taylor (1970).
7 North (1972) argues this case for psychiatrists. Indeed the increasing detachment of priests from secular life may mean that teachers and doctors may have to usurp this function.
8 Note Plowden (1967): 'The teacher is expected to be a good man and to influence children more by what he is than by what he knows . . . Teachers cannot escape the knowledge that children will catch values and attitudes from them'. Grace (1967): 'Everyone is now aware of the responsibility now given to teachers in the spheres of moral and ethical training.' But this is a parental function too. See Peck and Havighurst (1964): 'Parents must accept the security giving functions ordinarily performed by parents'; and Plowden (1967): 'Teachers must strive to serve as substitutes for parents' All this, says Whyte (1956) is demanded by parents.
9 Loukes (1965), p. 57, and Loukes (1966), p. 138.
10 Mead (1961).
11 Spens Report (1959), pp. 197 ff. The position of headmasters is a vexed one and has not been introduced here; see Goodwin (1968), But they are much maligned. Cohen (1971) found that older headmasters were less authoritarian and traditional than is generally supposed.
12 Waller (1965), p. 185.
13 Crowther Report (1959), para. 627.
14 Havighurst and Taba (1949), p. 41.
15 Oppenheim (1956), p. 287.
16 Peck and Havighurst (1964), p. 140.
17 See Morris (1958).
18 Kay (1968), Chapter 8.
19 Carstairs (1962), p. 55.
20 NAS (1972).
21 McPhail (1972), pp. 4–5. He cites May (1971) and The Schools Council (1968) as evidence confirming his findings.
22 Kay (1973).

Bibliography
BERG, L., *Look at Kids* (Penguin, 1972).
BRONFENBRENNER, U., *Two Worlds of Childhood* (Allen & Unwin, 1971).
CARSTAIRS, G. M., *This Island Now* (Hogarth Press, 1963).
CASTLE, E. B., *Moral Education in Christian Times* (Allen & Unwin, 1958).
COHEN, L., 'Age and Head Teachers Role Conception', in *Educational Research*, Vol. 14, No. 1, 1971.
COHEN, S., *Folk Devils and Moral Panics* (McGibbon & Kee, 1972).
COLEMAN, J. S., *The Adolescent Society* (Free Press, 1961).
CONNELL, R. W., 'Class Consciousness in Childhood', in *Australian and New Zealand Journal of Sociology*, Vol. 6, No. 2, 1970.

CROWTHER REPORT, *Fifteen to Eighteen* (HMSO, 1959).

DALE, R. R., 'Teachers Who Have a Good Influence: An Analysis of Opinion', in *Education for Teaching*, February 1967.

DANDURAND, P., 'Dynamique culturelle en milieu scolaire', in *Revue Française de Sociologie*, Vol. 13, No. 11, 1972.

DREW, D. E. and ASTIN, A. W., 'Undergraduate Aspirations: A Test of Several Theories', in *American Journal of Sociology*, Vol. 77, No. 6, 1972.

EATON, W. J., *Influencing the Youth Culture* (California Sage Pub., 1970).

ELLIOT, P., *The Sociology of the Professions* (Macmillan, 1972).

EPPEL, E. M. and EPPEL, M., *Adolescents and Morality* (Routledge & Kegan Paul, 1966).

FRASER, W. R., 'Moral Education in the U.K., the U.S.A. and the U.S.S.R.', in *Aspects of Education-One* (Univ. Hull Inst. Education, 1964).

FROMM, E., *The Fear of Freedom* (Routledge & Kegan Paul, 1960).

GOODWIN, F. J., *The Art of the Headmaster* (Ward Lock Educational, 1968).

GRACE, G. R., 'The Changing Roles of the Teacher', in *Education for Teaching*, February 1967.

HARGREAVES, D. H., *Interpersonal Relations and Education* (Routledge & Kegan Paul, 1972).

HAVIGHURST, R. J. and TABA, H., *Adolescent Character and Personality* (John Wiley, 1949).

HOYLE, E., *The Role of the Teacher* (Routledge & Kegan Paul, 1969).

JACKSON, J. (Ed.), *Professions and Professionalization* (Cambridge Univ. Press, 1970).

JAHODA, G., 'Development of the Perception of Social Differences in Children from Six to Ten', in *British Journal of Psychology*, May 1959.

JOHNSON, T. J., *Professions and Power* (Macmillan, 1972).

JUNG, C., *Two Essays on Analytical Psychology* (Routledge & Kegan Paul, 1953).

KAY, W., *Moral Development* (Allen & Unwin, 1968).

KAY, W., 'The Self Concept as a Moral Control', in *Journal of Moral Education*, Vol. 2, No. 1, 1972.

KAY, W., 'Some Primary School Teacher Attitudes to Moral and Religious Education', in *Journal of Moral Education*, Vol. 2, No. 3, 1973.

KING, E. J. (Ed.), *The Teacher and the Needs of Society in Evolution* (Pergamon, 1970).

LARSON, L. E., 'The Influence of Parents and Peers During Adolescence: The Situation Hypothesis Revisited', in *Journal of Marriage and the Family*, Vol. 34, No. 1, 1972.

LIPPETT, R., LEWIN, M. and WHITE, R. K., 'The Social Climate of Children's Groups', in Barker, Kounin and Wright (Eds), *Child Behaviour and Development* (McGraw-Hill, 1943).

LIPPETT, R. and WHITE, R. K., 'An Experimental Study of Leadership in Group Life', in Maccoby, Newcomb and Hartley (Eds), *Readings in Social Psychology* (Methuen, 1959).

LOUKES, H., *New Ground in Christian Education* (Student Christian Movement, 1965).

LOUKES, H., 'Religious Education in the Primary School', in *Religious Education 1944–84* (Allen & Unwin, 1966).

MCPHAIL, P., UNGOED-THOMAS, J. R. and CHAPMAN, H., *Moral Education in the Secondary School* (Longmans, 1972).

MAY, P., *Moral Education in School* (Methuen, 1971).

MEAD, G. H., *Mind, Self and Society* (Univ. Chicago Press, 1934).

MEAD, M., *Coming of Age in Samoa* (Penguin, 1943).

MEAD, M., *Growing Up in New Guinea* (Penguin, 1942).

MEAD, M., 'The School in American Culture', in Halsey, Floud and Anderson (Eds), *Education Economy and Society* (Free Press, Glencoe, 1961).

MORRIS, B., *Objectives and Perspectives in Education* (Routledge & Kegan Paul, 1972).

MORRIS, D., *The Human Zoo* (Corgi, 1969).

MORRIS, J. F., 'The Development of Adolescent Value Judgements', in *British Journal of Educational Psychology*, Vol. 28, Pt. 1, 1958.

MUSGROVE, F. and TAYLOR, P. H., *Society and the Teacher's Role* (Routledge & Kegan Paul, 1969).

NAS, *Violence in Schools and its Treatment* (National Association of Schoolmasters, 1972).

NEWCOMB, T. M. and HARTLEY, E. L., *Readings in Social Psychology* (Holt, 1947).

NORTH, M., *The Secular Priest* (Allen & Unwin, 1972).

OPPENHEIM, A. N., 'A Study of Social Attitudes of Adolescents', Unpublished Ph.D. thesis, London, 1956.

PARSONS, T., 'The School Class as a Social System', in P. I. Rose (Ed.), *The Study of Society* (Random House, 1967).

PECK, R. F. and HAVIGHURST, R. J., *The Psychology of Character Development* (John Wiley, 1964).

PLOWDEN REPORT, *Children and Their Primary Schools* (HMSO, 1967).

SCHOOLS COUNCIL ENQUIRY, *Young School Leavers* (HMSO, 1968).

SPENS REPORT, *Secondary Education* (HMSO, 1938).

STAINES, J. W., 'The Self-Picture as a Factor in the Class Room', in *British Journal of Educational Psychology*, Vol. XXVIII, June 1958.

STEEL, E. M., 'Criminality in Jeffersonian America—A Sample', in *Crime and Delinquency*, Vol. 18, No. 2, 1972.

SUGARMAN, B., 'Teenage Boys at School', Unpublished Ph.D. thesis, Princeton, 1966.

TAYLOR, G. (Ed.), *The Teacher as Manager* (National Council for Technical Education, 1970).

TEEVAN, J. J., 'Reference groups and pre-marital sexual behaviour', in *Journal of Marriage and the Family*, Vol. 34, No. 2, 1972.

TOFFLER, A. (Ed), *The Schoolhouse in the City* (Preager, 1968).

WALLER, W., *The Sociology of Teaching* (Wiley, 1965).

WHYTE, W. H., *Street Corner Society* (Univ. Chicago Press, 1955).

YARLOTT, G., *Education and Children's Emotions* (Weidenfeld & Nicolson, 1972).

Chapter 18

Some Problems Relating to Moral Education

It is argued below that moral education involves the teacher in the practice of attitude formation and change. This includes three primary elements, the communicator, the audience and the communication. In education these clearly refer to the teacher, the pupils and the curriculum. Having already discussed the former two, it is now necessary to discuss the last element.

The present educational system was evolved in rudimentary form in the static society of ancient Egypt. Passing through Greece and Rome it became our medieval heritage. Perpetuated by professions dependent upon accumulated wisdom from the past, its literati assumed that their function was to transmit this body of learning. Thus the corpus of knowledge was clearly defined, and for convenience was sliced into segments appropriate to professional needs. Even when new subjects, such as modern languages were incorporated into the curriculum, the rationale for their inclusion and the methods of instruction employed, were always derived from the existing, traditional body of knowledge.

During the present century this position has changed. A knowledge 'explosion' has shattered the traditional delineation of academic subjects; and psychological research has shown both that children learn actively rather than passively and also that they possess a refreshing reluctance to compartmentalize their knowledge. Consequently curriculum reform is a major educational industry.

In one sense moral education is in a strong position to claim a place in any new school curriculum. Parents, teachers and pupils all support this, and are encouraged to do so by its advocacy in every major official education report during this century. However, there are difficulties. Many teachers claim that it already occurs through the media of the present school lessons. Consequently they insist that no time-tabled lesson is needed. Others affirm that it should contain sex education; but naïve and maladroit handling of this evokes parental and public hostility. Still more wish to subsume it under the aegis of religious education, and thereby precipitate ideological squabbles. Current research is slowly eliminating these problems, but this only lays bare the fundamental question of taxonomy.

Where can moral education be placed in our new analyses of the curriculum?

The Unity of the Curriculum

There are two ways of eliminating an outmoded taxonomy of human knowledge. One is to devise new, more satisfying analyses: the other is to eliminate them by insisting that all knowledge is integrated. This does not mean that the former analyses are abolished. It merely means that the allocation of knowledge into compartments labelled History, Geography, Mathematics, Physics, Chemistry, Divinity, Psychology and Sociology will result not from the inertia of past centuries but the application of contemporary insights. These insights can approach the problem either from the vantage point of the pupil or the subject. Peterson first adopted the pupil-centred approach and suggested that curricular considerations should spring from the actual manner in which pupils approach knowledge. These he called the logical, empirical, moral and aesthetic, claiming that they were the primary modes of thinking (1). Consequently subjects should be classified accordingly.

Phenix proposed a similar scheme, based on his view that the aim of education is both a comprehension of the world and a recognition of meaning in all its aspects. He thus spoke of the realms of meaning as the natural divisions of knowledge. These are symbolics, empirics, aesthetics, synnoetics (personal relationships), ethics and synoptics. The first two refer to scientific understanding and the last one to history, theology and philosophy which, when applied to the other realms of meaning, have an integrative effect. Whitfield then developed this analysis and both listed the nature of the meaning derived from these realms, and identified the curricular element which could cultivate this (2), when children developed the appropriate skills, attitudes and interests.

Hirst approached the problem in a rather different way. Adopting a subject-centred vantage point he affirmed that all knowledge can be analysed into a finite number of distinct disciplines or forms (3); thus he approached the problem with human conceptual structures as his guide. By logical analysis he reached the conclusion that traditional taxonomies were largely accurate. Knowledge could be divided into the distinct disciplines familiar to us in the form of history, mathematics, science, etc. In addition to these *forms* there are, he claimed, *fields* of knowledge. The distinctive characteristic of such a field is that it is not a coherent epistemological unity, but draws its data from many disciplines. He then further argued that these fields of knowledge may be either theoretical or practical.

The educational approach, which considers criteria for the selection of material, is complementary to these psychological and philosophical analyses. Bruner, for example, considered that the subject matter should contribute to the growth and development of a democratic society. 'Then it should follow,' he argued, 'that a curriculum ought to be built around the great issues, principles, and values that a society deems worthy of the continual concern of its members' (4). Equally, the primary criterion of Phenix was that the material should cultivate comprehension and *meaning*. It should thus relate to the quality of life, rather than the logic of the curriculum, and so cultivate the inner lives of both teachers and pupils. Only three points need to be made here. First, philosophical analysis and psychological investigation are complementary activities in taxonomic studies and curriculum reform. Second, the coherence and integrity of the classical *forms* of knowledge, e.g. history, mathematics, etc., both determine the subject matter and assure their place in schools. Third, the criteria of Peterson, Bruner and Phenix are only applicable to *fields* of study. They must, of necessity, draw their material from recognized *forms* of knowledge, but the consequent integration necessarily constitutes a *field* of knowledge.

Thus we turn to the taxonomic investigations of the Schools Council Integrated Studies. They speak of truth strategies, rather than subjects, and claim that a curriculum is composed of four such areas each with its own technique for arriving at the truth in that area of knowledge. Thus they postulated four primary forms of knowledge: the arts; natural sciences; social sciences; and morals, religion and philosophy. Their insistence on integrated curricular work establishes these firmly as *fields* rather than forms of knowledge. For them, 'Integrated studies, are the exploration of any theme, area, or problem which requires the help of more than one school subject for its full understanding' (5). Like Bruner and Phenix they insist that the material used should endow our culture with meaning, and enable children to comprehend more fully their inner lives and personal relationships.

The Integration of Knowledge

Since Karl Mannheim dismissed liberal education as being 'too aloof from history to be really helpful' (6) the conflict has sharpened between those who want to make bigger things go faster and those who want to improve the quality of personal life. Hence many attempts are being made to bridge what have been derisively called 'the two cultures'. In education one attempt has taken the form of encouraging pupils to study both the arts *and* the sciences, and then defer specialization in either for as long as possible.

These taxonomies, or curricular analyses, are a current attempt to achieve the same end. In order to see this more clearly it is necessary, first, to show that Peterson's modes of thought, Phenix's realms of meaning, Hirst's categories of knowledge, and the Schools Council's truth strategies can all be correlated. Then if to this one adds Bloom's domains of response, a clear pattern emerges (see table 3).

Table 3. *Conflated Taxonomies of Knowledge*

	Affective	*Cognitive*
Bloom		
Peterson	Aesthetic	Empirical
	Moral	Logical
Phenix	Synnoetics	Symbolic
	Aesthetic	Empirical
		Synoptic
Hirst		Forms
		Fields
Schools Council	Arts	Natural Sciences
	Morals	Social Sciences
	Religious Understanding	Philosophy

In this structure it is immediately apparent that the differing elements in each taxonomy can be accommodated within the two-fold structure defined in Bloom's terminology. Thus all the varying categories can be listed as either affective or cognitive. In the *cognitive* realm one can place those curricular elements which cluster around a pupil's cerebral, conceptual, detached, objective comprehension of a subject-centred activity. Conversely the *affective* approach is necessarily subjective and pupil-centred and requires a committed and visceral response to curricular material. Thus although these analyses stress the unity of knowledge, this conflation indicates that such knowledge has two aspects.

The nomenclature describing these twin facets of the underlying unity of knowledge can be endlessly multiplied, but when resolved to their quintessence it is clear that the affective classification contains all those elements which are only comprehensible if the pupil or student makes a personal response. The cognitive elements, on the other hand, are completely comprehensible when approached logically, and may even demand that the learner adopts an impersonal approach to the subject.

The only observation to note here is the fact that although Hirst fits into such a conflation he does not satisfy this last requirement. He holds firmly to the view that knowledge is a unity, and appears to construct a taxonomy on the basis of philosophical criteria alone. Consequently man's affective response can be partially omitted. This is necessarily a consequence of constructing a taxonomy on the basis of philosophy without making recourse to psychological considerations. The inevitable consequence is that there is no secure place for moral education in his scheme.

However, this is catered for in the other taxonomies. Few reasons are provided, but those which are support the writer's view that the omission of moral education has resulted in a gross imbalance in school curricula. It must, however, be stressed that not only should curricula contain affective as well as cognitive elements, but also that *moral education as an integral part of any taxonomy must have both practical and theoretical components.* If these are divided from one another then moral education becomes effete. It is then either a study of ethics or a system of social control. Therefore one must view with grave concern many proposed courses in moral education which do not acknowledge this basic fact.

Moral Education Curricula

May, for example, insists that adequate moral education consists of ethical discussions alone. Bull goes a little further than this but stops at the point where his proposed course engenders mature moral judgement. McPhail goes even further and asserts that moral education must inculcate respect and concern for people. The weakness here lies in his assumption that when children know what they ought to do, they will in fact be able actually to do it. As we shall see below, this is a dangerous and false assumption to make. Although there are quantitative variations between these three all are qualititatively distinct from genuine moral education. Such curricular activity should not only provide moral insight but also lead children to the point where they are so committed to these insights that they are expressed in actual conduct.

These criticisms should not be construed as a complete denunciation of such curricula, but it must be stressed that courses in moral education which are limited to the cognitive element ought to be described as ethics rather than moral education. Therefore even the advanced work of McPhail must also be accepted as an interim proposition. As McPhail's work is neither based upon an integrated and coherent system, nor appears to consider, with any seriousness, the three basic problems cited below, it must of necessity be a temporary measure, filling a gap until a more firmly based and less expedient curriculum can be formulated. Perhaps the team working on that project deliberately chose to call their curricular 'lifeline', in order to stress this point! When somebody is in imminent danger of being drowned they are thrown a lifeline. This, obviously, is only intended to get them out of danger. Once on the shore the rescued individual has to face the other pressing problems of life. The real danger here lies in the fact that we may ignore the temporary nature of McPhail's propositions. We must be more rigorous with our temporary measures in moral education for so much more is at stake. If we fail we could easily witness the moral turpitude of succeeding generations of schoolchildren exposed to sustained courses, which are merely designed to encourage inquiry and discussion. The danger lies here— because the material is primarily moral in connotation we may be deceived into assuming that moral education is thereby assured.

Thus it must be stressed again that in moral education one must have at least two related dimensions—first that of ethics, and second that of morality. The former will be concerned with moral theories and the techniques for making valid moral judgements. The latter will be concerned with actual conduct and should be a necessary consequence of the former. This is not unique to moral education. Poetry, music, art and religion all have these two dimensions. All are comprised of a detached, objective factual content and a committed, creative, behavioural response. Some go even further and claim that this is true of education as a whole. Bruner, for example, argued that curricular material should be chosen on the criterion of whether it led to action (7). It would be infinitely easier to omit the latter, but alas it would not then be moral education.

There is, naturally, one final minor problem connected with the implementation of new taxonomies in specific schools. Obviously such new curricular activities would demand a much more flexible timetable than that which has hitherto catered for traditional subjects. Many headteachers may thus be apprehensive about the mode of catering for such curricular innovations. Davies has shown how a 'transverse matrix' can be used for this purpose. He presents it so convincingly, as a dynamic model well able to cater for such changes, that even the most timid administrator can be assured that chaos will not follow the introduction of new 'subjects' and 'activities'.

MORAL VALUES, IMPERATIVES AND CONDUCT

Before considering how the school may be instrumental in moral education three further problems must be faced. These are not only fundamental to both ethics and moral education but it is also probable that failure to solve them may emasculate any scheme of moral education. Despite this, contemporary proponents of moral education appear to be glossing over the difficulties distilled in these three problems. They are as follows:

1. The validation of moral values.
2. The naturalistic fallacy.
3. Moral motivation.

These three problems cohere. One has first to justify the validity of any basic moral value or principle. Having done that and decided which values and principles are valid the next task is to determine how moral imperatives can be derived from them. Many say that this is impossible and so dub this process the 'naturalistic fallacy', but since children *actually* do this every day one has to pass logically on to the next point. Here the problem revolves around the fact that when children know what they *should* do it does not follow that this is what they *would* do.

The complex ramifications of these basic problems may be simplified if one takes as a starting point the conclusion that a morally mature child must be autonomous, rational, altruistic and responsible. Of these the first may be taken for granted. Autonomy is, by definition, an essential pre-requisite of morality. Any action performed under duress cannot be classified as moral, in any normal sense of the word. It is true that a behaviourist would triumphantly proclaim at this point that autonomy is a 'possible impossibility' because all our actions and thoughts are merely conditioned responses to a wide range of stimuli. This is why Skinner assures us that we cannot claim to be free in any autonomous sense of the word, and that autonomous man is a pre-scientific myth. The usual riposte at this point is to observe that 'rats aren't chaps' and proceed to insist that his conclusions, reached by experimenting with pigeons and rats, cannot legitimately be applied to people. However, most would agree that the notion of autonomy is axiomatic in any discussion of morality.

Furthermore, since responsibility must be considered in the context of the should/would controversy, we are thus left with the problem of justifying reason and love as moral values.

Validating Rationality and Altruism
The approaches made to this question of value-validation are legion. The pragmatist dismisses them; the sociologist believes that they are irrelevant: and every other science appears to exclude them from the world of fact. Yet this is a false impression, it may give credence to the popular pejorative use of the term 'value-judgement', but it is not well founded. Young admitted that terms like love and loyalty should be used in a biological context. Julian Huxley expressed this view even more strongly by insisting that 'values and ideals are natural phenomena' (8). Waddington, however, is the most powerful antagonist of the traditional pragmatic, sociological view. Arguing from the basis of his studies in embryonic development he concludes starkly, 'It can be shown that values are facts, and it can be shown from the point of view of biology' (9).

However, granted that we may accept that love and reason are 'facts' how may they be validated? Why should we not advance the theory that it is better to hate than to love; and to be irrational rather than reasonable? The simplest answer to this is that provided by the existentialist. He says simply that we do not validate them until we are actually involved in a specific situation. For him there are no moral absolutes. Hence Genet, in his journal can say 'Evil be thou my good'. Such a view, of course, was expressed more crudely by the Marquis de Sade, and Simone de Beauvoir's sensitive biography shows how he concluded that criminal deviance alone gave a man the chance to affirm his autonomy. Hence this tragic figure committed himself to a life of depraved ruthlessness.

One comes a little closer, to a credible solution, with the theory of utilitarianism, which argues that by being kind and honest in society the members enable it to function efficiently—but this makes values *means* and not *ends*, and so does not justify them in themselves. However, it does point forward to what seems to be a viable principle. This may be called the process of 'self-authentication', extending beyond the 'coherence' principle exemplified in the phrase 'I am lying', where the internal incoherence means that it cannot be sustained, and moves into the area of sociology.

However, there appear to be three forms of this theory. The validation is found in social response, or in the values themselves, or in the interaction of society and these values. The first argues that such values evoke a common response or general consensus of opinion. This is the view of Griffiths who assumes that normalcy is a feature of any such population. The second is exemplified in the American Declaration of Independence wherein it is said that certain truths are 'self-evident'. Thomas Jefferson's full text runs, 'We hold these truths to be undeniable—they derive rights inherent and un-alienable—the preservation of life and liberty and the pursuit of happiness'.

The last is the one which concerns us here. It argues that in the dynamic interaction of persons in relationships, guided by these values, it will be apparent that the values authenticate themselves. Thus, for example, a discussion can only be sustained if the participants accept the tenets of logical discourse. If the discussion followed a haphazard, random policy of basing comments on *non sequiturs* and irrational conclusions, it would clearly founder. Therefore despite the almost universal distrust of reason alone, and Bertrand Russell's jibe that men fear thought as they fear nothing else on earth, reason can still be validated, by the principle of self-authentication.

This appears to apply equally to love as a value. The furore which followed Carstairs' comment that we ought to place charity before chastity, has now subsided and left us comprehending a little more clearly the reasons why St Paul called love the greatest value in this universe (10). Now Fletcher has applied this authenticating argument explicitly to love and claims that it is self-justifying. For this reason, it is argued that a society based on mutual concern would not disintegrate in the manner of one based on mutual, reciprocal hatred.

Yet this is not entirely satisfactory. When we make moral judgements and inculcate moral attitudes, values enter imperceptibly. Rationality, for example, is supported on rational grounds. Thus, a self-authenticating validation may be circular, but we can move one step away and argue the case for 'reason' by saying with Polanyi, that 'mind is the meaning of the body' (11), for implicit in this is the conviction that all phenomena have meaning. This is not far removed from Hampshire's view that such meaning is accessible to ratiocination and that 'it is the constructive task of the philosophy of mind to provide a set of terms in which ultimate judgements of value can be clearly stated' (12). This same assumption of inner coherence and validation, is also explicit in Murdoch's study of what she calls the 'Good'. Analysing our complex and disparate moral systems she affirms her belief that 'The concept Good stretches through the whole of it and gives it the only kind of unity which it can possess' (13).

Thus it can be seen that the principle of self-authentication is not entirely satisfactory. Hatred could be self-authenticating in a society which placed a premium on hostility, aggression and even social *anomie*. Thus one is led to conclude that these values are based on some form of personal commitment. Although this is then validated in practice, it does not authenticate the original response to life.

Here, of course, one enters the sphere of religious and ideological beliefs and therefore this point must be deferred until later, when we discuss the relationship between religious and moral education. For the moment, one point may be made in the context of this notion of 'insight'. There may be some element of human personality which recognizes these values by intuition and then substantiates them by experience. This at least is the view of Griffiths. He vigorously argues that such insight is not mystical, but is phenomenal and communicable. 'The fact that judgement often proceeds by illumination like seeing faces in the fire,' he argues, 'does not mean that it requires mystical insight which is incommunicable. Once the faces in the fire are seen, one can get someone else to see them who would never have done so on his own' (14).

The Naturalistic Fallacy
Having assumed that one may legitimately determine what *is* good and true, there follows the difficulty of legitimately deriving moral

imperatives from such statements. This is usually termed the 'natural-istic fallacy'. It argues that no factual premises can entail evaluative conclusions. Then in turn this terminology leads to the descriptive phrase which refers to this problem as that of 'ontology and values'.

The philosophy of the last two centuries has been dominated by the related dogmas of Hume's naturalistic fallacy and Descartes' total separation of mind and extension. It is therefore, not un-expected to find that Teilhard's rejection of Cartesian dualism also opens the way to resolving the problem of ontology and values (15). Central to these arguments is Teilhard's law of complexity-conscious-ness. This implies that man is a unitary whole who in his totality is *both* mind *and* extension: who may be perceived in different dimen-sions; or conceived of in terms of the 'within' of consciousness and the 'without' of materiality. Values and imperatives exist in the 'within' of man's self-reflective nature. The 'without' of materiality knows nothing of them. As the epitome of complexity-consciousness man is therefore the confluence of both dimensions. Thus with man perceived as a unitary whole in terms of the physical, *and* the psy-chical, matter *and* consciousness, mind *and* extension, a within *and* a without, it is not entirely gratuitous to conclude that one may also discern both ontology *and* values in the one phenomenon. Thus although there may be no logical nexus between 'is' and 'ought' there is an inherent and necessary psychological relationship.

To Teilhard's arguments one may add those of Jaspers. He believes that moral imperatives spring spontaneously from our dual nature as 'authentic' and 'empirical' beings. All conditional imperatives have a sociological origin in corporate expedience, and even when enshrined in the most venerable laws are transient procedural rules, which may be manipulated: but 'The unconditional imperative', he writes, 'comes to me as the command of my authentic self to my mere empirical existence. I become aware of myself as of that which I myself am, because it is what I ought to be' (16).

For reasons of this kind one may argue that it is not fallacious to deduce moral imperatives from moral statements. Indeed children regularly do this almost without thinking. When anybody says 'It is wrong to do that', it is naturally assumed that the statement means, 'Don't do it'.

The Should–Would problem
Finally, one must turn to the problem of moral responsibility. May believes that moral education is adequate if it only provides children with the techniques for making moral decisions. This view he then consolidates by arguing that it is not the duty of a moral educator to ensure that such convictions achieve behavioural expression.

Hirst provides an educational reaction to refute such a view of moral education. Even when speaking of education as the pursuit of knowledge he argues that 'What is being sought is, first, sufficient immersion in the concepts, logic and criteria of the discipline for a person to come to know the distinctive way in which it "works" by *pursuing these in particular cases*', and so continues 'Nor is it to imply that understanding in moral issues can be had *without participation* in practical pursuits' (17). What after all is the value of moral knowledge if one does not implement it?

This, at least, is the view of Scheffler who delicately ridicules the gentility of educational practices which only affect cognitive activity and not human values and behaviour. For him both educational and linguistic criteria impose this view, but he goes further. Commitment to moral values implies not only the practice of morality but the possession of moral convictions. His extended and complex argument can be compressed into one assertion. 'To learn that one should be honest', he argues, 'is to come to believe that one ought to (be honest). To teach someone that one ought to be honest thus involves not merely teaching him *to be* honest, but also trying to have him acquire the belief that one ought to be honest' (18). Thus moral education has two corollaries. First, that moral conduct follows as a consequence and, second, that this conduct springs from moral convictions.

This, curiously, can also find sociological support. In a recent publication Scott has presented a highly sophisticated thesis which does just that. Reduced to its essentials his argument is as follows. Moral learning and moral commitment must proceed together. If they do not, then the process of socialization is placed in jeopardy. It could be argued that one has here a more refined, socially orientated form of the utilitarian approach to morality: but Scott has seen clearly that socialization is not only contingent upon personal commitment to the *mores* of a given society; but that it also proceeds by the internalization of these norms.

However, some may argue that this is a bogus problem since it is merely a disguised discussion concerning human motivation. Hence, they may continue, it is not a human concern which is limited to the sphere of morality, but once this vantage point is adopted one seems to be on secure ground.

Psychologists and sociologists are gargantuan purveyors of motivational theories, but any collation of these will fall into a simple structure beginning with man's biological needs and ending with his highest aspirations. A tripartite analysis can simplify this. There appear to be three groups of such theories.

1. Need-reduction.
2. Stimulus-response.
3. Affective and cognitive dissonance.

The general theory that activity is determined by the 'need-reduction' of an individual has become well known through the work of Fleming. At the biological end of this spectrum the theories are vulnerable to many criticisms, even though much of our conduct can be explained in terms of physical appetites and needs. However, at the higher end they become much more respectable. Our need for love and consistency produces conduct which is approved by social consensus. Maslow's theory of a 'hierarchy of needs' meets most of the objections here for he both spans the whole band of needs and also asserts that many of these are unconscious.

The stimulus-response theory has been widely disseminated by Skinner; and the comments made earlier indicate much of the sterility of these theories for our understanding of man *qua* man. This view, that conduct results from a series of responses to a wide range of stimuli, has been refined by a number of psychologists. Some, like Hebb, emphasize the neural aspect. Others, like Mac-Kenzie, discuss the process whereby stimuli precipitate a need, which becomes a want, then an appetite, then a desire, then a wish and finally a will which issues in a behavioural drive towards action.

Theories concerned with dissonance have been given a recent boost by the surge of interest in attitude formation and change. Simply expressed, this theory argues that if there is an imbalance of any kind, our homeostatic physical and psychical systems will act in order to rectify it. This can range from the crudest affective levels to the highest forms of cognitive behaviour. Thus at the lower end one finds theories which argue that any environmental change will result in overt conduct, if it alters the affective state of the individual concerned. One sees this in any change of behaviour resulting either from the setting sun casting shadows on sun-bathers or the ending of a friendship between lovers. At its highest level it can affect spiritual and moral convictions. Thus a scientist, whose beliefs conflict with his scientific assumptions, will act to resolve the conflict.

Out of these theories Maslow's seems to be the most appropriate in an educational situation, for it implies not only that needs evolve with the individual but also that he strives towards the highest, and it is at this juncture that an important point must be made. Motivational theories are primarily concerned with explaining why children behave as they do. Important though this is, we are much more concerned with discovering *how* moral imperatives may result in actual behaviour.

Of course it can be argued that once a child knows the morally commendable course of action to take, he spontaneously follows it. Although contrary to all the research evidence (19) there are serious proponents of this view. Becker has shown how some eighteenth-century philosophers assumed that man was naturally moral and so could live 'the good life on earth instead of the beatific one after death' (20). Now Eibl-Eibesfeldt has revived this humanistic, idyllic naturalism. In a complex argument which rejects the current view that man is naturally aggressive, he says that we cannot act against our phylogenetic inheritance for this was built upon spontaneous love. Thus he concludes that we all respond 'to signals that release cherishing behaviour' (21).

Such a view ignores the blunt Pauline description of man as a creature who cannot refrain from indulging in prohibited activity, and finds difficulty in doing what he knows he ought to do. But this does lead to one way out of this *impasse*. Allport expresses the view that our behaviour results from the set of central determinants which, when integrated, form our personality. Thus whether the conduct is adaptive or expressive it results from the structure of our personality.

The work of Havighurst, Taba and Peck also make it clear that we normally behave in conformity with our personality, indeed they describe their work as a 'motivational theory of personality'. On this point Maslow is lyrical. Speaking of the 'self-actualizing' person he says, 'Such people love because they are loving persons, in the same way that they are kind and honest, as a strong man is strong without willing to be, as a rose emits perfume, as a cat is graceful, or a child is childish' (22).

Clearly the moral educator must therefore be involved in what can derisively be called 'personality engineering', but since such personality changes occur in all educative processes it is difficult to see why any objection should be raised to an educational procedure which makes this a conscious process designed for the highest good of society and its members.

However, one may be more precise than this. Human personality can be defined in terms of a number of motivational factors. Amongst these would be placed sentiments, motives, sanctions, beliefs, opinions, values, interests, traits, and attitudes; and each system of analysis has powerful, psychological advocates: but of these systems those which refer to traits and attitudes are the most valuable. Allport, for example, concludes that 'What a man is doing, or what he is trying to do, gives the fundamental testimony as to the nature of his traits' (23). Thus for him personality and conduct are a complex of traits.

This analysis can proceed still further. There are many who have concluded that attitudes, like their related traits, are the determinants of actual conduct. The evidence for this affirmation is provided elsewhere (24), but it does lead to an extremely important point. Both Cattell and Halloran have spoken of attitudes in similar terms. Cattell prefers to call them attitude-interests, but of these he remarks, 'these single attitudes are the individual bricks in the house of the total dynamic structure' (25). Halloran concludes that many social scientists 'have found it necessary to use the concept of moral attitude as the basic building block for social psychological theory' (26). Therefore attitude formation and change will presumably result in changed behaviour in the children concerned' (27). Indeed this sums up the central thesis of the present work. People behave as they do because they are the people they are! We have examined the ways in which a child's personality is moulded by society, home and school. It has been made abundantly clear that this personality then determines the degree to which a child *would* do what he knows he *should* do. Therefore both home and school must so foster the moral traits and attitudes of children that they are enabled to respond positively when they recognize such moral imperatives laid upon them.

Moral Ideas or Moral Action?

These three basic problems in moral education again highlight the fact that it has two aspects—the cognitive and the affective. Clearly any discussion concerned with value-validation constitutes the cognitive aspect. It is when one turns to consider the problem of deriving moral imperative from such evaluative data that the procedure, although requiring intellectual appraisal, also demands personal commitment. Thus one is concerned here with both cognitive and non-cognitive elements. Finally, any reference to the actualizing of moral decision leads plainly to the affective and conative area of a child's awareness.

To limit moral education to the first of these areas, or even only reluctantly allow it to enter the second, would result in an educational travesty. Morality, in company with music, art, poetry and religion, has a clearly defined cognitive element, but this does not exhaust its content for there are also the equally important non-cognitive areas.

This view has recently been highlighted, in an extreme form, by Jones. Distressed by the arid intellectualism of the average school curriculum he argued that non-cognitive elements are as equally essential. Thus for him both fantasy and feeling are necessary ingredients in a balanced educational diet. Jones may expose himself to those critics who would wish to insist that he overreacts to Bruner's emphasis on the cognitive processes in education, and does not therefore recognize that Bruner's work represents the most digested form of advanced research in this field, legitimately forming a stable base for any curriculum. However, it is difficult not to ultimately agree with Jones when he outlines his curricular principles. 'A credible psychology of instruction,' he argues, 'must at the very least be suggestive in respect to three types of students; those who are predisposed to lead with their thoughts; those who are predisposed to lead with their feelings, and those who are predisposed to lead with their fantasies' (28).

If this is true of education in general, then it is certainly true of moral education. It is not enough merely to *know* the good; one must be *committed* to it. One must not only *know*, one must also *feel* that a particular course of action is the right one to take, for education, of any kind, to be more than a system of instruction, one must make a total response with the whole personality. It must entail comprehension *and* commitment. If either is omitted, the process becomes an enervated caricature. Therefore, in its starkest form, one may simply say that moral education is only adequate if it both prepares children to reach their own moral decisions on the basis of valid criteria, and *also* enables them to implement such decisions.

This apparent preoccupation with ensuring that moral education results in actual moral conduct, and so does not merely produce ethically sophisticated delinquents, must not blind one to the fact that moral education must also contain a hard core of cognitive material. Here one may find a place for 'moral judgement'.

Two of the three problems discussed above highlight this element. Clearly any discussion of moral values will of necessity involve children in the exercise of moral judgement, but 'conscience' can also find a place, for any consideration which derives moral imperatives from value-statements will necessarily include the exercise of that inner, complex psychological element of personality called 'conscience'.

It is possibly the third basic moral problem which will prove to be the most difficult to overcome in practice, but the foregoing discussion may be of help there. If attitudes and traits are both constituent elements of our personality and also predisposing factors in our conduct, then moral educators will be involved in the formation and modification of their pupils' attitudes and traits.

It was argued earlier that the preconditions of morality are ultimately based on affective experiences, and the primary moral qualities upon cognitive processes, but it is equally possible to argue that both are traits or attitudes. Now having already abstracted 'conscience' and 'moral judgement' from the list our task is made easier. The preconditions of morality are immediately recognizable as moral qualities. Identity, self-acceptance, and the response to moral paradigms qualify as such. This analysis, of course, can be extended further and refined more fully. A child's identity is bound up with his roles, values, beliefs, opinions and relationships. Equally, the degree of self-acceptance is linked to his self-concept, his ideal-self and his self-image.

To this list one may now add the primary moral traits. These could be indexed, on trait analysis, in terms of personal gratification, and the degree to which a child treats people as people. His ability to formulate moral principles will also depend upon his personality traits, but this will be apparent when it comes to the application of these principles in actual conduct.

Thus one may now draw together the conclusions of both the present and the next chapter, where the attitudes and traits of personality are discussed. Here the discussion has included the view that a child's personality determines the nature of his conduct. Now since attitudes, in the technical sense, are merely more refined forms of traits, in that they refer to a narrower spectrum of referents, one may subsume traits under the category of attitudes and repeat the simple conclusion drawn above.

Moral education must have both a cognitive and a non-cognitive element. It must both impart the intellectual skills required to make valid moral judgements and also enable children actually to do what they know *ought* to be done. In such a situation it is logical to conclude that the 'should' of moral comprehension can become the 'would' of actual conduct. However, this requires the process of moral education to utilize those skills, which sociologists have discovered to be most effective in the process of attitude formation and change.

One final point needs to be emphasized. Reference has been made to the character modifications which may be required if pupils are to become morally mature. Hitherto such fundamental personality changes in a religious context have been described as 'conversions'. Those who have experienced this dramatic process, either in themselves or their acquaintances, both in its sudden or protracted form, can testify to the radical change of conduct which follows. Without demeaning the term may it not legitimately be concluded that we have hitherto been speaking of some such experience? If this is so, then adequate *moral education really requires a secular equivalent of conversion*. For at its lowest level both the religious and moral man accept the need for a radical change of life, in the pursuit of personal freedom.

Psychologists and sociologists have now laid bare many of the psychological mechanisms and social forces which influence this fundamental human experience. More recently, social psychologists have shown how attitudes (which it will be remembered are the 'basic buildings blocks of personality') can be both formed and modified. These psychologists, social psychologists and sociologists should now come to the aid of teachers so that the highest moral and social benefits of religious experience may be enjoyed by secular man.

Naturally, such a process must meet the charge that it is a subtle form of indoctrination. The arguments to show that indoctrination is characterized not by content or method but by the *aim* of the process, have been advanced elsewhere (29) and need not be repeated. If one may therefore take it that the *aim* is all important this charge can be met. How can the creation of autonomous agents, able to resist the blandishments of heteronomous authority, be called indoctrination? Furthermore such an aim has a built-in disclaimer of this charge. When a person is able to resist further heteronomous impositions upon his morality he is the kind of person such a process is intended to produce. Yet while he is unable to resist them he is equally the kind of person who needs the autonomy which results from maturity of character. Thus, logically, while the process is effective it is needed. When the process is complete the realization of the aim makes it redundant.

RELIGION AND MORALITY

One final problem remains to be considered, this concerns the relationship between religious education and moral education. Some say there is none, for each has different aims. Therefore they merely complement each other. The more sophisticated plead for a total severance, arguing that when a child's morality is supported by religious notions, it will collapse if religion is rejected in puberty. On the other hand, some say that many objectives of religious and moral education coincide for although religion and morality each make distinct contributions to human life, there is a large area of overlap. Even a brief perusal of modern religious education syllabuses makes this clear. Such a contention, they say, is supported by studies which reveal a correlation between religious and moral behaviour (30); by the persistence with which the two are constantly syncretized (31); and by the ease with which religious morality can be accommodated to the ethos of a secular society, without shedding any of its essentials. Such evidence proves little. In psychiatric circles there is a genuine, humorous statistic which shows that the national incidence of schizophrenia is correlated with the import and export of bananas. This, of course, only shows that the two are coincidental. The syncretic approach is equally invalid, for one can argue that even though religion may supply moral elements, it is a secondary source of this commodity.

One comes nearer to a solution by closely examining the essential nature of morality and religion. Leaving aside those ideological dogmas, which often masquerade as educational criteria, psychological and sociological investigations reveal a series of confluence points. Then by concentrating on Christianity and non-prescriptive morality, general observations can be made which are applicable to both. When this is done the immediate conclusion reached is that Christianity does not consist of subscription to an alleged divine law any more than morality consists of subscribing to a supposed ethical absolute. Neither consists of subscription to authoritarian dicta of any kind. Their essence lies in the affirmation that ultimate values (whose validation lies in the world of experience rather than speculation) are the only legitimate basis upon which to build our lives. Once this is recognized there follows a common commitment to these values, which is best described as an act of faith. Then, once committed, the truly religious or moral man feels under compulsion to express these convictions in his everyday life.

Since each demands commitment to such values, the adherents are then characterized not by a structured creed but by the generalized view that every aspect of life should be subordinated to the requirements of reason and compassion. How far one should stress the common sensitivity to what Smith calls 'life's mystery' cannot be known, but both recognize that life is pervaded by principles and values. Consequently the Christian lives by the application of perpetually valid moral principles to everyday life: and the moral atheist subscribes to a series of first-order principles which he applies situationally. Consequently both can then describe the ideal moral society as not only fraternal and familial but also based on political and economic justice. They may diverge when describing such a society. The atheist, for example, would employ a sociological as opposed to the theist's theological frame of reference. The former would speak of the brotherhood of man; the latter of the family of God—but they would both agree on essentials. It is these, rather than the thought-forms which contain them, which are of prime importance. However, if we view the problem from both psychological and sociological vantage points it is possible to be more specific and show that such convergence points exist.

The present volume has a sociological perspective. If to this one adds a psychological analysis (32) a clear picture emerges. Mature morality requires the establishment of moral preconditions, traits and attitudes. If we look at these in turn both the moral and religious content becomes self-evident.

The Preconditions of Morality
These, it will be remembered, are primarily the establishment of one's identity, the acceptance of our ambivalent nature, and the paradigmatic experiences which result from access to ideal figures. These clearly constitute three primary aims in religious education. Children are given a stable identity in the myth-form of God the father, they are thereby raised to the status of members of the human family. Consequently it is natural to observe that one keynote of Christianity is the theological affirmation that all are accepted by Christ in spite of their inadequacies. Finally, sociologists and philosophers have recently pointed to the overwhelming paradigmatic power of the person of Christ (33). He has now invaded pop-culture and is enjoying an unexpected popularity amongst most sub-cultures, through the medium of West End and New York musicals. For children the point is simple: they sing, 'For he is our childhood's pattern', and that is precisely the role of a paradigm in the process of identification.

Primary Moral Traits
In the above sociological analysis of higher- and lower-status morality, certain traits emerged as characteristic of moral maturity, these were moral judgement, deferred gratification, personalism, flexibility and dynamism. All are essential elements in moral growth. Again, each one can be disclosed as a contingent moral trait, the inculcation of which is one aim of religious education. Mature moral judgement is advocated in many forms in the New Testament but emerges most clearly in The Golden Rule (34), wherein Jesus argued that moral judgement should be based on equality and equity.

Deferred gratification too is built into the teaching of Christianity. Here it is advocated that present satisfactions should be deferred in order to attain a more lasting good. This can easily be derided as the irresponsible neglect of our present life, but in fact such is not the case. Both the teaching of the New Testament and the lives of its advocates show that this leads to a disciplined regimen in which no personal indulgence is allowed to interfere with the greater good of mankind.

Moral personalism is so central to Christian teaching that any reference is superfluous. It has for two millennia sustained and advocated a life-style in which people, their feelings, well-being and future welfare are all deemed to take precedence over every other consideration. The moral flexibility, inherent in Christian teaching has recently been made explicit by the new theology. It is now argued, for example, that the whole tenor of Christian ethical discourse resolves itself down to the proposition that legalism has been superseded by the enunciation of moral principles. Consequently the New Testament makes it clear that every Christian should seek to elucidate those principles which had hitherto been expressed through the medium of law.

Lastly the dynamism of this ideology is apparent in the teaching of Jesus. It is now generally accepted that when Jesus taught in parables and ended each by saying 'Go thou and do likewise', he was not, for example, advocating that we should pour oil and wine into the wounds of travellers, give all our money to the poor, or go out and look for a lost sheep. He was saying, 'In that parable I showed how the principle of love would operate under those particular circumstances. Now go away and apply these principles in your own lives.'

Primary Moral Attitudes

These have been defined as autonomy, rationality, altruism and responsibility. Like the other qualities enumerated above they are also central affirmations of Christian religious education (35). That Christ called men to exercise moral autonomy, is now clear. He rejected the view that we should subscribe blindly to the law, and insisted that His followers ought to accept moral and religious principles which they then applied, as free agents, without reference to any legal formulary.

That altruism is central to Christian teaching requires no explanation. Christianity is built upon the principle that love is a prime moral virtue. Nothing transcends it; and this transcendental form expresses the nature of ultimate reality, for 'God is love'. It is, therefore, incumbent upon all men to express this quality in their relationships.

However, Christians also believe that the cosmic principle of coherence and order, the *logos*, became incarnate in Christ. On this basis the early Christians stressed that the 'Faith' should be coherently comprehended and cogently expressed in comprehensive terms. They assumed that just as words indicated the nature and meaning of mind, so the *logos* (or word) was a revelation of ultimate reality. Furthermore, it was believed that the rational processes of the human mind also reflected this cosmic quality. As a consequence the natural theology of the medieval world resulted from the conviction that a coherent faith should be both accessible to, and comprehended by, rational processes. Finally, Christians accept the biblical view that each man is responsible for his neighbour's welfare, and that this obligation must issue in practical attempts to ensure the well-being of all men.

THE NEED FOR MORAL EDUCATION

Despite the many problems which attach themselves to any attempt to morally educate our children it is essential that schools should embark on this educational venture. We have seen that the new taxonomies provide it with an integrated place in emerging curricula, but these taxonomies could also become dysfunctional. By stressing the tremendous advances made in the sciences they can be mishandled in a gross and maladroit way. Because we live in a cyberculture it is mistakenly assumed that technical education must be intensified. This is true; but not entirely so. Contemporary technology has a built-in disclaimer of this fact.

Cybernetics will create more aesthetic and moral hunger, not less! When machines freed man from the tedium of physical labour, they liberated his mind, and cultures emerged which did not depend upon the degradation of a slave class. Today a comparable process has started. Computers, still only in their infancy, will ultimately free man from the drudgery of mental-calculation, data-storing, and decision making. Then, just as his mind was earlier liberated so now man's spirit could be freed. In this situation art, music, religion, morality and even hitherto unexplored powers of the human personality may flourish and enable us to become truly 'humanized'.

REFERENCES

1 See Archambault (1966), p. 122.
2 Whitfield (1971), pp. 18–19.
3 Hirst (1967), p. 76.
4 Bruner (1962).
5 Schools Council Integrated Studies (1972), p. 7. One should remember, however, that such integration can also take place within the pupils.
6 Mannheim (1954), p. 56.
7 Bruner (1972), Chapter 8.
8 Huxley (1964), p. 106.
9 Waddington (1970), p. 88.
10 I Corinthians 13:13.
11 Polanyi (1969), p. 79.
12 Hampshire (1959), p. 126.
13 Murdoch (1970), p. 97.
14 Griffiths (1958).
15 This idea is developed by Kay (1970, 1971).
16 Jaspers (1951), p. 55. cf. Freire (1970): 'Education is the process of becoming critically aware of one's reality in a manner which leads to effective action.'
17 Hirst (19666), pp. 132–3.
18 Scheffler (1966), pp. 93–4.
19 See Kay (1968), p. 187, *et al.* cf. Keniston (1970): 'Eveu the highest levels of moral reasoning do not alone guarantee truly virtuous behaviour'.

20 Becker (1958), p. 102.
21 Eibl-Eibesfeldt (1972), p. 137.
22 Maslow (1970), p. 198, but note his qualification that 'not *all* conduct reflects the character structure' (p. 56).
23 Allport (1959), p. 494.
24 See Kay (1968), Chapter 10. Kay (1969), pp. 33 ff.
25 Cattell (1965), p. 173.
26 Halloran (1967), p. 121.
27 There is, of course a less rigorous theoretical solution. Following the argument that schools, and moral educators, must allocate roles and encourage role playing, one can avoid this tedious and complex analysis. One has only to argue that if the allocated roles are so defined that not only the inherent benefits and privileges, but also the duties and responsibilities, are delineated and accepted, those playing these roles will be predisposed to do what they know they *ought* to do. This facile solution is currently applauded by some involved in the field of moral education, but it fails to distinguish between roles inherently connected with identity and those which are assumed at will. If the former is implied then 'personality engineering' is inevitable. If the latter, morality will become a psychological garment to be donned or shrugged off as circumstances demand.
28 See Jones (1972), Chapter 7, especially pp. 167 ff.
29 See Kay (1968), pp. 225 ff, and Snook (1972).
30 e.g. Wright and Cox (1971).
31 Hiroike (1966) has built a system of 'supreme morality' on a synthetic structure erected with the central teachings of the major world religions. This is the most potent moral force in contemporary Japan.
32 See Kay (1968) for an analysis of the primary moral attitudes.
33 Kay (1971).
34 The Golden Rule occurs in the Sermon on the Mount (*New English Bible*, Matthew 7:12), 'Always treat others as you would like them to treat you'.
35 This correlation appeared first in Kay (1969) and then in Wilson (1971).

Bibliography

ALLPORT, GORDON W., *Personality: A Psychological Interpretation* (Constable, 1959).
ALLPORT, GORDON W., *Pattern and Growth in Personality* (Holt, Rinehart & Winston, 1963).
ARCHAMBAULT, REGINALD D. (Ed.), *Philosophical Analysis and Education* (Routledge & Kegan Paul, 1966).
ARGYLE, MICHAEL, *The Scientific Study of Social Behaviour* (Methuen, 1959).
BEAUVOIR, SIMONE DE, *The Marquis de Sade* (Jahn Calder, 1963).
BECKER, CARL, *The Heavenly City of the Eighteenth-century Philosophers* (Oxford Univ. Press, 1958).
BLOOM, BENJAMIN S. (Ed.), *Taxonomy of Educational Objectives*: ACUE Handbook 1 'Cognitive Domain'; Handbook II 'Affective Domain' (Longmans, 1965).
BRUNER, JEROME S., *The Process of Education* (Harvard Univ. Press, 1962).
BRUNER, JEROME S., *Relevance of Education* (Allen & Unwin, 1972).
BULL, NORMAN, *Moral Education* (Routledge & Kegan Paul, 1969).
BULL, NORMAN, *The Way of Wisdom*: Book I 'Living With Others'; Book II 'Myself and Others' (Longmans, 1972).
CARSTAIRS, G. M., *This Island Now* (Hogarth Press, 1967).
CATTELL, RAYMOND B., *The Scientific Analysis of Personality* (Pelican, 1965).

DAVIES, T. I., *School Organizations: A New Synthesis* (Pergamon, 1969).

EIBL-EIBESFELDT, *Love and Hate* (Methuen, 1972).

FLEMING, CHARLOTTE M., *The Social Psychology of Education* (Routledge & Kegan Paul, 1961).

FLEMING, CHARLOTTE M., *Adolescence: Its Social Psychology* (Routledge & Kegan Paul, 1963).

FLETCHER, JOSEPH, *Situation Ethics* (Student Christian Movement, 1966).

FREIRE, P., 'The Adult Literacy Process as Cultural Action for Freedom', *Harvard Educational Review*, Vol. 40, No. 2, 1970.

GENET, JEAN, *The Thief's Journal* (Penguin, 1967).

GRIFFITHS, A. P., 'Justifying Moral Principles', in *Proceedings of the Aristotelean Society*, Vol. LVIII, 1957–8.

HALLORAN, J. D., *Attitude Formation and Change* (Leicester Univ. Press, 1967).

HAMPSHIRE, STUART N., *Thought and Action* (Chatto & Windus, 1959).

HAVIGHURST, R. J. and TABA, H., *Adolescent Character and Personality* (John Wiley, 1949).

HEBB, D. O., *The Organization of Behaviour* (Chapman & Hall, 1959).

HIROIKE, CHIKURO, *The Characteristics of Morality and Supreme Morality* (Institute of Moralogy, Japan, 1966).

HIRST, P. H., 'Liberal Education and the Nature of Knowledge', in R. D. Archambault (Ed.), *Philosophical Analyses and Education* (Routledge & Kegan Paul, 1966).

HIRST, P. H., 'The Curriculum', in *The Educational Implications of Social and Economic Change*, Schools Council Working Paper No. 12 (HMSO, 1967).

HUXLEY, JULIAN, *Essays of a Humanist* (Pelican, 1964).

JASPERS, K., *Way to Wisdom* (Gollancz, 1951).

JONES, RICHARD M., *Fantasy and Feeling in Education* (Penguin, 1972).

KAY, WILLIAM, *Moral Development* (Allen & Unwin, 1968).

KAY, WILLIAM, 'Compassionate Reasoning as the Basis of Morality', in *Lumen Vitae*, Vol. XXVI, No. 1, 1971a.

KAY, WILLIAM, 'Ontology and Values: I', in *Teilhard Review*, Vol. 5, No. 1, 1970.

KAY, WILLIAM, 'Ontology and Values: II', in *Teilhard Review*, Vol. 5, No. 2, 1971b.

KAY, WILLIAM, 'Religious Morality in a Secular Society', in *The Modern Churchman*, Vol. XVI, No. 2, 1973.

KENISTON, KENNETH, 'Student Activism, Moral Development and Morality', in *American Journal of Orthopsychiatry*, Vol. 40. No. 4, 1970.

LIFELINE—Generic term for 'Schools Council Moral Education Project' Curricula Material.

MACKENZIE, J. S., *A Manual of Ethics* (Univ. Tutorial Press, 1948).

MCPHAIL, PETER *et al.*, *Moral Education in the Secondary School* (Longmans, 1972).

MANNHEIM, KARL, *Diagnosis of Our Time* (Routledge & Kegan Paul, 1954).

MASLOW, ABRAHAM H., *Motivation and Personality* (Harper & Row, 1970).

MAY, PHILIP, *Moral Education in the School* (Methuen Educ., 1971).

MURDOCH, IRIS, *The Sovereignty of Good* (Routledge & Kegan Paul, 1970).

PECK, R. F. and HAVIGHURST, R. J., *The Psychology of Character Development* (John Wiley, New York, 1964).

PHENIX, PHILIP H., *The Realms of Meaning* (McGraw-Hill, 1964).

POLANYI, MICHAEL, *Personal Knowledge* (Routledge & Kegan Paul, 1958).

POLANYI, MICHAEL, *Knowing and Being* (Routledge & Kegan Paul, 1969).

SCHEFFLER, ISRAEL, *The Language of Education* (Chas. C. Thomas, 1966).

SCHOOLS COUNCIL INTEGRATED STUDIES, *Exploration Man* (Oxford Univ. Press, 1972).

SCOTT, JOHN G., *Internalization of Norms* (Prentice-Hall, 1972).

SKINNER, B. F., *Beyond Dignity and Freedom* (Cape, 1972).

SKINNER, B. F., *Science and Human Behaviour* (Free Press, 1953).

SMITH, J. W. D., *Religious Education in a Secular Setting* (Student Christian Movement), 1969).

SNOOK, I. A., *Indoctrination and Education* (Routledge & Kegan Paul, 1972).

TEILHARD, PIERRE DE CHARDIN, *The Phenomenon of Man* (Collins, 1960).

WADDINGTON, C. H., *Principles of Embryology* (Allen & Unwin, 1956).

WADDINGTON, C. H., 'The Need for Biological Ways of Thought', in *New Society*, 15 January 1970.

WHITFIELD, R. C. (Ed.), *Disciplines of the Curriculum* (McGraw-Hill, 1971).

WILSON, J. B., *Education in Religion and the Emotions* (Heinemann, 1971).

WRIGHT, D. and COX, E., 'Changes in Moral Belief in Relation to Religious Belief', in *British Journal of Social and Clinical Psychology*, Vol. 10, Pt. 4, November 1971.

YOUNG, J. Z., *Doubt and Certainty in Science* (Oxford Univ. Press, 1960).

YOUNG, J. Z., *An Introduction to the Study of Man* (Clarendon, 1971).

Part Three

Conclusion

Chapter 19

The Task of Moral Education

The foregoing empirically validated affirmations, concerning the influence of family and society and school on the moral education of children, lead to clear educational imperatives. If to this analysis one adds the evidence adduced in my psychological review of moral education (1) a comprehensive programme emerges which, on the basis of educational criteria, appears to constitute some fundamental elements in any formal programme of moral education. Our task, it seems, is to confirm and inculcate:

1. The preconditions of morality.
2. The primary moral traits.
3. The primary moral attitudes.

At first glance it seems that this could be merely a more sophisticated version of the rigid, authoritarian schemes which have posed as moral education in the past, but this is not so. That view of the morally educated man as obedient, conformist and rule-bound is clearly inappropriate in contemporary society where most moral questions are currently open-ended. Today we need to develop breadth of understanding, moral insight and autonomy. Only children who are thus equipped can be considered morally educated, for not only will they be able to formulate and implement moral decisions, but will do so by the application of those principles which are publicly held to be valid. Thus the prohibitive elements will be replaced by positive principles; and legal impositions will be ousted by autonomous decisions. Furthermore, such children will have a viable morality which will not be enervated by the perpetually shifting moral standards, and constantly modified *mores*, characteristic of a mobile, secularized, pluralistic society.

THE PRECONDITIONS OF MORALITY

It was seen above (see Chapter 3) that the preconditions of morality include the establishment of a sense of identity, the ability to accept oneself, the experience of identification, the development of informed conscience, and the sustained experience of personal achievement;

all of which are facilitated by the experiences of a loving home and a familial school.

Identity

The educational task of confirming a child's identity is both imperative and complex, but it cannot be avoided. The imperative arises because this assumption seems to imply that children should be allowed to indulge in personal individualism and anarchy. Peters expunges this view by observing that 'It is not enough to say that children should learn to be themselves at school; we must give them the equipment to find out properly what sort of selves they want to be' (2). This task is also complex, for as Wall argues, personal maturity is reached 'by the construction of four selves; social, sexual, vocational and philosophic' (3).

The practical need for this is obvious. Children must be enabled to so establish their ego-identity that they can live on terms of parity in the adult world for which they are destined. The full psychological analysis of this process has been mapped by Gergen, who then proceeded to disclose how crucial this is to our understanding of interpersonal behaviour. However, the sociological element must also be emphasized.

This awesome mystery of reflective self-consciousness has been the subject of innumerable learned tomes with Mead as perhaps the clearest exponent of this theme. He argued, 'The self, as that which can be an object to itself, is essentially a social structure and it arises in social experience' (4). This social reflection of the opinions, views, attitudes, traits and conduct of others is thus reflected in children and helps them to construct their identity. For this reason Cooley speaks of 'the looking-glass self', even though, for him constructive social interaction is needed to sustain this self.

Just as anarchic individualism is avoided by this process, so also is excessive conformism. Decades ago Durkheim made it clear that children find their identity in devotion to the group. These two aspects, of course, exactly complement each other. The group bestows identity and the self responds with attachment. In fact it is in this interaction that true identity and individuality is found. As Teilhard said 'Union differentiates' (5). We are only truly ourselves when united with others.

Clearly this is important. Since identity was first established in the familial society, so it must be nurtured in the school society. This therefore is one crucial task for every teacher.

Self-acceptance

The fact that children should also have their identity and self-respect enhanced by acceptance needs little elaboration. The sociological orientation of this notion is equally clear. Until others accept them, children find it difficult to accept themselves. Thus, in one sense a good school is a society in which a child can be bad but still accepted. This naturally affects a child's conduct. Dittes and Kelley, for example, found that the highest adherence to group norms was found amongst students who felt that they had been accepted for their own sake; as persons in their own right. Again, it must be emphasized that this does not indicate blind conformity. It reveals sensitive personal reciprocity. Being treated as persons they accord the same privilege to others.

The educational problem here is that of distinguishing between self-acceptance and self-complacency. This is a knotty problem, leading into the complex by-ways of incipient psychoses. But one clear point can be made. A simple distinction between the two seems to lie at the point where one distinguishes between accepting a child's limitations but condemning his failure to use his potential. Evangelicals speak of this when they say that we ought to hate the sin but love the sinner. This seems to clarify the point further. While rejecting all that is inimical to personal growth and maturation we can still accept the child, and thus enable him to do the same.

Paradigmatic Experiences
The presentation of paradigms (as individuals or groups) is the next educational necessity. Paradigmatic influences are now an undisputed element in any sociological consideration of conduct. As we have seen, these are provided first by the family: but even here the matter is more complex than would at first sight appear to be the case. Clearly parents are the first paradigms, but apparently siblings can also function in this role. Peck and Havighurst discovered this in Prairie City over a decade ago, but more recently Leventhal has developed this view on the basis of specific research. He found for example, that boys with older sisters are subject to their paradigmatic influence and so become more feminine in their traits and attitudes than boys with an older brother. They later modify their conduct, when the normal masculine process of identification takes over, but before that, the older sister is the dominant force.

Social class difference also emerge here. Cass, for instance, found that lower-status children have less positive attitudes to authority figures. Consequently their paradigms can be deviant and the resultant conduct socially aberrant. The one point which her superb survey does not develop is the apparent ambivalence of higher-status children to paradigms. They also admire socially deviant characters. Even in adult life one has only to note the popularity of highly aggressive, unfair, ill-tempered wrestlers, amongst the middle-class male viewers, to realize that there is some truth in this. Perhaps one ought therefore to distinguish between two forms of paradigm. There is, first, the fantasy figure whose escapades children admire, but whose values they reject. Then, second, the paradigms, who, by the process of identification, mould a child's self-concept (6).

Finally, it should be remembered that identification can be related to reference groups. Fenchel *et al.* for example, found a rigid hierarchy in the importance of student reference groups, and disclosed that here too conduct is determined by the norms of the dominant reference groups of each individual.

Again the educational implications are clear. Every possible means should be used to ensure that all children have access to paradigmatic figures. Consequently peer groupings should be such that adherence to them, as reference groups, results in socially creative conduct.

Conscience

Before passing on to consider the experience of success as an essential precondition of morality, brief reference must be made to the development of conscience. This was dealt with at length earlier in the present volume. Further consideration is out of place in a sociological study. All that one needs to add here is that many educators would agree with Berridge when she affirms that the most vital concern of schools should be 'The formation of a mature personal conscience' (7) Though how precisely one sets about this is not at all clear.

Success and Achievement

The need to achieve and experience success is not confined to the adult world. Children too need this positive reinforcement of their efforts. This not only endorses the saying that 'nothing succeeds like success', but also emphasizes the autonomous nature of the process. Both points have been empirically confirmed. Attiyeh and Lumsden found that educational success bred further achievement; and McClelland confirmed that self-reliance was an essential trait of the individual who fitted into an achieving society. At this point the developmental psychologist could enter the discussion. He would argue that maturation is only possible if each developmental stage is so successfully negotiated that it leads on to the next. Thus the sequential model of growth implies the necessity of achievement at each level and in each phase.

The educational implications of this are also obvious. Children should be given a chance to succeed in every area of their lives. Teachers alerted to this can then modify their demands, for, as Berrien has shown, achievement and satisfaction go hand in hand. One cannot rely simply on cognitive dissonance to alter a child's attitude to tasks he must accomplish under compulsion. Like Goldthorpe's affluent workers, he must have both a satisfactory view, and experience of, his work otherwise his self-respect is affected and subsequent underachievement follows.

It must be remembered too that failure to achieve success in school leads inevitably to a search for it elsewhere. This appears to be one function of adolescent gangs, with their stereotyped dress and *mores*. Sugarman speaks of this structure as the teenage role in contrast to the traditional pupil role. Hypothesizing that the former rejects school values, he tested for school achievement and found that 'underachievement tends to be associated with high commitment to the teenage role and low commitment to the pupil role' (8). This, as we shall see below, is extremely important. If the home and school do not establish these preconditions, then a delinquent gang subculture may do so.

This reference to school achievement is also important since it highlights a further point. Children can achieve either as persons or as scholars. Fortunately for the practitioner of moral education McDavid made a very important discovery here. Having confirmed that children may be divided into those who are approval orientated and those who are achievement orientated he showed that the former responded to teachers as persons while the latter directed their attention to the lesson content. This is the crucial point. For the purposes of moral development, approval is much more potent than achievement. Such approval orientated children were more conscious of others as persons and so responded within a complex of personal relationships which would sustain the approval which mattered so much to them. Again this does not mean that they were uncritical conformers. They were merely much more sensitive to people and relationships.

A SECOND CHANCE

Thus every infant school teacher facing her class must ensure that she is aware of the degree to which these preconditions of morality have been established in every child. She must furthermore make every effort to establish and confirm them in her pupils. This primary aim of moral education must be sustained throughout a child's social life.

Infant Experience
This clearly runs counter to the Freudian view that schools can do little by way of character development since all the crucial, formative experiences took place during the pre-school years (9). The most

thoroughgoing critic of this view is Allport. In a restrained but devastating demolition of this view he observes that 'Freud taught that the guidelines of a person's character are established by the age of three'. He then conflates the evidence which must lead one to conclude that the notion of a latency period is indeed 'a curious myth' (10) since children are far from latent between the age of six and thirteen years.

The Importance of Adolescence

This point, that growth is a sustained process, is taken up in the Plowden Report and developed further. There it is argued that while recognizing the importance of learning in infancy 'It would be surprising if at later ages limited periods at least of *maximum receptivity* did not occur for many skills and emotional developments' (11). Clearly this does not preclude the emergence of many 'growth spurts'; but since Roe found that the 'main personality characteristics are considerably stable by the age of sixteen years' (12) one is led to ask if there is a later period of maximum receptivity or malleability, which corresponds to infancy.

Considerable evidence points to the fact that there is. Most of this revolves around the central concept of identity, but all of it points to the fact that the personality of a child is most plastic when on the thresholds of both childhood and adulthood. The first prepares him for existence; the second prepares him for life. According to Anna Freud the balance between the id and the ego, established in infancy, is upset by sexual maturation. Thus in adolescence identity-instability emerges again. It is thus at this stage that children seek afresh for their identity and are thus in a period of maximum plasticity. It is for this reason that the welter of evidence accumulated by Nisbet and Entwistle is collated in a chapter entitled 'The New Birth'. Here they conflate much of the evidence available to confirm this view that children have a second chance to develop their personalities; and careful reading of this meticulously documented chapter makes it perfectly clear that it is a stage during which young adolescents can acquire the preconditions of morality as they develop their new identity.

Whether children actually realize the profound experience through which they are passing can never be known. Many are conscious of the fundamental changes taking place, but perhaps confuse them with physiological elements and so ignore the crisis. Or again it may be a simple defence mechanism which operates. Many of us are unaware of the significance of many crises until they have passed simply because if this awareness accompanied the intensity of these experiences, they might well become unbearable.

Two Critical Phases

All the evidence adduced above on the subject of identity need not be repeated here. Appeal can be made to perhaps the most cogent protagonist of this theme. Erikson has argued that there are eight stages of development, each characterized by a polarization of psychological traits. In adolescence, he argues, the primary task is to establish identity in the face of the role compulsion imposed by society and it is this which can diffuse a child's sense of identity.

He too believes that the growth spurt of adolescence is marked by genital maturity and can thus be equated with that of infancy. However, he sums up his position succinctly. 'In their search for a new sense of continuity and sameness, adolescents have to refight many of the battles of earlier years; and they are ever ready to install lasting idols and ideals as guardians of a final identity' (13). This does not detract from his conviction that infancy is a critical period in the development of identity. It merely emphasizes that there are two such critical phases.

It should be noted that all the essential elements are here. Identity is established; there is continuity with the self which had been accepted; and paradigmatic figures dominate. Here then is the second chance to establish the preconditions of morality. It is thus not surprising to find that this is also the phase during which conversions are most likely to occur. They may be to a religion, an ideology or simply a life-style, but the plasticity of the personality enables it to be moulded during this phase (14). This theme could be endlessly permutated. Prior to the resolution of this problem of identity, there are phases of self-estrangement, self-doubt, self-loathing, a feeling of inadequacy and a general sense of personal disintegration. Such considerations, however, belong properly to a discussion on the psychology of conversion and the current malaise of alienation. However, this does highlight the fact that any offer of identity, acceptance and moral paradigms can be assured of a massive response from young adolescents.

DELINQUENT SUBSTITUTES

The McCords discovered an obvious fact when their investigations revealed that parental rejection or deviance led children into criminality because they were compelled to establish their identity and achieve some success in an aberrant way, for example, by flouting authority. Thus if schools also fail to meet this need they are priming their pupils for delinquent conduct in sub-cultures which may satisfy these needs.

Delinquent Gangs

Cohen and Bennett have both reported that such satisfaction was found in the delinquent gang culture. Here, as Whyte had earlier shown, the gang made good this fundamental personal deficiency. The members were given an instant identity, confirmed by outward symbols ranging from stereotyped life-styles to standard modes of dress. The gang accepted such adolescents *just as they were*. Pop and underground sub-cultures provided readily accessible paradigms. Group norms were rigid and, although destructive and deviant, vandalist achievements and anti-social success are assured. Thus the candidate for gang memberships is, as Yablonsky found, quite literally a displaced person seeking social integration and personal assurance (15).

Violent Gangs

Although Yablonsky was prompted to write as a result of a brutal, lethal gang action he still pleads for the violent gang to be considered *sui generis* and argues that the gangs described by Whyte 'bear little resemblance to the violent gang of today' (16). However, it is difficult to accept his point. Nineteenth-century gangs were notorious for their criminal violence. At the turn of the century Hall, writing of London gangs, noted that 'amongst them murder was not infrequent'. Therefore, for our purposes the parallel is legitimate. In his report on the violent gang, Yablonsky reports on the Synanon Society, which attempts to rehabilitate such gang members within a non-delinquent sub-culture. Here the evidence supports our case. It describes in details how the therapy hinges upon establishing those moral preconditions which have been outlined above (17).

Social-class Differences

One other interesting series of conclusions also support the view that children deprived in this way are eager candidates for delinquent gang cultures. Miller noted that such gangs emerged in lower-status situations and thus confirmed Talcott Parsons' view that mother dominated working-class boys, deprived of the male paradigm, sought a substitute-father in the gang as 'a defence against feminine identification' (18). Then Bryant and his colleagues went further and showed that such delinquent members treated the gang as a family surrogate. Finally this primary function of the gang is confirmed by all the research reports which affirm that gang membership is a phase which significantly ends with courtship. Naturally the dominant gang members attempt to keep the group together, since it provides them with status and security. However, as Cloward and Ohlin have observed, such gangs inevitably break up when the members move towards another familial structure; one in which they believe that those elusive personal qualities will be found.

The task of the School

It is clear then that schools have this imperative task laid upon them. Where the homes fail, the schools must attempt to succeed. At the moment these two crucial periods appear to coincide with entry into the primary school and the early years of the secondary school. The Freudian counsel of despair must not be allowed to prevail. Schools must face this task and they must succeed. The alternative is, as we have seen, inevitable delinquency amongst the already deprived members of the community.

Nor must the schools forget that the constant habilitation of these moral preconditions, constitutes a life-long task. We must therefore not only meet these needs while the pupils are in our schools. We must also send them out equipped to continue their moral growth.

THE PRIMARY MORAL TRAITS

The above survey was extended in order to clarify the position since this element in moral education would apparently be most effectively disseminated through a pervasive familial school influence. One can see why this should be so. All the elements are primarily affective and interpersonal. Indeed one might go further and argue that they are merely an explication of the effects of genuine love. When turning to these primary moral traits, however, it can be seen that they could be aligned with the cognitive lives of children and could therefore lend themselves to some formal consideration within a school curriculum. These qualities, it will be remembered, were moral judgement, personal gratification, moral personalism, moral flexibility and moral dynamism.

Social-class Differences

The evidence used to support the presentation of these moral traits made it clear that they were positively correlated to social class. A review of the current process of embourgeoisement then gave some cause for hope, but it is clear that schools must augment the deficiencies of many homes in this respect. This is not to say that the bourgeoisie are inherently more moral than the plebeian element in any given population. It is merely an emphasizing of the stark fact that one segment of our population is deprived, and that this deprivation has deleterious effects on the development of personal morality.

Moral judgement

Thus the schools must attempt, by every means possible, to ensure that the moral judgement of children is encouraged to mature. They must develop that self-discipline which does not leave an individual child so much at the mercy of his whims and impulses that he perpetually seeks present gratification. They must insist on lessons which will ensure that the erosive materialism of society is countered by a value-system which places pre-eminent worth on people *qua* persons. There must be perpetual opportunities to comprehend that behind regulations lie accessible and reasonable principles. Finally, by whatever means possible, children should be enabled to implement their moral decisions so that the course of action which they know they *should* take is in fact the one which they would take.

Moral Dynamism and Flexibility

All of this, of course, must be done within the maturational limits of a child's development and thus the principle of 'readiness for morality' should be observed (19). But there are two other points which must be made here. Moral education is inadequate if it develops flexibility but no dynamism. That is, children must not only be helped to know what to do, but also enabled to actually do it. May disagrees with me on this point. He insists that 'Many would argue that to achieve the first of these is to have achieved success in moral education' (20). This may be true in religious education where it would be illegitimate to attempt to inculcate religious behaviour, but in my view the two activities are distinct.

Personality Changes

The second point is a development of this. If it is conceded that moral education must affect a child's actual conduct, then some means must be found of ensuring that it does. In arguing earlier (21) that the attitudinal model of morality helped here, it was assumed that our actions are consonant with our personalities, and these in turn may be defined in terms of attitudes. Hence moral education must of necessity be involved in a conscious and deliberate policy of attitude formation and change. This happens haphazardly anyway, so why not structure the process? Cox has rightly described this as 'a kind of personality engineering' (22). It is true that the term is emotive in that it implies that such a moral educator treats his pupils as an engineer treats his machines, but this is the case. In attempting to inculcate these primary moral qualities the teacher cannot avoid modifying his pupils' personalities. This is true of every learning situation. It would be naïve to assume that children's personalities are unaffected by the educational process, and when this is orientated specifically towards morality it is difficult to see how one can avoid this. Indeed it would follow from the foregoing argument that we ought to so mould children's personalities that they find it easier *actually* to do what they know they *ought* to do.

The Duty of the Schools

Finally, as the chapter on moral embourgeoisement made clear, this volume is not intended to be a broadside against those who despise the middle classes as decadent and undeservedly privileged. It is simply intended to show that when home and society are inadequate in these respects, the schools must take over their functions. In this process, the educational aim should be the universalizing of all the emotional and economic advantages enjoyed by middle-class children.

Nor is this intended to imply that the bourgeoisie are the epitome of all moral virtue. The evidence simply suggests that such children have a greater opportunity to maximize on our educational system and so become more morally mature in precisely the same way as they have similar opportunities to become more literate, numerate and socially upwardly mobile. Therefore, this function of the school goes beyond the bounds of education alone and becomes a potent factor in what optimists describe as our cultural evolution.

THE PRIMARY MORAL ATTITUDES

Before continuing to outline the general task of schools involved in moral education, it is appropriate, at this point, to make a simple observation. Establishing the preconditions of morality appears to resolve itself down to the proposition that children need emotional security. Equally, the primary moral traits appear to be amenable to the dictates of rational thought. In a sentence the former may depend upon love; the latter can develop through the application of reason.

This observation is important since such a juxtaposing of altruism and rationality appears to be a necessary corollary to any consideration of the primary moral attitudes. These, it will be remembered, are:

1. Moral autonomy.
2. Moral rationality.
3. Moral altruism.
4. Moral responsibility.

I have already argued that moral maturity is indexed by the degree to which a child is autonomous, rational, altruistic and responsible;

that it consists of the *co-existence* of these attitudes in a developed form, and that democratic processes may best inculcate them. Furthermore, these may be treated as attitudes for complex, technical reasons; but the simple educational implication is clear. Attitudes determine the quality of a child's conduct. Consequently, if these primary moral attitudes can be inculcated then there is a greater likelihood of moral education resulting in moral conduct. Clearly the explication of these attitudes could be indefinitely extended. For convenience we may present them (in the context of this book) in the following terms.

Moral autonomy

Autonomy is the attitude of a person whose identity is so secure that he can rely on the validity of his moral judgement, concerning a moral dilemma, and reach a conclusion independently of hetero-nomous guides. Yet he must also feel free to seek advice and weigh its merits, without considering himself to be under any compulsion emanating from the authority of his mentor.

Moral rationality

Rationality clearly refers to the willingness to discuss reasonably the moral obligations of interpersonal interactions, but we have seen that it involves more than this. It implies also that quality of moral flexibility which will enable a child to abstract moral principles from a welter of authoritarian dicta, but its essence seems to be in the development of personal autonomy. It marks the degree to which a child will not merely *act* independently, but will also *think* independently.

Moral altruism

Altruism is also a development of this progression. It reveals a concern for people, rather than objects, and places their needs on an equality with one's own. It does more. It adds a new dimension to moral thought since this activity is modified by concern for people. A purely rational and valid conclusion need not be implemented because it may have an adverse effect on the persons involved. Thus it marks the degree of moral personalism in a child, and is indexed by the degree to which other people are considered as ends in themselves.

Moral responsibility

Responsibility is a difficult attitude to define. On the negative side it obviously implies the willingness to accept culpability for one's actions. Positively expressed it must imply the sense of obligation which a moral decision imposes upon an individual. In the terminology of the present thesis, it implies a developed form of moral dynamism. Thus a person who had reached a moral decision on the basis of rationality and altruism ought then to implement the decision by acting upon it. Furthermore, such a situation also requires the exercise of deferred gratification since an individual's personal needs may have to be deferred in order to expedite the moral decision made.

The Self-actualizing Man

For any who might wish to pursue this exercise in conceptual clarification a little further, it is interesting to compare the four primary attitudes outlined above with the moral components presented by Wilson (23) and the facets of morality as described by Wright. Then it will be seen that a conflation appears to take place with no artificial straining of the concepts (see table 4).

Table 4. *Four primary moral attitudes compared with those described by Wilson and Wright*

Kay	Wilson	Wright
Autonomy	Autemp	Moral belief
Rationality	Dik, Gig, Phron	Moral insight
Altruism	Phil, Emp	Altruism
Responsibility	Krat	Resistance to temptation

As is apparent, from table 4 the key concept is creative autonomy. This in turn can lead to the notion of mental health. The work of Laing has now made it axiomatic, in psychoanalytical circles, that the schizoid personality, although considered sane (24) is still vulnerable because it has an insecure grasp of its own autonomy. Maslow has revealed how the autonomous man is essentially creative. He describes this man as 'self-actualizing'. His evidence reveals that such a person is not only mentally healthy but also actively creative and that 'this special type of creativeness is projected out upon the world or touches whatever activity the person is engaged in' (25). Clearly we have here supportive evidence for the argument that moral creativity is an element in mature morality.

Such a series of definitions suffers from all the limitations of brevity; but it ought to be noted finally that they make reference to all the primary moral qualities which have already been outlined above.

RATIONAL-ALTRUISM

The above reference to rationality and altruism in morality may now be developed further. It is axiomatic that a morally mature child must be autonomous since nobody can be either praise or blameworthy when acting under compulsion. Equally the morally mature person must at least intend to implement his moral decisions. The moral irresponsibility which does not consider this to be a necessary element of morality, disqualifies any claim to such maturity. It is here, between autonomy and responsibility that one enters a fascinating area of human activity. Hitherto, this has been referred to as 'compassionate reasoning' and I have elsewhere argued that this is a viable basis for mature morality (26), but now the analysis must be made more rigorous.

The Conflict between Reason and Love

At the moment one finds an apparent conflict in discussions on morality. On one side stand Wilson and Peters emphasizing that reason is the prime factor in morality. On this point the former is quite explicit. 'The most important point to be made', he argues, 'is that the appropriate attitude to morality is a *rational* one.' Peters states that 'Our moral life can be more or less rationally, intelligently and spontaneously conducted' (27). Yet on the other hand one finds Fletcher and Winnicott taking a diametrically opposed view in their consideration of ethics. The former argues that 'only one thing is intrinsically good; namely love; nothing else at all' (28).

The Reconciliation of Reason and Love

At first these positions appear to be irreconcilable. They are based on opposed views of man and cultural evolution. The protagonists of reason treat man as an essentially cerebral creature and trace his civilized growth from Athens, through the Age of Reason to the present cyberculture in which logic reigns supreme. Those who argue for the primacy of love tend to look upon man as a visceral creature and see all his cultural triumphs as a corollary of this fact. They argue that all human experience has its noumenal qualities, and culture advances when artists and innovators encapsulate and preserve these for the rest of mankind.

Such debunkers of reason are never short of supportive evidence. In a recent study of cigarette smoking Mausner and Platt observed that the millions who find valid 'reasons' for continuing this lethal practice are a proof of the inadequacy of Mills' picture of rational man. Teachers too can support this reaction against reason. Many would agree with the case-study of a child in whom intellectual activity appeared to be an impediment. Thus North observed 'He needs help in self-mastery other than through his intellect' (29). Thus the argument could continue with the ordinary man observing that all life's really important decisions are ultimately visceral in form; while the literati content themselves with expounding the D. H. Lawrence view that all valid arguments and motives originated in the solar plexus.

This is a false dichotomy. Not only does Wilson commit himself to the view that reason, in the matter of morals, includes consideration for feelings of others, but Fletcher dilutes his apparently uncomprising position by devoting a chapter to arguing that love should be reasonable and just. Both, therefore, appear to be converging upon common ground. Their difference is thus a matter of emphasis, and points forward to a profound and important development in our understanding of morality. One may develop this theme and argue that an entirely new moral attitude, or concept, can be distilled from this apparent conflict.

This we shall call rational-altruism. It is more than reason tinged with love; and more than love circumscribed by reason. It is a new quality in human experience, which may now be amalgamating in mankind and distilling a new quality which will be as essential for moral life as is water (a compound of hydrogen and oxygen) for physical survival.

Rational-altruism

To the evidence of Wilson and Fletcher one can add that already distilled from a consideration of the preconditions and primary qualities of morality where it was suggested that the preconditions of morality are established by the experience of love, and the primary traits of morality are amenable to reasoned discourse. Further confirmation may be adduced from the work of Norman and Sheila Williams. Basing their conclusions on the verbal responses of nearly 800 children, to moral-dilemma situations, they classified the answers within an orthogonal lattice structure. (This consists of dimensions placed at right angles to each other. Related responses are then located within the four frames.) Here each dimension constituted a continuum. The first ranged from self to other. The second from considering to obeying. Hence all the moral responses fell into the four following groups:

1. Self-considering.
2. Self-obeying.
3. Other-obeying.
4. Other-considering.

Considering the evidence with care it seems legitimate to conclude that the dimension which runs from self-considering to other-considering is really a measure of altruism. At its maximum it places the emphasis on concern for others. At its minimum it leads to egocentricity. Equally the dimension which begins with self-obeying and ends with careful considering could be thought of in terms of rationality. At its minimum this results in unquestioning obedience. When fully developed it leads to a rational consideration of the data provided with no reference to authoritarian dictates (see figure 6).

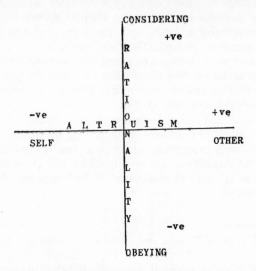

Figure 6. A model of complex orthogonal analysis

On this model it seems clear that the proposed orthogonal analysis of Mr and Mrs Williams is a further breakdown of this complex quality of rational-altruism.

Another research conclusion can now be inserted to advance the argument at this point. Those familiar with the publications emanating from The Committee on Human Development at the University of Chicago will have read the reports associated with the name of Havighurst. The most recent refers to the morally mature personality as rationally altruistic. If anything the authors emphasize the primacy of love and so disclose the fact that they are still thinking of separate entities. For them, however, it is still that disciplined, rational love which they agree 'is advocated by Christianity, as well as by other religions' (30).

One final element of parallel evidence can be fitted in here to clinch the argument. In outlining his maturational structure of human personality Freud had emphasized that there were two fundamental qualities around which the notion of maturity hinged. These he believed to be the ability to love and the capacity to apply one's mind to problem-solving in the course of daily work. Fromm much later took these over and applied them to man in contemporary society. As a result he concluded that Freud's scheme lent itself to a moral typology. His conclusions, based on clinical work, were then pellucidly clear. When autonomous man existed for himself, he said, the main attributes of his personality were the ability to love and the facility to reason. In fact the morally mature man was a compassionate, reasoning creature.

Thus one is led to an unavoidable conclusion. It is possible that an inchoate moral quality is about to emerge. Such a statement must be taken in the context of cultural evolution. Albright has recently drawn our attention to the fact that the passing of the pre-logical age and the emergence of logical thought inaugurated the modern age. May it not be that rational/altruism may herald the next phase in this evolution?

A New Phase in Cultural Evolution

This argument is sharpened when one realizes that we may now not merely be passing into a post-logical phase, as Korzybski thought, but may be coming to the end of a cultural era. This at least is the argument advanced by Teilhard and Coon, both of whom said that mankind was approaching the end of the Neolithic Age.

Thus, just as the use of reason led man into the Neolithic Age so the emergence of rational-altruism may lead him into a new moral age. In the first he mastered his material environment. In the emergent age he should be enabled to use this transcended form of reason to become as equally competent in the moral dimension of life. If this is true it leads on to a thrilling conclusion.

The neolithic or 'new-stone' age already spans man's development from primitive flint-chipping to our present technical cyberculture. The emergent moral age may have just as much potential. If this is so, then our present efforts to live moral lives could be considered as the moral equivalent of flint-chipping; and before us lies the inconceivable moral parallel to space technology.

This does not mean, of course, that technological evolution is expected to give way to moral evolution. Just as reason will be transcended and function as the moral force of rational-altruism, so also technology will be transformed for the good of mankind. The technocrats must still satisfy our basic needs and fulfil their ecological obligations. If not then men will still be cold, hungry and homeless, whether it be on a planetary or domestic scale: and it is extremely difficult to be moral when one is cold, hungry and homeless. This, at least, is one reason why there is such contemporary concern with world pollution and over-population.

However, the primary point is this. We may now be moving into this 'new value' age. The current preoccupation with the 'quality of life' only serves to underline this point. Maslow believes that his 'self-actualizing men', who are motivated by disciplined love, are the growing-tip of this evolutionary movement. He says that they are 'more natural, more human', but this uniqueness does not isolate them from mankind. 'They are closer to *both* their specieshood and to their unique individuality' (31).

All of this has enormous implications for moral education. It means that when all the aims and intentions have been distilled down to their essentials we are left with the two fundamental primary attitudes of love and reason. It is these which we must develop in children so that they spontaneously respond to people with love and to problems with reason. The exercise of reason implies autonomy and the employment of love makes responsibility a necessary corollary. Thus we return to the four primary moral attitudes, but we can now see that the distillation can go further. In the final analysis the aim of moral education should be simply that of teaching and helping children to love each other. All the rest follows from this when it is understood aright.

This does not mean that we inculcate emotional attachments. It implies that we must discover and implement those educational techniques which will enable us to produce autonomous children who display reasoned, responsible behaviour. If the foregoing arguments have any validity, this will also further the cultural evolution of mankind and perhaps hasten the day when homo sapiens may become homo moralis, the self-actualizing man whose conduct is characterized by this emergent moral quality of rational-altruism.

Having now reached this conclusion it is possible to add further confirmation of this point. This cannot be presented in the role of supportive arguments. These comments merely indicate that man has been feeling forward towards this point for centuries. Pascal for example, argued that 'The heart has reasons of which reason knows nothing'. Keats, possibly reflecting his early medical training, expressed the view that 'Axioms in philosophy are not axioms until they are proved upon our pulses'. Sir Herbert Read echoed this sentiment when he perpetually referred to what he called 'Felt-thought'. This must not be confused with D. H. Lawrence's 'philosophy of the blood', in which only visceral convictions had validity. His was a reaction against that excessive intellectualization which seemed to treat man as a cerebral creature whose feelings were relics of an animal past.

To underline the inadequacy of this view Clough wrote his bitter parody of the ten commandments which contained the vitriolic lines, 'Thou shalt not kill; but needst not strive officiously to keep alive'. Hence in his review of the biological techniques which could enhance man's intellect, Taylor observes that without a corresponding development in altruism 'the rapid improvement of intelligence might prove to have objectionable effects, even disastrous ones' (32). In more measured tones, Aldous Huxley argues that '*without progress in charity*, technological advance is useless. Indeed, it is worse than useless. Technological progress has merely provided us with more efficient means for going backwards' (33). For the simple fact is that any utopian society must be founded upon compassionate-reasoning. Only in such a system can individuals attain the ideal of self-realization and also share in its economic and technological triumphs while also under-writing each other in adversity.

Moral Education and Cultural Evolution

The conclusions of such a survey are self-evident. Although the establishment of the preconditions of morality constitutes a life-long task, in which the human personality perpetually proceeds towards self-realization, the moral educator has an important part to play. For him there are two critical phases which highlight his task. Thus in the early stages of both the primary and secondary phases of education teachers have unparalleled opportunities to act. Here they will help children to establish their identity and to accept the self thus identified. They can provide them with norms of conduct which may be verified by reference to an inwardly accepted value-system, and they can consolidate all this by enabling children to experience success and achievement in their personal relationships.

Furthermore, moral education should enable children to make mature moral judgements. It should provide them with the personal means of resisting any deleterious whims and impulses. The primary importance of persons *qua* persons should be emphasized. Children should also be provided with the skills to abstract moral principles from legalistic data. Finally they have to be given whatever assistance they may need to apply these principles in actual practice.

Finally the attitudes of autonomy, rationality, altruism and responsibility should be inculcated. Only in this way will children be enabled to adopt an autonomous stance in which they spontaneously respond to problems with reason, react intuitively to people with love, and implement moral decisions reached on the basis of rational-altruism. When rightly understood this resolves itself down to the proposition that *children must be taught to love one another* so that adult society may be characterized by compassionate reasoning.

This is equally the task of all institutions which are able to affect the quality of man's political and social life. They must utilize every means to ensure that man lives at peace with man. They must ensure that this is characterized not only by the negativism of refraining from violence and envy, but also by the positive expression of harmony and goodwill which rises above colour, class and creed. Therefore only one final point needs to be emphasized. Moral education is not needed merely to arrest the current wave of violence, arson, murder and delinquency. It is essential if we are *to advance the cultural evolution of mankind.* This note has been sounded already but needs to be heard again.

Maslow calls the morally mature man a self-actualizing person, and observes that one of his characteristics is his ability to take the long view. 'This impression of being above small things, of having a larger horizon, a wider breadth of vision, of living in the widest frame of reference, *sub specie aeternitatis,* is of the utmost social and interpersonal importance' (34). We need not aspire to such heights but can at least adopt a vantage point which provides a perspective whereby despite current pessimistic predictions, we may look forward optimistically to thousands of years of cultural evolution.

The neolithic age appears to be behind us. May we not hope that a neotimetic age (see p. 193) lies before us? If this is so, the perspective of our educational planning must be framed not by ten years, or ten decades or even by ten centuries. We must think in terms of the cultural age which now appears to be passing and view our efforts in the light of at least the ten millennia to come.

REFERENCES

1 Kay (1968).
2 Peters (1969), p. 12.
3 Wall (1968), p. 147.
4 Mead (1965), p. 139.
5 Teilhard (1960), p. 262.
6 Precisely how one may distinguish between them is problematic. In the former a child might well admire Socrates and Christ, yet be unaffected by either. Yet in the latter case the process of identification is, by definition, unconscious.
7 Berridge (1969), p. 13.
8 Sugarman (1967), p. 156.
9 cf. Peck and Havighurst (1964), 'by the age of ten—indeed perhaps much earlier—whatever character the child has he is likely to have for life' (p. 162), and Cronbach (1954), p. 194.
10 Allport (1967), pp. 208, 213.

11 Plowden (1967), para. 12.
12 Roe (1958), p. 252.
13 Erikson (1950), p. 174.
14 Psychological studies of adolescent conversions confirm this; see Starbuck (1895), James (1929) and Thouless (1950).
15 Some, of course, follow an 'isolate' path; see Morse (1965).
16 Yablonsky (1967), p. 24.
17 *op. cit.*, pp. 275–84.
18 Parsons (1954), p. 305.
19 See Kay (1968), p. 249.
20 May in *Spectrum*, Vol. 1, No. 3, p. 124.
21 Kay (1968), Chapter 9.
22 Cox in *British Journal of Educational Sociology*, Vol. 17, No. 169, p. 315.
23 The most sophisticated form appears in Wilson (1973) and does much to emasculate the view that he has given us 'a statement of his own general moral position' (see *Journal of Curriculum Studies*, Vol. 1, p. 175).
24 This need not mean any more than that such an individual can control his aggression and anxiety without resorting to psychoses, neuroses and moral disorders.
25 Maslow (1970), p. 171.
26 Kay (1971).
27 Wilson (1961), p. 164: his italics. Peters (1963), p. 49.
28 Fletcher (1966), p. 57.
29 North (1972), p. 93.
30 Peck and Havighurst (1964), p. 124; and they were thoroughgoing Freudians!
31 Maslow (1970), p. 178.
32 Taylor (1969), p. 166. This tension between feeling and thought is apparent in every aspect of cultural evolution. Abrams (1953) has traced this by contrasting the Augustan (intellectual) and Picaresque (romantic) tension in eighteenth-century literature, but the same pattern may be traced in the philosophy and theology of that and subsequent centuries.
33 Huxley (1957), p. 8.
34 Maslow (1970), p. 160.

Bibliography
ABRAMS, M. H., *The Mirror and the Lamp* (Oxford Univ. Press, 1953).
ALBRIGHT, W. F., *Archaeology and the Religion of Israel* (Johns Hopkins, 1953).
ALLPORT, GORDON, *Patterns and Growth in Personality* (Holt, Rinehart & Winston, 1967).
ATTIYEH, R. and LUMSDEN, K. G., *Micro-economics* (Prentice Hall, 1970).
BARRY, F. R., *Christian Ethics and Secular Society* (Hodder & Stoughton, 1966).
BENNETT, IVY, *Delinquent and Neurotic Children* (Tavistock Pubs., 1960).
BERRIDGE, DOROTHY M., *Growing to Maturity* (Burns & Oates, 1969).
BERRIEN, K. F., 'Homoeostasis Theory of Group Implications for Leadership', in L. Petrullo and B. M. Bass (Eds), *Leadership and Interpersonal Behaviour* (Holt, Rinehart & Winston, 1961).
BRYANT, H. A., DOBBINS, D. A. and BASS, B. M., 'Group Effectiveness, Coercion, Change and Coalescence Among Delinquents Compared to Non-delinquents', in *Journal of Social Psychology*, Vol. 61, 1963.
CASS, LORETTA K., 'An Investigation of Parent–Child Relationships in

Terms of Awareness, Identification, Projection and Control', in *American Journal of Orthopsychiatry*, No. 22, 1952.

CLOWARD, R. A. and OHLIN, L. E., *Delinquency and Opportunity—A Theory of Delinquent Gangs* (Routledge & Kegan Paul, 1961).

COHEN, A. K., *Delinquent Boys—The Culture of the Gang* (Routledge & Kegan Paul, 1956).

COOLEY, CHARLES H., *Human Nature and the Social Order* (Charles Scribner, New York, 1922).

COON, CARLETON S., *The History of Man* (Cape, 1962).

CRONBACH, L., *Educational Psychology* (Harcourt Brace, 1954).

DITTES, J. E. and KELLEY, H. H., 'Effects of Different Conditions of Acceptance upon Conformity to Group Norms', in *Journal of Abnormal and Social Psychology*, No. 52, 1956.

DURKHEIM, EMILE, *Moral Education* (Free Press, Glencoe, 1961).

ERIKSON, ERIK H., *Childhood and Society* (Norton, New York, 1950).

FENCHEL, G. H., MONDERER, J. H. and HARTLEY, E. L., 'Subjective Status and the Equilibration Hypothesis', in *Journal of Abnormal Social Psychology*, No. 46, 1951.

FLETCHER, J., *Situation Ethics* (Student Christian Movement, 1966).

FREUD, ANNA, *The Ego and the Mechanisms of Defence* (Hogarth Press, 1937).

FROMM, ERICH, *Man for Himself* (Routledge & Kegan Paul, 1956).

GERGEN, KENNETH J., *The Concept of Self* (Holt, Rinehart & Winston, 1971).

GOLDTHORPE, J. H., *The Affluent Worker in the Class Structure* (Cambridge Univ. Press, 1969).

HAVIGHURST, R. J. and TABA, H., *Adolescent Character and Personality* (John Wiley, New York, 1949).

HIRST, P. and PETERS, R. S., *The Logic of Education* (Routledge & Kegan Paul, 1970).

HUXLEY, ALDOUS, *Ends and Means* (Chatto & Windus, 1957).

JAMES, WILLIAM, *The Varieties of Religious Experience* (Longmans Green, 1929).

KAY, W., 'Compassionate Reasoning as a Basis for Morality', in *Lumen Vitae*, Vol. XXVI, No. 1, 1971.

KORZYBSKI, ALFRED H., *Science and Sanity* (Univ. Chicago Press, 1933).

LAING, R. D., *The Divided Self* (Penguin, 1965).

LEVENTHAL, F. M., *Respectable Radicals: George Howell and Victorian Working-Class Politics* (Weidenfeld & Nicolson, 1971).

LOUKES, HAROLD, *New Ground in Christian Education* (Student Christian Movement, 1965).

MCCLELLAND, D. C., *The Alienating Society* (Princeton, New Jersey, 1961).

MCCORD, J. and MCCORD, W., 'The Effects of Parental Role Models on Criminality', in *Journal of Social Issues*, Vol. 14, No. 3, 1958.

MCDAVID, J. W., 'Personal and Situational Determinants of Conformity', in *Journal of Abnormal and Social Psychology*, No. 58, 1959.

MASLOW, A. H., *Motivation and Personality* (Harper & Row, 1970).

MAUSNER, B. and PLATT, E. S., *Smoking* (Pergamon, 1972).

MEAD, G. H., *Mind, Self and Society* (Univ. Chicago Press, 1965: first published 1934).

MILLER, W. B., 'Lower Class Culture as a Generating Milieu of Gang Delinquency', in *Journal of Social Issues*, Vol. 14, 1958.

MORSE, MARY, *The Unattached* (Pelican, 1965).

NISBET, J. D. and ENTWHISTLE, N. J., *The Age of Transfer to Secondary Education* (Univ. London Press, 1966).

NORTH, M., *Personality Assessment Through Movement* (McDonald & Evans, 1972).

PARSONS, C. TALCOTT, *Essays in Sociological Theory* (Free Press, Glencoe, 1954).

PECK, R. F. and HAVIGHURST, R. J., *The Psychology of Character Development* (John Wiley, New York, 1964).

PETERS, R. S., 'Reason and Habit: The Paradox of Moral Education', in W. R. Niblett (Ed.), *Moral Education in a Changing Society* (Faber, 1963).

PETERS, R. S., *Ethics and Education* (Allen & Unwin, 1966).

PETERS, R. S. (Ed.), *Perspectives on Plowden* (Routledge & Kegan Paul, 1969).

PETERS, R. S. and HIRST, P., *The Logic of Education* (Routledge & Kegan Paul, 1970).

PLOWDEN REPORT, *Children and the Primary Schools* (HMSO, 1967).

READ, HERBERT E., *Education Through Art* (Faber, 1958).

ROE, M. C., 'Psychological Study of Values and Interests of Senior Grammar School Pupils with Reference to Preferences at Work', Unpublished Ph.D. thesis, London, 1958.

STARBUCK, E. D., *The Psychology of Religion* (New York, 1895).

SUGARMAN, BARRY, 'Involvement in Youth Culture, Academic Achievement and Conformity in School', in *British Journal of Sociology*, 1967.

TAYLOR, G. RATTRAY, *The Biological Time Bomb* (Panther, 1969).

TEILHARD, PIERRE DE CHARDIN, *The Phenomenon of Man* (Collins, 1960).

THOULESS, R. H., *An Introduction to the Psychology of Religion* (Cambridge Univ. Press, 1950).

WALL, W. D., *Adolescents in School and Society* (NFER, 1968).

WHYTE, W. H., *Street Corner Society* (Univ. Chicago Press, 1955).

WILLIAMS, NORMAN and WILLIAMS, SHEILA, *The Moral Development of Children* (Macmillan, 1970).

WILSON, J. B., *Reason and Morals* (Cambridge Univ. Press, 1968).

WILSON, J. B., *The Assessment of Morality* (NFER, 1973).

WINNICOTT, D. W., 'The Young Child at Home and at School', in *Moral Education in a Changing Society* (Faber, 1963).

WRIGHT, DEREK, *The Psychology of Moral Behaviour* (Pelican, 1971).

YABLONSKY, LEWIS, *The Violent Gang* (Pelican, 1967).

Author Index

(Please note that this does not include material contained in the bibliographies appended to each chapter.)

Subject Index